International Law of Victims

Carlos Fernández de Casadevante Romani

International Law of Victims

Springer

Carlos Fernández de Casadevante Romani
Facultad Ciencias Jurídicas y Sociales
Derecho Público II
Universidad Rey Juan Carlos
Madrid
Spain

ISBN 978-3-642-28139-6 ISBN 978-3-642-28140-2 (eBook)
DOI 10.1007/978-3-642-28140-2
Springer Heidelberg New York Dordrecht London

Library of Congress Control Number: 2012936804

Printed on acid-free paper

Springer is part of Springer Science+Business Media (www.springer.com)

To all the victims
Especially to my father and my uncle Ignacio, victims of the Basque nationalist terrorist organization ETA

Contents

Part One The Victims and International Law

Part One
The Victims and International Law

Some Previous Questions

The Approach of International Law to Victims

Traditionally, International Law has not paid sufficient attention to victims.[1] An explanation for this can be found in the particular nature of international law: States make, interpret and apply international law. Therefore, as a result of this and owing to the predominantly interstate structure of the international community, international norms have been created to respond to states' interests and goals. In this context, states have paid attention to persons or individuals only in some particular fields of international law.

This is the case, for example, with human rights, international criminal law (with regard to international criminal responsibility of individuals)[2] or international humanitarian law. But in each of these branches of international law, the way in which victims are considered differs. So, in international law of human rights, victims are considered when the State is the author of the breach of the international obligation, but this branch of international law does not consider the breach of international obligations in this field by non-state actors.[3]

Nevertheless, such an approach does not mean that only states breach human rights because non-state actors do so as well. Although this is an established fact, it has taken a lot of time for it to gain global recognition and acknowledgement in the international arena by international norms and by statements of international organs.[4] An example of this is the report to the Sub-Commission on the Promotion

[1] As Bottigliero clearly states, victims have been left on the periphery of domestic and international political agenda (cf. Bottigliero 2004, 2).

[2] See Fernández de Casadevante Romani (ed) (2011).

[3] On this issue, see Clapham (2006).

[4] An example of it are the resolutions adopted since 1994 onwards by the UN Commission on Human Rights under the title "Humans rights and terrorism". The UN Commission on Human Rights has also qualified terrorism as a violation of human rights (see resolutions 1994/46, 1995/43, 1996/47, 1997/42, 1998/47, 1999/27, 2000/30, 2001/37, 2002/35 and 2003/37). Also, the Sub-

C. Fernández de Casadevante Romani, *International Law of Victims*,
DOI 10.1007/978-3-642-28140-2_1, © Springer-Verlag Berlin Heidelberg 2012

and Protection of Human Rights submitted in 2001 by the Special Rapporteur on "Terrorism and Human Rights" K. KOUFA, where it states:

> 102. Terrorist acts, whether committed by States or non-State actors, may affect the right to life, the right to freedom from torture and arbitrary detention, women's rights, children's rights, health, subsistence (food), democratic order, peace and security, the right to non-discrimination, and any number of other protected human rights norms. Actually, there is probably not a single human right exempt from the impact of terrorism.[5]

Yes, on the one hand, non-state actors breach human rights but international law only pays attention and give legal consequences to the breaches of human rights by states. On the other hand, the responsibility of non-state actors for the breaches they have perpetrated is the concern of international criminal law and of international humanitarian law. In both cases, such breaches are envisaged from the perspective of the international criminal responsibility of the individual.

In contrast to the international law of human rights (where the author is always the state) in international criminal law and in international humanitarian law, however, individuals may be regarded as victims as a consequence of acts perpetrated by individuals (even by individuals exercising public functions) as well as by non-state actors. In both cases, international responsibility rests only with the individuals and victims are recognized. Nevertheless, the way in which they are recognized is inadequate.[6]

This situation guides Bottigliero to ask for reasons why victims of some of the worst crimes have received "second class" treatment or no justice at all because whereas victims of ordinary crimes can access established means for redress, the situation of victims of crimes and of violations on a grand scale (such as those perpetrated during a war, involving large numbers of victims) is more complicated.[7]

Taking these precedents into account, one can better appreciate the advances that the creation of the International Criminal Court (ICC) and the international criminal courts in the 1990s as well as the international norms

Commission on the Promotion and Protection of Human Rights (see resolutions 1994/18, 1996/20 and 1997/39). In 1993, this Sub-Commission had even condemned "the violations of human rights by the terrorist groups Sendero Luminoso and Movimiento Revolucionario Tupac Amaru" in Perou (resolution 1993/23).

[5] UN, Doc. E/CN.4/Sub.2/2001/31, p. 46. She drafted a preliminary report (E/CN.4/Sub.2/1999/27), a progress report (E/CN.4/Sub.2/2001/31), a second progress report (E/CN.4/Sub.2/2002/35), an additional progress report with two addenda (E/CN.4/Sub.2/2003/WP.1 and Add.1 and 2) and a final report (E(CN.4/Sub.2/2004/40). In fact, a lot of rights are concerned by terrorism: the right to liberty and security, the right to family life, the right of movement, the right to information, the right to fair trial, etc.

[6] This is the case of the statutes of the International Criminal Court (ICC) and of the international criminal courts of the former Yugoslavia and Rwanda. See also the Statute of the *Special Tribunal for Lebanon* and the rules and Procedure and Evidence of this tribunal, as well as the Statute of the Extraordinary Chambers in the Courts of Cambodia.

[7] Bottigliero, *op. cit.*, 5.

adopted in the last several years represent for the process of humanization of international law.

Previously, both international and domestic law had ignored the victim. Domestic law because the state's *ius puniendi* embodied in criminal law has traditionally had the criminal as the exclusive reference without considering the victim.[8] International law because its approaches on the matter of responsibility have been always focused upon the author of the wrongful act: the state (in international law of human rights), the individual or the state (in international humanitarian law) or the individual (in international criminal law), but always ignoring the victim.

Nevertheless, the characteristics of the legal context of the social and democratic rule of law together with the existence of an important number of treaties on human rights guide us to a reinterpretation of the aim of the criminal process quoted here. According to that reinterpretation, the criminal process is conceived of as an instrument of guarantee both for the person to whom the crime is attributed and for the victim. It is an instrument of guarantee for the accused because he/she cannot be condemned without destroying the principle of presumption of innocence through a fair process. But it is also an instrument of guarantee for the rest of the citizens and for the victims of crime. For the rest of the citizens because it is within the framework of criminal proceedings that the State exercises the jus puniendi that citizens have delegated to him. For the victims of crime because it is in the frame of the criminal process that victims shall be protected and adequately supervised on their rights. This is why the protection of victims of crime begins to be one of the specific aims of the criminal process.[9]

The panorama quoted here shows that, despite the relevance of this subject, victims have been either ignored or insufficiently considered by domestic as well as by international norms. But this panorama has begun to change since different international norms relating to victims have been progressively introduced. These are norms generally characterized by a certain concept of the respective victim, as well as by the enumeration of a list of rights to which the victim in question is entitled to. It is upon that list or catalogue of rights in favour of victims that an international statute of victims is built. In reverse, these catalogues of rights are obligations in the charge of States.

---

[8] As a consequence of such a concept, the criminal process has been understood in domestic law as an instrument to realize the state's *ius puniendi*. That is, the process through which the state's right to punish because of the commission of a criminal offence is realized. In this concept, the idea of the offence as an act causing damages to victims in their condition as concrete and individual citizens is not retained and victims neither appear nor are envisaged. This is why "allowing victims' participation in criminal proceedings and recognizing the right of the victims to be informed of progress in the case, serves to rebalance a criminal justice system that would otherwise only address the relationship between the State and the offenders and the rights of the defence" (UNODOC (2011), 33, para. 134).

[9] See Sanz Hermida (2009), pp. 25–28 et seq. As UNODOC states, "a system that merely punishes those persons convicted for criminal acts, while simultaneously ignoring the needs and interests of victims, cannot be considered as fulfilling its objectives" (UNODOC, *op. cit.*, 15, para. 56).

Most of these rights are common to all categories of victims. Others are, on the one hand, rights only related to a particular category of victims. Most of the rights are rights already existent in the international law of human rights. Consequently, they are not new but consolidated rights. On the other hand, they are also rights related to one another so that the breach of one implies the breach of all others related or connected to it.

These international norms related to victims are also recent. The most ancient were born in the 1980s. The most recent belong to 2006.

These are norms of an institutional, customary or conventional nature of a general or regional frame, all related to concrete categories of victims: victims of crime, victims of abuse of power, victims of gross violations of international human rights law, victims of serious violations of international humanitarian law, victims of enforced disappearance, victims of violations of international criminal law and finally victims of terrorism.

Most of these norms are of an institutional nature. This fact raises questions about their binding effects. Independent of this discussion and the doctrinal approaches traditionally related to it, it must be remembered that the absence of formalism in international law can also lead to international obligations rising from institutional norms. From another perspective, it should also be remembered that international treaties are frequently preceded by institutional norms adopted on the same subject as that of the future treaty.[10] This is why actual institutional norms relating to the different categories of victims could lead, in the future, to international treaties.[11] In the meantime, they show the existence of a consensus, on the part of states, on the necessity of taking certain victims into account. They also demonstrate recognition of the existence of victims by states and also by international organizations. Particularly, in the case of institutional norms that have been adopted without a vote, by consensus.

---

[10] Such a procedure is frequent in the field of international human rights law. For example, the Convention Against Torture of 1984 was preceded by the Declaration on the Protection of All Persons from being subjected to Torture and Other Cruel, Inhuman or Degrading Treatment or Punishment adopted by A/RES/3452 (XXX) of 9 December 1975. Also, the International Convention on the Elimination of All Forms of Racial Discrimination adopted and opened for signature by A/RES/2106 (XX) of 20 December 1965, which was also preceded by the Declaration on the Elimination of All Forms of Racial Discrimination adopted by A/RES/1904 (XVIII) of 20 November 1963. More recently, the International Convention for the Protection of All Persons from Enforced Disappearance adopted on 20 December 2006 by A/RES/61/177, which was preceded by the Declaration on the Protection of All Persons from Enforced Disappearance adopted by A/RES/47/133 of 18 December 1992.

[11] Actually, only two treaties exist and both concern victims of enforced disappearance, the United Nations International Convention for the Protection of All Person from Enforced Disappearance, 2006 (entry into force on 23 December 2010, in accordance with article 39(1) which reads as follows: "This Convention shall enter into force on the thirtieth day after the date of deposit with the Secretary-General of the United Nations of the twentieth instrument of ratification or accession") and the Inter-American Convention on the Forced Disappearance of Persons of 9 June 1994 (into force on 28 March 1996).

In any case, the problem of the legal effects of institutional norms on states is here a relative one because institutional norms relating to victims do not do anything other than reiterate the rights and obligations already existent in international law on human rights. From this point of view, they only express *lex data*. Questions, nevertheless, can arise with regard to those rights that could be qualified *de lege ferenda* rights.

Due to the plurality of the categories of victims envisaged by international norms and the particularism inherent to them, I would like to underline that that plurality of categories does not constitute an obstacle in the way of building a common minimal protection to each victim because the different categories of victims have the same common denominator: the fact of being victims as a consequence of a wrongful act that is a crime. This is why independent of the possible particularization and possible inclusion in a certain category as a result of the wrongful act suffered, the different categories of victims are *all of them*—at the same time that victims belong to a certain category of victims—victims of crime.[12] Consequently, they all have the same rights that belong to the international statute of victims of crime with regard to the criminal process. In addition, they also have other rights not linked to the criminal process but to their condition as victim. Most of them are rights common to all categories of victims as well as rights that are enshrined in other international norms.[13] This is in the case of the following: the right to effective access to law and justice, the right to administration of justice, the right to fair trial, the right to investigation, the right to compensation and reparation, the right to the protection of private and family life, the right to protection of the dignity and security and the right to information. Finally, there are other rights specifically connected to some particular categories of victims. This is in the case of those relating to the assistance to victims like the right to emergency and continuing assistance, the right to specific training for persons responsible for assisting victims, or the right to truth and to memory.

So, it is possible to state the existence of a common international legal statute for the victim (including all categories of victims) that is compatible and complementary with the particular international legal statute of each category of victims that is built in the international norms related to them. That is, an international legal statute for the victim made up of a catalogue of rights to which *all* victims are entitled.

It is an international legal statute, too, characterized by the victim's right to justice and to redress that has become an indispensable element of the efforts to protect individual human rights.[14]

---

[12] Only victims of abuse of power do not become victims as a consequence of a crime. According to UN Declaration of Basic Principles of Justice for Victims of Crime and Abuse of Power adopted by the General Assembly resolution 40/34 of 29 November 1985, they become victims through acts or omissions that do not yet constitute violations of national criminal laws but of internationally recognized norms relating to human rights.

[13] Basically norms belonging to international law of human rights.

[14] See Bassiouni (2002), 136.

This statement shall be completed with the fact that most of these rights are not other than the particularization with regard to the victims of rights already existent in international law on human rights where international treaties declare that *everyone* is entitled to them. This is a very important element reinforcing the international legal statute of the victim.

With this new approach, the practically exclusive preoccupation of the criminal system of justice, which focused on the search for the crime's author as well as on the sanction applied to that criminal conduct before the commission of a crime, ends. It has been a situation in which the other face of the crime—the victim—never appeared. Fortunately, due to the work of many victims' organizations, this panorama has begun to change.[15]

As we will see, it is a panorama characterized by the following elements. First, international norms take victims into account. Concerning its legal nature, only a minority of them have a conventional source,[16] whereas the great majority has an institutional nature. With regard to the differences in the problems that institutional norms belonging to international organizations of co-operation present to determine their legal effects, institutional norms adopted inside the European Union have the advantage of being clearly binding on the Member States because of the obligations imposed on them by the constitutive treaties.

Second, with regard to its territorial scope, some of these norms have been adopted in the UN, whereas the others have been adopted in the European (Council of Europe and European Union) and in the American regional system (OAS).

Third, they are all international norms of a recent date.

Fourth, there does not exist an only formal concept of victim but so many concepts as categories of victims.[17] As we will see, some international norms related to victims opt for a general concept of victim. This approach makes it possible to include in it other particular categories of victims not expressly envisaged or not sufficiently developed by the particular norm in question. In any case, the interaction between the different international norms related to victims makes it possible to base it on a general, wide concept of victim.

Five, those international norms envisage eight categories of victims: victims of crime, victims of abuse of power, victims of gross violations of international human rights law, victims of serious violations of international humanitarian law, victims of enforced disappearance, victims of violations of international criminal law, victims of trafficking and victims of terrorism.

---

[15] See Cario, "Terrorisme et droit des victimes", in SOS Attentats, *op. cit.*, 345.

[16] So the European Convention on the Compensation for Victims of Violent Crimes adopted on 24 November 1983 (entered into force on 1st February 1998), the United Nations International Convention for the Protection of All Persons from Enforced Disappearance, adopted on 20 December 2006 (into force on 23 December 2010) and the Inter-American Convention on enforced disappearance of persons, on the 9th July 1994 (this convention entered into force on 28 March 1996).

[17] I say nearly because there is no international norm giving a definition of victim of terrorism.

Six, each category of victim can be generally individualized according to the elements such as the nature of the breach, its perpetrator, the nationality or place of the victim as well as its interests and specific needs.[18] Nevertheless, all victims have in common the fact of being victims of a previous wrongful act (a crime or the breach of an international obligation) attributed to an individual or group of individuals or to a State.

Seven, as a consequence of it nearly all victims are victims of a crime. At the same time, they are also victims belonging to the category of victim that is determined by the wrongful act in question.

In the following pages, I will study both existent international norms related to the different categories of victims and international treaties (of a general or universal scope as well as of a regional scope) on human rights, as well as international case laws on matters handled by international organs of human rights (international courts and body treaties on human rights). This task will be done, first, to know, examine and describe the international law related to victims. Second, with the aim of trying to build a general, global concept of victim (independent of the category to which the victim belongs) on the basis of the common elements present in the existent definitions. Finally, to determine a common catalogue of the rights of victims in general, valid for any category of victim, built upon the existent international norms. A catalogue that is compatible with particularism envisaged in the international norms related to victims with regard to each category of victim.

The International Norms Related to Victims

Like the birth of the international human rights law, the relatively recent interest in victims finds its origin in the social situation created after World War II. As a consequence of this dramatic experience, a legislative policy began to coordinate measures to revitalise the status of the victim, in particular, within the criminal proceedings. This initiative became more intense in the 1980s. States and international organizations began to codify law on the matter. An ensemble of international norms solely concerned with victims and their rights began to emerge. They are international norms of a different nature (most of them institutional norms). They are also norms of a different territorial range (general or universal and regional). Still most of the rights building the international statute of the victim are still rights enshrined in international treaties; mainly human rights treaties ratified by the large majority of states.

As we will see, the international statute of victims built on such norms have a more acute legal effect on the framework of the European Union as a consequence

[18] See Almqvist (2006), 6.

of the legal binding effects the norms, created inside this frame of integration, have upon State members. Its obligatory character is undisputable and this fact is a great advantage with regard to the norms adopted in International Organizations of cooperation such as the UN or, in the regional frame, the Council of Europe or the Organization of American States.

Nevertheless, despite the deficiencies that institutional norms of International Organizations of cooperation present the fact is that most of the rights making up the international statute of victims have their origin in international treaties of human rights. As a consequence of it, almost all of these rights have become customary obligations binding States.

International Norms of a General or Universal Scope: United Nations

In the *general or universal frame* of the UN, there are, at the moment, seven international norms related to six categories of victims. First, the General Assembly Resolution 40/34 adopted on 29 November 1985, the *Declaration of Basic Principles of Justice for Victims of Crime and Abuse of Power.*[19] Second, related to victims of enforced disappearance, the *Declaration on the Protection of All Persons from Enforced Disappearance* adopted by the General Assembly of the United Nations in its resolution A/RES/47/133 of 18 December 1992. That was recently followed on 20 December 2006 by resolution A/RES/61/177 that the General Assembly adopted as the *International Convention for the Protection of All Persons from Enforced Disappearance.*[20] Third, General Assembly Resolution 60/147 adopted on 16 December 2005 through which the *Basic principles and guidelines of the right to a remedy and reparation for victims of gross violations of international human rights law and serious violations of International Humanitarian Law*[21] adopted by the UN Commission on Human Rights on 19 April 2005, by Resolution 2005/35, were adopted. Finally, and with regard to victims of violations of international *criminal* law (war crimes, crimes against humanity and genocide), the *Statute of the International Criminal Court* (ICC) adopted by the Conference of Rome on 17 July 1998, and the *Statutes* of the international criminal courts *ad hoc* for the *former Yugoslavia* and for *Rwanda* adopted by Security Council resolutions in the frame of Chap. VII of the Charter.

---

[19] Adopted by General Assembly Resolution 40/34 of 29 November 1985 it is based on Article 18 of the Universal Declaration on Human Rights, adopted and proclaimed by General Assembly Resolution 217 A (III) of 10 December 1948. Article 8 contains the right of everyone to an effective remedy by the competent national tribunals for acts violating the fundamental rights granted him by the constitution or by law. See Bassiouni (2003), 134–185.

[20] See http//:www2.ohchr.org

[21] UN E/CN.4/2005/L.10/Add. 11. It was adopted by a recorded vote of 40 to none, with 13 abstentions.

Consequently, six categories of victims are envisaged by these norms: victims of crime, victims of abuse of power, victims of gross violations of international human rights law, victims of serious violations of international humanitarian law, victims of enforced disappearance and victims of violations of international criminal law.

As it can be appreciated, no international norm related to victims of terrorism has yet been adopted by UN. It is a regrettable lack. In particular because of the many terrorist attacks that have taken place and continue take place in the international community. Despite this reality, the action of the UN with respect to victims of terrorism has been unfortunately limited to expressions of mere courtesy deprived of any legal obligations. This is the case of General Assembly resolutions showing the General Assembly's solidarity with victims of terrorism or requesting the Secretary-General to seek the views of Member States on the possible establish ment of a United Nations voluntary fund for victims of terrorism. This position is similar to the attitude of the Security Council[22] and the Commission on Human Rights.[23]

These statements of the UN are very poor and unsatisfactory. It is evident that the UN cannot remain deaf to the pleas for justice for victims of terrorism; victims who in most corners of our little planet do not have the most basic human rights[24]; victims who furthermore have never called for revenge. On the contrary, they have placed their trust in the state to deliver the justice that is their due.

In consequence, it is the responsibility of the UN itself to urge and promote international norms recognising and guaranteeing victims of terrorism the effective enjoyment of their human rights. This is particularly true of their effective right to justice and to redress. This is why associations of victims of terrorism call for such actions.[25] This is also what elementary considerations of justice demand. I will deal with this question later.[26]

An initial approach to the norms related to the categories of victims quoted here reveals two things. On the one hand, the recent attention paid by international law—that is by states—to victims. On the other hand, the progressive legal approach to the problem on the basis of categories of victims that result from different wrongful victimizing acts.

---

[22] See its resolution 1566 (2004), adopted on 8th October 2004 that considers the possibility of establishing an international fund to compensate victims of terrorist acts and their families. Also resolution 1624 (2005) of 14 September which reaffirms "its profound solidarity with the victims of terrorism and their families"; or resolutions 1611 (2005) of 7 July and 1618 (2005) of 4 August, in which it expresses "its deepest sympathy and condolences to the victims. . .. and their families" of the terrorist attacks that took place in London and Iraq, respectively.

[23] See resolution 2003/37 of the Commission on Human Rights adopted on 23 April 2003 and related to the establishing of an international fund to compensate victims of terrorist acts.

[24] Among them, the effective right to justice or the right to redress. This is the case of situations described in the preceding footnote. They all lead, *de facto,* to deny victims of terrorism their effective right to justice and, as a consequence, their right to redress.

[25] See Bou Franch and Fernández de Casadevante Romani (2009).

[26] See chapter "Special Reference to the Victims of Terrorism" of this book.

In a certain way, the manner in which international law pays attention to the victim is similar to the way in which the protection of several groups (women, children, disabled persons) or the fight against certain practices breached of human rights (torture, race discrimination, discrimination of women, enforced disappearance, etc.) has been done in international law of human rights.

With regard to the first aspect, that is, the recent attention given by states to victims it must be remembered that the *Declaration of Basic Principles of Justice for Victims of Crime and Abuse of Power* of 29 November 1985 is the first international norm related to victims adopted in the UN. On the one hand, it is an international norm of a general or universal character. On the other hand, it is a norm related only to two categories of victims: victims of crime and victims of abuse of power. Later other international norms taking into account other categories of victims followed this Declaration.

In addition to the concepts of victim of crime and victim of abuse of power, the Declaration of 1985 also includes a catalogue of rights. They are the right of access to justice and fair treatment linked to the prompt redress of victims and to the necessary adaptation of judicial and administrative mechanisms to the needs of victims, and the rights of restitution, compensation and assistance.

A few years later, the Declaration of 1985 was followed by the *Declaration on the Protection of All Persons from Enforced Disappearance* adopted by the General Assembly of the United Nations in its resolution A/RES/47/133 of 18 December 1992. Related to the same practice of enforced disappearance, the Declaration of 1992 was recently followed on 20 December 2006 in the resolution A/RES/61/177 by the General Assembly adopting the *International Convention for the Protection of All Persons from Enforced Disappearance.*[27]

In contrast to the Declaration of 1992, the Convention of 2006 contains a definition of "enforced disappearance". So, according to article 2:

> For the purposes of this Convention, 'enforced disappearance' is considered to be the arrest, detention, abduction or any other form of deprivation of liberty by agents of the State or by persons or groups of persons acting with the authorization, support or acquiescence of the State, followed by a refusal to acknowledge the deprivation of liberty or by concealment of the fate or whereabouts of the disappeared person, which place such a person outside the protection of the law.[28]

---

[27] It entered into force on 23 December 2010. As stated earlier, it is the only treaty related to victims in the general or universal frame. In the regional frame, it was preceded by the Inter-American Convention of the 9th July 1994 (this convention entered into force on 28 March 1996) on enforced disappearance of persons. See its text at http://www.oas.org/juridico/spanish/Tratados/a-60.htlm.

[28] According to Article 1: "1. Any act of enforced disappearance is an offence to human dignity. It is condemned as a denial of the purposes of the Charter of the United Nations and as a grave and flagrant violation of the human rights and fundamental freedoms proclaimed in the Universal Declaration of Human Rights and reaffirmed and developed in international instruments in this field. 2. Any act of enforced disappearance places the persons subjected thereto outside the protection of the law and inflicts severe suffering on them and their families. It constitutes a violation of the rules of international law guaranteeing, inter alia, the right to recognition as a person before the law, the right to liberty and security of the person and the right not to be

At the same time, both the 1992 Declaration and the 2006 Convention list a catalogue of rights to which victims of enforced disappearance are entitled. These are the following: the right to justice (which includes the right to a prompt and effective judicial remedy), the right to know the truth regarding the circumstances of the enforced disappearance, the progress and results of the investigation and the fate of the disappeared person and, in connection with it, the right to seek for, to receive and to spread information[29]; the right to form and participate freely in organizations and associations concerned with attempting to establish the circumstances of enforced disappearances and the fate of disappeared persons, and to assist victims of enforced disappearance and, finally, the right to obtain reparation and prompt, fair and adequate compensation.

The 2006 Convention gives to reparation a double content. On the one hand, it covers material and moral damages.[30] On the other hand, "where appropriate" it covers other forms of reparation such restitution, rehabilitation, satisfaction (including restoration of dignity and reputation) and guarantees of non-repetition.

These rights are complemented by the *International Convention for the Protection of All Persons from Enforced Disappearance* with a catalogue of obligations on the charge of states. They are the following: the obligation to make the offence of enforced disappearance punishable by appropriate penalties "which take into account its extreme seriousness",[31] the obligation to investigate all enforced disappearance, the obligation to establish its competence to exercise jurisdiction over this kind of offence, the obligation to take the necessary measures to ensure that the term of limitation for criminal proceedings is of long duration, is proportionate to the extreme seriousness of this offence and commences from the moment when the offence of enforced disappearance ceases, taking into account its continuous nature; the principle *aut dedere aut iudicare*, the obligation not to regard the offence of enforced disappearance as a political offence or as an offence connected with a political offence or as an offence inspired by political motives, the obligation not to refuse a request for extradition based on such an offence, the obligation not to

subjected to torture and other cruel, inhuman or degrading treatment or punishment. It also violates or constitutes a grave threat to the right to life."

[29] According to Article 18 of the 2006 Convention, any person with a legitimate interest, such as relatives of the person deprived of liberty, their representatives or their counsel, has access to at least the following information: The authority that ordered the deprivation of liberty; the date, time and place where the person was deprived of liberty and admitted to the place of deprivation of liberty; the authority responsible for supervising the deprivation of liberty; the whereabouts of the person deprived of liberty, including, in the event of a transfer to another place of deprivation of liberty, the destination and the authority responsible for the transfer; the date, time and place of release elements relating to the state of health of the person deprived of liberty; and in the event of death during the deprivation of liberty, the circumstances and cause of death and the destination of the remains.

[30] See Fernández Sola (2008), 411.

[31] In Article 7.

justify an offence of enforced disappearance invoking an order or instruction from any public authority, civilian, military or other, etc.[32]

In line with international treaties on human rights, the 2006 Convention establishes an international body—the Committee on Enforced Disappearances—and envisages the three classical techniques of control (reports, interstate communications and individual communications to which it adds a new technique that is an innovation in this field: the *request*. Effectively, according to Article 30.1:

> 1. A request that a disappeared person should be sought and found may be submitted to the Committee, as a matter of urgency, by relatives of the disappeared person or their legal representatives, their counsel or any person authorized by them, as well as by any other person having a legitimate interest.

If the Committee, according to Article 30.1, found that the request submitted to it as a matter of urgency is not manifestly unfounded; does not constitute an abuse of the right of submission of such requests; has already been duly presented to the competent bodies of the State Party concerned, such as those authorized to undertake investigations, where such a possibility exists; is not incompatible with the provisions of the Convention; and the same matter is not being examined under another procedure of international investigation or settlement of the same nature; then, it shall request the State Party concerned to provide it with information on the situation of the persons sought, within a time limit set by the Committee.[33]

In the light of the information provided by the State Party concerned in accordance with the fulfilment of the conditions quoted here, and according to Article 30.3, the Committee "may transmit recommendations to the State Party, including a request that the State Party should take all the necessary measures, including interim measures, to locate and protect the person concerned in accordance with this Convention and to inform the Committee, within a specified period of time, of measures taken, taking into account the urgency of the situation. The Committee shall inform the person submitting the urgent action request of its recommendations and of the information provided to it by the State as it becomes available".

At least, Article 30.4 states that the Committee shall continue its efforts to work with the State Party concerned for as long as the fate of the person sought remains unresolved. The person presenting the request shall be kept informed.

Like the UN Convention against Torture and Other Cruel, Inhuman or Degrading Treatment or Punishment of 10 December 1984, the *International Convention for the Protection of All Persons from Enforced Disappearance* also includes as a technique of control a visit to the State Party concerned in the practice of enforced disappearance.[34] So, according to Article 33, "if the Committee receives reliable information

---

[32] These obligations are all similar to those existent inside the UN Torture Convention against Torture and Other Cruel, Inhuman or Degrading Treatment or Punishment of 10 December 1984.

[33] See Article 30.2.

[34] Cf. Article 23. But in contrast to the UN Torture Convention against Torture and Other Cruel, Inhuman or Degrading Treatment or Punishment of 10 December 1984 that gives States Parties the possibility of not accepting this kind of visits (cf. Article 28), the International Convention for the

indicating that a State Party is seriously violating the provisions of this Convention, it may, after consultation with the State Party concerned, request one or more of its members to undertake a visit and report back to it without delay".

Like in the UN Convention against Torture and Other Cruel, Inhuman or Degrading Treatment or Punishment, here, the Committee on Enforced Disappearances shall notify the State Party concerned, in writing, of its intention to organize a visit, indicating the composition of the delegation and the purpose of the visit. The State Party shall answer the Committee within a reasonable time.

Article 28 introduces an innovation with regard to international treaties on human rights because it makes express reference to cooperation with all relevant organs, offices and specialized agencies and funds of the United Nations, with the treaty bodies instituted by international instruments, with the special procedures of the United Nations and with the relevant regional intergovernmental organizations or bodies, as well as with all relevant State institutions, agencies or offices working towards the protection of all persons against enforced disappearances. It also envisages consultations with other treaty bodies instituted by relevant international human rights instruments, in particular, the Human Rights Committee instituted by the International Covenant on Civil and Political Rights, with a view to ensuring the consistency of their respective observations and recommendations.

A short time before the *International Convention for the Protection of All Persons from Enforced Disappearance* and also recently UN General Assembly had adopted another norm related to this category of victims. It is an institutional norm: GA 60/147 resolution of 16 December 2005 adopting the *Basic Principles and Guidelines on the Right to a Remedy and Reparation for Victims of Gross Violations of International Human Rights Law and Serious Violations of International Humanitarian Law* previously adopted by the Commission on Human Rights in its resolution 2005/35 of 19 April 2005 and by the Economic and Social Council in its resolution 2005/30 of 25 July 2005, in which the Council recommended to the General Assembly that it adopt the Basic Principles and Guidelines.[35]

With regard to its *object*, it is constituted by two categories of victims: victims of gross violations of international human rights law and victims of serious violations of international humanitarian law. It shall be added that this norm was adopted with any negative vote, which is indicative of the unanimous agreement of its members about its content: the rights of victims to a remedy as well as to redress.

From the point of view of its legal effects and even as an institutional norm within the framework of the UN, it should be noted that the *Basic Principles and Guidelines on the Right to a Remedy and Reparation for Victims of Gross Violations of International Human Rights Law and Serious Violations of International Humanitarian Law* does not do more than formulate legal obligations into a

Protection of All Persons from Enforced Disappearance does not allow States Parties not to accept the competence of the Committee on Enforced Disappearances. To the effect of the visits envisaged by Article 33, the competence of this Committee is compulsory.

[35] As seen, it is an institutional norm previously adopted by two other organs in the UN.

force in international treaties on human rights with universal and regional scope, as well as in treaties belonging to international humanitarian law and to international criminal law. In this line and as it is stated in the preamble of such basic principles and guidelines, they

> do not entail new international or domestic legal obligations but identify mechanisms, modalities, procedures and methods for the implementation of existing legal obligations under international human rights law and international humanitarian law which are complementary though different as to their norms.[36]

This outlook of the international norms related to victims adopted in the UN is complemented by the *Statute of the International Criminal Court* approved in Rome on 17 July 1998 with regard to victims of violations of international criminal law (crimes of war, crimes against humanity and genocide). The Statutes of the International Criminal Courts for the *former Yugoslavia* and for *Rwanda* adopted by the Security Council should also be added. In contrast to the Statute of Rome that envisages the participation of victims of the crimes in the jurisdiction of this Court on the occasion of the activation of the prosecutor's jurisdiction, the statutes of two international criminal courts *ad hoc* only allow the participation of victims as witnesses.

Despite the supposed progress that all these international norms related to the different categories of victims there is not yet an international norm of universal or general scope related to victims of terrorism[37] or an international treaty of universal scope related to victims in general.[38] It is also true that such a treaty would only bind State Parties and that this kind of treaty would show a most serious engagement on the matter by these states. But in any case a general or universal treaty on victims of terrorism or on victims in general would constitute great progress in the matter.

In my opinion, the most relevant fact of the international law actually in force related to victims is that the rights that the different international norms contain are rights firmly consolidated through the different treaties on human rights. Yes, the victim is a 'natural person' and as such is entitled to the rights that international treaties on human rights proclaim with regard to "everyone". They are rights, too, that states have the charge to guarantee and to makes that they become effective.

On the other hand and on the same lines, the rights that international norms related to victims proclaim, are most of them, not other than personal basic rights that bind states also as norms of customary nature. In other words, the international

---

[36] In paragraph seven.

[37] See chapter "Special Reference to the Victims of Terrorism" of this work.

[38] As already stated there is only one treaty of general or universal scope *stricto sensu* related to victims; the International Convention for the Protection of All Persons from Enforced Disappearance not yet in force. I said *stricto sensu* because the Statute of the ICC is a treaty of general or universal scope. At the regional level, there are two treaties: the European Convention on the Compensation of Victims of Violent Crimes adopted on 24 November 1983 and the Inter-American Convention on enforced disappearance of persons, of 9th July 1994.

norms that I examine in this work only particularize with regard to victims a list of human rights already in force in international law on human rights by conventional and by customary norms. Consequently—the majority of them—they are not rights of *lege ferenda* but *lex data*. I will prove it later when I discuss the catalogue of rights built into the international legal statute for victims.

As we see now, in the *regional frame* the situation differs. On the one hand, the existing norms relating to victims in this regard are limited to Europe and to the Americas. At the same time, with regard to Europe, these norms come from two different international organizations: the Council of Europe (an international organization of cooperation) and the European Union (an international organization of integration) with the consequence that its norms are of a different nature compared to the legal norms of each of them. Basically this means that only the institutional norms adopted inside the European Union have a clear binding legal effect.[39]

As far as the *American* continent is concerned, there actually only exists one international norm on victims that was adopted by OAS.[40]

On the other hand, the situation differs because of the categories of victims envisaged by such norms: victims of crime, victims of terrorism and victims of enforced disappearance.

Third, it also differs because of the different legal nature of the existent norms: a plurality of institutional norms and only two of a conventional nature.

At least, as I have just stated, the international norms adopted in the framework of the Council of Europe and of the EU differ in their legal effects as a consequence of the legal nature of the international organization from which those norms come: cooperation in the case of the Council of Europe; integration in that of the EU.

International Norms of a Regional Scope

Europe: The Council of Europe and the European Union

In the European regional framework, as in its work in the field of human rights, the Council of Europe has also been pioneering with regard to victims with the *European Convention on the Compensation of Victims of Violent Crimes* adopted

---

[39] There is no doubt about the binding effects of norms adopted by the EU because it is clearly stated in the foundational treaties (cf. article 288 of the Treaty on the Functioning of the European Union

(*Official Journal of the European Union* (*OJEU*) C 115 of 9 May 2008).

[40] Remember, the Inter-American Convention on enforced disappearance of persons, of the 9th July 1994.

This Convention entered into force on 28 March 1996. That is, in accordance with its article XX, on the thirtieth day from the date of deposit of the second instrument of ratification.

on 24 November 1983.[41] It is the sole international treaty on victims existing in Europe although only related to one category: the victims of violent crimes. This Convention has been preceded by previous work of the Council of Europe, which focused upon different international institutional norms related to victims. They are basically resolutions and recommendations. This is the case with *Resolution 77 (27) On the Compensation of Victims of Crime* adopted by the Committee of Ministers on 28 September 1977, which is based upon reasons of equity and social solidarity with the aim of laying down guiding principles with a view to harmonising national provisions in this field. With respect to *compensation of victims of crime Resolution 77 (27)* takes into account the fact that the possibilities of compensation that are available to victims of crime are often insufficient, in particular, when the offender has not been identified or is without resources. This is why it lays down a group of guiding principles (like those regarding the prompt compensation of victims of crime; the subsidiary compensation by the state when it cannot be ensured by other means, etc.) that will be developed by Member States. Later, in its *Recommendation (83) 7*, adopted on 23 June 1983 *On Participation of the Public in Crime Policy* the Committee of Ministers underlined the need for a crime policy which takes account victims' interests and formulates some measures.[42]

After the 1983 Convention, the Council of Europe moved forward by taking into account *The Position of the Victim in the Framework of Criminal Law and Procedure* through *Recommendation No. R (85) 11*, of 28 June 1985.[43] This Recommendation changes the perspective of compensation of victims of violent crimes that is found in the 1983 *European Convention on the Compensation of Victims of Violent Crimes* and focuses on victims rights' in the framework of criminal law and procedure. From this point of view, *Recommendation (85) 11* takes into account not only the traditional perspective of the legal justice system, focused on the relationship between the state and the offender, but also focuses its attention on the needs and interests of victims through a catalogue of guidelines. It recommends that Member States review their legislation and practice in accordance with a series of guidelines, all of which consider the position of the victim in the following fields: in respect of the police and in respect of the prosecution, in questioning of the

[41] European Convention on the Compensation of Victims of Violent Crimes, Convention No. 116, adopted on 24 November 1983, entered into force on 1 February 1998. This Convention is actually ratified by 27 of the 47 Member States of the Council of Europe. Italy, Greece and Poland are some of the states of the European Union that have not ratified the Convention.

[42] For the text, see www.coe.int. After the European Convention on the Compensation of Victims of Violent Crimes of 1983, the Committee of Ministers of the Council of Europe took other recommendations on victims. Cf., for example, the following: No. R (85) 11 E On the position of the victim in the framework of criminal law and procedure, adopted on 28 June 1985; No. R (87) 21 E On assistance to victims and the prevention of victimisation, adopted on 17 September 1987; No. R (93) 1 E On effective access to the law and to justice for the very poor adopted on 8 January 1993; and No. R (97) 13 concerning intimidation of witnesses and the rights of the defence adopted on 10 September 1997.

[43] See www.coe.int.

victim, the information that should be given to victims in the framework of court proceedings, compensation of victims, the protection of victim's privacy, as well as the special protection that should be given to victims against intimidation and the risk of retaliation by the offender whenever this appears necessary.

On 17 September 1987, the Committee of Ministers adopted *Recommendation No. R (87) 21 On the Assistance to Victims and the Prevention of Victimisation.* By that it recommends a broad battery of measures to the Member States. This institutional norm was followed in 2006 by *Recommendation (2006) 8* of the Committee of Ministers *On Assistance to Crime Victims* which was adopted on 14 June. These Recommendations form the corner stone for the Council of Europe's *European Convention on the Compensation of Victims of Violent Crimes*, which expounds in its preamble on reasons of equity and social solidarity to deal with two situations. On the one hand, that of victims of intentional crimes who have suffered bodily injury or impairment of health and of dependants of persons who have died as a result of such crimes. On the other hand, and as a consequence of the precedent, the need to introduce or develop schemes for compensation for these victims by the state in whose territory such crimes were committed, in particular when the offender has not been identified or is without resources. To achieve its objectives, the 1983 Convention contains "minimum provisions" to compensate victims of crimes. They consist of a general principle and some rules concerning the scope of victim's compensation. According to that general principle, compensation shall be paid by the state on whose territory the crime has been committed[44] when compensation is not "fully available" from other sources.[45] As far as the scope of the victim's compensation is concerned it shall cover "at least the following items: loss of earnings, medical and hospitalisation expenses and funeral expenses, and, as regards dependants, loss of maintenance".[46] The 1983 Convention allows States Parties, if necessary, to set for any or all elements of compensation "an upper limit above which and a minimum threshold below which such compensation shall not be granted".[47] It also allows States Parties to reduce or refuse victim's compensation on account of the applicant's situation.[48] The victim's compensation may also be reduced or refused in the following three situations: on account of the victim's or the applicant's conduct before, during or after the crime, or in relation to the injury or death; on account of the victim's or the applicant's involvement in organized crime or his membership in an organization which engages in crimes of violence; or

[44] See Articles 2, 3 and 4 of the European Convention on the Compensation of Victims of Violent Crimes, see note 26.

[45] Article 2, *ibid.*

[46] Article 4, *ibid.*

[47] Article 5, *ibid.*

[48] Article 7, *ibid.*

if an award or a full award would be contrary to a sense of justice or to public policy (*ordre public*).[49]

Nevertheless, the 1983 Convention does not cover all victims of crime. According to article 3, compensation shall be paid by the state on whose territory the crime was committed only to two groups of persons: (a) to nationals of the States Parties to the Convention; (b) to nationals of all Member States of the Council of Europe who are permanent residents in the state on whose territory the crime was committed. As a result of this approach, three groups of persons are *excluded* from a possible compensation even if they are victims of a crime committed in the territory of a State Party to the Convention: (a) the nationals of Member States of the Council of Europe ware not parties to the Convention; (b) the nationals of Member States of the Council of Europe who are not permanent residents in the state on whose territory the crime was committed; and (c) the nationals of third states.

It should not be forgotten that the Council of Europe is an international organization of cooperation. This means that the efficacy of its action is conditioned by the political will of Member States. With regard to the 1983 Convention, this means that the efficacy of its objectives depends not only on the ratification of the treaty by the Member States of the Council of Europe but also on the adoption of all national measures necessary to implement the treaty by the relevant States Parties.[50] It is obvious that the step forward represented by the 1983 Convention is a weak one, as it excludes three groups of persons. Further, the reluctance of Member States in accepting and executing the resolutions and recommendations adopted by the Committee of Ministers should be remembered.

As mentioned earlier, after the1983 Convention *Recommendation No. R (85) 11*, adopted on 28 June 1985 on *The Position of the Victim in the Framework of Criminal Law and Procedure* changes the perspective of compensation of victims of violent crimes that is found in the 1983 Convention analyzed hand focuses on victims rights' in the framework of criminal law and procedure. So it takes into account the traditional perspective of the legal justice system, focused on the relationship between the state and the offender, and it also focuses its attention on the needs and interests of victims through a catalogue of guidelines.

To make an evaluation of the action of the Council of Europe with regard to victims of crime, several circumstances should be taken into account. First, as stated earlier, in the case of the Council of Europe we are in the typical context of an international organization of cooperation. This is an organization to which member states do not transfer competences to be exercised by it. As known in this kind of international organization, the effectiveness of the measures adopted depends to a large extent on the will of member states. In the case of the *European Convention on the Compensation of Victims of Violent Crimes* adopted on 24 November 1983,

[49] Article 8, *ibid.*

[50] Because the 1983 Convention is not a self-executing one.

the effectiveness of its goals depends on the ratification of the treaty by the Council of European Member States'. It also depends on the executive measures such states have to adopt in domestic law because in international law—and it is the case of the 1983 Convention—what is usual is that treaties are not *self-executing* but *not self-executing*. That is, needing national measures in order to be applied. But in this case, too, the fact is that only 25 of the 47 Member States of the Council of Europe have ratified this Convention. In other words, the effectiveness of this treaty, like that of others, depends on the double attitude of states: on the one hand, its will to ratify the treaty; on the other hand, the adoption of the national measures that are necessary to apply it. But both circumstances need a lot of time and without them it is impossible to achieve the goals the treaty is intended for.

Second, it is obvious that the progress the 1983 Convention pursues to compensate victims of violent crimes becomes weak by the exclusions it contains with regard to the three groups of victims quoted here.

The slowness of states in the acceptance and execution in domestic law of the resolutions and recommendations adopted by the Committee of Ministers should also be taken into account here. It is a weakness inherent to international institutional norms but it does not exempt the addressee states from their obligation of accepting the legal effects such norms contain. At the same time, this weakness does not prevent states from delaying their fulfilment.

In any case, it must be recognized that the Council of Europe has been a pioneer in the field of victims of crime and that its action has pointed out to the *EU* the way to follow. Examples of this are the recent legislative measures adopted by the European Union focused in the Treaty of Amsterdam. They are basically two: the *Council Framework Decision (2001/220/JHA) of 15 March 2001 on the Standing of Victims in Criminal Proceedings*[51] and the *Council Directive 2004/80/EC of 29 April 2004 Relating to Compensation to Crime Victims*.[52] I will analyze this later.

But the Council of Europe has also been a pioneer with regard to *victims of terrorism*. Yes, as different from victims of crime—with regard to whom we have just examined a plurality of international norms of general or universal as well as of regional scope—the only international norm actually entirely dedicated to victims of terrorism is the *Guidelines on the Protection of Victims of Terrorist Acts* adopted by the Committee of Ministers of the Council of Europe on 2 March 2005[53] with the aim of addressing the needs and concerns of the victims of terrorist acts "in identifying the means to be implemented to help them and to protect their fundamental rights while excluding any form of arbitrariness, as well as any discriminatory or racist treatment".[54] These Guidelines reaffirm the *Guidelines on Human*

[51] OJEC L 82 of 22 March 2001. This Framework Decision has been qualified as "a milestone in the development of victims' rights" as well as "the first so-called 'hard law' instrument covering a wide range of victims' rights available at the international level" (Pemberton and Groenhuijsen, p. 1).

[52] OJEC L 261 of 6 August 2004.

[53] *Council of Europe*, Committee of Ministers-CM/Del/Dec(2005)917.

[54] Paragraph h) of the preamble, *ibid.*

Rights and the Fight against Terrorism, adopted on 11 July 2002 at the 804th meeting of the Ministers' Deputies, "as a permanent and universal reference".[55]

With regard to its *legal nature*, is it a binding norm? What kind of international norm is it? The answer is neither easy nor unequivocal. The Guidelines themselves underline the aim of inviting states to cooperate. The last paragraph of the preamble "invites member states to implement" the Guidelines and "ensure that they are widely disseminated among all authorities responsible for the fight against terrorism and for the protection of the victims of terrorist acts, as well as among representatives of civil society." But despite this invited character that could lead one to conclude that these guidelines are not binding, it is necessary to take into account other elements allowing the support of an affirmative conclusion on its binding effect upon Member States of the Council of Europe. One of these elements is the fact that the Guidelines reiterate with regard to victims of terrorism a catalogue of rights most of which are actually in force. So, for most parts it is not dealing with rights *ex novo* (that in fact these guidelines do not create) but with international obligations strongly consolidated in many international treaties.[56] Furthermore, most of the rights proclaimed are of a customary nature.

Therefore, and independent of the binding or not binding character of this institutional norm inherent to its own legal nature, it can be concluded that the most part of the Guidelines bind member states because they do nothing other than reaffirm international obligations actually binding states through conventional or through customary ways.

If the weakness of the legal action developed by the Council of Europe is remembered—from the point of view of the legal effects—it will be easier to understand the importance of the action developed inside the *EU*. As already stated, as different from the Council of Europe, in the case of the EU we are confronted by an international organization of integration. That is, an international organization to which member states have transferred competences; even legislative competences binding on member states.

As stated earlier, the legislative measures adopted by the European Union on victims are: the *Council Framework Decision (2001/220/JHA) of 15 March 2001*

[55] Paragraph e) of the preamble, *ibid.*

[56] As stated earlier, this is the case in the general or universal frame for both the International Covenant on Civil and Political Rights and the International Covenant on Economic, Social and Cultural Rights. Also, in the regional frame of the European Convention on Human Rights, the American Convention on Human Rights of 22 November 1969 and of the African Charter on Human and Peoples' Rights of 27 June 1981. The Guidelines of the Council of Europe contain a catalogue of rights to which victims of terrorism are entitled: right to emergency assistance, right to continuing assistance, right to investigation and prosecution, right to an effective access to the law and to justice, right to administration of justice, right to compensation, right to protection of the private and family life of victims of terrorist acts, right to protection of the dignity and security of victims of terrorist acts, right to information for victims of terrorist acts, and the right to a specific training for persons responsible for assisting victims of terrorist acts.

on the Standing of Victims in Criminal Proceedings and the *Council Directive 2004/80/EC of 29 April 2004 Relating to Compensation to Crime Victims.*

The *Council Framework Decision of 15 March 2001* is adopted under Title VI of the Treaty of the European Union (TEU): "Provisions on Cooperation in the Fields of Justice and Home Affairs". With regard to its binding effects, its dispositions refer to article 34.2.b) TEU according to which the Council can adopt,

> framework decisions for the purpose of approximation of the laws and regulations of the Member States. Framework decisions shall be binding upon the Member States as to the result to be achieved but shall leave to the national authorities the choice of form and methods. They shall not entail direct effect.

As a result, all Member States are obliged to adopt all national measures that are needed to give effectiveness to the standing of victims in criminal proceedings envisaged by this Council Framework Decision. It underlines its harmonising nature, "to the extent necessary to attain the objective of affording victims of crime a high level of protection, irrespective of the Member State in which they are present."[57] It really responds to the needs underlined in the conclusions of the European Council meeting in Tampere on 15 and 16 October 1999, in particular point 32 thereof, that stipulated that "minimum standards should be drawn up on the protection of the victims of crimes, in particular on crime victims' access to justice and on their right to compensation for damages, including legal costs. In addition, national programmes should be set up to finance measures, public and nongovernmental, for assistance to and protection of victims."[58]

The approaches taken by this Council Framework Decision are the following. First, it considers that the victim's needs should be considered and addressed in a comprehensive, coordinated manner, avoiding partial or inconsistent solutions that may give rise to secondary victimization.[59] Second, it states that its provisions are not confined to attending to the victim's interests under criminal proceedings proper but they also cover certain measures to assist victims before or after criminal proceedings, which might mitigate the effects of the crime.[60] Third, the Council Framework Decision also considers that the rules and practices as regards the standing and main rights of victims need to be approximated, with particular regard to the right to be treated with respect, the right to provide and receive information, the right to understand and be understood, the right to be protected at the various stages of procedure and the right to have allowance made for the disadvantage of

[57] Cf. para. 4 of the preamble of the Council Framework Decision 2001/220/JHA, see note 51. It "codifies rules at the supranational level concerning the legal position of victims that are binding concerning the domestic legal order of the member states" (Pemberton and Groenhuijsen, "Developing victims' rights...", *op. cit.*, 1).

[58] Cf. para. 3, *ibid.*

[59] Cf. para. 5, *ibid*

[60] Cf. para. 6, *ibid.*

living in a different Member State from the one in which the crime was committed.[61] Finally, the Council Framework Decision envisages the involvement of specialized services and victim support groups before, during and after criminal proceedings, as well as the fact that suitable and adequate training should be given to persons coming into contact with victims; a training that "is essential both for victims and for achieving the purposes of proceedings."[62]

Council Directive 2004/80/EC of 29 April 2004 constitutes the culmination on the European Union level of the initiative taken by the Council of Europe with its *Convention on the Compensation of Victims of Violent Crimes*, the object of both being the complete compensation of victims of crime. This is why both norms build up a system of cooperation between states to facilitate access to compensation to victims of crimes in cross-border situations. The victims of crime should not be disadvantaged by the fact of having suffered the crime in a state[63] other than the state where the victim is habitually resident. It is obvious that this objective is easier to achieve with *Council Directive 2004/80/EC* than with the Convention of 1983 because the Council Directive is binding upon all Member States while the Convention of 1983 is only binding for States Parties and the Directive entered into force on the twentieth day following its publication in the Official Journal of the European Union. To achieve its objectives, *Directive 2004/80/EC* builds its action upon *two fundamental principles*—the principle according to which victims of crimes in the European Union should be entitled to fair and appropriate compensation for the injuries they have suffered, and this regardless of where in the European Union the crime was committed.[64]

But as in the European Convention of 1983, a gap remains because the Directive does not cover all victims not habitually resident in a Member State of the European Union.[65]

The other principle is that of territoriality. According to it compensation shall be paid by the competent authority of the Member State on whose territory the crime

---

[61] Cf. para. 8, *ibid.*

[62] Cf. para. 11, *ibid.*

[63] A State Party to the Convention of 24 November 1983, see note 41, or a Member State of the European Union.

[64] A principle mentioned in para. 6 of the preamble, Council Directive 2004/80/EC, see note 52: "Crime victims in the European Union should be entitled to fair and appropriate compensation for the injuries they have suffered regardless of where in the European Union the crime was committed". It is also formulated in article 1: "Member States shall ensure that where a violent intentional crime has been committed in a Member State other than the Member State where the applicant for compensation is habitually resident, the applicant shall have the right to submit the application to an authority or any other body in the latter Member State."

[65] As stated earlier, the European Convention of 1983 does not cover three groups of victims: nationals of all Member States of the Council of Europe not parties to the Convention; nationals of all Member States of the Council of Europe not habitually resident in the state in which the crime has been committed; and nationals of third states. See page 20 of the present work.

has been committed.[66] The idea behind this is the freedom of movement existing in the European Union linked to the objective of suppression, between Member States, of all obstacles to it. When European Union law guarantees to a person the freedom of movement, the protection of that person from any harm in the Member State in question, has to be guaranteed. This is the corollary of the freedom of movement.

This is why the Directive envisages several measures with the aim of realizing the objective of an effective compensation.[67] It constitutes "minimum standards on the protection of the victims of crime, in particular on crime victims' access to justice and their rights to compensation for damages, including legal costs."[68] At the same time, the Directive establishes a system of cooperation to facilitate the access of victims of crime to compensation in cross-border situations. This system of cooperation is structured upon the regimes actually existing in most of the Member States being built upon the European Convention of 1983. The Directive adds to it a new mechanism of compensation in all Member States. Such a system of cooperation is based on two principles. On the one hand, it should be ensured that victims of crime could always turn to an authority in the Member State where they reside. Any practical and linguistic difficulties that occur in a cross-border situation should be eradicated; on the other hand, it should include the provisions necessary for the victim to find the information needed to make the application and to allow for efficient cooperation between the authorities involved.[69]

Nevertheless, recent works of the Commission Staff underline the fact that the current European Union legislation is inadequate to meet the needs of victims. The issues identified are covered by the two following problems: on the one hand, existing European Union legislation is inadequate to improve the situation of victims because it is vague, does not contain concrete obligations and is not enforceable, and has therefore been poorly implemented by the Member States.[70] On the other hand, the needs of victims of crime are not sufficiently addressed in the Member States because victims do not get recognition and respect, protection, support, effective access to justice, or effective access to compensation and restoration.[71]

---

[66] A principle ruled in article 2 Council Directive 2004/80/EC, see note 52.

[67] Cf. CJEU, *Cowan Case*, Case 186/87, European Court Reports 1989, 195.

[68] Para. 3 of the preamble, Council Directive 2004/80/EC, see note 52.

[69] Cf. *ibid.*, paragraphs 12 and 13.

[70] In the opinion of Pemberton, A. and Groenhuijsen, M.S., "the transposal of Framewotk decision articles in domestic legislation and the enforcement of victims' rights paints a considerably less encouraging picture. It might be an overstatement to call the implementation of the Framework Decision a failure, but at least one may conclude, …, that the impact has not been qualitatively different from previous soft-law instruments" ("Developing victims' rights…", *op. cit.*, 2). In this regard, see Groenhuijsen and Pemberton, 43–59.

[71] Cf. COMMISSION STAFF WORKING PAPER, Executive summary of the Impact Assessment Accompanying the document Communication from the Commission to the European Parliament, to the Council, to the European economic and social Committee and to the Committee of the Regions—Strengthening victim's rights in the EU {COM(2011) 274 final}and {SEC(2011) 580 final}, Brussels, 18.5.2011, SEC(2011) 581 final, p. 6.

At the least, the consequences of crime and not meeting the needs of victims also have significant hidden costs, including important financial and health costs.[72]

With regard to *the first problem*, the Commission Staff's working papers underline that both *Framework Decision 2001/220/JHA on the standing of victims in criminal proceedings* and *Directive 2004/80/EC on the compensation of crime victims* are inadequate because of the following elements. First, the level of implementation by the Member States of these two pieces of legislation has been mixed. Second, "whilst the scope of the Framework Decision covers most of the rights of victims of all types of crime and is overall still relevant, any new action needs to cover a wider range of rights and obligations on the Member States given the growing awareness and changing judicial culture to address not only the rights and needs of the prosecuted but also those of the victims".[73] This is why the scope of EU legislation on victims needs to be updated in light of new research and findings on victims, in particular with regard to mutual recognition of protection measures, and access to justice. Third, the Framework Decision suffers from ambiguous drafting, weak obligations and infringement possibilities.[74] The Framework Decision has not been effective in meeting, or moving towards the desired outcomes of addressing the needs of victims and achieving minimum standards for victims across the EU because no Member State can claim to have fully implemented the Framework Decision. According to the Commission Staff Working Paper of 18 May 2011, the ineffectiveness of this legislation is due to ambiguous drafting, a lack of concrete obligations and a lack of infringement possibilities against Member States.[75]

With regard to the second problem—that is, the needs of victims of crime that are not sufficiently addressed in the Member States—the Commission Staff Working Paper classifies the needs of victims into five categories: the need to be recognized and treated with respect and dignity[76]; the need to be protected[77]; the need to be

[72] *Ibid.*, 2.

[73] *Ibid.*

[74] *Ibid.*, 4.

[75] Cf. *ibid.*, 2. About the implementation of this Framework Decision, see the excellent study of APAV, *Project Victims in Europe. Implementation of the EU Framework Decision on the standing of victims in the criminal proceedings in the Member States of the European Union*, Lisbon, 2009.

[76] Victims "need to be recognised as victims and for their suffering to be acknowledged. Victims also need to be treated with dignity and respect in all communications with all persons involved in the judicial process. Particular attention should be given to the needs of vulnerable victims, e.g. children, disabled person, victims of sexual violence. Indirect victims (e.g. family members) also need to be recognised as the consequences of the crime affect them too." (*ibid.*).

[77] Victims "need to be protected to prevent further crime or intimidation from the offender. For victims of chronic violence, security is both their primary need in reporting a crime, but also their primary concern." Victims also "need to be protected from secondary victimisation during proceedings due to poor treatment in connection with and during the judicial process." (*ibid.*).

supported[78]; the need to access justice[79]; and the need for access to compensation and restoration.[80]

According to the Commission Staff, the fact that these needs generally are not sufficiently or adequately met in the Member States is the key problem that the proposed measures—a new Directive on the matter—will address.[81] On the other hand in the opinion of the doctrine, the Framework Decision, "although it was intended to approximate the victims' position across the European Union, has ended up widening the gap between member states with more advanced victims' rights and those in which they have still to meet the most basic requirements".[82]

The primary drivers for the identified problems quoted here are: non-prioritization of victims and a lack of knowledge about their needs, rooted in historical and cultural attitudes; a lack of enforcing mechanisms for victims' rights and a lack of practitioner knowledge of victims' issues.

The general objectives of the future Directive on victims of crime, actually in discussion, are "to facilitate the establishment of a European area of freedom, security and justice and the development of mutual trust between criminal justice authorities, by ensuring that the rights of victims are fully respected throughout the EU, whilst also respecting the rights of the defence, and that citizens can circulate freely without being treated differently should they fall victim to crime."[83]

More precisely, the Commission Staff Working Paper distinguishes between *specific* and *operational* objectives. As *specific objectives* it quotes:

---

[78] In the immediate aftermath of a crime, victims "need support mainly through emergency assistance together with psychological first aid. Support during the subsequent judicial process, whether legal, emotional or practical, is also often needed by and crucial to victims, and in particular vulnerable victims. Support may be needed both in the short and long term as a consequence of the crime." (*ibid*., 3).

[79] Victims "must be given access to justice, such as accessibility of court processes, availability of adequate legal representation in criminal trials, access to more informal legal processes and the right to review a decision on whether or not to prosecute the offender. Victims must also be able to understand the information received and the proceedings." (*ibid*.).

[80] Victims "must be given the choice to access restorative justice services, as a complement to the normal judicial process. Restorative justice gives victims an opportunity to confront their offenders face to face and allows offenders account for what they have done. This process helps victims to get on with their lives." (*ibid*.).

[81] The cause, "the fact that some of its norms are phrased in vague, open fashion, making it difficult to ascertain whether member states have, in fact, complied with them" (Pemberton and Groenhuijsen, "Developing victims' rights…", *op. cit*., 3). Concerning its evaluation, "in 2009, seven years after the deadline for transposition of most Framework Decision articles, still no EU Member State had correctly done so" (*ibid*., 9).

[82] Pemberton and Groenhuijsen, "Developing victims' rights…", *op. cit*., 10. Such analysis guides both authors to say that "albeit a hard law instrument in nature" this Framework Decision "has not had qualitatively different effects from previous soft-law instruments" (*ibid*.). See also Groenhuijsen and Pemberton, 43–59.

[83] *Ibid*., 5.

- To ensure that victims are recognized and treated with respect and dignity[84];
- To ensure that victims are protected[85];
- To ensure that victims are supported[86];
- To ensure that victims have effective access to justice[87]; and
- To ensure that victims have access to compensation and restoration.[88]

To achieve it, the proposed measures will establish "minimum standards on victims' rights, which will improve the general environment for protecting all victims of all types of crime in EU law and policy, including for instance victims of terrorism and road traffic crimes."[89]

Consequently, the new legal step on the matter in the EU will soon be a *Directive of the European Parliament and of the Council establishing minimum standards on the rights, support and protection of victims of crime*, now at the stage of a Proposal.[90] This proposal aims to ensure that the wide-ranging needs of victims of crime are respected and met. For this, it establishes minimum standards on victims' rights, which will improve the general environment for protecting victims in EU law and policy, and it also sets out the horizontal framework for addressing the needs of all victims of crime, irrespective of the type of crime or the circumstances or place in which it was committed.

An additional relevant element is that all provisions in this proposal are also applicable to family members of a victim—that is, *indirect victims*—whose death has been caused by a criminal offence "since such persons have specific and

---

[84] The *operative objectives* in this regard are: to ensure that the needs of indirect victims are met; to ensure that all police, prosecutors, judges and court staff who come into contact with victims receive appropriate victims training; and the establishment of needs assessment mechanisms for all victims to identify the needs of victims and vulnerable victims and their needs.

[85] The *operative objectives* in this regard are: to ensure that victims do not lose the protection they have been given when they travel or move abroad; to ensure that contact between the offender and victim is avoided during proceedings.

[86] The *operative objective* in this regard is to ensure that effective victim support services are available

[87] The *operative objectives* in this regard are: to ensure that all victims are able to attend trial; to ensure that all victims are assisted in understanding their rights, obligations and the proceedings; and to ensure that all victims have a right to have prosecution decisions reviewed.

[88] The *operative objective* in this regard is to ensure all victims have access to effective Restorative Justice Services

[89] Cf. COMMISSION STAFF WORKING PAPER, *op. cit.*, 6.

[90] European Commission, COM(2011) 275/2. For this, it will build on and complement existing instruments, in particular Council Directive 2011/36/EU on preventing and combating trafficking in human beings, and protecting victims, in Council Directive on combating the sexual abuse, sexual exploitation of children and child pornography presently under negotiation or in Council Framework Decision of 2002/475/JHA on combating terrorism as modified by Council Framework Decision 2008/919/JHA of 28 November 2008.

legitimate interests in the proceedings beyond those of family members of surviving victims and are often recognized as representatives of the victim"[91]

Following the conclusions of the impact assessment accompanying this proposal, the new directive—a directive containing concrete obligations on the charge of Member States on the rights of victims—will replace *Council Framework Decision 2001/220/JHA on the standing of victims in criminal proceedings*. This is why the proposal, at the same time that it maintains a number of provisions of it[92] also adds, new articles introducing substantives changes to it. They concern the following issues.

First, the *definition* of direct[93] and indirect victim[94] is accompanied by that of other situations envisaged in the proposal. This is the case in the following: "family members",[95] "non-marital cohabitee",[96] "registered partner",[97] "restorative justice services",[98] "child"[99] and "a person with disability".[100]

Second, four *rights are recognized as related to victims for the provision of information and support*: the right to receive information from the first contact with a competent authority (Article 3), the right of victims to receive information about

[91] *Ibid.*, 6.

[92] This is the case of the following articles of the proposal: Article 9 (right to be heard), Article 12 (right to legal aid), Article 14 (right to the return of property), Article 15 (right to decision on compensation from the offender in the course of criminal proceedings), Article 16 (rights of victims resident in another Member State) and Article 25 (co-operation and co-ordination of services).

[93] That is, "a natural person who has suffered harm, including physical or mental injury, emotional suffering or economic loss directly caused by a criminal offence".

[94] That is, "the family members of a person whose death has been caused by a criminal offence".

[95] According to Article 2.b), "'family members' means the spouse, non-marital cohabitee, registered partner, the relatives in direct line, the brothers and sisters, and the dependants of the victim".

[96] According to Article 2.c), "'non-marital cohabitee' means a person who is living with the victim on a stable and continuous basis without that relationship being registered with an authority".

[97] According to Article 2.d), "registered partner' means the partner with whom the victim has entered into a registered partnership, on the basis of the legislation of a Member State".

[98] According to Article 2.e), "'restorative justice services' means services which have as their objective to bring together the victim and the accused with a view to reaching a voluntary agreement between them on how the harm arising from the offence can be addressed".

[99] According to Article 2.f), "'child' means any person below 18 years of age".

[100] According to Article 2.g), "'a person with disability' means a person who has a physical, mental, intellectual or sensory impairment which, in interaction with various barriers, may hinder the full and effective participation in society on an equal basis with others."

their case (Article 4), the right to understand and to be understood (Article 5) and the right to interpretation and translation (Article 6).[101]

Third, the right of victims to *access victim support services*. To this regard, unlike the Guidelines of the Council of Europe, Article 7 of the proposal for a Directive conceives this right as an obligation on the charge of Member States, which "shall ensure that victims and their family members, in accordance with their needs, have access to free of charge confidential victim support services".[102] This support should be available "from the earliest possible moment after the commission of as crime irrespective of whether it has been reported" and provided in a variety of ways.[103]

Fourth, in the framework of *victims' participation in criminal proceedings*, the proposal for a Directive includes four victims' rights: the right of victims to have their complaint acknowledged (Article 8)[104]; the right to have any decision not to prosecute reviewed for which Member States shall ensure that victims are provided with sufficient information to decide whether to request a review of any decision not to prosecute (Article 10)[105]; the right to safeguards in the context of mediation and other restorative justice services (Article 11), which includes the establishment on the charge of Member States of standards to safeguard the victim from intimidation or further victimization, to be applied when providing mediation or other restorative justice services[106]; and the right to reimbursement of expenses incurred as a result of victims' participation in criminal proceedings, including as a result of their attendance at the trial (Article 13).

---

[101] It is of the European Commission that "the purpose of these Articles is to ensure that victims receive sufficient information in a form they can understand to enable them to fully access their rights and to ensure they feel treated in a respectful manner. Such information should be available from the moment a victim makes a complaint of a criminal offence as well as on a regular basis throughout criminal proceedings and in relation to the progress of the case. Sufficient detail should be provided to enable victims to make informed decisions about their participation in proceedings and how to access their rights, in particular when deciding whether to request a review of the decision not to prosecute." (COM(2011) 275/2, 7).

[102] This right including a minimum of such services shall provide (cf. Article 7.2 of the proposal).

[103] Cf. COM(2011) 275/2, 7.

[104] According to the legal elements of the proposal, the purpose of this Article is to ensure that "when a person makes a complaint of a crime, the victim is provided with an official acknowledgment which they can refer back to in any future communications." (*ibid.*).

[105] In order to enable the victim "to verify that that established procedures and rules have been complied with and that a correct decision has been made to end a prosecution in relation to a specific person".

[106] Article 11 lists a minimum content of such standards." (*ibid.*, 8). Precise mechanisms for a review are left to national law but it is established that such a review should "as minimum" carried out by a person or authority different to the one that took the original decision not to prosecute. It is important to say that in such cases, participation of the victim "should be voluntary which also implies that the victim has sufficient knowledge of the risks and benefits to make an informed choice." (*ibid.*).

Fifth, the proposal for a Directive takes into account and gives great importance to the *vulnerability of victims* providing to this issue five articles (Articles 18–23) in the frame of Chap. 4 entitled "Recognition of vulnerability and protection of victims". So, Article 18 identifies four categories of vulnerable victims: children, persons with disabilities, victims of sexual violence and victims of human trafficking; its purpose being "to ensure that victims are not prevented from attending the trial and seeing justice done, due to their own financial limitations".[107]

Vulnerable victims once specified, Articles 19–23 list several rights linked to their protection: the right to avoidance of contact between victim and offender (Article 19),[108] the right to protection of victims during questioning in criminal investigations in order to prevent secondary victimization (Article 20), the right to protection of vulnerable victims during criminal proceedings (Article 21) and the right to protection of child victims during criminal proceedings (Article 22).[109]

With regard to this issue of the different categories of vulnerable victims envisaged by this proposal, it is surprising that the absence among them of the victims of terrorism, a category of vulnerable victims ignored by this proposal even after having declared in the legal elements of the proposal concerning this Article 18 that "victims of terrorism require particular attention in any assessment given the varying nature of such acts ranging from acts of mass terrorism to targeted terrorism against individuals".[110] Consequently, they are relegated to the general provision of Article 18.3 according to which Member States "shall ensure that all other victims receive a timely and individual assessment, in accordance with national procedures, to determine whether they are vulnerable, due to their personal characteristics or the circumstances or the type or nature of the crime, to secondary and repeat victimization or intimidation."

I find this approach inadequate with regard to victims of terrorism. In my opinion, they should be included in this Proposal for a Directive as another category of vulnerable victims and not excluded from this inclusion for separate treatment in a specific directive, which is the most adequate way to reinforce the international legal statute.

Finally, in the framework of Chap. 6 entitled "General Provisions", Article 24 of the Proposal for a Directive refers to the *training of practitioners*. Here, unlike the *Guidelines on the Protection of Victims of Terrorist Acts* adopted by the Committee of Ministers of the Council of Europe on 2 March 2005—which only say that States "should encourage specific training for persons responsible for assisting victims of

---

[107] *Ibid.*

[108] Which could be achieved "by various means such as establishing separate waiting areas, and controlling the arrival of victims and the accused. Best practice and guidance offered to public officials can also act as an important source of information on how to assist in avoiding contact." (*ibid.*, 10).

[109] Article 23 (right to protection of privacy) also included in this Chapter of the proposal was already recognized in the precedent norms of the EU.

[110] European Commission, COM(2011) 275/2, 9.

terrorist acts, as well as granting the necessary resources to that effect"[111]—Article 24 of the Proposal for a Directive goes further imposing upon Member States a legal obligation. So, they "shall ensure" that staff related to the victims (police, prosecutors, court staff, members of the judiciary, persons providing victim support and restorative justice services) receive both general and specialist training to sensitize them to the needs of victims and to deal with them in an impartial, respectful and professional manner.[112] In the same line, Member States shall also ensure that victim support and restorative services are provided in an impartial, respectful and professional manner.

From a global perspective, the new Directive will reinforce the legal statute of victims of crime inside the EU including in it a list of rights more developed and enriched than in the first EU legal norm on the matter: the replaced *Council Framework Decision 2001/220/JHA on the standing of victims in criminal proceedings*.[113] Nevertheless, once adopted, "it remains to seen whether it becomes effective in practice. Even when it has been transposed in national legal order, challenges remain, in the sense that enforcement of EU-inspired national provisions may be insufficient or lacking together".[114]

---

[111] On point No. XI.

[112] The legal elements of the proposal speak of "training requirements for public officials who come into contact with victims". It adds that "the level, type and frequency of training including any specialist training should be determined in accordance with the extent and nature of the officials' contact with victims as well as, in particular, whether they are in contact with specific groups of victims." Training should cover "issues which will assist officials to treat victims in a respectful manner, to identify protection needs and to provide them with appropriate information to help them cope with proceedings and access their rights" as well as issues "such as awareness of the negative effects of crime on victims and the risk of causing secondary victimisation, skills and knowledge, including special measures and techniques, required to assist victims and minimise any trauma to the victim in particular from secondary victimisation, recognising and preventing intimidation, threats and harm to victims, the availability of services providing information and support specific to the needs of victims and the means of accessing these services." (*ibid.*, 11).

[113] In opinion of Pemberton and Groenhuijsen, "even in comparison to earlier soft-law instruments the draft Directive is more concrete as well as more ambitious. Instead of being a set of minimum standards, it represents a significant advance on even the highest level of victims' rights available" (Pemberton and Groenhuijsen "Developing victims' rights…", *op. cit.*, 13). Moreover, being a stronger instrument than a framework decision, it has "more possibilities to review the progress in implementation and to sanction non-compliers. Individual complainants can use the provisions of a Directive, but not a Framework Decision, to bring a case before the European Court of Justice" (*ibid.*, 11).

[114] *Ibid.*, 14. In this sense, "it is highly questionable whether transposal into law should be the most relevant criterion in the assessment of the position of victims of crime. For many of the norms, it is not the legislative provision, but enforcement in practice that matters. It is often not much use to have a law asserting a right to support or to receive information, if the actual support or reception of information in practice is not secured" (*ibid.*, 3).

America: The Organization of American States (OAS)

In the American regional sphere, the only existing international norm related to victims—in this case to one category of victims—is the *Inter-American Convention on Forced Disappearance of Persons* of 9 July 1994.[115] It contains a definition of "forced disappearance"[116] but not of "victim". Thus, the definitions existing in the other international norms may be useful. The Convention contains obligations of States Parties many of which are also present in other international treaties as, for example, the *United Nations Convention against Torture and Other Cruel, Inhuman or Degrading Treatment or Punishment* of 10 December 1984. Namely the obligation to adopt the legislative measures that may be needed to define the forced disappearance of persons as an offence and to impose an appropriate punishment commensurate with its extreme gravity; the obligation not to consider the forced disappearance of persons a political offence for purposes of extradition; the obligation to include the forced disappearance of persons among the extraditable offences in every extradition treaty entered into between States Parties; the obligation of States Parties to take the necessary measures to establish its jurisdiction over the crime of forced disappearance when the alleged criminal is within its territory and it does not proceed to extradite him; the non-admission of the defence of due obedience to superior orders or instructions that stipulate, authorize, or encourage forced disappearance as a cause of exclusion of individual criminal responsibility; the consideration of this Convention as the necessary legal basis for extradition with respect to the offence of forced disappearance when State Parties make extradition conditional on the existence of a treaty and receive a request for extradition from another State Party with which it has no extradition treaty; etc.

As a novelty, in the first paragraph of Article VII, this Convention states that criminal prosecution for the forced disappearance of persons and the penalty judicially imposed on its perpetrator shall not be subject to statutes of limitations. Nevertheless, such a statement is next limited by paragraph two when it states that if there should be a norm of a fundamental character preventing application of the stipulation quoted here, the period of limitation shall be equal to that which applies to the gravest crime in the domestic laws of the corresponding State Party.[117]

In contrast to the *International Convention for the Protection of All Persons from Enforced Disappearance* of 20 December 2006, the *Inter-American*

---

[115] It entered into force on 28 March 1996. For the text, see http://www.oas.org/juridico/english/treaties/a-60.htlm.

[116] According to article II: "For the purposes of this Convention, forced disappearance is considered to be the act of depriving a person or persons of his or their freedom, in whatever way, perpetrated by agents of the state or by persons or groups of persons acting with the authorization, support, or acquiescence of the state, followed by an absence of information or a refusal to acknowledge that deprivation of freedom or to give information on the whereabouts of that person, thereby impeding his or her recourse to the applicable legal remedies and procedural guarantees."

[117] One can imagine that the reference to "a norm of a fundamental character" shall be interpreted as a norm of constitutional level.

Convention on enforced disappearance of persons lacks the treaty body and the classical control techniques that are usual in international law on human rights. With regard to the treaty body and in contrast, too, to the *Inter-American Convention to Prevent and Punish Torture* of 9 December 1985,[118] the *Inter-American Convention on Forced Disappearance of Persons* of 9 July 1994 submits to the techniques of control and to the bodies charged with it in the frame of the American Convention on Human Rights. So Article XIII states:

> For the purposes of this Convention, the processing of petitions or communications presented to the Inter-American Commission on Human Rights alleging the forced disappearance of persons shall be subject to the procedures established in the American Convention on Human Rights and to the Statue and Regulations of the Inter-American Commission on Human Rights and to the Statute and Rules of Procedure of the Inter-American Court of Human Rights, including the provisions on precautionary measures.

This is, it may be recalled, the way in which the American Convention on Human Rights conceived the intervention of the Inter-American Commission and of the Inter-American Court of Human Rights. As i known, the competence of the Inter-American Commission on Human Rights is compulsory with regard to individual petitions containing denunciations or complaints of violation of this Convention by a State Party and facultative with regard to communications in which a State Party alleges that another State Party has committed a violation of a human right set forth in this Convention. On the contrary, the jurisdiction of the Inter-American Court of Human Rights is facultative for both types of petitions and communications. This is why it can only intervene when the concerned state has recognized as binding with regard to it the jurisdiction of the Court on all matters relating to the interpretation or application of the American Convention on Human Rights.

But the *Inter-American Convention on Forced Disappearance of Persons* introduces a novelty not envisaged by other international treaties on human rights. Perhaps as a consequence of the gravity of the conduct of enforced disappearance that in certain cases is qualified as a crime against humanity. So Article XIV of the Inter-American Convention clearly states that without prejudice to the provisions of Article XIII related to the procedure of petitions and communications presented before the Inter-American Commission in which a forced disappearance is alleged:

> ...when the Inter-American Commission on Human Rights receives a petition or communication regarding an alleged forced disappearance, its Executive Secretariat shall urgently and confidentially address the respective government, and shall request that government to provide as soon as possible information as to the whereabouts of the allegedly disappeared person together with any other information it considers pertinent, and such request shall be without prejudice as to the admissibility of the petition.

The shortage of international norms related to victims in the American regional system shall be complemented by a rich and abundant jurisprudence of the

[118] Article 8, paragraph three, of this Convention states: "After all the domestic legal procedures of the respective State and the corresponding appeals have been exhausted, the case may be submitted to the international fora whose competence has been recognized by that State."

Inter-American Court of Human Rights on the matter.[119] This jurisprudence has taken place within the framework of the American Convention on Human Rights and it binds all States Parties to that Convention. Through it, the Inter-American Court has specified and systematized the content of the rights protected by the American Convention. From the point of view of this work, special attention shall be paid to those rights directly related to victims. In the case, for example, of the constructions of the Inter-American Court on the *right of access to justice* in relation to which it has stated that this right is not limited to the formal institution of domestic proceedings, but it also involves the assurance within reasonable time of the right of alleged victims or their relatives to have every necessary step taken to know the truth and punish those responsible for the events.[120] Moreover, the Court says that access to justice constitutes a peremptory norm of International Law and, as such, "it gives rise to the States' *erga omnes* obligation to adopt all such measures as are necessary to prevent such violations from going unpunished, whether exercising their judicial power to apply their domestic law and International Law to judge and eventually punish those responsible for such events, or collaborating with other States aiming in that direction".[121]

The same occurs with the *obligation to investigate, to prosecute and to punish violations* of the American Convention; obligation that is intimately linked to the right of victims (or its relatives) of such violations to be heard and to take part in the proceedings in order to establish the truth of the facts and to punish those responsible for it as well as to the right to a prompt and effective judicial remedy before competent judges or tribunals.

The same is true in the case concerning *redress* that Article 63.1 of the American Convention recognizes victims of violations of it.[122] On this matter, the Inter-American Court reiterates international jurisprudence and underlines that it is a principle of international law, which jurisprudence has considered "even a general concept of law," that every violation of an international obligation which results in harm creates a duty to make adequate reparation.[123]

---

[119] I will analyze it on Part II of the present work.

[120] I/A Court H.R., *Case of La Cantuta v. Peru,* Merits, Reparations and Costs. Judgment of November 29, 2006. Series C No. 162, para. 149. That is in the same line of what it had stated in the following cases: *Case of the "Mapiripan Massacre"*, Judgement of September 15, 2005. Series C No. 134, para. 216; *Case of the Serrano-Cruz Sisters,* Judgement of March 1, 2005. Series C No. 120, para. 66, and *Case of 19 Tradesmen,* Judgement of July 5, 2004. Series C No. 109, para. 188.

[121] I/A Court H.R., *Case of La Cantuta v. Peru,* Merits, Reparations and Costs. Judgement of November 29, 2006. Series C No. 162, para. 160.

[122] According to it: "1. If the Court finds that there has been a violation of a right or freedom protected by this Convention, the Court shall rule that the injured party be ensured the enjoyment of his right or freedom that was violated. It shall also rule, if appropriate, that the consequences of the measure or situation that constituted the breach of such right or freedom be remedied and that fair compensation be paid to the injured party."

[123] I/A Court H.R., *Case of Velásquez-Rodríguez v. Honduras.* Reparations and Costs, Judgement of July 21, 1989. Series C No. 7, para. 25.

The Inter-American Court has also the precise *content* of redress (that consists of full restitution—*restitutio in integrum*—), its *modalities* (individual and collective), the *damages* that shall be redressed (material and moral) and has clearly stated the *incompatibility* with redress of the amnesty provisions. So, the Court

> considers that all amnesty provisions, provisions on prescription and the establishment of measures designed to eliminate responsibility are inadmissible, because they are intended to prevent the investigation and punishment of those responsible for serious human rights violations such as torture, extrajudicial, summary or arbitrary execution and forced disappearance, all of them prohibited because they violate non-derogable rights recognized by international human rights law.[124]

Moreover, it is in the Inter-American Court of Human Rights that some violations of human rights (like extra-legal execution or forced disappearance) are *crimes against humanity*:

> In this regard, the Court will emphasize that the acts committed in La Cantuta to the detriment of the victims of extra-legal execution or forced disappearance, are crimes against humanity that cannot go unpunished, are non-extinguishable and cannot be the subject-matter of amnesty.[125]

On the other hand, the jurisprudence of the Inter-American Court of Human Rights stated under the American Convention also spreads its effects both upon the *Inter-American Convention to Prevent and Punish Torture* of 9 December 1985 and the *Inter-American Convention on enforced disappearance of persons*, of 9th July 1994. Upon the first because the Inter-American Court of Human Rights has stated its own competence to interpret and to apply it as well as to declare the responsibility of a State that has agreed to be obliged by this Convention and has also accepted the jurisdiction of the Inter-American Court of Human Rights. As the Court itself explains, as some member countries of the Organization of American States were still not parties to the American Convention and had not accepted the jurisdiction of the Court, the drafters of the Convention against Torture decided not to include in it an article that made express and exclusive reference to the Inter-American Court in order not to indirectly bind them to the former Convention and the aforementioned jurisdictional organ.[126]

The possibility of ratifying or adhering to the Convention against Torture was opened to the greatest number of States by means of a general clause. What was considered important was to attribute the competence for applying the Convention against Torture to an international organ, whether this was a commission, a committee, an existing tribunal or one that would be created in the future.[127]

---

[124] I/A Court H.R., *Case of Barrios Altos v. Peru*. Merits, Judgement March 14, 2001. Series C No. 75, para. 41.

[125] I/A Court H.R., *Case of La Cantuta v. Peru,* Merits, Reparations and Costs. Judgement of November 29, 2006. Series C No. 162, para. 225.

[126] I/A Court H.R., *Case of the "Street Children" (Villagrán-Morales et al.) v. Guatemala. Merits.* Judgement of November 19, 1999. Series C No. 63, para. 247.

[127] *Ibid.*, para. 248.

But the jurisprudence of the Inter-American Court of Human Rights also spreads its effects upon the *Inter-American Convention on Forced Disappearance of Persons* because in Article XIII this Convention expressly states that for the purposes of it, the processing of petitions or communications presented to the Inter-American Commission on Human Rights alleging the forced disappearance of persons shall be subject to the procedures established in the American Convention on Human Rights and to the Statute and Regulations of the Inter-American Commission on Human Rights as well as to the Statute and Rules of Procedure of the Inter-American Court of Human Rights, including the provisions on precautionary measures.

References

Almqvist J (2006) Facing the victims in the global fight against terrorism, working paper. FRIDE 18:6

Bassiouni Ch (2003) Reconnaissance internationale des droits des victimes In: SOS Attentats (eds) Terrorisme, victimes et responsabilité pénale internationale. Calmann-Lévy, Paris, 134–185

Bottigliero A (2004) Redress for victims of crimes under international law. M. Nijhoff, Leiden

Bou Franch V, Fernández de Casadevante Romani C (2009) La inclusión del terrorismo entre los crímenes internacionales previstos en el Estatuto de la Corte Penal Internacional. (Una propuesta del Colectivo de Víctimas del Terrorismo en el País Vasco, COVITE, para la Conferencia de Revisión del Estatuto de la Corte Penal Internacional), Valencia

Clapham A (2006) "The *jus cogens* Prohibition of Torture and the Importance of Sovereign State Immunity", in the collective work *Promoting Justice, Human Rights And Conflict Resolution Through International Law. Liber Amicorum Lucius Caflish*, M. Nijhoff Pub., Leiden, 2007, pp. 151–169

Fernández de Casadevante Romani C (ed) (2011) Derecho Internacional de los Derechos Humanos, 4th edn. Madrid, Dilex

Fernández de Casadevante Romani C, Mayordomo Rodrigo V (2011) Código de normas internacionales relativas a las víctimas, Tecnos, Madrid

Fernández Sola N (2008) El derecho a la reparación de las víctimas de desaparición forzada: hacia la justicia a través del Derecho internacional. R.E.D.I LX:411)

Groenhuijsen MS, Pemberton A (2009) The EU framework decision on victims. Does hard law make a difference ? Eur J Crime Crim Law Crim Justice 17:43–59

Pemberton A, Groenhuijsen MS (2012) "Developing victim's rights within the European Union: past, present and future", in Kirchhoff G. et al (eds.) *Proceedings of the 13th World Society of Victimology Symposium*, Wolf Legal Publishers, Nijmegen, p. 1

Sanz Hermida AMª (2009) Víctimas de delitos: derechos, protección y asistencia. Iustel, Madrid

UNODOC (2011) The Criminal justice response to support victims of acts of terrorism. United Nations, New York

The International Categories of Victims

The International Concept of Victim: Almost as Many Concepts of Victim as Categories of Victims

The first thing that must be underlined is the non-existence of an international concept of victim. On the contrary, there are almost as many definitions as categories of victims envisaged by international norms. The exception is constituted by victims of terrorism because no definition exists both in the system of the UN[1] and in the regional systems.[2]

The result of this situation is a plurality of definitions. In any case, the non-existence of an international concept of victim is not so important because from the different elements present in such definitions it is possible to conclude the existence of a series of common denominators. On the contrary, those gaps can be filled by resorting to international norms on victims of crime because all victims—except victims of abuse of power, accordingly to the definition contented in the *Declara tion of Basic Principles of Justice for Victims of Crime and Abuse of Power*[3]–are victims as a consequence of a crime.

As stated before, the international norms actually related to victims fall into several categories: victims of crime, victims of abuse of power, victims of gross violations of international human rights law, victims of serious violations of international humanitarian law, victims of enforced disappearance, victims of violations of international criminal law, victims of trafficking and victims of terrorism. The different definitions of the concept of victim existing in these

[1] Inside UN, there is no international norm defining victims of terrorism.

[2] In the European regional system only, the definition given by the *Guidelines on the Protection of Victims of Terrorist Acts* and adopted by the Committee of Ministers of the Council of Europe on 2 March 2005. In the American and in the African regional systems, no definition of victims of terrorism exists.

[3] It was adopted on 29 November 1985 by a General Assembly Resolution 40/34.

C. Fernández de Casadevante Romani, *International Law of Victims*,
DOI 10.1007/978-3-642-28140-2_2, © Springer-Verlag Berlin Heidelberg 2012

international norms will be examined in order to be able to conclude the possibility of building or not building a general concept of victim that could be shared by all categories of victims independent of the definitions quoted here, or, at least, the elements present in all of these definitions.

The Different International Categories of Victims

Victims of Crime

The first time victims of crime received attention from international law took place inside the UN. This was through General Assembly Resolution 40/34 adopted on 29 November 1985 containing the *Declaration of Basic Principles of Justice for Victims of Crime and Abuse of Power*.[4] More recently, other international norms belonging to the European regional frame have paid attention to it.[5]

The General or Universal System of United Nations

The general frame established by the General Assembly *Declaration of Basic Principles of Justice for Victims of Crime and Abuse of Power* states several principles related to this category of victims: access of victims to justice and fair treatment, restitution, compensation and assistance. General Assembly Resolution 40/34 also contains a concept of "victim" that includes three categories of persons: first, persons who, individually or collectively, have suffered harm. Second, it includes the immediate family or dependants of the direct victim and third, persons who have suffered harm in intervening to assist victims in distress or to prevent victimization.[6] According to the Declaration,

> 1. "Victims" means persons who, individually or collectively, have suffered harm, including physical or mental injury, emotional suffering, economic loss or substantial impairment of their fundamental rights, through acts or omissions that are in violation of criminal laws operative within Member States, including those laws proscribing criminal abuse of power.
>
> 2. A person may be considered a victim, under this Declaration, regardless of whether the perpetrator is identified, apprehended, prosecuted or convicted and regardless of the familial relationship between the perpetrator and the victim. The term "victim" also

---

[4] Adopted on 29 November 1985 by General Assembly Resolution 40/34 it is based on Article 8 of the Universal Declaration of Human Rights, which states the right of everyone "to an effective remedy by the competent national tribunals for acts violating the fundamental rights granted him by the constitution or by law."

[5] This is the case of norms adopted by the Council of Europe and the European Union.

[6] There is a similar definition in the ICC Rules of Procedure and Evidence as well as in the Statute of this Court. They also envisage a special protection for victims in the procedures before the ICC.

includes, where appropriate, the immediate family or dependants of the direct victim and persons who have suffered harm in intervening to assist victims in distress or to prevent victimization.[7]

They are, in all cases, victims acquiring this condition as a consequence of acts or omissions that are in violation of criminal laws operative within Member States, including those laws proscribing criminal abuse of power.

As can be appreciated, criminal laws operative within Member States constitute the standard, the violation of which gives rise to the condition of victim.[8] From this point of view, the criminalization in the domestic law of acts such as terrorism, genocide, crimes of war and crimes against humanity—as well as others—would make possible a much more expanded concept of victim because it is the states' domestic criminal law, which leads to the categorization of victims as persons having suffered harm through acts or omissions that are in violation of criminal laws operative within the concerned state. Consequently, it would be very helpful for victims if states take all necessary steps and measures to ensure that such acts (as well as others envisaged by the international norms relating to victims and not yet included as offences under national law) become offences under national law.[9]

In the opinion of Fernández Sola with reference to persons who have suffered harm in intervening to assist victims in distress or to prevent victimization, the General Assembly Declaration opens the door to the international protection of persons, associations and collectives of human rights that in the defence of it become victims as a consequence of the attacks of the same groups and forces responsible for the victimization in question.[10]

---

[7] The third paragraph of this definition adds: "3. The provisions contained herein shall be applicable to all, without distinction of any kind, such as race, colour, sex, age, language, religion, nationality, political or other opinion, cultural beliefs or practices, property, birth or family status, ethnic or social origin, and disability."

[8] In the same way article 1 para. 1 of Recommendation (2006) 8 of the Committee of Ministers adopted on 14 June 2006. For the purpose of this recommendation, article 1 para. 1 states that: "Victim means a natural person who has suffered harm, including physical or mental injury, emotional suffering or economic loss, caused by acts or omissions that are in violation of the criminal law of a member state. The term victim also includes, where appropriate, the immediate family or dependants of the direct victim."

[9] It would be also very helpful from the triple perspective of the *Declaration of Basic Principles of Justice for Victims of Crime and Abuse of Power*. That is persons who have suffered harm (direct victims) as well as the immediate family or dependants of the direct victim and persons who have suffered harm in intervening to assist victims in distress or to prevent victimization (both, indirect victims).

[10] Fernández Sola also underlines that this category of victims has already been protected by the Inter-American Court of Human Rgihts in the case *of Nogueira de Carvalho et al. v. Brazil* (I/A Court H.R., *Case of Nogueira de Carvalho et al. v. Brazil. Preliminary Objections and Merits.* Judgement of November 28, 2006, Series C No. 161). The concept of the European Court of Human Rights is more restrictive (see Chapter IV of the present work).

In this article, the author makes only refence to victims of enforced disappearance (cf. Fernández Sola (2008), 403).

The European Regional System: The Council of Europe and the European Union

In the European regional system, the work of the *Council of Europe* on victims—like its work on human rights earlier—has preceded that of the former European Community that is today the European Union. On victims also through a treaty: the *European Convention on the Compensation of Victims of Violent Crimes* adopted on 24 November 1983, actually ratified by 47 states. More recently, the *European Union* has also focused its attention on this category of victims through *Council Directive 2004/80/EC of 29 April 2004 Relating to Compensation to Crime Victims.*[11] The aim of both the Convention and the Directive is compensation to victims in cross-border situations, that is persons living in a Member State of the European Union or in a State party to the1983 European Convention become victims of crime in the territory of another Member State of the European Union or of another State party to the1983 European Convention. What both legal instruments look for is that victims are compensated even in cross-border situations. In other words, the cross-border situation does not become an obstacle to compensate crime victims.

As all Member States of the EU are also members of the Council of Europe, we are faced with two situations. On the one hand, that of the states bound both by the Council Directive and 1983 European Convention and on the other hand, that of the Member States of the EU only bound by the Council Directive.[12]

Article 2 of the *European Convention on the Compensation of Victims of Violent Crimes of 24 November 1983* states that when compensation is not fully awarded from other sources States Parties shall compensate,

(a) those who have sustained serious bodily injury or impairment of health directly attributable to an intentional crime of violence;
(b) the dependants of persons who have died as a result of such crime.[13]

More recently, *Council Framework Decision (2001/220/JHA)* of 15 March 2001[14] gives, inside the European Union for the first time, a concept of "victim". According to article 1 a), "victim" is,

[11] *OJEC* L 261 of 6 August 2004. This Directive was done on the basis of the principle of subsidiarity of Article 5 of European Union's Treaty "since the objective of facilitating access to compensation to victims of crimes of cross-border situations cannot be sufficiently achieved by the Member States because of the cross-border elements and can therefore, by reason of the scale or effects of the action, be better achieved at Community level,. . ." (paragraph 15 of its preamble).

[12] The Council Directive has the advantage of binding all Member States of the EU. So, Member States of the EU that are not parties to the 1983 European Convention are, at least, bound in that way to compensate crime victims in cross-border situations.

[13] This obligation to compensate victims of violent crimes persists even if the offender cannot be prosecuted or punished, see article 2 para. 2.

[14] OJEC L 82 of 22 March 2001.

> a natural person who has suffered harm, including physical or mental injury, emotional suffering or economic loss, directly caused by acts or omissions that are in violation of the criminal law of a Member State.[15]

Victims of Abuse of Power

This category of victims is the object of the General Assembly *Declaration of Basic Principles of Justice for Victims of Crime and Abuse of Power* adopted on 29 November 1985. According to it, victims of abuse of power are persons

> who, individually or collectively, have suffered harm, including physical or mental injury, emotional suffering, economic loss or substantial impairment of their fundamental rights, through acts or omissions that do not yet constitute violations of national criminal laws but of internationally recognized norms relating to human rights.[16]

Consequently, as different from crime victims who are also objects of this Declaration, in the case of victims of abuse of power the standard of victimization is constituted by international law on human rights, the acts in question being not violations of domestic criminal law (they are neither offences nor crimes) but of internationally recognized norms relating to human rights. Despite this concretion, the Declaration does not contain any additional information concerning that kind of conduct.

On the contrary, the Draft UN Convention on Justice and Support for Victims of Crime and Abuse of Power defines "abuse of power" as "acts or omissions that are not violations of national criminal laws but are violations of internationally recognized *jus cogens* norms".[17]

However, this accuracy is not satisfactory. First, because the concept of norm of *jus cogens* (peremptory norm of international law) has a very specific content, which describes the international responsibility of the State (which is not a criminal responsibility). Second, because generally behaviours violative of peremptory norms when committed by individuals or non-State actors constitute international crimes subject to international criminal law. This is the case for genocide, torture, enforced disappearances, extrajudicial executions, terrorism, crimes against humanity and war crimes. Third, because these international crimes tend to be criminal offences in domestic law of States. Last but not least, because even though those behaviours were not typified as crimes in the criminal law of the State, they

---

[15] It also contains a definition of "victim support organization". That is: "a non-governmental organization, legally established in a Member State, whose support to victims of crime is provided free of charge and, conducted under appropriate conditions, complements the action of the State in this area" (article 1 lit. b). Some time later, on 29 April 2004, the Council Directive 2004/80/EC relating to compensation of victims was adopted, see note 36. This Directive is founded upon the principles of subsidiarity and beyond what is necessary in order to achieve that objective."

[16] Point No. 18 of the Declaration.

[17] On Article 2 (b). The Draft is of 8 February 2010 and has been drawn up by the World Society of Victimology.

would continue to be international crimes subject to the principle of universal justice and international jurisdiction.

In other words, it is difficult to find an example of a violation of a norm of *jus cogens* that would not constitute violation of the criminal law of the State and that—as noted by the draft Convention—can be described as abuse of power. But even if there were, it would always be an international crime. Abuse of power, as it is defined in the draft Convention, is incompatible with the concept of *jus cogens* and the consequences attributed by international law to the violation of such peremptory norms.

Victims of Gross Violations of International Human Rights Law and Serious

Violations of International Humanitarian Law

More recently on 16 December 2005, the General Assembly adopted Resolution 60/147 that contains UN Commission on Human Rights Resolution 2005/35 on the *Basic Principles and Guidelines of the Right to a Remedy and Reparation for Victims of Gross Violations of International Human Rights Law and Serious Violations of International Humanitarian Law.*[18] Here, two categories of victims are envisaged: victims of gross violations of international human rights law and victims of serious violations of international humanitarian law.

This Declaration distinguishes two types of victims: *direct* and *indirect victims. Direct victims* are,

> persons who individually or collectively suffered harm, including physical or mental injury, emotional suffering, economic loss or substantial impairment of their fundamental rights, through acts or omissions that constitute gross violations of international human rights law, or serious violations of international humanitarian law.[19]

On the other hand, and with regard to *indirect victims*, the Basic Principles and Guidelines state that,

> Where appropriate, and in accordance with domestic law, the term 'victim' also includes the immediate family or dependants of the direct victim and persons who have suffered harm in intervening to assist victims in distress or to prevent victimization.[20]

---

[18] Doc. E/CN.4/2005/L.10/Add.11. The resolution was adopted within the Commission on Human Rights by a recorded vote of 40 votes to none, with 13 abstentions. See A/RES/40/34, Annex, B. para. 18.

[19] A/RES/40/34, Annex, V.8.

[20] *Ibid.*, Annex, V.8. So, in the same line that the definition given in General Assembly *Declaration of Basic Principles of Justice for Victims of Crime and Abuse of Power* adopted on 29 November 1985.

At least it should be added here that the condition of the victim exists regardless of whether the perpetrator of the violation is identified, apprehended, prosecuted, or convicted and regardless of the familial relationship between the perpetrator and the victim.[21]

Victims of Violations of International Criminal Law

International criminal law envisages victims of the following crimes: crimes of war, crimes against humanity, genocide, enforced disappearance, extrajudicial executions, terrorism and torture. In contrast to other fields of international law already quoted here, the crime is committed by a natural person and never a State because in international law the State is not criminally responsible. In consequence crimes are always committed by a natural person even if the person has committed the crime while exercising state functions. Immunity cannot be invoked to exclude international criminal responsibility. The aim of the immunity recognized by international law to persons exercising state functions is only to guarantee the exercise of state functions, i.e., to protect state sovereignty.[22]

It is obvious that the only immunity international law recognizes in such persons is the guarantee of the free exercise of state functions, of state sovereignty. But sovereignty protected by international law cannot be used or invoked to legally justify the commission of international crimes. Neither those committed on the occasion of the exercise of state functions because it is obvious that within the attributions of sovereignty there is not—and there can never be—the commission of international crimes. How can be international law be invoked to justify the commission of international crimes that this same legal order prohibits? How can international law be invoked to elude the international criminal responsibility that such commission implies?

In other words, it is clear that crimes such as genocide, crimes of war, crimes against humanity, enforced disappearance, extrajudicial executions, or the practice of torture, for example, do not belong to the performance of state functions. Consequently, being conduct banned by international law, immunity recognized by international law cannot be used to grant any type of *impunity* on the basis of state sovereignty.

Nevertheless, unfortunately, the International Court of Justice (ICJ)—the principal judicial organ of the UN—has not yet arrived at such a conclusion. On the contrary, in the *Case concerning the Arrest Warrant of 11 April 2000 (Democratic Republic of the Congo v. Belgium)*, it stated:

> 54. The Court accordingly concludes that the functions of a Minister for Foreign Affairs are such that, throughout the duration of his or her office, he or she when abroad enjoys full immunity from criminal jurisdiction and inviolability. That immunity and that inviolability

---

[21] *Ibid.* Annex, V.9.

[22] On this matter cf. Fernández de Casadevante Romani (2010), 373–378.

> protect the individual concerned against any act of authority of another State which would hinder him or her in the performance of his or her duties.[23]

It is the opinion of the ICJ that if a Minister for Foreign Affairs is arrested in another State on a criminal charge, he or she would clearly thereby be prevented from exercising the functions of his or her office. So, the consequences of such impediment to the exercise of those official functions would be equally serious, regardless of whether the Minister for Foreign Affairs were, at the time of arrest, present in the territory of the arresting State on an official visit or a private visit, regardless of whether the arrest relates to acts allegedly performed before the person became the Minister for Foreign Affairs or to acts performed while in office, and regardless of whether the arrest relates to alleged acts performed in an official capacity or a private capacity. Furthermore, the ICJ adds that even the mere risk that, by traveling to or transiting another State, a Minister for Foreign Affairs might be exposing himself or herself to legal proceedings could deter the Minister from traveling internationally when required to do so for the purposes of the performance of his or her official functions.[24]

I do not agree with these statements of the ICJ. First, if according to the Court in conventional international law there is any provision specifically defining the immunities enjoyed by Ministers for Foreign Affairs, it is also true that conventional international law gives a lot of examples of situations in which it is clearly stated that specific acts can be prosecuted independent of the official functions performed by the person realizing or ordering such conduct.[25]

Second, it is also true that neither customary international law nor conventional international law conceives states immunity of jurisdiction as a protective shield of conduct such as those envisaged by the Arrest Warrant. Effectively, as it can be clearly deduced from the analysis done by the ICJ, conduct violating human rights or international humanitarian law cannot be qualified either as "acts performed in an official capacity" or as "acts performed in the exercise of state functions", nor as acts founded on the sovereignty, independence and equality of States. To hold to the contrary amounts to an outrage because it signifies not only that the state or its organs can torture or incite racial hatred or commit genocide but also

[23] ICJ, *Arrest Warrant of 11April 2000 (Democratic Republic of the Congo v. Belgium), Judgment, I.C.J. Reports 2002*, p. 22. It also states that no distinction can be drawn between acts performed by a Minister for Foreign Affairs in an "official" capacity, and those claimed to have been performed in a "private capacity", or, for that matter, between acts performed before the person concerned assumed office as Minister for Foreign Affairs and acts committed during the period of office. As known, in this case the arrest warrant concerned the Minister for Foreign Affairs of the Democratic Republic of the Congo—Mr. Yerodi—to whom the commission of several international crimes were attributed.

[24] Cf. *ibid.*, para. 55, 22.

[25] That is the case, for example, of Article VI of the 1948 Convention on the Prevention and Punishment of the Crime of Genocide, of Article 17 of the Statute of the ICC, of Articles 5 and 7 of the 1984 UN Torture Convention and of Articles 8 and 9 of the Draft Code of Crimes Against the Peace and Security of Mankind.

that international law gives legal hedge to such conduct[26]. This is not so because international law does not protect such conduct nor does it lead to the conclusion that such acts are under the protection of the immunity of jurisdiction because of the sole fact that they are committed by state organs.

It should immediately be added that any such conduct can be considered as an act inherent to state functions. On the contrary, they are all acts qualified as international crimes by international law. Moreover, they are all acts that breach peremptory norms or *jus cogens* existent in international law on human rights and in international humanitarian law prohibiting, for example, torture, genocide, racial hatred, crimes of war, crimes against humanity, enforced disappearances and extra-judicial executions.[27]

At least, in the line of one of the arguments of the ICJ, nothing prevents another Minister or another representative of the state concerned to perform the functions that the Minister for Foreign Affairs, who is the object of the Arrest Warrant, cannot perform. Through this way, the Minister for Foreign Affairs concerned could not be arrested.

Nevertheless, despite the developments that have taken place in the recent years with regard to the immunity of heads of state, heads of government and ministers, this field of international law does not yet pay enough attention to the legal status of victims. Neither the statute of the ICC nor the statutes of the international criminal courts for the former Yugoslavia and Rwanda recognize any active *locus standi* of victims of crimes in order to initiate criminal proceedings before these courts or to become parties in the proceedings. Despite these shortcomings, the statute of the ICC constitutes an advance with regard to the current situation of victims. It recognizes victims' rights more actively than the statutes of the criminal courts for the former Yugoslavia and Rwanda, which merely envisaged victims as witnesses.[28] Concretely, Article 19.3 of the ICC-statute, e.g. authorizes victims to submit observations to the Court.[29]

---

[26] The Arrest Warrant refers to "various speeches inciting racial hatred" and to "particularly virulent remarks" allegedly made by the Minister for Foreign Affairs Mr. Yerodia during "public addresses reported by the media" on 4 August and 27 August 1998. These speeches "allegedly had the effect of inciting the population to attack Tutsi residents of Kinshasa: there were dragnet searches, manhunts (the Tutsi enemy) and lynchings. The speeches inciting racial hatred thus arc: said to have resulted in several hundred deaths, the internment of 7 Tutsis, summary executions, arbitrary arrests and unfair trials." (*Warrant of 11April 2000 (Democratic Republic of the Congo v. Belgium), Judgment, I.C.J. Reports 2002*, paragraph 67, 28.)

[27] See Carnerero (2007); Esposito (2007); M. Cosnard, "Quelques observations sur les décisions de la Chambre des Lords du 25 Novembre 1998 et du 24 Mars 1999 dans l'affaire Pinochet", *RGDIP*, 1999/2, 309 et seq.; Ch. Dominice, "Quelques observations sur l'immunité de juridiction pénale de l'ancien Chef d'Etat", *RGDIP*, 1999/2, 298 et seq.

[28] The framework of the *Extraordinary Chambers in the Courts of Cambodia* allows for the victim to participate in the proceedings as a *partie civile*.

[29] Article 19 para. 3 states: "The Prosecutor may seek a ruling from the Court regarding a question of jurisdiction or admissibility. In proceedings with respect to jurisdiction or admissibility, those who have referred the situation under article 13, as well as victims, may also submit observations to the Court".

The International Criminal Court (ICC)

The Statute adopted in the Rome Conference on 17 July 1998 and the Rules of Procedure and Evidence[30] guide the functioning of the ICC. The Statute is the first international treaty related to an international criminal court that expressly takes victims into account, although it does not arrive at the point of authorizing victims to directly ask for the intervention of the Court.

In relation to the concept of victim, the very wide concept contained in Rule 85 of the Rules of Procedure and Evidence of the ICC should be underlined. This definition is wider compared to other categories of victims made in other international norms quoted previously. According to the Rule 85,

> For the purposes of the Statute and the Rules of Procedure and Evidence:
> (a) "Victims" means natural persons who have suffered harm as a result of the commission of any crime within the jurisdiction of the Court;
> (b) Victims may include organizations or institutions that have sustained direct harm to any of their property which is dedicated to religion, education, art or science or charitable purposes, and to their historic monuments, hospitals and other places and objects for humanitarian purposes.

The difference here is that the wide-ranging concept present in Rule 85 does not demand that the victim becomes the direct object of the criminal offence. This is why some authors consider that the concept quoted here in Rule 85 covers all natural and legal persons who have directly or indirectly suffered harm as a result of the commission of any crime within the jurisdiction of the ICC.[31] As stated, in contrast to the international criminal courts for the former Yugoslavia and Rwanda, the statute of the ICC, and the Rules of Procedure and Evidence of the ICC, expressly envisage victims.[32] The ICC statute refers to victims in arts 68, 75 and 79.[33] The Rules of Procedure and Evidence envisage victims and witnesses in Section III of Chapter 4.

According to article 15, the Prosecutor may initiate investigations *proprio motu* on the basis of information on crimes within the jurisdiction of the Court. If certain conditions are fulfilled, the Prosecutor concludes that there is a reasonable basis to

[30] About the ICC, see Carnerero (2011), 521 et seq. *In extenso* see O. Triffterer, *Commentary on the Rome Statute of the International Criminal Court –Observers' Notes, Article by Article-*, 2008.

[31] So for example, Gozzi and Laborde (2005), 297 et seq.

[32] The Rules of Procedure and Evidence of the ICC is an instrument for the application of the ICC-Statute.

[33] Related to the protection of victims and witnesses and their participation in the proceedings (article 68), the reparations to victims (article 75) and to the Trust Fund that should be established for the benefit of victims of crimes and of families of such victims within the jurisdiction of the ICC (article 79). In respect of these articles see, for example, the commentaries of D. Donat-Cattin, "Article 68. Protection of victims and witnesses and their participation in the proceedings", 1275 et seq.; "Article 75. Reparation to victims", 1399 et seq.; M. Jennings, "Article 79. Trust Fund", 1439 et seq., in: O. Triffterer, *Commentary on the Rome Statute of the International Criminal Court –Observers' Notes, Article by Article*, 2008.

proceed with an investigation, he or she shall submit to the Pre-Trial Chamber a request for authorization of an investigation, together with any supporting material collected. This is the moment when an intervention of victims in the form of a representation to this Chamber takes place in accordance with the Rules of Procedure and Evidence. Afterwards, if upon examination of the request and the supporting material given to it by the Prosecutor as well as the observations made by victims, this Pre-Trial Chamber considers that there is a reasonable basis to proceed with an investigation, and the case appears to fall within the jurisdiction of the Court, it shall authorize the commencement of the investigation, without prejudice to subsequent determinations by the Court with regard to the jurisdiction and admissibility of a case.[34]

According to Article 43 paragraph 6 of the Statute, the Registrar of the ICC shall set up a *Victims and Witnesses Unit* within the Registry.[35] This Unit shall provide, in consultation with the Office of the Prosecutor, "protective measures and security arrangements, counselling and other appropriate assistance for witnesses, victims who appear before the Court and others who are at risk on account of testimony given by such witnesses."

As a general principle, Rule 86 establishes that the needs of all victims[36] (and witnesses) shall be taken into account during the procedure before the ICC. Article 68 of the Statute and Rules 87 and 88 are dedicated to the protection of victims and witnesses.[37] According to article 68.1, the Court shall take appropriate measures to protect the safety, physical and psychological well-being, dignity and privacy of

---

[34] In accordance with article 15 para. 3, which states: "If the Prosecutor concludes that there is a reasonable basis to proceed with an investigation, he or she shall submit to the Pre-Trial Chamber a request for authorization of an investigation, together with any supporting material collected. *Victims may make representations to the Pre-Trial Chamber, in accordance with the Rules of Procedure and Evidence.*" (emphasis is added).

[35] Article 12,4 of the Statute of the *Special Tribunal for Lebanon* establishes within the Registry a section for victims and witnesses ("Section III, Rights of the accused and victims"). It provides for the participation in the proceedings respecting the rights of the accused (cf. Article 17) and organizes their compensation (cf. Article 25). On the other hand, the rules of Procedure and Evidence of this Special Tribunal envisage the participation of victims and their protection (pursuant Article 28 of the Statute of this Special Tribunal).

[36] The reference to victims is precise: "in particular, children, elderly persons, persons with disabilities and victims of sexual or gender violence". According to Rule 86: "A Chamber in making any direction or order, and other organs of the Court in performing their functions under the Statute or the Rules, shall take into account the needs of all victims and witnesses in accordance with article 68, in particular, children, elderly persons, persons with disabilities and victims of sexual or gender violence".

[37] According to Rule 87 para. 1: "Upon the motion of the Prosecutor or the defense or upon the request of a witness or a victim or his or her legal representative, if any, or on its own motion, and after having consulted with the Victims and Witnesses Unit, as appropriate, a Chamber may order measures to protect a victim, a witness or another person at risk on account of testimony given by a witness pursuant to article 68, paragraphs 1 and 2. The Chamber shall seek to obtain, whenever possible, the consent of the person in respect of whom the protective measure is sought prior to ordering the protective measure."

victims and witnesses.[38] So, in line with article 68 paragraph 2, Rules 87 and 88 allow *in camera* proceedings, as well as other measures such as those relating to prevent the release of the identity or the location of a victim.[39] On the other hand, in line with article 68 paragraph 2, Rule 88 states that upon the motion of the Prosecutor or the defence, or upon the request of a witness or a victim or his or her legal representative, if any, or on its own motion, and after having consulted with the Victims and Witnesses Unit, as appropriate, it is possible for the Court, to take into account the views of the victim or witnesses, to order special measures. Similarly, the Court can order that a counsel, a legal representative, a psychologist or a family member shall be permitted to attend during the testimony of the victim or the witness. Finally, apart from the special measures envisaged in Rule 88, also included is the duty that the Court takes into consideration that violations of the privacy of a witness or victim may create risk to his or her security. The Court will be vigilant in controlling the manner of questioning a witness or victim so as to avoid any harassment or intimidation, paying particular attention to attacks on victims of crimes of sexual violence.

Victims can also participate actively in the proceedings. According to article 68 paragraph 3 "where the personal interests of the victims are affected, the Court shall permit their views and concerns to be presented and considered at stages of the proceedings deemed to be appropriate by the Court and in a manner which is not prejudicial to or inconsistent with the rights of the accused and a fair and impartial trial." Such views and concerns may be presented by the legal representatives of the victims where the Court considers it appropriate, in accordance with the Rules of Procedure and Evidence. Rule 89 adds that the victim or a person acting with the consent of the victim, or a person acting on behalf of a victim can present their views and concerns through written application to the Registrar, who shall transmit the application to the relevant Chamber.

Victims can freely choose a legal representative but when there are a number of victims, for the purposes of ensuring the effectiveness of the proceedings, the Court may request the victims or particular groups of victims to choose a common legal

---

[38] It is an exception with regard to the principle of public hearings of article 67 of the Statute.

[39] Rule 87 para. 3 states: "A Chamber may, on a motion or request under subrule 1, hold a hearing, which shall be conducted in camera, to determine whether to order measures to prevent the release to the public or press and information agencies, of the identity or the location of a victim, a witness or other person at risk on account of testimony given by a witness by ordering, *inter alia*: (a) that the name of the victim, witness or other person at risk on account of testimony given by a witness or any information which could lead to his or her identification, be expunged from the public records of the Chamber; (b) that the Prosecutor, the defense or any other participant in the proceedings be prohibited from disclosing such information to a third party; (c) that testimony be presented by electronic or other special means, including the use of technical means enabling the alteration of pictures or voice, the use of audio-visual technology, in particular videoconferencing and closed-circuit television, and the exclusive use of the sound media; (d) that a pseudonym be used for a victim, a witness or other person at risk on account of testimony given by a witness; or (e) that a Chamber conducts part of its proceedings in camera".

representative or representatives. It is also envisaged that, when a victim or group of victims lack the necessary means to pay for a common legal representative chosen by the Court, it may receive assistance from the Registrar, including financial assistance when this is required.[40]

According to Rule 91 paragraph 2, the victim and his or her representatives attend and participate in the proceedings. It can also request the questioning of a witness, an expert or the accused; questioning which must be requested by the Court.[41] Moreover, victims as well as their representatives shall be notified of all the proceedings before the Court. Therefore, to allow victims to apply for participation in the proceedings in accordance with Rule 89, the Court shall notify victims concerning the decision of the Prosecutor not to initiate an investigation or not to prosecute pursuant to article 53.[42] Consequently, the Court shall notify victims regarding its decision to hold a hearing to confirm charges. With regard to the competences of the Secretary of the ICC, the latter shall notify victims or their legal representatives who have already participated in the proceedings or, as far as possible, those who have communicated with the Court in respect of the case in question, about all proceedings before the Court. Rule 93 authorizes the Chamber to seek the views of victims or their legal representatives on any issue. It also can seek the views of other victims, as appropriate.

One of the most innovative aspects of the Statute of the ICC concerns victims compensation envisaged in article 75 of the Statute. To make it possible to provide reparation for victims, article 79 of the Statute of the ICC creates a Trust Fund for the benefit of victims which is obtained from money and other property collected through fines or forfeiture to be transferred.

As can be seen, the way in which the Statute of the ICC and, moreover, the rules of Procedure and Evidence envisage victims of international criminal law constitutes a significant advance in international law. Its recognition of the victim as an actor in the criminal proceedings is innovative. In contrast to the statute of the ICC, we will see now that the statutes of the two International Criminal Tribunals give victims reduced prominence, conceiving them only as witnesses.

The International Criminal Tribunals for the Former Yugoslavia and for Rwanda

As mentioned, in contrast to the statute of the ICC, the statutes of the two Criminal Tribunals give victims reduced prominence, conceiving them only as witnesses. More concretely, as witnesses of the Prosecutor, they cannot receive any compensation from these Tribunals. Both Tribunals do not envisage a particular

---

40 See Rule 90.

41 See Rule 91 para. 3.

42 See Rule 92 para. 2.

status to the victims. Still it must be added that a major role of victims in these Tribunals becomes difficult due to the nature of, both crimes of war and crimes against humanity that were committed; crimes that concern a great number of victims. But it is also difficult because of the accusatory legal nature of the proceedings, so that an active role for the victims in the proceedings could have a negative effect on the role given to the Prosecutor in both statutes.[43] It is the Prosecutor who manages public action with the aim of the defence of public international order and repression against crime. The consequence of it is that both statutes have foreseen a set of measures to protect victims in their role as witnesses but it does not envisage a particular statute of victim. So, it is the Prosecutor who manages international public action of the victim but this one cannot set itself up as civil part.

The position of victim in the process is more delicate. Being conceived as witness, the victim cannot participate by himself or herself in the procedure: they have to swear before testifying, they can express themselves only within the frame of the questioning and contra-questioning (inside the limits inherent to it), they have no access to the elements of proof, they can only assist in the questioning of other witnesses but from the bench that are reserved for the public and they cannot receive reparation for the damage suffered.

There are three reasons guiding this system. On the one hand, the accusatory legal nature of the proceedings established by the statutes of both Tribunals. That is, a proceeding in which prosecution (with a repressive aim) and defence are placed under the arbitral look of the judge. On the other hand, the imperatives of repression in international criminal justice are the most important because its first objective is investigation and transferral of the affected before a court and, once there, to punish or to absolve. The protection of the fundamental rights of the accused in the moment of the drafting of both statutes gave into the consideration that an active role for the victims in the proceedings could have a negative effect on the role given to the Prosecutor in both statutes.

Victims of Enforced Disappearance

The General or Universal System of the United Nations

The blight of enforced disappearances has only recently attracted the attention of international law both in the general or universal system of the United Nations and in the regional systems, but in this last case only in the American regional system.

[43] In this respect, see C. Jorda, "L'accès des victimes à la justice pénale internationale" and C. Tournaye, "L'apport des Tribunaux *ad hoc* pour la répression du terrorisme", both in: SOS Attentats, see note 6, 416 et seq.

In the general or universal system of United Nations, two international norms related to victims of enforced disappearance have been built. On the one hand, the *Declaration on the Protection of All Persons from Enforced Disappearance* and on the other hand, the *International Convention for the Protection of All Persons from Enforced Disappearance* adopted on 20 December 2006 by resolution A/RES/61/177 of the General Assembly.[44]

As we will see, the way in which the general or universal system of United Nations faces up to enforced disappearances is similar to that of other international treaties of this general system. A way characterized by the fact that the treaty is preceded in time by a declaration of the UN General Assembly on the same subject as that of the future treaty. It is the same case, for example, in the field of international law of human rights that this sector of norms faced the fight against torture. Here, the *Convention Against Torture of 1984* was preceded by the *Declaration on the Protection of All Persons from being subjected to Torture and Other Cruel, Inhuman or Degrading Treatment or Punishment* adopted by A/RES/3452 (XXX) of 9 December 1975.[45]

This kind of proceeding shows clearly the way in which the birth of international obligations took place in a concrete field without regulation or with an incipient regulation through norms of *soft law*. In such cases, the initiative comes always or almost always from the UN General Assembly or from another organ of this international organization, being the legal instrument of an institutional norm adopting the form of a "Declaration" that, for its part, is preceded by other institutional norms drawn up inside the United Nations. Then, generally more late than quickly, the legal work begun with the institutional norm concerned marks its end with an international treaty of a general or universal character. In the meanwhile, regional initiatives can contribute to the acceleration or consolidation of the legal process. On occasions, it is also the general or universal initiative which promotes and gives place to posterior regulations.[46]

With regard to enforced disappearances the *Declaration on the Protection of All Persons from Enforced Disappearance* was preceded by resolution A/RES/33/173

[44] It is, until today, the only international treaty at the general or universal level relating to a category of victims. The 1992 Declaration and the 2006 Convention, see note 4, contain the following catalogue of rights: right to justice (which includes the right to a prompt and effective judicial remedy); the right to know the truth regarding the circumstances of the enforced disappearance; the progress and results of the investigation and the fate of the disappeared person; the right of access to all information concerning the person deprived of liberty; the right to form and participate freely in organizations and associations concerned with attempting to establish the circumstances of enforced disappearances and the fate of disappeared persons; and, at least, the right to obtain reparation and prompt, fair and adequate compensation.

[45] See note 10 of the first chapter of this book.

[46] It is the case of the UN Commission on Human Rights in relation to Resolution 2005/35 of 19 April 2005 containing the *Basic Principles and Guidelines of the Right to a Remedy and Reparation for Victims of Gross Violations of International Human Rights Law and Serious Violations of International Humanitarian Law* (Doc. E/CN.4/2005/L.10/Add.11).

of 20 December 1978, in which the General Assembly "... expressed concern about the reports from various parts of the world relating to enforced or involuntary disappearances, as well as about the anguish and sorrows caused by those disappearances, and called upon Governments to hold law enforcement and security forces legally responsible for excesses which might lead to enforced or involuntary disappearances of persons."[47] The same *Declaration on the Protection of All Persons from Enforced Disappearance* underlines in its preamble the need of an international treaty on the matter:

> Bearing in mind that, while the acts which comprise enforced disappearance constitute a violation of the prohibition found in the aforementioned international instruments, it is none the less important to devise an instrument which characterizes all acts of enforce disappearance of persons as very serious offences and sets forth standards designed to punish and prevent their commission.

As a consequence, the General Assembly considered it necessary to adopt a specific legal instrument with the above-mentioned result.

But the legal answer to the seriousness of enforced disappearance is not limited to the adoption of the International Convention. Both, the Declaration and the International Convention qualify the practice of enforced disappearance as a crime against humanity. The Declaration, in paragraph four of its preamble,

> Considering that enforced disappearance undermines the deepest values of any society committed to respect for the rule of law, human rights and fundamental freedoms, and that the systematic practice of such acts is of the nature of a crime against humanity.

The International Convention, in paragraph five of its preamble states that enforced disappearance always constitutes a crime and "in certain circumstances defined in International Law" enforced disappearance also constitutes "a crime against humanity."[48] Article 5 of the Convention categorically states,

> The widespread or systematic practice of enforced disappearance constitutes a crime against humanity as defined in applicable International Law and shall attract the consequences provided for under such applicable International Law.

The *Inter-American Convention on Forced Disappearance of Persons* of 6 September 1994 states in paragraph six of its preamble, "that the systematic practice of the forced disappearance of persons constitutes a crime against humanity."

The conception and qualification of enforced disappearance as a crime against humanity is also considered in the *General Comment of the Working Group on*

---

[47] Para. 5 of the preamble. The same is true in the case of other international norms quoted by this Declaration like A/RES/43/173 of 9 December 1988 and the Principles on the Effective Prevention and Investigation of Extra-legal, Arbitrary and Summary Executions, set forth in the Annex to the Economic and Social Council resolution 1989/65 of 24 May 1989, endorsed by the General Assembly in its resolution A/RES/44/162 of 15 December 1989 (cf. *ibid.*, para. 10).

[48] Para. 5 of the preamble of the International Convention for the Protection of All Persons from Enforced Disappearance.

Enforced or Involuntary Disappearances. In its General Comment, the Working Group underlines that a crime against humanity is always committed in a certain context, such as: the existence of an attack against any civilian population, the widespread and systematic character of this attack and the knowledge the perpetrator has of the attack. These are elements which can be found in article 7 of the Statute of the ICC.[49]

Due to the fact that the ICC Statute is actually ratified by more than a hundred states and has been incorporated into the statutes of other international criminal courts as well as international hybrid courts the Working Group concludes that the definition of the crime against humanity made in article 7 of the Statute of the ICC "now reflects customary International Law and can thus be used for interpretation."[50]

With regard to the concept of victim, the *International Convention for the Protection of All Persons from Enforced Disappearance* of 20 December 2006 qualifies as victim,

> the disappeared person and any individual who has suffered harm as the direct result of an enforced disappearance.[51]

Consequently, this Convention only envisages *direct victims* and, within this, *two types* of victims. On the one hand, the disappeared person; on the other hand, any individual who has suffered harm as the direct result of an enforced disappearance. Despite this limit and, in line with what was stated earlier, it is possible to enlarge this restricted concept of victim by resorting to other international norms relating to victims. Basically, because enforced disappearance is a crime—a very serious crime—thanks to the door opened by the UN *Declaration of Basic Principles of Justice for Victims of Crime and Abuse of Power* adopted by General Assembly resolution 40/34 of 29 November 1985, quoted above, which also envisages indirect victims.

---

[49] According to article 7 para. 1 ICC-Statute: "For the purpose of this Statute, 'crime against humanity' means any of the following acts when committed as part of a widespread or systematic attack directed against any civilian population, with knowledge of the attack: (a) Murder; (b) Extermination; (c) Enslavement; (d) Deportation or forcible transfer of population; (e) Imprisonment or other severe deprivation of physical liberty in violation of fundamental rules of International Law; (f) Torture; (g) Rape, sexual slavery, enforced prostitution, forced pregnancy, enforced sterilization, or any other form of sexual violence of comparable gravity; (h) Persecution against any identifiable group or collectivity on political, racial, national, ethnic, cultural, religious, gender as defined in paragraph 3, or other grounds that are universally recognized as impermissible under International Law, in connection with any act referred to in this paragraph or any crime within the jurisdiction of the Court; (i) Enforced disappearance of persons; (j) The crime of apartheid; (k) Other inhumane acts of a similar character intentionally causing great suffering, or serious injury to body or to mental or physical health."

[50] See under www2.ohchr.org/english/issues/disappear/index.htm.

[51] Article 24 para. 1.

However, to make this possible it is necessary to include the crime of enforced disappearance in the criminal code of the concerned state. Otherwise, the restricted definition will persist.[52]

The American Regional System: The Organization of American States (OAS)

As just stated, the only international norm related to enforced disappearance of persons in the regional systems concerns the American continent: the *Inter-American Convention on Forced Disappearance of Persons* of 6 September 1994. This Convention does not have a concept of "victim of enforced disappearance". Nevertheless, as suggested earlier, this gap can be resolved by resorting to other international norms related to victims of crime, in general, or to some crimes or offences, in particular, because enforced disappearance of persons is a crime,[53] to be more exact, a very serious crime. But this solution, as stated earlier, requires that the concerned state categorize enforced disappearance of persons as a crime in its domestic order.

Victims of Trafficking

On the *Protocol to Prevent, Suppress and Punish Trafficking in Persons, especially Women and Children* supplementing the *United Nations Convention against Transnational Organized Crime*, both adopted by General Assembly resolution 55/25 on 15 November 2000,[54] there is no specific definition of victim of trafficking, but that the determination of the status of victim is made by reference to the offence of trafficking in persons defined in Article 3.a) of the said Protocol. According to it:

> For the purposes of this Protocol:
> (a) "Trafficking in persons" shall mean the recruitment, transportation, transfer, harbouring or receipt of persons, by means of the threat or use of force or other forms of coercion, of abduction, of fraud, of deception, of the abuse of power or of a position of vulnerability or

[52] In the opinion of N. Fernández Sola, this lack could also be covered by way of the third category of victims envisaged by the UN Declaration of 1985, that is, "persons who have suffered harm in intervening to assist victims in distress or to prevent victimization." In his opinion, this category could be helpful to protect persons, associations and groups engaged with human rights which become victims of attacks of forces or groups responsible for enforced disappearance, see Fernández Sola (2008), 403 et seq.

[53] For example, UN *Declaration of Basic Principles of Justice for Victims of Crime and Abuse of Power* adopted by General Assembly resolution 40/34 of 29 November 1985 or Resolution 2005/35 of 19 April 2005 containing the *Basic Principles and Guidelines of the Right to a Remedy and Reparation for Victims of Gross Violations of International Human Rights Law and Serious Violations of International Humanitarian Law* (Doc. E/CN.4/2005/L.10/Add.11).

[54] The Convention entered into force on 29 September 2003. The Protocol, on 25 December 2003.

> of the giving or receiving of payments or benefits to achieve the consent of a person having control over another person, for the purpose of exploitation. Exploitation shall include, at a minimum, the exploitation of the prostitution of others or other forms of sexual exploitation, forced labour or services, slavery or practices similar to slavery, servitude or the removal of organs;[55]

Accordingly, any person who is the object of the practice defined in Article 3.a) can be brought under the status of victim of trafficking.

In the *European regional frame*, and inside the Council of Europe, the *Convention on Action against Trafficking in Human Beings* held in Warsaw on 16 May 2005[56] defines the concept of victim by reference to "trafficking of human beings" defined in Article 4.a). So Article 4.e) states:

> 'Victim' shall mean any natural person who is subject to trafficking in human beings as defined in this article.

And according to Article 4.a):

> For the purposes of this Convention:
> a) "Trafficking in human beings" shall mean the recruitment, transportation, transfer, harbouring or receipt of persons, by means of the threat or use of force or other forms of coercion, of abduction, of fraud, of deception, of the abuse of power or of a position of vulnerability or of the giving or receiving of payments or benefits to achieve the consent of a person having control over another person, for the purpose of exploitation. Exploitation shall include, at a minimum, the exploitation of the prostitution of others or other forms of sexual exploitation, forced labour or services, slavery or practices similar to slavery, servitude or the removal of organs;

As for the *European Union*, the Directive 2011/36/EU of the European Parliament and of the Council of 5 April 2011 on preventing and combating trafficking in human beings and protecting its victims, and replacing the Council Framework Decision 2002/629/JHA[57] nor does it contain a specific definition of victim of trafficking but the determination of that status should be done with reference to the criminal offences related to trafficking in human beings referred to in Article 2.[58]

---

[55] Specifying Article 3.d) that: "'Child' shall mean any person under eighteen years of age."

[56] The Convention entered into force on the 1st February 2008.

[57] *OJEU* L 101, of 15 April 2011.

[58] According to which: "1. Member States shall take the necessary measures to ensure that the following intentional acts are punishable: The recruitment, transportation, transfer, harbouring or reception of persons, including the exchange or transfer of control over those persons, by means of the threat or use of force or other forms of coercion, of abduction, of fraud, of deception, of the abuse of power or of a position of vulnerability or of the giving or receiving of payments or benefits to achieve the consent of a person having control over another person, for the purpose of exploitation. 2. A position of vulnerability means a situation in which the person concerned has no real or acceptable alternative but to submit to the abuse involved. 3. Exploitation shall include, as a minimum, the exploitation of the prostitution of others or other forms of sexual exploitation, forced labour or services, including begging, slavery or practices similar to slavery, servitude, or the exploitation of criminal activities, or the removal of organs. 4. The consent of a victim of trafficking in human beings to the exploitation, whether intended or actual, shall be irrelevant where any of the means set forth in paragraph 1 has been used. 5. When the conduct referred to in paragraph 1 involves a child, it shall be a punishable offence of trafficking in human beings even if

Victims of Terrorism

Contrary to the other categories of victims analyzed in Chapter II, I will devote the next Chapter III instead of a paragraph to victims of terrorism. Various are the reasons of this choice. First, in contrast to the preceding six categories of victims (victims of crime, victims of abuse of power, victims of gross violations of international human rights law, victims of serious violations of international humanitarian law, victims of enforced disappearance and victims of violations of international criminal law), there is no international norm of a general or universal character related to them. The only exception is given in the European regional system by the *Guidelines on the Protection of Victims of Terrorist Acts* adopted on 2 March 2005 by the Committee of Ministers of the Council of Europe.[59]

Second, my choice is also justified by the fact of the non-existence in international law of an international concept of "victim of terrorism"[60] as well as by the fact that this definition is also conditioned by the concept of "terrorism" on which no consensus exists in the international community except for the definition given by the UN Security Council. Both questions deserve to be answered and, as I will show in the following pages, both problems can be resolved. It is related to the concept of terrorism by resorting to the elements present in the definition given by the UN Security Council in international treaties on the matter. From here the gap can be closed. On the other hand, the concept of "victim of terrorism" can be built both from the existing elements in the definition of victim contained in the international norms related to the different categories of victims quoted above and from the existing definition of terrorism.

As we will see, this task is much easier within the framework of the European Union because the existing norms in this regional system delimit in a more complete way what is understood by "terrorism", "terrorist organization" and "acts of terrorism". On this basis, it is also easier to build the concept of "victim of terrorism".

In any case what is surprising is that the United Nations has not yet adopted any international norm related to victims of terrorism either through its principal organs (the General Assembly or the Security Council) or through its subsidiary organs (Commission on Human Rights). On the contrary, it has paid attention to victims of crime, to victims of gross violations of international human rights law and to victims of serious violations of international humanitarian law. Having focused its attention on the fight against terrorism, the United Nations—and with it, its Member States—has forgotten the weaker and more directly affected by terrorism: the victims terrorism creates.

It is true that victims of terrorism are also victims of crime and at the same time victims of serious violations of human rights because terrorism is both a crime and

---

none of the means set forth in paragraph 1 has been used. 6. For the purpose of this Directive, 'child' shall mean any person below 18 years of age."

[59] Council of Europe, Committee of Ministries-CM/Del/Dec(2005) 917.

[60] It only exists in the frame of the Council of Europe.

a violation of human rights. But the reason for which victims of terrorism deserve a different treatment is due also both to the nature of the terrorist act and to the specific needs of the victims of terrorism. With regard to the first element, the characteristics terrorist acts share are underlined in paragraph 3 of Security Council resolution 1566 (2004)—as well as in other international norms—adopted under Chapter VII of United Nations Charter, which I will analyze in the following pages.[61]

With regard to the specific needs of the victims of terrorism, as UNODOC recently remembered, most of the acts considered as terrorism "inflict largescale human and material devastation". Moreover, such acts "impact not only the direct victims, who may be physically injured or killed, but may also have lasting effects on indirect victims, such as their dependents or relatives, as well as vicarious victims, which may include members of the broader public".[62] This is why it concludes that "any difference in treatment afforded to victims of acts of terrorism, as distinct from victims of other crimes, should be based upon their specific needs".[63]

The same is valid with regard to the way victims of terrorism are treated in the legal field by the EU. In my opinion, victims of terrorism do not have to be included within the category of victims of crime but need a distinct treatment. I have already outlined the reasons.

In my opinion, the *Proposal for a Directive establishing minimum standards on the rights, support and protection of victims of crime*, actually in discussion by the EU[64] is *inadequate* from the perspective of victims of terrorism: *on the one hand* because it is not intended for them, but in general, for victims of crime. As a result, it does not give visibility to the victims of terrorism.

It is true that terrorism is a crime and as a result, that victims of terrorism are also and at the same time victims of crime. However, as I have already said, terrorism is not a simple crime (like murder, for example) and the victims of terrorism are not simple victims of crime. No. Terrorism is a serious violation of human rights, an international crime and its victims are *macrovictims*.[65] Terrorism, in contrast to other offences, directly attacks the structure of the State and seeks to defeat it to impose by force a totalitarian project. Terrorizing society is the means to achieve this.

On the other hand, this Proposal for a Directive is not only limited to victims of crime but also, with respect to them, does not intend to establish or pick up a catalogue of rights which they are holding, but simply provide "minimum standards on the rights, support and protection of victims of crime"; minimum standards that Member States can improve.

---

[61] See 71 et seq. of the present work.

[62] UNODOC (2011), p. 93, para. 375.

[63] *Ibid.* See also paragraphs 376–379.

[64] European Commission, COM(2011) 275/2.

[65] As noted by BERISTAIN, all crimes of terrorism are of a greater tragic gravity than similar crimes in the same genus (a terrorist murder is more serious than murder). For this reason, their victims deserve the name of macrovictims. (See Beristain (2004), p. 35). De este autor vid. también *Victimología. Nueve palabras clave*, Tirant lo Blanch, Valencia, 2000, y *Transformación del Derecho Penal y la Criminología hacia la Victimología*, ARA Editores, Perú, 2008.

Third, the victims of terrorism are not a simple category of "vulnerable" victims. In this regard, the Proposal for a Directive falls short. Also, despite the fact that in Recital No. 18 of the Proposal for a Directive, it is stated that "victims of terrorism require particular attention in any assessment—in order to determinate their vulnerability—given the varying nature of such acts ranging from mass acts of terrorism to targeted terrorism against individuals",[66] later, in the corresponding article—article 18, entitled "Identification of vulnerable victims"—the victims of terrorism are not identified as a vulnerable category.[67]

In any case, even if you include them, limiting the treatment of victims of terrorism to their inclusion in the category of vulnerable victims is insufficient and unsatisfactory because as I have already said, the victims of terrorism are not a simple category of vulnerable victims or simple victims of crime.

Fourth, the Proposal for a Directive does not grant the rights claimed by the victims of terrorism. It is obliged to provide, within the right to information, information to victims of any change in the implementation of the judgment: prison privileges, benefits, changes in level, etc. In this regard, article 4 (titled, "Right to receive information about his case") only provides notification to the victim, when it has so requested:

- Of any decision ending the criminal proceedings instituted as a result of the complaint of a criminal offence made by the victim,
- The decision not to proceed with or to end an investigation or a prosecution, or a final judgement in a trial, including any sentence;
- Information enabling the victim to know about the state of affairs of the criminal proceedings instituted as a result of the complaint of a criminal offence made by the victim, unless, in exceptional cases the proper handling of the case may be adversely affected;
- The time and place of the trial;
- The time when the person prosecuted or sentenced for offences concerning them is released from detention.

[66] European Commission, Brussels 18.5.2011, SEC(2011) 275 final, 17.

[67] Article 18 says: "1. For the purposes of this Directive, the following categories of victims are considered to be vulnerable due to their personal characteristics: (a) Children; (b) Persons with disabilities. 2. For the purposes of this Directive, the following categories of victims are considered to be vulnerable due to the nature or type of crime to which they have fallen victim: (a) Victims of sexual violence; (b) Victims of human trafficking. 3. Member States shall ensure that all other victims receive a timely and individual assessment, in accordance with national procedures, to determine whether they are vulnerable, due to their personal characteristics or the circumstances or the type or nature of the crime, to secondary and repeat victimization or intimidation. 4. Member States shall ensure that all vulnerable victims as identified in paragraphs 1, 2 and 3, receive a timely and individual assessment, in accordance with national procedures, to determine which special measures as provided in Articles 21 and 22 they should benefit from. Such an assessment shall take into account the wishes of the vulnerable victim including where they do not wish to benefit from special measures. 5. The extent of the assessment may be adapted according to the severity of the crime and the degree of apparent harm suffered by the victim."

These gaps and more are explained precisely by the general character of this Proposal for a Directive[68]; generality that is incompatible with the special treatment in a specific international norm which—as other categories of victims—is also required by the victims of terrorism. The Proposal for a Directive itself is aware of that and says so explicitly in the concluding paragraphs of its explanatory memorandum: on the one hand, when it states—without concrete them—that "victims of terrorism will benefit from improved mechanisms for identifying their needs, keeping them informed of proceedings and providing adequate protection during proceedings"; on the other hand, when it states that "looking to the future, action in relation to specific categories of victims such as victims of terrorism and organized crime is also envisaged. In particular, analysis of the existing gaps in the protection of victims of terrorism is due to take place with a view to improving the situation of victims of terrorism in Europe".[69]

At least, if we compare the rights listed in the Proposal for a Directive and those listed in the *Guidelines on the Protection of Victims of Terrorist Acts* adopted by the Committee of Ministers of the Council of Europe on 2 March 2005, we see that neither the right of emergency assistance nor the right to continuing assistance is envisaged by the proposal. This last, on article 7, only takes into account the right to access free of charge confidential victim support services. The same concerns the right to investigation and prosecution that is neither envisaged by the proposal.

Both texts have in common the lack of references to two rights closely linked to victims of terrorism: the right to the truth and the right to memory.

References

Beristain A (2004) Protagonismo de las Víctimas de hoy de mañana (Evolución en el campo jurídico penal, prisional y ético). Tirant lo Blanch, Valencia

Carnerero R (2007) La inmunidad de jurisdicción penal de los Jefes de Estado extranjeros. Iustel, Madrid

Carnerero R (2011) La Corte Penal Internacional. In: Fernández de Casadevante Romani C (dir.) Derecho Internacional de los Derechos Humanos, p 521

Esposito C (2007) Inmunidad del Estado y Derechos Humanos. Civitas, Madrid

Fernández de Casadevante Romani C (2010) Derecho Internacional Público, 2003. M.D. Evans, International Law: 373–378

Fernández Sola N (2008) El derecho a la reparación de las víctimas de desaparición forzada: hacia la justicia a través del Derecho internacional. Revista Española de Derecho Internacional 60:403

Gozzi MH, Laborde JP (2005) Les Nations Unies et le droit des victimes du terrorisme. Revue Internationale de Droit Pénal 76:297

UNODOC (2011) The criminal justice response to support of acts of terrorism. United Nations, New York

[68] I say general character because it only envisages victims of crime. That is, of all crime.

[69] European Commission, Brussels 18.5.2011, SEC(2011) 275 final, 4.

Special Reference to the Victims of Terrorism

Victims of Terrorism and International Law: From Ignorance to Recognition

The answer of international law to terrorism has been, for a long time, very weak. Consequently, until recently, interest has not been shown nor has attention been paid by the international community to victims of terrorism. The proof of this is the fact that until the 1993 Vienna World Conference on Human Rights the relationship between terrorism and human rights did not attract the attention of the United Nations.[1] Since 1994, the UN General Assembly's resolutions concerning terrorism appear under the title "human rights and terrorism."[2] At the same time, the resolutions adopted on the matter are characterized by the affirmation "that the most essential and basic human right is the right to life" and by the General Assembly's concern "at the gross violations of human rights perpetrated by terrorist groups."[3] They also declare the General Assembly's solidarity with victims of terrorism and request the Secretary-General of the UN to seek the views of Member States on the possible establishment of a United Nations voluntary fund for victims of terrorism as well as for ways and means to rehabilitate the victims of terrorism and to reintegrate them into society.

[1] From 1972 to 1991, the General Assembly examined this matter under the title: "Measures to prevent international terrorism which endangers or takes innocent human lives or jeopardizes fundamental freedoms and study of the underlying causes of those forms of terrorism and acts of violence which lie in misery, frustration, grievance and despair and which cause some people to sacrifice human lives, including their own, in an attempt to effect radical changes."

[2] The starting point was A/RES/49/185 of 23 December 1994.

[3] There are a lot of General Assembly resolutions qualifying terrorism as a violation of human rights, see A/RES/48/122 of 20 December 1993; A/RES/49/185 of 23 December 1994; A/RES/50/186 of 22 December 1995; A/RES/52/133 of 12 December 1997; A/RES/54/164 of 17 December 1999 and A/RES/56/160 of 19 February 2001. See Fernández de Casadevante Romani and Jiménez García (2005), 116 et seq.

C. Fernández de Casadevante Romani, *International Law of Victims*,
DOI 10.1007/978-3-642-28140-2_3, © Springer-Verlag Berlin Heidelberg 2012

From 1994 onwards, the UN Human Rights Commission also began to adopt resolutions under the title "human rights and terrorism"; resolutions containing references to victims of terrorism.[4] It also requested the Sub-Commission on the Promotion and Protection of Human Rights to undertake a study on the issue of terrorism and human rights in the context of its procedures. The Special Rapporteur stated in this respect,

> 102. Terrorist acts, whether committed by States or non-State actors, may affect the right to life, the right to freedom from torture and arbitrary detention, women's rights, children's rights, health, subsistence (food), democratic order, peace and security, the right to non-discrimination, and any number of other protected human rights norms. Actually, there is probably not a single human right exempt from the impact of terrorism.[5]

The same connection between terrorism and human rights is made by the High Commissioner for Human Rights in his report to the General Assembly according to Resolution 48/142 entitled "Human rights: a unity framework report."[6] It states that terrorism "is a threat to the most fundamental human right, the right to life" and that "the essence of human rights is that human life and dignity must not be compromised and that certain acts, whether carried out by State or non-State actors, are never justified no matter what the ends."[7]

By now it is clearly established that terrorism is a violation of human rights. In this context, it must be added that terrorism is not an ordinary violation of human rights. On the contrary, it is an *international crime*.[8] This is why victims of terrorism request the inclusion of this crime among the crimes coming under the jurisdiction of the ICC or, as another alternative, to judge its most serious aspects (murder, torture, enforced disappearance of persons, persecution and other inhuman acts of a similar character intentionally causing great suffering, or serious injury to body or to mental or physical health) as crimes against humanity. This course of action is possible, because as underlined by the President of the ICC, although the

---

[4] The UN Commission on Human Rights has also qualified terrorism as a violation of human rights (see resolutions 1994/46, 1995/43, 1996/47, 1997/42, 1998/47, 1999/27, 2000/30, 2001/37, 2002/35 and 2003/37). Also, the Sub-Commission on the Promotion and Protection of Human Rights (see resolutions 1994/18, 1996/20 and 1997/39). In 1993, the Sub-Commission had even condemned "the violations of human rights by the terrorist groups Sendero Luminoso and Movimiento Revolucionario Tupac Amaru" in Peru (resolution 1993/23).

[5] Doc. E/CN.4/Sub.2/2001/31 of 27 June 2001, 46. The Special Rapporteur drafted a preliminary report (Doc. E/CN.4/Sub.2/1999/27 of 7 June 1999), a progress report (Doc. E/CN.4/Sub.2/2001/31 of 27 June 2001), a second progress report (Doc. E/CN.4/Sub.2/2002/35 of 17 July 2002), an additional progress report with two addenda (Doc. E/CN.4/Sub.2/2003/WP.1 and Add.1 and 2 of 8 August 2003) and a final report (Doc. E/CN.4/Sub.2/2004/40 of 25 June 2004). In fact, a lot of rights are infringed by terrorism: the right to liberty and security, the right to family life, the right to movement, the right to information, the right to a fair trial, etc.

[6] Doc. E/CN.4/2002/18 of 27 February 2002, paras 3 and 4.

[7] *Ibid.*, paras 2 and 5.

[8] Cf. P. Kirsch, "Terrorisme, crimes contre l'humanité et Cour pénale internationale", in: SOS Attentats, see note 6, 111.

Statute of the ICC does not include terrorism among the crimes within the jurisdiction of the Court, this crime could be considered a crime against humanity of the type of those envisaged in Article 7 of the Statute of the ICC so that, *a priori*, nothing hinders the ICC from taking them up if the other elements guiding the jurisdiction of this international court are present.[9]

The fact of not dealing with terrorism either as an independent crime or as a type of crime against humanity leads to impunity and denies victims of terrorism their effective right to justice when the State will not or cannot guarantee it.[10] In consequence, it is the responsibility of the United Nations itself to urge and promote international norms recognizing and guaranteeing victims of terrorism the effective enjoyment of their human rights. This is especially true for their effective right to justice and to redress. This is why victims of terrorism call for such actions.[11]

In short, although the Commission on Human Rights has reiterated "its unequivocal condemnation of all acts, methods and practices of terrorism, regardless of their motivation, in all their forms and manifestations, wherever, whenever and by whoever committed, as acts aimed at the destruction of human rights, fundamental freedoms and democracy"[12] and although bearing in mind that "the most essential and basic human right is the right to life",[13] as well as "profoundly deploring the large number of civilians killed, massacred and maimed by terrorists in indiscriminate and random acts of violence and terror, which cannot be justified under any circumstances,[14] what is true is that in contrast to the Council of Europe[15] United Nations has paid far less attention to victims of terrorism. Also that this attention

[9] The High Commissioner on Human Rights states that terrorism is a crime against humanity in para. 4 of his Report to the General Assembly according to Resolution 48/142 entitled "Human rights: a unity framework report" (Doc. E/CN.4/2002/18 of 27 February 2002).

[10] This is the case, for example, when the crime of terrorism has been amnestied or has been prescribed according to domestic law and the prescription has taken place as a consequence of the passivity of the State to investigate the crime or in the instruction of the indictment. Impunity also takes place, e.g. in case of failed States. The causes are many and all lead to impunity.

[11] See Bou Franch and Fernández de Casadevante Romani (2009).

[12] For example, in resolutions 2002/35 and 2004/44 about "Human Rights and Terrorism" and in resolutions 2003/68 and 2004/87 about "Protection of Human Rights and Fundamental Freedoms while Countering Terrorism."

[13] So, for example, in resolutions 2002/35 and 2004/44 entitled "Human Rights and Terrorism" and in resolutions 2003/68 and 2004/87 about "Protection of Human Rights and Fundamental Freedoms while Countering Terrorism." see *ut supra* note 4.

[14] *Ibid.*

[15] The attention of the Council of Europe to victims of terrorism is specified in its Guidelines on the Protection of Victims of Terrorist Acts adopted by the Committee of Ministers on 2 March 2005. It contains measures and services that are granted independent of the identification, arrest, prosecution or conviction of the perpetrator of the terrorist act. They concern emergency and continuing assistance, investigation and prosecution, effective access to law and to justice, administration of justice, compensation, protection of the private and family life of victims of terrorist acts, protection of the dignity and the security of victims of terrorist acts, information for victims of terrorist acts, specific training for persons responsible for assisting victims of terrorist acts and the

has been limited to expression of mere courtesy deprived of any legal obligation.[16] More precisely, what is true for the General Assembly is also true for the Security Council[17] and the Commission on Human Rights.[18]

So, although terrorism is an international crime that seriously violates human rights, the paradox is that, unlike other categories of victims, no international norm on victims of terrorism and their rights has yet been adopted inside the UN.

On the contrary, with regard to the other types of victims, several international norms have been adopted as has been shown to take into account most of the different categories of victims. To change this situation, it is urgent that in particular the United Nations, in line with the actions concerning the other categories of victims being mentioned, and like the acts carried out by the Council of Europe, promote an international norm affirming the status of victims of terrorism. That is to say, a statute made up of a catalogue of rights inherent to the condition of victims of terrorism based upon the effective right to justice and the prevention of impunity, connected to the jurisdiction of the ICC. It is the only way in which the "universal" right to justice of each victim of terrorism can be guaranteed.[19]

Yes, it is evident that the UN cannot remain deaf to the pleas for justice of victims of terrorism; victims who in most corners of our little planet do not have the most basic human rights[20] and victims who, besides, have never called for revenge. On the contrary, they have placed their trust in the state to deliver the justice that is their due.

Consequently, it is the responsibility of the UN itself to urge and promote international norms recognizing and guaranteeing victims of terrorism the effective enjoyment of their human rights. This is especially true of their effective right to

possibility for states to increase protection of this category of victims (Council of Europe, Committee of Ministers-CM/Del/Dec(2005)917).

[16] Contrary to the silence of the UN with regard to victims of terrorism, it has frequently—and correctly—pointed out the obligation of states to respect human rights when combating terrorism. In this line, the Commission on Human Rights on 21 April 2005 appointed, for a period of 3 years, a Special Rapporteur on the Promotion and Protection of Human Rights and Fundamental Freedoms while countering terrorism. This shows a clear and concrete endorsement by Member States of the need to make the honouring of human rights commitments an integral part of the international fight against terrorism, http://www.un.org/spanish/terrorism/terrorismhr.shtml.

[17] See *ut supra* page 11, note 22.

[18] See resolution 2003/37 of the Commission on Human Rights adopted on 23 April 2003 and related to the establishing of an International Fund to compensate victims of terrorist acts.

[19] Without the intervention of the ICC, most victims of terrorism would lack, *de facto*—as is the situation today—their right to justice because its effective exercise depends upon the correct functioning of state structures and presently many states affected by terrorism are either failed states or states in which the effective exercise of this right is impossible because of the weakness of the existent state structures. In such conditions, the right to redress is also impossible. As a consequence, many victims of terrorism lack basic human rights.

[20] Among them, the effective right to justice or the right to redress. This is the case of situations described in the preceding footnote. They all lead, *de facto*, to deny victims of terrorism their effective right to justice and, as a consequence, their right to redress.

justice and to redress. This is why victims of terrorism associations call for such actions.[21] This is also what elementary consideration of justice demands.

Fortunately, it seems that the time for victims of terrorism in the legal field of United Nations is also coming because the objective of addressing the rights of the victims of terrorism has been included very recently in the agenda of the UN. Thus, from his first report, the new Special Rapporteur for the Promotion and the protection of human rights and fundamental freedoms while countering terrorism—Mr. Emmerson—expresses his commitment to pay special attention to the rights of direct and indirect victims of acts of terrorism as well as to the duties of States with respect to actual and potential victims.[22] Still more, he advances a catalogue of rights of victims of terrorism; a catalogue that is conceived as an obligation on the charge of States.

For the first time, in the framework of the United Nations it is clearly stated that "any sound, sustainable and comprehensive strategy for combating terrorism requires the recognition of the suffering of victims of terrorist acts".[23] Also, that States "have important duties in this regard".[24]

Moreover, also for the first time, it is underlined that the first obligation of any State is "to protect the lives of its citizens and of all individuals within its territory and subject to its jurisdiction"; an obligation that has the following consequences:

> the duty to take reasonable measures, within the lawful and proportionate exercise of State powers, and in a manner consistent with the protection of human rights, to prevent the materialization of a real and immediate risk to life; the duty to conduct thorough, independent and impartial investigations when it is plausibly alleged that this primary positive obligation has been violated; the duty to investigate and bring to justice the perpetrators of acts of terrorism in a manner consistent with international standards on the protection of human rights; and the duty to afford adequate reparation to direct and indirect victims of terrorism in cases where, on inquiry, it is established that the State has failed to discharge its primary obligation to take reasonable steps to prevent violations by non-State actors of the right to life or the right to physical security.[25]

Independent of these rights that States have with respect to "its citizens and of all individuals within its territory and subject to its jurisdiction", the Special Rapporteur emphasizes that States also have "broader duties with respect to supporting the victims of terrorism".[26] And this, "even in cases where the relevant authorities have done all that can reasonably be required of them, within the lawful and

[21] Regarding this question, See Bou Franch and Fernández de Casadevante Romani (2009).

[22] Vid. UN General Assembly, *Promotion and protection of human rights and fundamental freedoms while countering terrorism*, 18 August 2011, (A/66/310, para. 20, 5)

[23] *Ibid.*, 6.

[24] *Ibid.*

[25] *Ibid.*

[26] *Ibid.*, para. 21, 6.

proportionate exercise of their powers, to prevent acts of terrorism from occurring".[27] That is, even without fault on their charge.

In this new approach, the Special Rapporteur considers it essential that the protection of the rights of the victims of terrorism be perceived "as a genuine legal duty resting primarily with States"[28]; a duty implying concrete obligations on the charge of States.

It is a new step and, at the same time, a radical change of the perspective with which the fight against terrorism was treated before: a fight where victims were not present—were invisible—and a fight where the UN and Member States always put the accent on the *voluntary basis* of the action relating to the assistance and needs of victims of terrorism. I would like to honour the success Spanish associations of victims of terrorism have had in this new approach.[29]

That different perspective is highlighted by the Special Rapporteur Mr. Emmerson:

> Whereas the United Nations Global Counter-Terrorism Strategy makes a pledge to Member States to only "consider putting in place, on a voluntary basis, national systems of assistance that would promote the needs of victims of terrorism and their families and facilitate the normalization of their lives",[30] the Special Rapporteur considers that States are bound by an international human rights obligation to provide for such assistance to victims of terrorism, including their families.[31]

The importance of this change is great: we are facing an international human rights obligation to provide assistance to victims of terrorism, "including their families"—that is, direct and indirect victims—which is a broader content. Effectively, in view of the Special Rapporteur:

> the obligation goes further than that and *includes, but is not limited to*, the duty to prevent acts of terrorism; the duty, if they have occurred, to properly investigate, publicly disclose the truth and bring the perpetrators to justice; the duty to investigate any allegations of culpable failure on the part of State authorities, in the lawful and proportionate exercise of their powers, to take reasonable steps to prevent acts of terrorism; legal recognition of victims of terrorism; pecuniary compensation, including for moral damages sustained; rehabilitation; provision of health care and psychosocial and legal assistance; ensuring a safe environment for the return or, if impossible, the resettlement of persons displaced by acts of terrorism or counter-terrorism measures; provision of moral support; and fostering good community relations and providing human rights education as a means of furthering tolerance.[32]

---

[27] *Ibid.*

[28] *Ibid.*, para. 23, 7.

[29] See Fundación Miguel Angel Blanco (2010, 2011).

[30] http://www.ohchr.org/EN/Issues/Terrorism/Pages/Statements.aspx.

[31] UN General Assembly, *Promotion and protection of human rights and fundamental freedoms while countering terrorism, op. cit.*, para. 24, 7.

[32] *Ibid.*, para. 24, 7. Italics are mine.

Although included in the list quoted above, the Special Rapporteur pays special attention to the issue of reparation. It considers that reparation schemes put in place on the national level should follow certain principles and list some of them "by way of example". According to him:

> Reparation schemes should aim at full restitution and foresee individual and collective reparation for both victims of counter-terrorism measures by the State and victims of terrorist acts, and follow a participatory approach. National reparation mechanisms must be independent and provide for adequate, effective and prompt reparation, which includes their being readily accessible and their taking a gender perspective into account. Compensation must never become a substitute for bringing perpetrators to justice or for revealing the truth in compliance with applicable international human rights obligations. States may also choose to provide financial assistance to organizations supporting victims of terrorism in order to comply with their international obligations vis-à-vis victims of terrorism.[33]

So, finally and after too much time, victims of terrorism and their rights begin to be the subject of work in the United Nations. I would be aware that this work prefigured, as in other categories of victims, in the adoption of a declaration of the General Assembly and later in an international treaty on the rights of the victims of terrorism.

In contrast to the general or universal system of the UN just described which is characterized by the non-existence of international norms on victims of terrorism, the progressive emergence of victims within the framework of the *European Union* took a further step on victims of terrorism with the Council Framework Decision of 13 June 2002 on combating terrorism (2002/475/JHA).[34] In its article 10, it takes into account the protection and assistance given to victims of terrorism. According to this article and related to the concept of "terrorist offences" which is developed in the long list of article 1 of this Council Framework Decision, article 10 states that Member States shall ensure that investigations into, or prosecution of, offences covered by this Framework Decision are not dependent on a report or accusation made by a person subjected to the offence, "at least if the acts were committed on the territory of the Member State."[35]

As already stated, the most important role in the matter—as in the more general field of human rights and in the more particular area of compensation for victims of crime and of prevention of torture—has been fulfilled by the Council of Europe, which until today is the only international organization to have adopted an international norm on victims of terrorism: the *Guidelines on the Protection of Victims of Terrorist Acts* adopted on 2 March 2005 by the Committee of Ministers.[36] These Guidelines are founded upon the principle that States "should ensure that any person who has suffered direct physical or psychological harm as a result of a terrorist act as well as, in appropriate circumstances, their close family can benefit

[33] *Ibid.*, para. 25, 7.

[34] *OJEC* L 164 of 22 June 2002.

[35] Article 10 para. 1, *ibid.*

[36] Council of Europe, Committee of Ministers-CM/Del/Dec(2005) 917.

from the services and measures prescribed by these Guidelines".[37] These are services and measures that are granted to victims of terrorism independent of the identification, arrest, prosecution or conviction of the perpetrator of the terrorist act. They include emergency and continuing assistance, investigation and prosecution, effective access to the law and to justice, administration of justice, compensation, protection of the private and family life of victims of terrorist acts, protection of the private and family life of victims of terrorist acts, information for victims of terrorist acts, specific training for persons responsible for assisting victims of terrorist acts as well as the possibility for states of adopting more favourable services and measures to victims of terrorist acts.

In that Guidelines, the UN has the model that international norms promoted within its framework should follow.

The Concept of Victim of Terrorism

Due to the clear link between both concepts, before dealing with the question relating to the concept of victim of terrorism, the definition of terrorism will be dealt with. Concerning this last, and as stated earlier, international law has all the elements to include in this concept all acts actually considered by international law as terrorists. With regard to the concept of "victim of terrorism", it shall be immediately specified that the non-existence of such a concept does not really constitute an obstacle, although its existence would be very helpful to particularize a concrete legal statute for this category of victims.

Yes, that gap does not constitute an obstacle. On the one hand, because it is possible to affirm the existence of a general concept of victim from the definitions contained in the international norms in force related to the different categories of victims; a concept whose elements are present in those definitions. On the other hand, because, as also stated, all victims—independent of the category to which they belong—have in common the fact of being victims as a consequence of a wrongful act (the victimizer fact) that is a crime. This is why independent of its possible particularization and of its possible inclusion in a certain category of victims depending on the type of criminal act suffered, the different categories of victims are at the same time both victims belonging to a concrete category of victims as well as victims of a crime; also victims of terrorism. Consequently, they all have the same rights inherent to the legal standing of victims in criminal proceedings. Additionally, they have rights not directly linked to the criminal proceedings but to their condition as victims. They are, most of them, rights that are common to the different categories of victims deriving from other international norms. At least victims also have rights inherent to the category of

[37] These persons are considered victims for the purposes of these Guidelines. The Guidelines make option for a broaden concept of victim.

victim to which they belong. These are rights recognized by international norms related to the category of victim concerned.

As opposed to the situation characterizing general international law, in the European regional system—particularly from the perspective of Member States of the European Union—the non-existence of a general concept of terrorism is in a certain way covered by the qualification as "terrorist offences" of the acts listed in Council Framework Decision (2002/475/JHA) of 13 June 2002[38]; a list which was completed by Council Framework Decision (2008/919/JHA) of 28 November 2008 adding other offences linked to terrorist activities such as public provocation to commit terrorist offences, recruitment for terrorism and training for terrorism.[39]

So far as the Council of Europe is concerned, we can see that the *Guidelines on the Protection of Victims of Terrorist Acts* adopted on 2 March 2005 by the Committee of Ministers do not contain a concept of terrorism. Despite that, such Guidelines give the consideration of victim of terrorism to any person who, as a result of a terrorist act, has suffered direct physical or psychological harm as the result of a terrorist act as well as, in appropriate circumstances, their close family.

A Previous Question: The Concept of Terrorism

On the occasion of the international fight against terrorism and, more concretely and as an example, of the qualification of terrorism as a crime against humanity by the statute of the ICC[40] as well as the concept of "victim of terrorism", this task is always going to be difficult due to the fact that a binding definition of terrorism does not exist. Still practically, all forms of terrorism are prohibited by the thirteen international conventions on terrorism actually in existence as well as by customary international law.[41] Indeed, in international law there is no field or sector in which terrorism is not forbidden. It is a prohibition that exists independent of the context in which the terrorist activity takes place: in time of war or in time of peace. In time of war, the international norms applied to international and non-international armed conflicts expressly prohibit the resort to terrorism against combatants and the

[38] *OJEU* L 164 of 2 June 2002.

[39] *OJEU* L 330 of 9 December 2008.

[40] Regarding this question, see Bou Franch and Fernández de Casadevante Romani (2009).

[41] This aspect is also underlined by the Report of the High Level Panel on Threats, Challenges and Change. Again, it was stated that practically all forms of terrorism are prohibited by the thirteen international conventions on terrorism actually existent as well as by customary international law, the Geneva Conventions or the ICC Statute, see Press Release SG/SM/8891 of 23 September 2003.

civilians. Such a prohibition derives clearly from the Geneva Conventions of 1949[42] as well as from its additional Protocols of 1977.[43]

Furthermore, International Humanitarian Law makes no distinction between crimes of war and crimes against humanity, so that the violation of one of its norms can be qualified as crime of war or as crime against humanity. More recently, in 1986, the ICJ recalled its statement in the *Corfu Channel* case in the line that existent prohibitions in the frame of international humanitarian law (prohibitions also appertaining to customary international law) are applicable both in peacetime and in wartime as "certain general and well recognized principles, namely: elementary considerations of humanity, even more exacting in peace than in war".[44]

In time of peace, terrorism is an international crime that is prohibited. The thirteen existing international treaties actually relating to terrorism[45] cover most of the various forms of terrorism and oblige states to take necessary measures to ensure that such acts are defined as offences under national law. It has to be remembered that the Geneva Conventions as well as their Protocols and the thirteen international treaties specifically related to terrorism are complementary. This means that these last are also applicable in peacetime and in international or internal armed conflicts.

To complete this description, it is necessary to add that terrorism is also envisaged by international criminal law.[46] Terrorism is one of the most serious international crimes. Even if it is not expressly qualified as a crime under the jurisdiction of the ICC, much of the acts envisaged by the international treaties relating to terrorism are, at the same time, acts appertaining to the "crime against humanity".[47]

---

[42] In this regard, see arts 27, 33 and 34 of the Fourth Geneva Convention Relative to the Protection of Civilian Persons in Time of War of 12 August 1949. As an example, article 33 states: "No protected person may be punished for an offence he or she has not personally committed. Collective penalties and likewise all measures of intimidation or of terrorism are prohibited. Pillage is prohibited. Reprisals against protected persons and their property are prohibited." See also article 51 para. 2 of Additional Protocol I to the Geneva Conventions of 12 August 1949, and relating to the Protection of Victims of International Armed Conflicts of 8 June 1977, and arts 4 and 13 of Additional Protocol II to the Geneva Conventions of 12 August 1949, and relating to the Protection of Victims of Non International Armed Conflicts of 8 June 1977.

[43] So, for example, article 51 para. 2 of Protocol I, which states, "The civilian population as such, as well as individual civilians, shall not be the object of attack. Acts or threats of violence the primary purpose of which is to spread terror among the civilian population are prohibited." Also, article 13 para. 2 of Protocol II.

[44] I.C.J. Reports 1949, 22. This statement was recalled in the *Case concerning Military and Paramilitary Activities in and against Nicaragua, Merits*, ICJ Reports 1986, 114, para. 218.

[45] Security Council Resolution S/RES/1377 (2001) of 12 November 2001 obliges states to rapidly ratify these treaties.

[46] In this respect, see Cassese (2008), 162 et seq.; Bollo Arocena (2004).

[47] International legal doctrine and jurisprudence agree on this matter. In this line also, the president of the ICC, *ut supra* p. 62 et seq. In Spain, the non-prescription of crimes of terrorism has been recently ruled by a bill (Ley Orgánica) modifying the Criminal Code. It concerns terrorist offences with result of death or serious injuries.

To prosecute before the ICC, those terrorist acts actually defined as crimes against humanity, according to article 7 of the ICC Statute, it would be necessary that the Prosecutor proves the four elements, which constitute a crime against humanity. First, the commission of certain acts; second, those acts have been committed as part of a widespread or systematic attack. Third, the attack was directed against any civilian population in application or execution of the politics of a state or of an international organization. Finally, the knowledge the author of such acts had of the fact that such acts were part of a widespread or systematic attack.[48] As an international crime, the principle *aut dedere aut iudicare* applies. It can be concluded that acts of terrorism are generally envisaged, defined and incriminated,[49] which will be further examined now.

The Concept of Terrorism in the Frame of United Nations

In the framework of general or universal international law, the Security Council's Resolution 1566 (2004), even though it does not contain a general definition of "terrorism", lists several acts considered as being acts of terrorism by different international treaties. The listing of such acts is made with reference to the existing international treaties on terrorism. This list of acts in Resolution 1566 (2004) is made "Acting under Chapter VII of the Charter of the United Nations", i.e., in exercise of the Security Council's primary responsibility for the maintenance of international peace and security conferred upon it by Article 24 of United Nations Charter[50] and with the binding effects that resolutions adopted under Chapter VII of the Charter have. The Security Council in operative paragraph 3,

> 3. Recalls that criminal acts, including against civilians, committed with the intent to cause death or serious bodily injury, or taking of hostages, with the purpose to provoke a state of terror in the general public or in a group of persons or particular persons, intimidate a population or compel a government or an international organization to do or to abstain from doing any act, which constitute offences within the scope of and as defined in the international conventions and protocols relating to terrorism, are under no circumstances justifiable by considerations of a political, philosophical, ideological, racial, ethnic, religious or

[48] Kirsch, see note 8 of the present chapter. In practice, only some acts of terrorism are excluded from the jurisdiction of the ICC, e.g. those committed in time of peace which do not fulfil the constitutive elements of the qualification of a crime against humanity. Doucet (2005), 271 et seq.

[49] See Doucet (2005).

[50] Article 24 states: "1. In order to ensure prompt and effective action by the United Nations, its Members confer on the Security Council primary responsibility for the maintenance of international peace and security, and agree that in carrying out its duties under this responsibility the Security Council acts on their behalf". Article 25 adds: "The Members of the United Nations agree to accept and carry out the decisions of the Security Council in accordance with the present Charter".

> other similar nature, and calls upon all States to prevent such acts and, if not prevented, to ensure that such acts are punished by penalties consistent with their grave nature.[51]

As may be seen in this paragraph, there is no definition *stricto sensu* of terrorism. Operative paragraph 3 of Resolution 1566 (2004) present several aspects. On the one hand, it is the first time that this organ of the United Nations refers to terrorism in such detail. An analysis of operative paragraph 3 reveals that it embraces all *criminal acts* including those against civilians and also against the military.[52] These acts are committed *with the intent* to cause death or serious bodily injury or to take hostages. They are committed *with the purpose* of creating a state of terror in the general public or in a group of persons or particular persons, intimidating a population or compelling a government or an international organization to do or to abstain from doing any act. These acts *constitute offences* within the scope of and as defined in the international conventions and protocols relating to terrorism.[53] Finally, they are criminal acts that are *under no circumstances justifiable* by considerations of a political, philosophical, ideological, racial, ethnic, religious or other similar nature. Consequently, the Security Council calls upon all states to prevent such acts and, if not prevented, to ensure that such acts are punished by penalties consistent with their grave nature.

With regard to the reference to international conventions and protocols relating to terrorism, it should be mentioned that some of these treaties, even if they do not directly refer to terrorism, have as their subject a series of acts actually considered as being terrorism. This is the case with wrongful acts against the safety of the civil

---

[51] In the opinion of L.M. Hinojosa Martínez, this definition is not technically precise, see his work Hinojosa Martínez (2008), 604.

[52] Even though there is no express reference to military personnel, it can be included since resort to terrorism is prohibited in International Humanitarian Law, see *ut supra* p. 69 et seq. See also article 4 para. 2 lit. d of Additional Protocol II, according to which acts of terrorism against "all persons who do not take a direct part or who have ceased to take part in hostilities, whether or not their liberty has been restricted", are and shall remain prohibited at any time and in any place whatsoever.

[53] Convention for the Suppression of Unlawful Seizure of Aircraft of 16 December 1970; Convention for the Suppression of Unlawful Acts against the Safety of Civil Aviation of 23 September 1971; Convention on the Prevention and Punishment of Crimes against Internationally Protected Persons of 14 December 1973; International Convention against the Taking of Hostages of 17 December 1979; Convention on the Physical Protection of Nuclear Material of 3 March 1980; Protocol for the Suppression of Unlawful Acts of Violence at Airports Serving International Civil Aviation, supplementary to the Convention for the Suppression of Unlawful Acts against the Safety of Civil Aviation of 24 February 1988; Protocol for the Suppression of Unlawful Acts against the Safety of Fixed Platforms Located on the Continental Shelf of 10 March 1988 and its Protocol for the Suppression of Unlawful Acts against the Safety of Fixed Platforms Located on the Continental Shelf of 14 October 2005; Convention on the Marking of Plastic Explosives for the Purpose of Detection of 1 March 1991; International Convention for the Suppression of Terrorist Bombings of 15 December 1997; International Convention for the Suppression of the Financing of Terrorism of 9 December 1999; International Convention for the Suppression of Acts of Nuclear Terrorism of 13 April 2005.

aviation and wrongful acts at airports serving international civil aviation[54]; and the use of unmarked and undetectable plastic explosives.[55]

Together with these international Conventions, there are others that directly envisage terrorist acts. According to them, the following acts are qualified as terrorist acts,

1. The "intentional commission of a murder, kidnapping or other attack upon the person or liberty of an internationally protected person, a violent attack upon the official premises, the private accommodation or the means of transport of an internationally protected person likely to endanger this person or his or her liberty", "a threat to commit any such attack", "an attempt to commit any such attack" and "an act constituting participation as an accomplice in any such attack;"[56]
2. The seizure, detention and threat of a person "to kill, to injure or to continue to detain another person in order to compel a third party, namely a State, an international intergovernmental organization, a natural or juridical person, or a group of persons, to do or abstain from doing any act as an explicit or implicit condition for the release of the hostage;"[57]
3. The unlawful and intentional deliverance, placement, discharging or detonating of "an explosive or other lethal device in, into or against a place of public use, a State or government facility, a public transportation system or an infrastructure facility" with the intent to cause death or serious bodily injury or with the intent to cause extensive destruction of such a place, facility or system, "where such destruction results in or is likely to result in major economic loss;"[58]
4. The possession of radioactive material or the making or possession of a device with the intent to cause death or serious bodily injury or with the intent to cause substantial damage to property or to the environment, as well as the use in any way of radioactive material or a device, or the use or damage of a nuclear facility in a manner which releases or risks the release of radioactive material with the intent to cause death or serious bodily injury or with the intent to cause substantial damage to property or to the environment; or with the intent to

[54] That constitutes the subject of the Montreal Convention for the Suppression of Unlawful Acts against the Safety of Civil Aviation of 23 September 1971, UNTS Vol. 974 No. 14118.

[55] That constitutes the subject of the Convention on the Marking of Plastic Explosives for the Purpose of Detection, see note 175. Its object is to control and limit the use of unmarked and undetectable plastic explosives (negotiated in the aftermath of the 1988 Pan Am flight 103 bombing). With this aim, States Parties are obliged within their respective territories to ensure effective control over "unmarked" plastic explosives.

[56] See article 2 para. 1 lit. a of the Convention on the Prevention and Punishment of Crimes against Internationally Protected Persons of 14 December1973, UNTS Vol. 1035 No. 15410.

[57] Article 1 para. 1 of the International Convention against the Taking of Hostages of 17 December 1979, UNTS Vol. 1316 No. 21931.

[58] Article 2 para. 1 of the International Convention for the Suppression of Terrorist Bombings of 15 December 1997, UNTS Vol. 2149 No. 37517.

compel a natural or legal person, an international organization or a state to do or refrain from doing an act[59];

5. The intentional commission of "an act without lawful authority which constitutes the receipt, possession, use, transfer, alteration, or dispersal of nuclear material and which causes or is likely to cause death or serious injury to any person or substantial damage to property." Also, the theft or robbery of nuclear material in order to compel a natural or legal person, international organization or state to do or to refrain from doing any act, as well as the attempt to commit any of the offences just described[60];
6. The provision or collection of funds "with the intention that they should be used or in the knowledge that they are to be used, in full or in part, in order to carry out an act which constitutes an offence within the scope of and as defined in one of the treaties listed in the annex"[61] or "any other act intended to cause death or serious bodily injury to a civilian, or to any other person not taking an active part in the hostilities in a situation of armed conflict, when the purpose of such act, by its nature or context, is to intimidate a population, or to compel a government or an international organization to do or to abstain from doing any act;"[62]
7. The unlawful and intentional seizure or exercise of control over a ship by force, threat or any other form of intimidation to commit an act of terrorism; to perform an act of violence against a person on board a ship if that act is likely to endanger the safe navigation of the ship; to place a destructive device or substance aboard a ship; and other acts against the safety of ships.[63] Also, the use of a ship as a device to further an act of terrorism; the transport on board a ship of various

[59] Article 2 para. 1 of the International Convention for the Suppression of Acts of Nuclear Terrorism of 13 April 2005. This Convention includes as an offence the threat to commit the offences quoted here (see article 2 para. 2).

[60] Article 7 para. 1 of the Convention on the Physical Protection of Nuclear Material of 3 March 1980, UNTS Vol. 1456 No. 24631.

[61] Convention for the Suppression of Unlawful Seizure of Aircraft of 16 December 1970; Convention for the Suppression of Unlawful Acts against the Safety of Civil Aviation of 23 September 1971; Convention on the Prevention and Punishment of Crimes against Internationally Protected Persons of 14 December 1973; International Convention against the Taking of Hostages of 17 December 1979; Convention on the Physical Protection of Nuclear Material of 3 March 1980; Protocol for the Suppression of Unlawful Acts of Violence at Airports Serving International Civil Aviation of 24 February 1988, supplementary to the Convention for the Suppression of Unlawful Acts against the Safety of Civil Aviation of 23 September 1971; Convention for the Suppression of Unlawful Acts against the Safety of Maritime Navigation of 10 March 1988; Protocol for the Suppression of Unlawful Acts against the Safety of Fixed Platforms Located on the Continental Shelf of 10 March 1988 and its Protocol for the Suppression of Unlawful Acts against the Safety of Fixed Platforms Located on the Continental Shelf of 14 October 2005; International Convention for the Suppression of Terrorist Bombings of 15 December 1997.

[62] Article 2 para. 1 of the International Convention for the Suppression of the Financing of Terrorism of 9 December 1999, UNTS Vol. 2178 No. 38349.

[63] See article 3 of the Convention for the Suppression of Unlawful Acts against the Safety of Maritime Navigation of 10 March 1988, UNTS Vol. 1678 No. 29004.

materials knowing that they are intended to be used to cause, or in a threat to cause, death or serious injury or damage to further an act of terrorism; as well as the transporting on board a ship of persons who have committed an act of terrorism[64];

8. The unlawful and intentional seizure or exercise of control over a fixed platform by force or threat thereof or any other form of intimidation; the performance of an act of violence against a person on board a fixed platform if that act is likely to endanger its safety; the destruction of a fixed platform or the causing of damages to it which is likely to endanger its safety; the placement or causing to be placed on a fixed platform, by any means whatsoever, of a device or substance which is likely to destroy that fixed platform or likely to endanger its safety; the injuring or killing of any person in connection with the commission or the attempted commission of any of the offences just described.[65]

Consequently, although there is no generally accepted definition of terrorism, it is possible to build an objective definition of terrorism based upon the commission of concrete acts that comprehend the great majority of terrorist acts. Such concrete acts are those envisaged by the international conventions quoted above.[66] Despite the value of this catalogue of acts considered as criminal offences made by reference to the international treaties on terrorism, it should be added that such a catalogue does not cover all forms of terrorism. In other words, there are forms of terrorism other than those envisaged in the treaties quoted here. Such is the case of urban violence, extortion or political prosecution which was denounced, e.g. by the Human Rights Commissioner of the Council of Europe in its report regarding the visit to the Autonomous Basque Community (Spain) in February 2001.[67]

The Concept of Terrorism in the Frame of the European Union

As stated above, in the frame of the European Union the nonexistence of a generally accepted concept of terrorism is to some extent covered by the qualification as "terrorist offences" of the acts listed in Council Framework Decision (2002/475/

[64] See the Protocol to the Convention for the Suppression of Unlawful Acts against the Safety of Maritime Navigation of 14 October 2005.

[65] See article 2 para. 1 of the Protocol for the Suppression of Unlawful Acts against the Safety of Fixed Platforms Located on the Continental Shelf of 14 October 2005, UNTS Vol. 1678 No. 29004.

[66] Cf. Hinojosa Martínez (2008), 60.

[67] Cf. Council of Europe, The Commissioner for Human Rights, Report by Mr. Alvaro Gil-Robles, Commissioner for Human Rights, on his visit to Spain and the Basque Country 5–8 February 2001 for the Committee of Ministers and the Parliamentary Assembly, Strasbourg, 9 March 2001, CommDH (2001) 2. In this respect, see Fernández de Casadevante Romani (2006). Also, Lozano Contreras (2001–2002), 17 et seq.

JHA) of 13 June 2002. Article 1 lists a series of intentional acts which are considered "terrorist offences" and oblige Member States to take necessary measures to ensure that such acts are defined as offences under national law.[68] Such acts are[69]:

- Seriously intimidating a population,
- Unduly compelling a Government or international organization to perform or abstain from performing any act,
- Seriously destabilizing or destroying the fundamental political, constitutional, economic or social structures of a country or an international organization.

According to article 1, the following intentional acts shall be deemed to be "terrorist offences":

(a) Attacks upon a person's life which may cause death;
(b) Attacks upon the physical integrity of a person;
(c) Kidnapping or hostage taking;
(d) Causing extensive destruction to a Government or public facility, a transport system, an infrastructure facility, including an information system, a fixed platform located on the continental shelf, a public place or private property likely to endanger human life or result in major economic loss;
(e) Seizure of aircraft, ships or other means of public or goods transport;
(f) Manufacture, possession, acquisition, transport, supply or use of weapons, explosives or of nuclear, biological or chemical weapons, as well as research into, and development of, biological and chemical weapons;
(g) Release of dangerous substances, or causing fires, floods or explosions, the effect of which is to endanger human life;
(h) Interfering with or disrupting the supply of water, power or any other fundamental natural resource, the effect of which is to endanger human life;
(i) Threatening to commit any of the acts listed in (a) to (h).

As can be seen, terrorism is not exhaustively described.[70] This is why Council Framework Decision (2008/919/JAH) of 28 November 2008 provides "for the criminalization of offences linked to terrorist activities in order to contribute to the more general policy objective of preventing terrorism through reducing the

---

[68] According to article 1 of the Council Framework Decision 2002/475/JHA, "Each Member State shall take the necessary measures to ensure that the intentional acts referred to below in points (a) to (i), as defined as offences under national law, . . .".

[69] Article 4 also envisages the fact of inciting or aiding or abetting an offence referred to in article 1 para. 1 and in articles 2 or 3.

[70] From the perspective of Spain, some criminal acts present in the terrorist acts of the Basque terrorist nationalist organization ETA remain outside this catalogue. This is the case with political prosecution (which can lead to exile). Extortion is covered by the revision by the Council Framework Decision 2008/919/JHA of 28 November 2008.

dissemination of those materials which might incite persons to commit terrorist attacks."[71] By this, states are obliged to take the necessary measures to ensure that offences linked to terrorist activities include the following acts:

(a) Public provocation to commit a terrorist offence;
(b) Recruitment of terrorists;
(c) Training of terrorists;
(d) Aggravated theft with a view to committing one of the offences listed in Article 1(1) of the Council Framework Decision (2002/475/JHA) of 13 June 2002, on combating terrorism, quoted here;
(e) Extortion with a view to the perpetration of one of the offences listed in Article 1(1) of the Council Framework Decision (2002/475/JHA) of 13 June 2002, on combating terrorism, quoted here;
(f) Drawing up false administrative documents with a view to committing one of the offences listed in Article 1(1)(a) to (h) and Article 2(2)(b) of the Council Framework Decision (2002/475/JHA) of 13 June 2002, on combating terrorism, quoted here.

The Concept of Terrorism in the Frame of Other Regional Systems

The European regional system is not the only with international regulation on terrorism. On the contrary, there are actually seven international treaties adopted in the frame of other regional systems. Most of them have a definition of terrorism as well as a description of acts considered terrorist acts. As we will see, these treaties have in common with the Security Council Resolution 1566 (2004) and with both Council Framework Decisions (2002/475/JHA) of 13 June 2002 and (2008/919/JAH) of 28 November 2008 the fact of underlying in terrorist acts the presence of the following elements:

- They are all criminal acts that are fulfilled with a concrete intention and purpose,
- These criminal acts are under no circumstances justifiable.

The treaties in question are the following: the Arab Convention on Suppression of Terrorism, of 22 April 1998, adopted in the frame of the *Arab League*[72]; in the frame of the *Cooperation Council For Arab States Of The Gulf*, the Convention against Terrorism of 4 May 2004[73]; the Convention of the Organization of the Islamic Conference on combating international terrorism of the 1st July 1999, adopted in the frame of the *Islamic Conference Organization*[74]; in the *African regional system*, the Convention on the Prevention and Combating

---

[71] Paragraph 7 of its preamble, *OJEU* L 330 of 9 December 2008.

[72] See Article 1.2 in https://www.unodc.org.

[73] Article 1 defines both"terrorist act"and"terrorist offence"*ibid.*

[74] See Article 1.2, *ibid.*

of terrorism, of 14 July1999 and its Protocol of 2004[75]; in the *Asiatic regional system* and adopted in the frame of the *South Asian Association for Regional Cooperation* (*SAARC*), the Regional Convention on Suppression of Terrorism of 4 November 1987 and the Additional Protocol to it of 6 January 2004[76]; in the frame of the *Association of South East Asian Nations* (*ASEAN*), the ASEAN Convention on Counter-Terrorism of 13 January 2007.At least, in the *American regional system*, the Inter-American Convention Against Terrorism, of 2002.[77]

From these treaties, only three do not have a definition of terrorism: the SAARC Regional Convention on Suppression of Terrorism of 4 November 1987, the ASEAN Convention on Counter-Terrorism of 13 January 2007 and the Inter-American Convention Against Terrorism of 2002. Nevertheless, the SAARC Regional Convention on Suppression of Terrorism of 4 November 1987 contains a list of acts that shall be considered as terrorist acts.[78] Except for these differences all the treaties have concurrent and common points.

Consequently, There Are Sufficient Elements to Build a Concept of Terrorism

In the frame of the United Nations as well as in the regional frame of the European Union, there are sufficient elements to conclude which acts may be actually qualified as terrorism. In the case of the United Nations, Resolution 1566 (2004) of the Security Council states that terrorist acts are criminal acts committed against civilians and the military with a concrete intentional element: that of causing death or serious bodily injury, or taking of hostages. These are acts with a concrete purpose: that of provoking a state of terror in the general public or in a group of persons; intimidating a population or compelling a government or an international organization to do or to abstain from doing any act. Such criminal acts committed against civilians and the military are under no circumstances justifiable. Such criminal acts committed against civilians and the military with the intention and purpose quoted above actually constitute criminal offences which are defined as such in international treaties on terrorism; treaties which comprehend the great majority of terrorist acts.[79]

[75] See Article 1.3 of the Convention. *ibid.*

[76] See Article 1 of both treaties. *ibid.*

[77] It does not contain a definition of terrorism and makes a remission to the international treaties on terrorism.

[78] In Article 1.e). In Article 1.f), it also envisages the attempt and the conspiracy to commit such acts. *ibid.*

[79] They are annexed to Security Council Resolution S/RES/1566 (2004) of 8 October 2004.

In the case of the European Union, the benefits deriving from Council Framework Decisions (2002/475/JHA) of 13 June 2002, and (2008/919/JAI) of 28 November 2008 are more obvious because they oblige Member States to take the necessary measures to ensure that the intentional acts referred to become punishable as criminal offences. This is why it is possible to conclude that the legal frame built in the European Union constitutes a big advance both from the point of view of the definition of terrorism and of its consequences in the legal field.

The international treaties existing in the different regional systems follow the same line. As can be seen most of them contain definitions both of "terrorism" and of "terrorist acts" and the others make a remission to the acts envisaged by the existent international treaties on terrorism. That is the treaties to which point 3 of the Security Council resolution 1566 (2004) adopted in the frame of Chapter VII of the Charter refers to.

The analysis of the legal body constituted by Security Council resolution 1566 (2004), by Council Framework Decisions (2002/475/JHA) of 13 June 2002, and (2008/919/JAI) of 28 November 2008, as well as by the treaties existing in the different regional systems allow one to conclude the existence in all these international norms of *common elements*. These are the ways in which it defines terrorism or the acts considered as terrorist, the intention and purpose of such acts as also the statements that are under no circumstances justifiable.

With regard to the first element, its *definition* or *description*, those international norms quoted above underline the fact that they are always acts of violence or the threat of use of violence against civilians and the military. Second, all of it underline the existence of an *intentional element*: such acts of violence are realized for the advancement of an individual or collective criminal agenda, with the aim of causing death or serious bodily injury or aiming to cause damage to the environment or to public or private installations or property, or to natural resources or to the cultural heritage. Third, all international norms quoted above emphasize that such criminal acts are realized with a *concrete purpose* consisting either in seriously terrorizing or intimidating a population, or an attempt on the life, freedom and security of the population, or disrupting any public service, the delivery of any essential service to the public or to create a public emergency; or in unduly compelling a Government or international organization to perform or abstain from performing any act.

At least all international norms quoted above underline that terrorist acts are *under no circumstances justifiable*.

Consequently, with the existing elements to achieve the goal, it should not be so difficult to arrive at a consensus on the international general definition of terrorism. In particular because the *political* element of the discrepancy—that is resorting to armed force in the defence of the right to self-determination or against the occupant of a territory—is already covered in international law. In other words, even in such cases international law does not authorize the resort to terrorism. It allows resorting to armed force, but it is an armed force within the framework of international law: an armed forced that should be managed respecting the international obligations existing on the matter. Clearly, international law never authorizes the resort to terrorism.

The Lack of a Concept of "Victim of Terrorism": Proposals

As stated earlier, in contrast to other categories of victims which have a definition of victim that is based in the international norms related to them, in the case of victims of terrorism the non-existence of concrete international norms related to them has as a consequence given rise to the non-existence of a concept of what such victims are. This is why I have criticized the passivity of the UN on the matter and why I ask for legal action from the UN promoting an international norm on victims of terrorism on the lines of those others adopted by this international organization with regard to other categories of victims such as victims of crime, victims of abuse of power, victims of gross violations of international human rights law, victims of serious violations of international humanitarian law and victims of enforced disappearance.

In the interim, the lack of an international concept of "victim of terrorism" can be filled by different ways. On the one hand, by reference to the international norms containing a definition of terrorism or containing a list of acts considered "terrorist acts". In such cases, it is clear that persons becoming victims of such acts—acts that are qualified by the concerned international norms as terrorist—fulfil the requirement of victims of terrorism.[80] On the other hand, and on the same lines, persons who are targets of the criminal acts prohibited by the international treaties on terrorism that are annexed to Security Council Resolution 1566 (2004) as well as by four of the regional treaties quoted earlier also fulfil the requirement of victims of terrorism.[81] At least, the obligation on the charge of states to take necessary measures to ensure that the international acts referred to become punishable as criminal offences lead to the conclusion that, once such legal action is taken, victims of such criminal offences become victims of terrorism. On the contrary, the lack of such legal action by states would prevent victims of the concerned criminal offences from being qualified as victims of terrorism. In other words, to make it possible the legal action of states in domestic law is indispensable.

At the same time, that the states take legal action in domestic law by necessary measures to ensure that the international acts referred to in the different treaties on terrorism (and on other international crimes) become punishable as criminal offences would also enlarge the concept of the victim. Through this, a larger number of victims would benefit from the statute inherent to the different categories of victims actually existent.[82] And this from the double perspective adopted by

[80] The same is the case of the Security Council Resolution 1566 (2004) (S/RES/1566), of Council Framework Decisions (2002/475/JHA) of 13 June 2002 and (2008/919/JHA) of 28 November 2008, and of the international treaties existing in the different international regional systems.

[81] The Convention of the Organization of the Islamic Conference on combating international terrorism of the 1st July 1999, adopted in the frame of the *Islamic Conference Organization*; the Regional Convention on Suppression of Terrorism of 4 November 1987, adopted in the frame of the *South Asian Association for Regional Cooperation* (*SAARC*); the ASEAN Convention on Counter Terrorism of 13 January 2007, in the frame of the *Association of South East Asian Nations* (*ASEAN*) and the Inter-American Convention Against Terrorism, of 2002, adopted in the frame of the *American regional system*.

[82] Because all these norms require that states take the necessary measures to ensure that the international acts referred into become punishable as criminal offences in domestic law.

international norms on victims—on the one hand, *direct victims*: that is victims having suffered harms and on the other hand, *indirect victims*: that is the immediate family or dependants of the direct victim and persons who have suffered harm in intervening to assist victims in distress or to prevent victimization.

But what is important is that in all these cases we are confronted by victims of crime. In some of them moreover, we are confronted by victims of very serious crimes.

As a consequence of all this, we can conclude that the non-existence in international law of a concrete definition of "victim of terrorism" does not constitute a real obstacle because this lack can be filled by reference to the universal and regional international norms on terrorism.

Complementarily, the determination of the type of victim (if direct or indirect) can also be done by reference to the General Assembly *Declaration of Basic Principles of Justice for Victims of Crime and Abuse of Power*, adopted on 29 November 1985, because terrorism is an infringement of criminal domestic law.

Although the propositions I have put forward could be useful to fill the gaps actually existing in the matter, it is obvious that the best solution would be a specific international norm on victims of terrorism. In the meanwhile, as stated, it is possible to determine which persons fulfil at a given moment the requirement of victims of terrorism. Complementarily, such persons would also be victims of crime as well as victims of gross violations of international human rights law and consequently benefit from the rights that international norms recognize as due to these categories of victims.

The Proposal for a Directive of the European Parliament and of the Council establishing minimum standards on the rights, support and protection of victims of crime: an inadequate response for victims of terrorism

As we have seen, to date the work developed by the European Union in the field of victims has failed to pay adequate care to the victims of terrorism, having devoted its attention almost exclusively to victims of crime. With regard to them, *Proposal for a Directive of the European Parliament and of the Council establishing minimum standards on the rights, support and protection of victims of crime*,[83] actually in discussion by the EU, will substitute Council Framework Decision 2001/220/JHA of 15 March 2001 *on the standing of victims in criminal proceedings*.[84] It is a Proposal for a Directive containing a catalogue of rights to which victims of crime are entitled. Obviously victims of terrorism, in their status as victims of

[83] European Commission, Brussels 18.5.2011, SEC(2011) 580 final. About this Proposal for a Directive cf.Pemberton and Groenhuijsen.

[84] *OJ*, L 82, of 22 March 2001.

crime—the crime of terrorism—can also invoke such rights but it is important to underline that terrorism is not an ordinary crime but a crime that seriously violates human rights as well as an international crime.

With regard to the past as well as to the actual regulation on the matter, the Proposal for a Directive constitutes an advance from the perspective of victims' international legal statute because it is now through a clearly binding norm—a directive—that Member States will be obliged to safeguard the exercise of a catalogue of rights broader and more specific with regard to the victims of crime than that currently existing in the aforementioned Framework Decision.[85]

In addition, the Proposal for a Directive is not confined to proclaim a series of rights but its aim is broader in that it also includes "support and protection" of the category of victims it envisages: victims of crime.

This is why I consider that the *Proposal for a Directive of the European Parliament and of the Council establishing minimum standards on the rights, support and protection of victims of crime* is *inadequate* from the perspective of the victims of terrorism: on the one hand because it is not intended for them, but in general, for victims of crime.[86] As a result, it does not give visibility to the victims of terrorism and visibility is important. Particularly because, in contrast to other categories of victims, victims of terrorism become victims as instruments used by terrorists groups or associations to combat democracy and to attack the structure of the State seeking to defeat it imposing by force a totalitarian project. Terrorizing society is the means to achieve this. This is why victims of terrorism are not like other categories of victims. It is true, as already said, that terrorism is a crime and as a result, that victims of terrorism are also and at the same time victims of crime. However terrorism is not a simple crime (like murder, for example) nor are the victims of terrorism simple victims of crime. No. Terrorism is a serious violation of human rights and an international crime. This is why victims of terrorism are defined as *macrovictims*.[87]

Consequently, recognition of victims of terrorism is, overall, recognition of the fundamental values of democracy and the rule of law; values that are only possible in democratic societies and that need to be protected.

On the other hand this Proposal for a Directive is not only limited to victims of crime but, with respect to these, its intention is not to establish or pick up a catalogue of rights which they are holding, but simply "minimum standards on the rights, support and protection of victims of crime"; minimum standards that Member States can improve.

---

[85] Cf.Pemberton and Rasquete.

[86] Its title is clear: *Proposal for a Directive of the European Parliament and of the Council establishing minimum standards on the rights, support and protection of victims of crime.*

[87] As noted by Beristain, all crimes of terrorism are of a greater tragic gravity than similar crimes in the same genus (a terrorist murder is more serious than murder). For this reason, their victims deserve the name of macrovictims. (See Beristain 2004, 35.) See also Beristain (2000, 2008).

Third, the victims of terrorism are not a simple category of "vulnerable" victims. In this regard, the Proposal for a Directive falls short. Despite the fact that in Recital No. 18 of the Proposal for a Directive it is stated that "victims of terrorism require particular attention in any assessment—in order to determinate their vulnerability—given the varying nature of such acts ranging from mass acts of terrorism to targeted terrorism against individuals"[88] later, in the corresponding article—article 18, entitled "Identification of vulnerable victims"—the victims of terrorism are not identified as a vulnerable category.[89]

In any case, even if we include victims of terrorism in the category of vulnerable victims, limiting the treatment of victims of terrorism to their inclusion in that category is insufficient and unsatisfactory because, as I have already said, the victims of terrorism are not a simple category of vulnerable victims or simple victims of an ordinary crime but victims of a crime seriously violating human rights as well as an international crime—a crime committed to terrorize society as the means of attacking the State and destroying democracy in order to impose by force a totalitarian project.

Fourth, the Proposal for a Directive does not list the rights claimed by the victims of terrorism. It is merely a case, within the right to information, of providing information to victims of any change in the implementation of the judgment: prison privileges, benefits, changes in level, etc. In this regard, article 4 (titled, "*Right to receive information about his case*") only provides notification to the victim, when it has so requested, of the following issues:

- Of any decision ending the criminal proceedings instituted as a result of the complaint of a criminal offence made by the victim,
- The decision not to proceed with or to end an investigation or a prosecution, or a final judgement in a trial, including any sentence;
- Information enabling the victim to obtain information of the state of affairs of the criminal proceedings instituted as a result of the complaint of a criminal offence made by the victim, unless, in exceptional cases the proper handling of the case may be adversely affected;
- The time and place of the trial;
- The time when the person prosecuted or sentenced for offences concerning them is released from detention.

These gaps and more are explained precisely by the general character[90] possessed by this Proposal for a Directive because it is only intended for victims of crime;

[88] European Commission, Brussels 18.5.2011, SEC(2011) 275 final, 17.

[89] Article 18 only considers as vulnerable victims "due to their personal characteristics" the following: Children and Persons with disabilities. On point 2 it states: "For the purposes of this Directive, the following categories of victims are considered to be vulnerable due to the nature or type of crime to which they have fallen victim: (a) Victims of sexual violence; (b) Victims of human trafficking."

[90] General character because it only envisages victims of crime. That is, *all* kinds of crime.

generality that is *incompatible* with the special treatment in a specific international norm which—like other categories of victims—are also required by the victims of terrorism.

The Proposal for a Directive itself is aware of that and says so explicitly in the concluding paragraphs of its explanatory memorandum: on the one hand, when it states—without concretising them—that "victims of terrorism will benefit from improved mechanisms for identifying their needs, keeping them informed of proceedings and providing adequate protection during proceedings"; on the other hand, when it states that "looking to the future, action in relation to specific categories of victims such as victims of terrorism and organised crime is also envisaged. In particular analysis of the existing gaps in the protection of victims of terrorism is due to take place with a view to improving the situation of victims of terrorism in Europe".[91]

At least, if we compare the rights listed in the Proposal for a Directive and those listed in the *Guidelines on the Protection of Victims of Terrorist Acts* adopted by the Committee of Ministers of the Council of Europe on 2 March 2005, we see that neither the right of emergency assistance nor the right to continuing assistance are envisaged by the proposal. This last, on article 7, only takes into account the right to access free of charge confidential victim support services. The same concerns the right to investigation and to prosecution that is not envisaged by the proposal.

On the other hand, both texts have in common the lack of references to two rights closely linked to victims of terrorism and victims of serious violations of human rights: the right to the truth and the right to memory.

The Need for a Specific International Norm on the Victims of Terrorism

The analysis I have done confirms, in my opinion, the need for both the UN and the European Union to develop an international norm on the international legal statute of victims of terrorism. That is, a catalogue of rights to which this category of victims is entitled.

As I have also stated, it is not a difficult task since both international organizations do not have to do anything else but follow the path outlined by the Council of Europe with its *Guidelines on the Protection of Victims of Terrorist Acts*, adopted by the Committee of Ministers on 2 March 2005. That is, Guidelines containing both a general concept of victim of terrorism and a catalogue of services, measures and rights which the victims of terrorism are entitled to.

As I have already said and will address more broadly later, in my opinion the above-mentioned catalogue of rights must be completed with the other two directly

[91] European Commission, Brussels 18.5.2011, SEC(2011) 275 final, 4.

linked to the victims of serious violations of human rights: the right to the truth and the right to memory.

The need for this specific international norm on victims of terrorism is justified, we must insist, by the very nature of the terrorist act: an act that constitutes a serious violation of human rights—an international crime—which aims at terrorizing the population in general and compelling a Government to act or fail to act in a certain sense to achieve the imposition by force of a totalitarian political project that the terrorist group pursues.

On the other hand, and from the *victimological perspective*, the victims of terrorism are not simple victims of crime but macrovíctims. Including victims of terrorism within the more general category of victims of crime is therefore negative because it aids to ignore them, preventing their visibility. In other words, they help to make them—once more—invisible. In this case, in the legal field.

Finally, the development of a particular international norm for the victims of terrorism also has pedagogical virtues for the democratic system and their societies because it highlights the fragility of democracy and the need for recognition of those who, being innocent, have been unjustly slaughtered by those availing of democracy, seeking to annihilate her and, with it, its system of freedoms to impose a totalitarian political project on society as a whole. For terrorists, the victims are only the means to achieve it and the maximum possible terror is the instrument for which society crease at will.

References

Beristain A (2000) Victimología. Nueve palabras clave, Tirant lo Blanch, Valencia

Beristain A (2004) Protagonismo de las Víctimas de hoy de mañana (Evolución en el campo jurídico penal, prisional y ético). Tirant lo Blanch, Valencia

Beristain A (2008) Transformación del Derecho Penal y la Criminología hacia la Victimología. ARA Editores, Perú

Bollo Arocena MD (2004) Derecho Internacional Penal Estudio de los Crímenes internacionales y de las técnicas para su represión. Servicio Editorial de la Universidad de País Vasco, Bilbao

Bou V, Fernández de Casadevante Romani C (2009) La inclusión del terrorismo entre los crímenes internacionales previstos en el Estatuto de la Corte Penal Internacional. MINIM, Valencia

Cassese A (2008) International Criminal Law:162

Doucet G (2005) Terrorisme: définition, juridiction pénale internationale et victims Victimes et Terrorisme. Revue International de Droit Penal 76:271

Fernández de Casadevante Romani C, Jiménez García F (2005) Terrorismo y Derechos Humanos. Una aproximación desde el Derecho Internacional. Dykinson, Madrid

Fernández de Casadevante Romani C (2006) La nación sin ciudadanos: el dilema del País Vasco. Dilex, Madrid

Fundación Miguel Angel Blanco, International Action (2010) Terrorism: a crime against humanity. Palais des Nations, Geneva

Fundación Miguel Angel Blanco, International Action (2011) Terrorism: a crime against humanity. Palais des Nations, Geneva

Hinojosa Martínez LM (2008) La financiación del terrorismo y las Naciones Unidas. Tecnos, Madrid

Lozano Contreras F (2002) Enforcement of the Notion of Due Diligence in the Report of the Human Rights Commissioner of the Council of Europe Regarding his Visit to the Autonomous Basque Community. Spanish Yearbook of International Law 8:17

Pemberton A, Groenhuijsen MS. Developing victim's rights within the European Union: past, present and future. In: Kirchhoff G, et al (eds) Proceedings of the 13th World Society of Victimology Symposium. Wolf Legal Publishers, Nijmegen

Pemberton A, Rasquete C. Victims in Europe-Assessment of the implementation on the Framework Decision on the standing of victims in criminal proceedings: preliminary results. In: Hartmann J (ed) Perspektiven professioneller Opferhilfe. VS Verlag, Wiesbaden, pp 99–112

The Existence of Common Elements in the Different Definitions of Victim

The recognition of the condition of victim is important because it has legal consequences. The most important of it is the attribution to the victim of a catalogue of rights that, at the same time, are obligations on the charge of states. Additionally, such recognition is also important because states, international organizations, NGOs and private companies are called upon by international norms to treat victims with respect and compassion as well as in a manner which respects their personal security, their private as well their family life.[1]

From this perspective, the determination of which persons are entitled to the condition of victim is a relevant question. Nevertheless, in international law there does not exist a unique definition of victim but almost as many definitions as categories of victims. In any case, this lack does not constitute a problem. On the one hand, because almost all categories of victims envisaged by international norms become victims as a consequence of a crime, is the hypothesis envisaged by the UN General Assembly resolution 40/34 adopted on 29 November 1985 which contains the *Declaration of Basic Principles of Justice for Victims of Crime and Abuse of Power*.[2] On the other hand, because the existence of a common definition of victim is not necessary to determine the rights that make part of the international legal statute of victims. In reality, like in other fields, the definition of who fulfils the condition of victim in a concrete case is a question of common sense. It is the group of persons directly targeted by the concerned criminal act.

Consequently, the lack of such a common definition can be filled by the definition of victim from the UN General Assembly Resolution 40/34 quoted earlier; a resolution reflecting the consensus of the international community on the matter.

[1] See Bassiouni (2002), 134–185.

[2] The only victims who do not become victims as a consequence of a crime are victims of abuse of power. That is, "persons who, individually or collectively, have suffered harm, including physical or mental injury, emotional suffering, economic loss or substantial impairment of their fundamental rights, through acts or omissions that do not yet constitute violations of national criminal laws but of internationally recognized norms relating to human rights".

C. Fernández de Casadevante Romani, *International Law of Victims*,
DOI 10.1007/978-3-642-28140-2_4, © Springer-Verlag Berlin Heidelberg 2012

Moreover, this definition has been reiterated by the UN General Assembly Resolution 60/147 of 16 December 2005 adopting the *Basic Principles and guidelines of the Right to a Remedy and Reparation for victims of Gross Violations of International Human Rights Law and Serious Violations of International Humanitarian Law*, which were contained in Resolution 2005/35 adopted by the Commission on Human Rights on 19 April 2005. This reiteration shows evidence of the great degree of agreement that exists over the definition of victim.[3]

As stated in the preceding pages, international norms related to the different categories of victims have in common the fact of envisaging both *direct* and *indirect* victims, this last category including the immediate family or dependents of the direct victim. From this perspective, therefore, the different passive subjects of victimization are covered.

With regard to the concept of *direct victims*, the different definitions existing in the international norms on the matter quoted earlier have in common the following elements:

They are natural persons who individually or collectively have

- Suffered harm (including physical or mental injury),
- Emotional suffering,
- Economic loss or
- Substantial impairment of their fundamental rights.

And this, as a consequence of:

- Acts or omissions that are in violation of criminal laws operative within the State where such acts or omission take place;
- Having intervened to assist victims in distress or
- Having intervened to prevent victimisation.

Consequently, and it is a previous condition affecting the concept of victim, it is necessary that states take all necessary steps and measures to ensure that such victimizing acts become offences under their own national law.

As it can be appreciated, in all cases envisaged by international norms we are in confronted by victims acquiring such a condition as a consequence of acts or omissions that are in violation of criminal laws operative within states including those laws proscribing abuse of power. Therefore, the qualification of a victim is subject to the previous legislative action of the state adopting the necessary measures to make such acts become criminal offences under national law. In other words, it is necessary for a positive legislative action on the charge of the state. It is the *conditio sine qua non*. Without such a previous legislative action, both the recognition as a victim and the enjoyment of the rights as victims recognized by international norms are impossible.

[3] Doc. E/CN.4/2005/L.10/Add.11. In the same line cf. S. Zappalá, *op. cit.*, 228. The resolution was adopted within the Commission on Human Rights by a recorded vote 40 votes to none, with 13 abstentions.

From the perspective of the present work, the legislative task I have referred to concern not only offences in general but also all victimizing acts envisaged by international norms related to the different categories of victims. That is terrorism, genocide, crimes against humanity, crimes of war, enforced disappearances, extra-judicial executions, torture as well as other human rights serious violations envisaged by international norms and not envisaged by the Criminal Codes of the concerned states. In all such cases, we are confronted by particularly serious acts that, however, have not become criminal offences under national law in all states. This is why it is so important that the international norms quoted here oblige states to take all necessary steps and measures to ensure that such acts become criminal offences under national law. Without these steps and measures under national law, the international norms remain ineffective.

Such steps and measures once taken under national law the definition of victim of the UN General Assembly resolution 40/34 adopted on 29 November 1985 which contains the *Declaration of Basic Principles of Justice for Victims of Crime and Abuse of Power* will spread its effects. And this in the triple dimension it contains: persons who have suffered harm (direct victims), the immediate family or dependents of the direct victim (indirect victims) and persons who have suffered harm in intervening to assist victims in distress or to prevent victimisation (also indirect victims).[4]

As a consequence of all this, both the initiative and the responsibility to arrive at a more or less extended concept of (direct and indirect) victim as well as to make it possible for victims to profit from the rights attributed to them by the international norms depend entirely on the action of States in the national law of each state. The other side of this situation is the inequality between victims because only victims of acts ruled as criminal offences in national law will be able to invoke and exercise the rights recognized as theirs by international norms.

In the *International Law of Human Rights*, the condition of being classified as a direct victim depends on what is written in the treaty. In other words, only persons claiming to be victims of a violation of the rights set forth in the concerned treaty by a State Party in the concerned treaty can present an application before the international treaty bodies envisaged in international treaties on human rights. Here, the state is the reference. On the one hand, because in International Law of Human Rights only state violations are envisaged and, on the other hand, because the concerned state must be party to the treaty and should have a accepted the competence of the international body established by the treaty. Therefore, only victims of violations of human rights envisaged by a treaty to which the concerned

[4] The protection of this last category of victims can be founded on the jurisprudence of the Inter-American Court of Human Rights (cf. N. Fernández Sola, "El derecho a la reparación. . ., *op. cit.*, 403).

state is Party and the competence of the treaty body of which has been accepted by that state will be able to claim before it by the way of individual applications.[5]

In the concrete case of the *European Convention for the Protection of Human Rights and Fundamental Freedoms* of 4 November 1950 Article 34 expressly states that only the eprson who claims to be the victim of a violation of the rights set forth in the Convention or the Protocols thereto by one of the High Contracting Parties (a person, non-governmental organisation or a group of individuals) has competence to present an application before the European Court of Human Rights (ECHR). On this question, the ECHR has stated that the concept of victim is interpreted autonomously and irrespective of domestic concepts.[6] It has also stated that the concept of victim does not imply the necessary existence of a prejudice. In other words, the existence of a violation of the Convention is conceivable even in the absence of prejudice.[7] Finally, the ECHR has underlined that, like the other provisions of the Convention, the term "victim" in Article 34 must also be interpreted in an evolutive manner in the light of conditions in contemporary society.[8] Nevertheless the person who is personally responsible for the violation cannot ask to be recognized as victim.[9]

With regard to the concept of *indirect victim*, according to Court's established case-law, the word "victim" in the context of Article 34 of the Convention denotes the person directly affected by the act or omission in issue.[10] Nevertheless on a

[5] On this question cf. Fernández de Casadevante Romani (2011), in C. Fernández de Casadevante Romani, *Derecho Internacional de los Derechos Humanos*, *op. cit.*, 67 et seq. On the concrete case of Spain, see Fernández de Casadevante Romani (2010).

[6] Like, for example, such as those concerning an interest or capacity to act. In addition, "in order for an applicant to be able to claim to be a victim of a violation of the Convention, there must be a sufficiently direct link between the applicant and the harm which they consider they have sustained on account of the alleged violation (see, among other authorities, *Tauira and Others v. France*, no. 28204/95, Commission decision of 4 December 1995, Decisions and Reports (DR) 83-B, p. 112; *Association des amis de Saint-Raphaël et de Fréjus and Others v. France*, no. 38192/97, Commission decision of 1 July 1998, DR 94-B, p. 124; *Comité des médecins à diplômes étrangers v. France and Others v. France* (dec.), nos. 39527/98 and 39531/98, 30 March 1999)" (*Gorraiz Lizarraga and others v. Spain*, Judgement of 27 April 2004, 35, *ECHR 2004-III*.

[7] Cf., in particular *Marckx v. Belgium*, Judgement of 13 June 1979, ECtHR serie A no 31, § 27, *Inze v. Austria,* Judgement of 28 October 1987, serie A n° 126, § 32).

[8] Cf. ECHR *Gorraiz Lizarraga and others v. Spain*, 38, *ECtHR 2004-III*. In this case, the Court adds: "And indeed, in modern-day societies, when citizens are confronted with particularly complex administrative decisions, recourse to collective bodies such as associations is one of the accessible means, sometimes the only means, available to them whereby they can defend their particular interests effectively. Moreover, the standing of associations to bring legal proceedings in defence of their members' interests is recognized by the legislation of most European countries. That is precisely the situation that obtained in the present case. The Court cannot disregard that fact when interpreting the concept of "victim". Any other, excessively formalistic, interpretation of that concept would make protection of the rights guaranteed by the Convention ineffectual and illusory."

[9] Cf. ECHR, *Paşa et Erkan Erol v.Turkey*, nº 51358/99, Judgement of 12 December 2006.

[10] Cf., ECHR *Amuur v. France*, Judgement of 12 December 2006, ECtHR *Recueil 1996-III*, 36.

case-by-case basis, the ECHR has accepted applications from "potential" victims, that is, from persons who could not complain of a direct violation.[11] On the contrary, it is the stand of the Court that mere suspicions or conjectures are not sufficient to acquire the condition of victim.[12]

But next to the direct victims are also indirect victims. With regard to the concept of *indirect victims*, international norms related to the different categories of victims as well as international case-laws on the matter consider the immediate family or dependents of the direct victim as indirect victims.[13]

From the perspective of victims of terrorism and with regard to this question of indirect victims, the *Guidelines on the Protection of Victims of Terrorist Acts* adopted by the Committee of Ministers of the Council of Europe on 2 March 2005 quotes case-laws of the ECHR to justify the inclusion of a family member of a "disappeared person" in the concept of indirect victim. Specifically, his Judgement of 10 May 2001 in *Cyprus v. Turkey* where the Court stated:

> 156. The Court recalls that the question whether a family member of a "disappeared person" is a victim of treatment contrary to Article 3 will depend on the existence of special factors which give the suffering of the person concerned a dimension and character distinct from the emotional distress which may be regarded as inevitably caused to relatives of a victim of a serious human-rights violation. Relevant elements will include the proximity of the family tie – in that context, a certain weight will attach to the parent-child bond –, the particular circumstances of the relationship, the extent to which the family member witnessed the events in question, the involvement of the family member in the attempts to obtain information about the disappeared person and the way in which the authorities responded to those enquiries. The Court further recalls that the essence of such a violation does not so much lie in the fact of the "disappearance" of the family member but rather in the authorities' reactions and attitudes to the situation when it is brought to their attention. It is especially in respect of the latter that a relative may claim directly to be a

---

[11] So, with regard to telephone tapping, in *Klass and others v. Germany*, Judgement of 6 September 1978, série A n° 28. Here in paragraph 34, the Court accepts "that an individual may, under certain conditions, claim to be the victim of a violation occasioned by the mere existence of secret measures or of legislation permitting secret measures, without having to allege that such measures were in fact applied to him. The relevant conditions are to be determined in each case according to the Convention right or rights alleged to have been infringed, the secret character of the measures objected to, and the connection between the applicant and those measures". For a case concerning extradition, *Soering v. United Kingdom*, Judgement of 7 July 1989, serie A nº 161). With regard to measures restricting the distribution of information on abortion to women of child-bearing age cf. *Open Door y Dublin Well Woman v. Ireland*, Judgement of 29 October 1992, serie A n° 246-A, § 44).

[12] So, for example in a case of absence of a formal expulsion order in *Vijayanathan et Pusparajah v. France*, Judgement of 27 August 1992, serie A nº 241-B, § 46; alleged consequences of a parliamentary report see *The Chrstian Federation of Jehovah's Witnesses in France v. France* (déc.), n° 53430/99, CEDH 2001-XI; a potential fine on an applicant company in *Senator Lines v. EU States (GC)* (déc.), n° 56672/00, ECtHR 2004-IV).

[13] This is the case, for example, of a case-law of the Inter-American Court of Human Rights. The General Assembly *Declaration of Basic Principles of Justice for Victims of Crime and Abuse of Power*, adopted on 29 November 1985, also includes as indirect victims persons who have suffered harm in intervening to assist victims in distress or to prevent victimization.

victim of the authorities' conduct (see *Çakici v. Turkey* [GC], no. 23657/94, § 98, ECHR 1999-IV).[14]

An analysis of the case-laws of the ECHR shows that the Court accepts an individual application from a person considered an *indirect victim*, where there is a personal and specific link between the direct victim and the applicant. So, under the basis of Article 2 (right to life), the Court accepted an application from the victim's wife and from a dead man's nephew.[15] Under Article 3 (prohibition of torture), it accepted an application from the mother of a man who disappeared while in custody[16]; under Article 6.1 (fair trial) with regard to the right to defend a deceased spouse's reputation and to the length and fairness of proceedings[17]; under Article 6.2 (everyone charged with a criminal offence shall be presumed innocent until proved guilty according to law) the Court accepted an application in a case concerning the widow of a defendant who was the victim of a breach of his right to be presumed innocent[18]; and under Article10 (freedom of expression) the ECHR also accepted an application concerning the interests of the applicant's widow.[19]

In cases where the direct victim who has filed a lawsuit dies, his death does not carry in an automatic way the cancellation of the application since the Court recognizes the rightful claimants of the deceased (next of kin or heirs)—and these in the case when it is a universal legatee—the power to decide whether to continue with the matter. To the Court, it corresponds to an opportunity to continue with its examination for the protection of human rights. In any case, it is necessary that the motives are considered as transferable.[20]

Finally the analysis of international norms on the different categories of victims shows that both the concepts of *direct* and of *indirect* victim are informed by *three*

---

[14] ECHR, Judgement of 10 May 2001, *Cyprus v. Turkey*, 156. See a critic of this judgement in N. Fernández Sola, *op. cit.*, 404.

[15] Cf. ECHR, *McCann and others v. United Kingdom*, Judgement of 27 September 1995, série A nº 324, and *Yaşa v. Turkey*, Judgement of 2 September 1998, *Recueil des arrêts et décisions 1998-VI*, § 66.

[16] Cf. ECHR, *Kurt v. Turkey*, Judgement of 25 May 1998, *Recueil des arrêts et décisions* 1998-III. However in *Çakıcı v. Turkey* (under Article 3), the ECHR did not accept the inclusion of a family member of a "disappeared person" inside the concept of indirect victim (cf. [GC], n° 23657/94, § 98–99, ECtHR 1999-IV).

[17] Cf. ECHR, *Brudnicka and others v. Poland*, n° 54723/00, § 26 et seq., ECtHR 2005-II, and *Marie-Louise Loyen et Bruneel v. France*, n° 55929/00, Judgement of 5 July 2005.

[18] Cf. ECHR, *Nölkenbockhoff v. Germany*, Judgement of 25 August 1987, serie A nº 123, § 33.

[19] Cf. ECHR, *Dalban v. Romania* [GC], n° 28114/95, § 39, ECtHR 1999-VI.

[20] Cf. ECHR. *Thévenon v. France* (cancellation), n° 2476/02, Judgement of 28 February 2006; *Karner v. Austria*, n° 40016/98, parágrafos 25 y siguientes, ECtHR 2003-IX and, *a contrario*, *Fairfield and others v. United Kingdom* (déc.) nº 24790/04, Judgement of 8 March 2005. Regarding the transferability of the reasons, cf. ECHR *Marie-Louise Loyen et Bruneel v. France, and, a contrario, Sanles Sanles v. Spain* (déc.), n° 48335/99, ECtHR 2000-XI et *Biçand others v. Turkey*, n° 55955/00, § 22, Judgement of 2 February 2006.

fundamental principles. On the *one* hand, the principle according to which the condition of the victim is independent of whether the perpetrator is identified, apprehended, prosecuted or convicted and regardless of the familial relationship between the perpetrator and the victim.[21] On *the other* hand, the principle of non-discrimination. According to it, the rights linked to the condition of victim are applied without distinction of any kind, such as race, colour, sex, age, language, religion, nationality, political or other opinion, cultural beliefs or practices, property, birth or family status, ethnic or social origin, and disability. *Last but not least*, the principle of respect for both the private and family life of victims according to which victims should be treated with compassion and respect for their dignity.[22]

So it is possible to conclude that actually international law recognizes the existence of both direct and indirect victims. International norms related to the different categories of victims particularize both concepts in terms of the function of the concrete category of victims but this fact does not prevent them from affirming that in general the elements these definitions contain are common and that its application covers the gaps existing with regard to some categories of victims. This is the case, for example, for victims of terrorism (non-existence of concept) or for victims of enforced disappearance (in its definition there is no reference to indirect victims).

In any case, as stated earlier, it is indispensable that the concerned State should take necessary measures to ensure that the acts envisaged by international norms on victims constitute criminal offences in national law. Without this, victims of such acts will not be able to invoke the rights of victims recognized by international norms because they do not fulfil the definition of victim according to national law.

[21] In the frame of the UN, this principle can be found in the General Assembly Resolution 60/147 of 16 December 2005 adopting the *Basic Principles and guidelines of the Right to a Remedy and Reparation for victims of Gross Violations of International Human Rights Law and Serious Violations of International Humanitarian Law* (Doc. E/CN.4/2005/L.10/Add.11). In the frame of the Council of Europe, the principle of non-discrimination is formulated both in the *Guidelines on the Protection of Victims of Terrorist Acts* adopted on 2 March 2005 by the Committee of Ministers, in the *European Convention on the Compensation of Victims of Violent Crimes* adopted on 24 November 1983 and in Recommendation (2006) 8 of the Committee of Ministers *On Assistance to Crime Victims*.

[22] This principle is stated both in paragraph 4 of UN the General Assembly Resolution 40/34 adopted on 29 November 1985 containing the *Declaration of Basic Principles of Justice for Victims of Crime and Abuse of Power*, in Article 2 of *Council Framework Decision (2001/220/JHA)* of 15 March 2001 *on the Standing of Victims in Criminal Proceedings* (*OJEU* L 81 of 22 March 2001) and in the *Guidelines on the Protection of Victims of Terrorist Acts* adopted on 2 March 2005 by the Committee of Ministers of the Council of Europe.

References

Bassiouni Ch (2003) Reconnaissance internationale des droits des victimes in the collective work of SOS Attentats: Terrorisme, victimes et responsabilité pénale internationale. Calmann-Lévy, Paris, pp 134–185

Fernández de Casadevante Romani C (dir.) (2010) España y los órganos internacionales de control en materia de derechos humanos

Fernández de Casadevante Romani C (2011) El Derecho Internacional de las Víctimas. Porrúa, México

Part Two
The Rights Recognized to Victims by International Norms

A Previous Question: The Legal Nature of Victims' Rights

The Legal Nature of Victims' Rights

As we have seen in Part One of the present work, most of the international norms related to the different categories of victims are of an institutional nature and only three are treaties.[1] So far as the first one is concerned, they are almost all institutional norms adopted in the frame of international organizations of co-operation, whereas a minority have been adopted in the frame of the European Union. The European Union is an international organization of integration to which Member States have ceded competences in different material fields. Within these competences, there are also legislative competences and this is why norms of the European Union bind Member States that they are obliged to fulfil.

Consequently, the problems and questions that ordinarily arise with regard to international institutional norms in reality are only problems and questions linked to international institutional norms adopted in the frame of international organizations of cooperation, for example, the UN, the Council of Europe and the OAS. From the perspective of the present work, all three are International Organizations having adopted norms related to the different categories of victims.

The principal question that emerges is the following: Are the norms of this type of International Organization binding? Do they produce legal effects on Member States to which these norms are directed?

Certainly, the problem is not new and it cannot be carried out as a sector of international doctrine traditionally does,[2] by basing this on *a priori* considerations

---

[1] So the European Convention on the Compensation of Victims of Violent Crimes adopted on 24 November 1983 (entered into force on 1st February 1998), the United Nations International Convention for, the Protection of All Person from Enforced Disappearance, adopted on 20 December 2006 (not yet in force) and the Inter-American Convention on enforced disappearance of persons, of the 9th July 1994 (this convention entered into force on 28 March 1996).

[2] Cf. Macgibon, "Means for the Identification ...", *op. cit.*, 10 et seq. Vid. Also Roucunas (1987-VI), p. 9 et seq.; Sepulveda (1990), 444 et seq.; Abbot and Snidal 421–456.

C. Fernández de Casadevante Romani, *International Law of Victims*,
DOI 10.1007/978-3-642-28140-2_5,

that exclude the institutional norms, which are generally speaking the resolutions of the United Nations General Assembly, as capable of having such effects. In my opinion, the answer to this question depends on the analysis of the constitutive treaty of the International Organization and on a number of factors as, for example, the content of the norm, its language, the procedure for its approval, how it was adopted, and consequently, the attitude of the States towards the institutional norm in question.

On the contrary, it is convenient to take into account that the context in which the problem arises finds its origin in the process of progressive institutionalization of the International Community as a consequence of the appearance of International Organizations. This process, which has changed the tendency to decentralization and the lack of institutionalization that was a characteristic of International Law before the Second World War, has a strong effect on the formation of international norms and one of its signs is the influence of those Organizations in making International Law more positive. In this regard, the pre-eminent position of the State in the formation of international norms has been influenced by the phenomenon of the International Organizations. This has had a twofold effect. On the one hand, traditional proceedings for drafting of International Law by the States—fundamentally treaties and custom—has been modified due to the action of International Organizations in the process of formation of international treaties and custom. Thus, in the framework of the United Nations resolutions of the General Assembly, these had important repercussions as regards the formation of customary norms: by declaring an international custom, by giving final shape to customary norms in the process of formation, or by constituting the starting point of an international custom. Therefore, interaction among the norms was brought about.

In the second place, for some time, the Laws arising from the action of International Organizations, that is to say, the institutional norms, have been added to the traditional results of the aforementioned process (treaties and customs). In other words, the shaping of the individual consent and the consensus of the States institutionalized within the framework of the International Organizations acquire a new field of action with a normative manifestation, which is different from treaty and custom. This manifestation is the institutional norm.

This is why, as Carrillo Salcedo correctly emphasizes, it is not possible today to analyse the drafting of International Law unless we take into account the influence the International Organizations have had on making international legal norms more positive.[3]

As I have stated earlier, the question is whether the legal value or force of the institutional norms arises especially with reference to those norms of international organizations whose constitutive treaty makes no mention of this or if they are considered to be merely recommendable.

[3] Vid. Carrillo Salcedo, *Curso…*, *op. cit.*, 123.

When the constitutive treaty clearly specifies the legal value of the acts of the organisation, the reply is contained in the constitutive treaty itself. This is the case of the Treaty on the Functioning of the European Union where article 288 clearly specifies that regulations, directives and decisions are binding with regard to the Member States.[4] The same is true of the framework of the UN as regards some decisions of the General Assembly.[5]

However, the constitutive treaties of International Organizations which address or specify the legal force or value of the norms created by the Organization constitute the exception, while the general rule is silence or the description of such acts as "recommendations", "decisions", etc. This is the case of UN General Assembly resolutions as well as of institutional norms adopted in the frame both of the Council of Europe[6] and of the OAS.[7] It is also the case of some norms specifically adopted on victims in the frame of UN by the General Assembly and by the Commission of Human Rights.[8]

With regard to UN General Assembly resolutions, some doctrinal sectors maintain that these are mere recommendations as, otherwise, the Charter would have expressly stated this as does article 25 regarding the Resolutions of the Security Council. However, in my opinion, the answer is not so simple. As Sir F. Vallat

[4] A reinforced binding character due to the principles of primacy, immediate and uniform application enshrined in the case law of the ECCJ. About these questions, see Blokker (1999), p. 45 et seq. Related to the Organization of African Unity, see Maluwa (2000), 201 et seq.

[5] Thus, for example, those decisions regarding the approval of the general budget of the Organisation and those concerning the specialized agencies (article 17), the choice of non-permanent members of the Security Council, the election of members of the Economic and Social Committee of the Trusteeship Council, the admission of new members to the United Nations, the suspension of the rights and privileges of the Members, the expulsion of Members (article 18), the decisions regarding the establishment of subsidiary institutions (article 22), those concerning the Trusteeship System and those which affect the Trusteeship Council (articles 85 and 87).

[6] On this question Article 15 of the Statute of the Council of Europe states: "a) On the recommendation of the Consultative Assembly or on its own initiative, the Committee of Ministers shall consider the action required to further the aim of the Council of Europe, including the conclusion of conventions or agreements and the adoption by governments of a common policy with regard to particular matters. Its conclusions shall be communicated to members by the Secretary General. b) In appropriate cases, the conclusions of the Committee may take the form of recommendations to the governments of members, and the Committee may request the governments of members to inform it of the action taken by them with regard to such recommendations."

[7] On this question Article 59 of OAS Charter states: "Decisions of the General Assembly shall be adopted by the affirmative vote of an absolute majority of the Member States, except in those cases that require a two thirds vote as provided in the Charter or as may be provided by the General Assembly in its rules of procedure."

[8] So, the Basic Principles and Guidelines of the Right a Remedy and Reparation for Victims of Gross Violations of International Human Rights Law and Serious Violations of International Humanitarian Law, adopted on 19 April 2005 by Resolution 2005/35 and later by the General Assembly on 16 December 2005 through Resolution 60/147 (UN E/CN.4/2005/L.10/Add. 11).

states, to say that the Assembly only has powers to discuss and recommend "would be a gross simplification".[9]

Basically, the underlying problem involves the judicial effects of the institutional norms drawn up by the General Assembly. The plan to solve this through the simple analysis of the Charter does not adapt to the nature of the International Community at the present time, one of whose structures is characterized precisely by the existence of common interests, and this occasionally leads to the fact that States that do not manifest their consent to the formation of a norm are bound by this norm as a result of the general consensus on the norm. In fact, in the social structure of common interests, we see a derogation of the absolute nature that the sovereignty of the State had as regards the structure of juxtaposition, so, third party States can be affected by the consent to be bound made by a considerable number of States. One example of this derogation of state sovereignty, a consequence of the social structure of common interests, is clearly seen in the multilateral treaties and the International Conferences which deal with questions of common interest for the International Community as a whole.[10]

In this context, the determination of the obligatory nature of the legal norm must be done based on the linking of this norm to the legal system which provides it with its force and which, in the event, can lay down sanctions in order to ensure respect for its norms. In our case, this system is the international one and in it, the formation of the international norms takes place through a process involving the individual consent of the state and the general consensus of the States, and it is the interaction between both stages which gives rise to the international norm in question. Therefore, the individual consent of the State and the general consensus within an International Organization gives rise to an institutional norm. The existence of both elements which demonstrate the attitude of the State as regards the institutional norm in question is a determining factor, and not the term conferred by the constitutive treaty—i.e. the Charter ("recommendation" or "decision").

Thus, the obligatory nature of the norm cannot depend on the degree of discretion or the power of appreciation which this grants to its receptor, but the attitude the receptor adopts. That the norm grants its receptor a wide degree of discretion or appreciation does not mean that it is not obligatory, thus it is correct to talk of the existence of norms which are more or less obligatory.[11] If this involves a norm, the norm is binding. It is another matter if, due to the extent of the discretion or the power of appreciation granted by the norm, in practice it is difficult to determine whether or not the receptor has complied with the obligation contained therein. Therefore, the problems arise at the time of application.

---

[9] Vallat (1959-II), 225 et seq. *Vid.* also Roucunas, *op. cit.*, 174 et seq.

[10] Which leads Reuter to state that "when the consent or the institutions arise from a sufficiently representative set of states mainly interested in one question, the consent or institution can sometime generate effects for third party states" (*Principes de Droit...*", *op. cit.*, 448 et seq.).

[11] *Vid.* Jacque (1991-II), 388.

In this context and with regard to the UN, it should be stressed that there is a contrast as regards the legal force of the resolutions of the General Assembly and the practice of this institution of the United Nations which, from its creation, has adopted over 6,000 resolutions.[12] In accordance with this doctrinal sector, if the Resolutions of the General Assembly lack legal force or the obligatory legal effects, can it be accepted that the General Assembly has carried out this regulatory task while it is aware of the effects of its Resolutions? The analysis of this practice demonstrates the opposite. Moreover, it clearly shows that in most occasions the institutional norm of the General Assembly precedes the treaty.[13] In other words, it highlights the effect the institutional norm has in the process of formation of conventional norms.

The above considerations shows the mistakes involved in avoiding the problem from pre-determined positions such as those which exclude an International Organization of cooperation from adopting resolutions with binding legal effects for its Members when the constitutive treaty does not say anything about this. In contrast to these positions, I find it more pertinent to make a detailed analysis of each resolution in the light of the factors quoted above.[14]

As I have mentioned above, the problem I am treating now shall be addressed from another more satisfactory perspective. This would start from the study of the process of formation of international norms, and this process cannot be understood properly if one starts with pre-conceived notions such as those described above or those referred to in article 38 of the Statutes of the ICJ considering that these contain the formal sources of International Law.[15]

As stated above, the formation of international norms in the International Community, and, therefore, the rights and obligations contained in them, are founded on the two fundamental elements quoted above, which, respectively, constitute the initial and final phases of the process of formation: the individual consent of the State and the general *consensus* of a plurality of States. Although this is true it is also a fact that in the International Community the State no longer acts in isolation, but within a dimension of association, and this fact has repercussions in the process for the formation of norms. In this context, the aforementioned process

[12] Although as P.M. Dupuy points out, in fact, the debate is restricted to a limited number of these (cf. *Droit International Public*, *op. cit.*, 277).

[13] See note 10 of the present work.

[14] Like the content of the norm, its language, the procedure for its approval, how it was adopted, and consequently, the attitude of the States towards the institutional norm in question. With regard to General Assembly resolutions, Sloan points out that given the difficulty or perhaps the impossibility of "making generalisations which cover all the resolutions, one has to consider all the circumstances involving a determined resolution before making an evaluation" (Sloan, *op. cit.*, 42).

[15] For example, Barberis and Shaw (1991).

of formation necessarily transcends the individual basis of consent to constitute the expression of the social group as a whole, or particular groups of States.[16]

Among these elements, the first one, the individual consent of the State constitutes the necessary, initial momentum for the process of formation of norms. The norm does not arise from this consent. The final moment, and thus the moment when the norm arises, takes place when the general *consensus* of the States is reached. Or, in other words, when there is a plurality of individual consent to being obliged by the same norm. Thus, the plurality of individual consent is transformed into a consensus of the States.

This way of addressing the process of the formation of international norms was used by the ICJ in the cases of the *North Sea Continental Shelf* and the *Fisheries Jurisdiction* in which it stated that in the process of the formation of the Law at international level, the crystallizing of the norm (its birth) takes place when there is general assent (*consensus*) of the States.[17]

In addition, this conception is put into effect in a particular way within the institutional dimension of the International Community today as a result of the evolution of the Community itself and it is characterized by the relational aspect, the sovereignty, having moved towards the institutional factor, and new channels for the production of consensus having been created. This is what happens within the International Organizations and Conferences so that in these environments the crystallization of *consensus*, the birth of the norm, is facilitated by the new dimension which State sovereignty has at the present time.

In my opinion from this perspective, the legal effects of the institutional norms adopted in the frame of international organizations of cooperation can be addressed in a more satisfactory way. According to it, the analysis of the conduct of the member States, manifested in the way the document is adopted, provides a satisfactory response to the first question which was posed at the start of this section. Together with this conduct, the examination of other factors will facilitate the interpretation of the will of the States regarding the document of the Organization and will make it possible for its legal effects to be determined.

The ICJ has also made statements along the same lines. For example, its advisory opinion regarding the Case of the *Legal Consequences for States of the Continued Presence of South Africa in Namibia (South-West Africa) notwithstanding Security Council Resolution 276 (1970)*, in which it stated that,

> For it would not be correct to assume that, because the General Assembly is in principle vested with recommendatory powers, it is debarred from adopting, in specific cases within

[16] Vid. González Campos, Sánchez Rodriguez and Andrés Sáenz de Santa Maria, *op. cit.*, 90.

[17] See ICJ, *Reports 1974*, 23. With regard to the second matter, *see* ICJ *Reports 1969*, 38. The non-existence of this consensus means that the 10-mile rule has not acquired "the authority of a general rule of international law" but, at any rate, it could not be used against Norway "inasmuch as she has always opposed any attempts to apply this to the Norwegian coast" (*Fisheries case*, ICJ, *Reports 1951*, 131).

> the framework of its competence, resolution which make determinations or have operative design.[18]

In addition, its advisory opinion concerning *Certain Expenses of the United Nations*, stated that,

> the functions and powers conferred by the Charter on the General Assembly are not confined to discussion, consideration, the initiation of studies and the making of recommendations; they are not merely hortatory. Article 18 deals with '*decisions*' of the General Assembly 'on important questions´. These 'decisions' do indeed include certain recommendations, but others have dispositive force and effect.[19]

If United Nations practice is examined, it can be seen that the General Assembly adopts different types of documents: Resolutions, Recommendations, Declarations and Decisions.[20] The following deals with the examination of this practice.

As regards the first, it is possible to classify them into four large blocks:

- Declarative Resolutions on customary norms.
- Resolutions which crystallize the customary norms *in statu nascendi.*
- Resolutions *de lege ferenda* which constitute the starting point for a custom.
- Resolutions interpreting the Charter.[21]

The *declarative resolutions* of customary norms generally appear under the title of "Declaration", and its subject is the affirmation of an existing rule of law, and it also constitutes a means for determining or interpreting international law, a proof of international custom or the statement of general principles of law.[22]

Despite the fact that the status of the resolutions called "Declarations" do not differ from other resolutions, this particular type of resolution can serve to stress the importance of the norms announced. As the Institute of International Law (IIL) points out in its Cairo Resolution, the appeal to declarations is usually convenient for dealing globally with a matter or to announce principles intended to influence the progressive development of international law.[23] As an example, Resolution 2625 (XXV) of the General Assembly on October 24, 1970 can be included. It contains the *Declaration on Principles of International Law concerning Friendly Relations and Cooperation among States in Accordance with the Charter of the United Nations*. With regard to this, in the case of *Military and Paramilitary Activities in and against Nicaragua*, the ICJ stated that it is not a repetition or a specification of the commitment assumed by the States in the Charter,

[18] ICJ, *Reports 1971*, 50.

[19] ICJ, *Reports 1962*, 163. The part in italics is from the original.

[20] It can also draw up and adopt conventions which are annexed to the resolution in question.

[21] The Institute of International Law (IIL) takes in the different types of documents under the form of recommendations (Resolution of the Cairo meeting, September 13–21, 1987, Vol. 62-II, 1987, 273 et seq.

[22] Cf. *ibid.*, Conclusion 4.

[23] Cf. *ibid.*, Conclusion 12.

> The effect of consent to the text of such resolutions cannot be understood as merely that of a 'reiteration or elucidation´ of the treaty commitment undertaken in the Charter. On the contrary, it may be understood as an acceptance of the validity of the rule or set of rules declared by the resolution by themselves.[24]

At doctrinal level, different characteristics have been given for these types of Resolutions. Some have pointed out that declarative Resolutions are not only declarations of an existing text. On the contrary, this type of Resolution serves to define, formulate, re-formulate, clarify, specify and authenticate a text, as well as to corroborate the rule contained in it.[25] Thus, "if all, or nearly all, of the members of the United Nations say that this is the law, as in the case of interpretative resolutions, it would require strong evidence of conflicting practice to maintain the contrary".[26] In other words they can contribute to the development of new norms.[27]

Others have highlighted the fact that declarative resolutions are a source of rules of international law similar to the consensus in the conferences for the codification and progressive development of International Law,[28] and they have also stated that as regards general International Law, these have the same value as declarative conventions, that is to say, if they can contribute to precision in the sense of practice (the material element of custom) on the one hand, and on the other the unanimous adoption or adoption by a large majority could be a proof of the *opinio iuris* (the spiritual element of international custom).[29] A third opinion defends the view that the resolutions which crystallize customary norms do not create law but constitute an authorized proof of its existence.[30]

With regard to victims, the UN General Assembly has adopted two Declarations which meet the systematizing, codifying and declarative characteristics underlined both by the IIL and by the ICJ. At the same time, both Declarations are the first international norms on the matter they deal with. They are the *Declaration of Basic Principles of Justice for Victims of Crime and abuse of Power* adopted on 29

---

[24] ICJ, *Reports 1986*, paragraph 188. Along the same lines, the ICJ mentions the resolution of the Sixth Inter-American Conference held on February 18, 1928, which condemned aggression and Resolution 78 of the General Assembly of American States (OAS), adopted on April 21, 1972 regarding the principles of non-intervention and the free determination of peoples.

[25] *Vid.* Sloan, *op. cit.*, 69.

[26] *Ibid.*

[27] Cf. Zappalá (2009), p. 226. In its opinion, this is the case of GA Resolution 60/147 of 16 December 2005 adopting the *Basic Principles and Guidelines of the Right a Remedy and Reparation for Victims of Gross Violations of International Human Rights Law and Serious Violations of International Humanitarian Law.*

[28] *Vid.* Jiménez de Aréchaga (1978-I), 31.

[29] An example of this is the statement from the ICJ in the case concerning *Military and Paramilitary Activities in and against Nicaragua* (cf. ICJ, *Reports 1986*, 100). In this regard, vid. Pastor Ridruejo, *Curso de ..., op. cit.*, 175.

[30] Castañeda (1970-I), 171.

November 1985 by GA Resolution 40/34[31] and the *Declaration on the Protection of All Persons from Enforced Disappearance* adopted on 18 December 1992 by GA Resolution 47/133.[32] In my opinion, both Declarations constitute the codification of an ensemble of norms recognizing the rights of victims.[33]

Thus, the origin of what has been said above regarding the interest and the current importance of this question can be seen. Moreover, the wealth produced by its analysis based on the practice of the General Assembly contrasts with the lack of doctrinal presentations which are restricted to discarding the fact that the institutional norms can have obligatory legal effects. The study of the practice and the appeal of the methods of analysis we have chosen prove precisely the contrary: the repercussion which these Resolutions of the General Assembly have in the formation of International Law and their effect on the sectors of these regulations referred to in their content.

The second group of resolutions of the General Assembly concerns the resolutions called resolutions *"crystallising"* the customary norms which are in the process of being formed and which contribute to the consolidation of the customary norm. This is the case, for example, of Resolution 1962 (XVIII) which contains the *Declaration on Principles Governing the Activities of States in the Exploration and Use of Outer Space* adopted unanimously by the General Assembly of the United Nations on December 13, 1963. The Declaration which is the subject of this Resolution contains the legal principles, which at that time reflected the International Law accepted by the members of the United Nations, and crystallized the general consensus that had been manifested in previous years as regards the general regime concerning freedom of activity in outer space. Later, these principles were codified by the *Treaty on the Principles Governing the Activities of States in the Exploration and Use of Outer Space, Including the Moon and Other Celestial Bodies.*[34]

Another example which should be quoted is the resolution belonging to the second group, Resolution 2749 (XXV) of December 17, 1970, which contains the *Declaration of the General Assembly on the Principles Governing the Sea-Bed and the Ocean Floor, and the Subsoil Thereof, Beyond the Limits of National Jurisdiction*, which proclaims that the resources are the "common heritage of mankind". In accordance with the analytical viewpoint that we have adopted above, the general consensus of the States, which was manifest in the voting on this Declaration accepting the legal status of the common heritage of mankind that it contains as regards the seabed, has the consequence that all the States have the right to share the

---

[31] A/RES/40/34.

[32] A/RES/47/133.

[33] In the same line cf. Zappalá (2009), 226, and Th. Van Boven, "The right to a remedy as contained in international instruments: access to justice and reparation in treaties and the new United Nations principles", in *ibid.*, 46.

[34] Approved by the General Assembly on December 19, 1966, it was signed in London, Moscow and Washington on January 27, 1967. It has been in force since October 10, 1967.

resources of the seabed in the area located beyond national jurisdiction. Later, the principles contained in Resolution 2749 (XXV) were codified in 1982 by the Convention of the United Nations on the Law of the Sea which again reveals the transcendence or the effects that the resolutions of the General Assembly have apart from what is said of these in the Charter. This fact also gives a good example of a few gaps in the doctrinal positions, which maintain that the resolutions of the General Assembly only have the effect of recommendations. As in the previous case, the resolutions of this second group also belie this.[35]

As stated earlier, this is also the case of GA Resolution 60/147 of 16 December 2005 adopting the *Basic Principles and Guidelines on the Right to a Remedy and Reparation for Victims of Gross Violations of International Human Rights Law and Serious Violations of International Humanitarian Law*, which where contained in Resolution 2005/35 adopted by the Commission of Human Rights on 19 April 2005.[36]

The last group of resolutions is made up of those that have a constitutive or generating effect, also called *de lege ferenda*. These are resolutions that through their adoption can be the basis for the practice of the States. They are thus transformed into customary International Law and constitute landmark norms in a process for the creation and drafting of International Law by stages, and their legal value depends on the acceptance they receive in the practice of the States.[37]

The 1987 Cairo Resolution of the Institute of International Law includes the following categories in these types of Resolutions:

- Resolutions that contribute to the creation of an international custom;
- Resolutions that contribute to the emergence of general principles of law;
- Resolutions that restrict the field of negotiations regarding a multilateral treaty, which is of general interest, especially those that provide rules to be included in a future treaty;
- Resolutions that establish policy determining the substance of a future customary or conventional law.[38]

An example of this is Resolution 1514 (XV) of the General Assembly of December 14, 1960. This contains the *Declaration on the Granting of Independence to Colonial Countries and Peoples* and was classified by the ICJ in its

[35] Thus, Part XI of the 1982 Convention defines the legal regime of the International Zone of the seabed and ocean bed and includes and develops the principles of Resolution 2749 (XXV) and sets up an International Organisation (The International Authority on the Sea and Ocean Beds) responsible for organizing and controlling activities in the Zone in accordance with the Convention.

[36] See *ut supra* note 33.

[37] Cf. Carrillo Salcedo, *Curso...*, *op. cit.*, page 131. The italics are from the original. *Vid.* also Sloan, *op. cit.*, 70.

[38] IIL (1987), 279.

advisory opinion on the *Namibia Case* as "a further important stage in the development of customary law".[39]

Another group is made up of the *interpretative* Resolutions of the Charter. In Sloan's opinion, "the Charter is binding on its members as a treaty and its principles are binding on all States as general international law. Authentic interpretations would have obligatory force equal to the Charter itself and authoritative interpretations would carry almost the same weight".[40]

By virtue of article 10 of the Charter, the General Assembly can discuss and make recommendations on any matter within the framework of the Charter and its competence regarding the interpretation of the Charter is very wide. This interpretation can be explicit (as declarative resolutions) or implicit (as a decision or recommendation invoking provisions within the Charter), but in both cases they have the same legal effect as regards the member states.[41]

There are no discrepancies with regard to the competence of the General Assembly to interpret the Charter through *interpretative resolutions*. We have referred to its extent as a result of the empowerment contained in article 10 to discuss and make recommendations on any matter within the framework of the Charter. As regards the effect on the attitude of the States, it is considered that this interpretation is generally accepted when there is a unanimous or almost unanimous vote for the aforementioned resolution.[42] Thus, it has been said that "every interpretation holds within it the seeds of development. This is true whether it purports to be strictly textual or is frankly teleological. Interpretations may explain, clarify, elaborate, develop or supplement the Charter, or they may slip into modification or informal amendment. The line between interpretation and modification, like the line between codification and development, is a thin one and the distinction is often difficult, if not impossible, to make. Development often takes place under the guise of interpretation and the test of general acceptability remains the best guide in either case".[43]

Finally, with regard to the *Recommendations*, in the opinion of Sir F. Vallat, "to say that recommendations of the General Assembly are not as a rule binding on States, does not mean that they are of no legal effect whatever. Resolutions may be strong evidence of the proper interpretation of the Charter or of generally accepted principles of international law".[44] As far as Sloan is concerned, even the

[39] ICJ, *Reports 1971*, 31. Cf. Also, the advisory opinion of the ICJ on the *Western Sahara* Case (*Reports 1975*, especially page 32). This Resolution was repeated and developed in subsequent Resolutions, 1541 (XV), 1980 (XVII) and 2625 (XXV). In opinion of B. Sloan, these types of resolutions also constitute a "species of General Assembly resolutions based on established practice outside the express provisions of Chapter IV of the Charter" (*op. cit*, 140).

[40] *Ibid.*, 57.

[41] Vid. *ibid.*, 57 et seq.

[42] Cf. SLOAN, *op. cit.*, page 59. This presumption could only be destroyed if the rejection of the resolution were to be proved by subsequent practice (ibid.).

[43] *Ibid.*, 60.

[44] Vallat, *op. cit.*, 231.

recommendations which have this characteristic *strictu sensu* involve obligations as regards cooperation, good faith and assistance, obligations applicable as regards all the recommendations validly adopted "without special regard to the size of the vote. The hortatory effect of recommendations will be strengthened by unanimity or near unanimity. Recommendations will also have value as precedents and may gain binding force through acceptance or estoppel".[45]

The same can be said with regard to the recommendations of the Committee of Ministers of the *Council of Europe*. With regard to the question I am dealing with now Article 15.b) of the Statute of London states:

> b. In appropriate cases, the conclusions of the Committee may take the form of recommendations to the governments of members, and the Committee may request the governments of members *to inform it of the action taken by them with regard to such recommendations*.[46]

As it can be appreciated, despite being qualified as "recommendations", the conclusions of the Committee of Ministers adopting such norms display legal effects, the principal of which is the obligation of the State to adopt the measures requested by the concrete recommendation. This obligation is reinforced by the power the Committee of Ministers has of inviting the governments of Member States to inform it of the action taken. If recommendations did not have legal effects, Member States would not be obliged to give effect to it or to inform the Committee of Ministers of the action taken with regard to it.

From the studies carried out, it can be deduced that institutional norms have legal effects within the internal order of the International Organization in question. Second, that in the concrete case of the UN, General Assembly resolutions are part of the customary process and have contributed to its acceleration.[47] Finally, the determination of the legal effects of the institutional norm depends more on the analysis of the will of the State manifested in its behaviour with regard to the international norm, rather than its denomination.[48]

Thus, we are always dealing with a norm.[49] Consequently, it always has legal effects.

---

[45] Sloan, *op. cit.*, 140. He adds that "at least in some circumstances the obligation does go further and is a duty not only to *consider* in good faith but to *act* in good faith as well. Such duty arises out of the obligations of co-operation implicit in organizational theory and expressly stated in Articles 1(3), 2(5) and 56 of the Charter of the UN" (*ibid.*, 125).

[46] Italics are mine.

[47] Cf. Jaque, *op. cit.*, 397.

[48] Cf. in this regard Carrillo Salcedo, *Curso . . .*, *op. cit.*, 132 et seq. Yes, The General Assembly is almost a universal forum in which the presence of almost all the States which make up the International Community, and it facilitates the operability of the process for drafting the institutional norm. Within the Assembly, the states manifest their attitude as regards the resolution at the same time and collectively through adopting the resolution. This resolution may contain a norm of International Law, which already exists or is emerging, or which might be the basis and starting point for the progressive development of International Law (cf. Jiménez de Aréchaga, *op. cit.*, 34.)

[49] Vid. Virally (1984). Especially 299.

Criteria for Determining the Attitude of the State and the Legal Effects of the Institutional Norm

Although dealing with special reference to the UN General Assembly institutional norms, the approach I have taken in the previous pages on the legal effects of the institutional norms is valid for all types of institutional norms of International Organizations of cooperation. Nevertheless, it is necessary to insist on the fact that the determining factor on the matter is the will of the State manifested within the International Organization as regards the institutional norm in question. Whether this individual consent of the State exists or not is what will determine whether the norm has crystallized or not through the general *consensus* of the States which participate in the international organization.[50]

To determine the will of the State, and therefore, the legal effects of the resolution, we can use the following techniques or criteria: the draft, the terms used, the content or the subject of the institutional norm, the procedure or way in which it is adopted, the context in which the resolution is drawn up and adopted, the intention of the states and the subsequent practice of the States.[51]

As far as the *content* or *subject* of the resolution is concerned, according to P.M. Dupuy the debate is restricted to a reduced number of resolutions (including the *declarations* adopted on the occasion of important international conferences convoked by the UN) and their regulatory character has been clearly established.[52] This is the case of Resolutions 2625 (XXV) and 3314 (XXIX).

The 1972 Declaration of Stockholm and 1992 Declaration of Rio de Janeiro are good examples of the usefulness of the criteria we are putting forward. It should be remembered that the legal effects of the former were put in doubt by the doctrine immediately after its adoption. The fact that this was by *consensus* was significant taking into account the obligations codified by the Stockholm Declaration, which had already been affirmed by international case law.[53] But the same questions arise for the 1992 Declaration of Rio with regard to those aspects that imply innovation in comparison with the pre-existing regime. There is no doubt that the passage of time and the practice of the States will contribute to consolidating these obligations and to reinforcing the legal effects of the Declaration.

---

[50] On this question from the perspective of the protection of human rights, see Carrillo Salcedo (1993). Especially 173–175.

[51] The ICJ refers to these criteria in the case of the *Legal Consequences for States regarding of the Continued Presence of South Africa in Namibia (South-West Africa) notwithstanding Security Council Resolution 276 (1970)* (Vid. ICJ, *Reports 1971*, 50).

[52] Vid., Dupuy, *Droit…*, *op. cit.*, 279.

[53] For example, Principle 21 which contains the obligation on prevention.

The *analysis of the content* involves three types of questions. The first concerns the legal or political nature of the resolution.[54] In the second place, the analysis of the terms to know whether it declares or recommends.[55] Finally, the nature of the question dealt with by the resolution (if this is new or has already been regulated by the International Community), which would allow us to establish whether it is a resolution that declares or crystallizes an already existing norm or in is the process of formation or is the starting point for a new norm.

The *procedure* or *form of adoption* of the resolution enables us to know the attitude of the Member States as regards the norm. In this respect, some authors endeavour to disassociate the act of adoption of the resolution (procedural aspect) from the content. Thus, the procedural act of adoption would have no consequences as regards the text contained in the resolution.[56] In my opinion, this disassociation is not possible as the adoption of the resolution is made with reference to its content. The attitude of the State at the time of the adoption of the resolution is determined by its content and by the text; therefore, the conduct observed at the time of the adoption is also the conduct manifested with regard to the text of the resolution.[57]

[54] In Carrillo Salcedo's opinion, as a result of its political nature, the General Assembly adopts many resolutions, which are clearly political in content "most of the time by majority, which naturally has little legal significance as concerns the process for the drafting of the general legal norms" (*Curso . . ., op. cit.*, 130).

[55] At doctrinal level, some authors choose to put institutional norms at the same level as conventional norms for the purposes of interpretation, and propose that the analysis of the content be done by analogy in accordance with the rules of the 1969 and 1986 Vienna Conventions. B. Sloan (*op. cit.* page 129) adds that "when the resolution contains a binding decision expressly authorized by the Charter or if this constitutes an agreement, it would seem reasonable to apply the rule of where it constitutes an agreement, it would appear reasonable to apply the treaty rule on *travaux préparatoires*" (preparatory works). Virally maintains that the acceptance of the adoption of a resolution also constitutes acceptance of the terms of the resolution "so it is necessary to formulate reservations in order to disassociate, in the event of consensus" ("Résolution et . . ..", *op. cit.*, 304.

[56] The adoption of a resolution would only express "an informal agreement regarding the text among all the states which, through their representatives, have contributed to this adoption", whether by majority, unanimously or by consensus (Virally, "Résolution et . . .", *op. cit.*, 301).

[57] Thus, Virally himself is inclined to recognize that the adoption of the resolution confers on the regulatory provisions of the text a legal authority which is above its formal classification, and he states that the resolution is of a *mixed nature*: "formally it is a unilateral act of the committee of the conference which produced it. Due to the conditions of its adoption, it expresses the content of the inter-governmental agreement and is thus of a conventional colouring" ("Résolution et . . .", *op. cit.*, 301 et seq.)

From the time that the consent to be bound by the resolution and the *consensus ad idem* are manifested within the General Assembly, the legal effects arise.[58]

On adoption by *voting*, this expresses the agreement of the states which *vote in favour*. The favourable votes must include both the States whose support might be necessary for the effective application of the resolution and the States of all the economic and legal systems.[59] That is to say, it must be a *representative vote* of the majority in question so that those proposing the resolution or those who invoke it for regulatory objectives may endeavour to make it "the expression of a collective *opinio iuris*, which is creative or simply demonstrates a regulatory intention attributable to the international community as a whole".[60]

The majority is essential. In fact, it is not the same for the resolution to be the subject of a general agreement and ample consensus among the States belonging to the main legal systems (which grants greater relevance and legal authority) which, on the contrary, finds opposition from a sufficiently representative minority (which will prevent the resolution from having legal effects).[61]

In any case, it is evident that the State that votes *in favour* of the resolution will adhere to the validity of the norm or set of norms declared by the resolution.[62]

Obviously, the States which vote *against* are free from the legal effects of the resolution voted by a majority. This is initially true, but it should be added that this refusal may be affected by the general consensus as regards the resolution in question on condition that the criteria for the manner of adoption of the institutional norm are respected.

As regards those who *abstain*, the doctrinal opinions diverge between those who maintain that these States do not oppose but disassociate from the agreement[63] and

---

[58] Following this line of thought, the resolution of the IIL at its Cairo meeting in 1987 in its conclusion number 13 states: "A law declaring resolution, adopted without negative vote or abstention, creates a presumption that the resolution contains a correct statement of law. That presumption is subject to rebuttal". And Conclusion number 14 adds: "In situations where a rule of customary law is emerging from State practice or where there is still doubt whether a rule, though already applied by an international organ or by some States, is a rule of law, a resolution adopted without negative vote or abstention may consolidate a custom or remove doubts that might have existed" (*op. cit.*, 283–285).

[59] Cf. Sloan *op. cit.*, 131.

[60] Cf. Dupuy, *Droit . . .*, *op. cit.*, 279 et seq.

[61] Vid. in this regard, Carrillo Salcedo, *Curso . . .*, *op. cit.*, 130. Other criteria apart from the representative nature is, according to P. M. Dupuy, the establishment of a control mechanism, which is more or less institutionalized for the monitoring of the resolution by the member states. This control could consist of a periodical examination of the conditions of application laid down in the resolution by an institution of the Organisation (*Droit...*, *op. cit.*, 280)

The criteria of the representative nature appear backed by the IIL in its Cairo Resolution, "The authority of a resolution is enhanced when it is adopted by a representative majority that includes the main legal systems" (*op. cit.*, 285).

[62] As stated by the ICJ in the case of *Military and Paramilitary Activities in and against Nicaragua* (ICJ, *Reports 1986*, para. 188)

[63] Cf. Virally, "Résolution. . .", *op. cit.*, 301.

those who consider that abstention is the same as acquiescence.[64] As was the case in the criteria examined above, the reply in the cases of negative votes and abstentions is determined by the number of negative votes or abstentions because if these are substantially or qualitatively significant the effect of stating the law or creating rules by the resolution would be weakened.[65]

If the resolution is adopted by *consensus*, this shows the unanimity of the agreement of the States concerning the content of the norm, and the authority of the resolution is thus reinforced.[66] Jacque states that if the vote on a resolution implies that there is already agreement on the content of the resolution among the members of the majority, this agreement is even more evident when the resolution is adopted by *consensus*. The same happens when reservations are formulated regarding the resolution by some States. This indicates that they grant a certain value to the commitment contained in the resolution as they feel the need to be more specific.[67] These reservations do not produce legal effects when it is a matter of resolutions that state existing law.[68]

From the viewpoint of the interpretation, the resolution adopted by *consensus* or by a unanimous vote will have a particular interpretation as proof of an *opinio iuris* in the customary process: it may testify to a political agreement. But it will be necessary to make a wider examination of the context in order to affirm that we are in the presence of a legal agreement and not a political one.[69]

In the cases of adoption of the resolution by *consensus*, the absence of protests can mean an acceptance of the resolution where each state commits itself given that the objection of a single State would be sufficient for the resolution not to be adopted. In other words, the acceptance of the consensus means that each Member State participates individually in the adoption of the resolution, which leads Virally to state that this is why the Member States of the institution which pronounces by

---

[64] Sloan, *op. cit.*, 131.

[65] Vid. IIL, *op. cit.*, 285.

[66] In accordance with Conclusion number 16 of the Resolution of the IIL of 1987, at the Cairo session, "the authority of a resolution is enhanced when it is adopted by consensus".

The Declaration of Stockholm in 1972 constitutes an example of a Resolution adopted by consensus.

It should be added that when the resolution is voted unanimously, it force seems, in principle, greater than when it is adopted by consensus.

[67] Vid. Jacque, *op. cit.*, 398. This author describes this agreement as "an informal legal agreement among states", which must be deduced from the examination of the circumstances involved in the adoption of the resolution (*ibid*).

[68] As concerns the reservations, the Cairo Resolution of the IIL in its Conclusion number 17, states that "Where a resolution may be subjected to reservations either in the explanations of votes or in other statements, the effect of such reservations is to qualify or limit the extent of approval by the reserving State. Depending on its contents a reservation may mean less than rejection of the rule. It may be merely an expression of doubt. If a resolution expresses existing law, a State cannot exclude itself from the binding force of that law by making a reservation" (*op. cit.*, 285)

[69] Vid. Jacque, *op. cit.*, 398.

consensus "cannot disassociate from the agreement made in this manner except as regards particular points and through active conduct, by formulating reservations before or after the adoption of the resolution".[70]

But it should not be forgotten that great resolutions are adopted through negotiation procedures, which are similar to great general treaties. This means that the resolutions are prepared in restricted groups and are then submitted to the plenary institution. Generally, they are discussed and voted on article by article and, more and more frequently, the states explain their vote to specify their positions clearly. This process of drafting the resolution shows the existence of an exchange of points of view and a meeting of wills within the Assembly, which is very similar to what takes place in the drafting of multilateral treaties.[71] Pastor Ridruejo hit the nail on the head when he stressed the characteristic of *consensus*: "the proposal of the resolution made by the President of the Organisation has been drafted through consultations, negotiations and transactions among the delegations concerned, that is to say, it is the subject of a compromise, so, when the President submits it to the institution, he already knows that it will not give rise to objections". These objections are understood to be those that are sufficiently substantial to prevent the adoption of the resolution given that practice shows that the state delegations can express minor objections (which adopt the form of reservations) but do not involve the intention to prevent the formation of the resolution.[72]

A third criteria is the *intention* of the States, which can be deduced from the language employed in the drafting of the resolution; if it is clearly imperative, is recommendatory, uses the conditional tense, leaves a wide discretionary margin to the states, etc.[73]

The importance of the drafting as regards the resolutions of the General Assembly has also been stressed by international case law. Thus, the ICJ in the case of *Military and Paramilitary Activities in and against Nicaragua* states that,

---

[70] Vid. Virally, "Résolution ...", *op. cit.*, 303.

[71] Which leads P.M. Dupuy to state that in such cases, whether it is wished or not, "it is a matter of the expression of a meeting of wills, although rather diluted... which is facilitated by the organic framework of the intervention, whose nature is conventionally deaf and difficult to respond to" (*op. cit.*, 281)

[72] J.A. Pastor Ridruejo, *Curso...*, *op. cit.*, 710. Also Carrillo Salcedo who, after he had stressed the negotiation process of the resolution among the states which make up the political groups which constitute the General Assembly, he states that "when this negotiation becomes fruitful and makes the adoption of a resolution possible by consensus or by general agreement, the resolution in question is in fact a concerted judicial act of a non-conventional nature, that is to say, an agreement between states expressed at a judicial act as distinct from an international agreement, with undeniable legal value as a new procedure for drafting legal norms in contemporary International Law..." (*Curso...*, *op. cit.*, 134)

[73] The IIL in Conclusion number 10 of the Cairo Resolution of 1987 highlights as criteria for appreciating the intention of states both the drafting and the context of a resolution as these help to determine the scope of the norm, and adds that the presence of "references to international law or equivalent phrases, or the deliberate omission, are relevant but not in themselves" (IIL, *op. cit.*, 281). Vid. Also Amerasinghe (1994), 175 et seq.

> ..., just as the wording of certain General Assembly declarations adopted by States demonstrates their recognition of the principle of the prohibition of force as a definitely matter of customary international law, some of the wording in those declarations operates similarly in respect of the right of self-defence (both collective and individual).[74]

In addition, as I have stated above, the *mode of adopting* the resolution, by voting (unanimously or by majority) or by consensus, also constitutes an indication of the intention of the States as regards the resolution.

The last criteria is *subsequent practice*, which places the resolutions of the General Assembly of the United Nations in relationship with custom[75] (with the three manifestations that we have just explained in the previous pages: declarative resolutions on customary norms, resolutions which crystallize the customary norms *in statu nascendi* and resolutions *de lege ferenda* which constitute the starting point for a custom). Practice, in this case, takes in both the resolution itself and the votes of the States which reflect their positions with regard to the resolution.[76]

The subsequent practice of the States as regards the resolution in question also allows us to confirm the attitude of these States concerning the legal value of the resolution and the interpretation of the Charter. It should not be forgotten that the Charter is a living text and thus the subsequent practice enables us to know the contemporary interpretation of the Charter made by current members.[77]

Considering the profundity of the changes that have occurred, the analysis of the subsequent practice of the States concerning the resolutions of the General Assembly acquires a new dimension. Thus, it is also useful to consider "the frequency and density of the repetition of certain principles through voluntary repetitive resolutions", both in the course of the sessions of the General Assembly and other plenary meetings of universal International Organizations such as the IWO, the WHO or the FAO.[78]

---

[74] ICJ, *Reports 1986*, para. 193.

[75] Vid. Carrillo Salcedo, *Curso ...*, *op. cit.*, 130.

[76] According to Sloan, the "resolutions -or at least the votes of States on resolutions- are a part of state practice", and constitute "a material source of customary law and must be taken into account in considering the current state of the law" (*op. cit.*, 74) And he adds, the "resolutions are evidence" (*ibid.*, 85).

[77] From this perspective, the changes that have occurred in the international community since the Charter was drafted are evident. The balance consigned to the Charter after the Second World War has been extensively altered, first, due to the universalizing of the Community itself as a result of decolonization and, more recently, due to the disappearance of the Soviet block and the subsequent break up of the USSR and other East-Europe States. The Charter is the same but the context in which it is applied has changed profoundly. So, some of the provisions (for example, Chapter VII) recover vitality and the Organization is confronted with new challenges. Within the framework of this Chapter, the provisions of the Charter concerning the prohibition of the use of force and the protection of human rights receive new applications, and questions arise such as the control of the legality of the acts of the Security Council.

[78] Dupuy, *Droit...*, *op. cit.*, 283. Sloan adds other factors such as the time and the circumstances, "the international climate in which the resolution was adopted must influence its weight" (*op. cit.*, 128). These changes give rise to another problem which is the replacement of the commitments

Although it is true that the United Nations Charter points out that the General Assembly can only adopt "decisions" and "recommendations", this does not prevent this institution from adopting other kinds of decisions ("declarations") or from the declarations and recommendations having obligatory legal effects. All the resolutions, independently of their names, have legal effects. The scope of these resolutions and their precision will have to be determined case by case by recourse to the criteria examined.

How can this conclusion be reconciled with the absence of provisions in the Charter expressly capacitating the General Assembly to create a law with binding legal effects? As it is true that the sovereignty of the State has only the limitations accepted by the States themselves—except for the limitation deriving from *ius cogens*—and that the will of the state reflected in the Charter does not state anything with regard to creation of law by the General Assembly, it is no less true that, in the General Assembly, the process for the formation of the institutional norms takes place through the channels and procedures laid down in the Charter. These procedures, in which the States have an active participation, channel the opinions of the majority and provide them with a regulation expression (which is the institutional norm).[79] The individual consent of each State and the *consensus ad idem* of the generality of the states are manifest and are crystallised through the procedures laid down in the Charter. At the meetings of the General Assembly, consent and consensus produce the institutional norm. But this is not the only thing. The institutional norm created in this way also expresses the *opinio iuris* of the States in the General Assembly. This is one of the more relevant aspects resulting from the institutionalization of the international community. Unlike the past, at the present time, it is not a reduced group of states (the Great Powers), which express the will of the International Community. On the contrary, it is practically all this community represented in the General Assembly—independent of the degree of power and economic development—that participates in the drafting of this norm of international law, which is the institutional norm.

The phenomenon that I have just described has also been specified as Pastor Ridruejo points out by a displacement of the centre of gravity of the material element of the custom, the practice, towards the spiritual element or *opinio iuris*, as a result of the demands made by the universalizing, democratization and socialization of international law. Today, the important thing is not always the practice or the material element of the custom, but the *opinio iuris* or legal conviction. And this *opinio iuris generalis* "is also adequately manifested through the resolutions of the General Assembly of the United Nations".[80]

and the text of the past by new individual and collective consent. Cf. also Amerashinge, "Interpretation of texts...", *op. cit.*, 198 et seq.

[79] Vid. Dupuy, *Droit...*, *op. cit.*, 290.

[80] Pastor Ridruejo, *Curso...*, *op. cit.*, 177. One of the results of the current situation after the changes that have occurred is the new leading role not only of the Great Powers but of all States of the International Community and the role they play in the General Assembly. This has led to the fact that international law declarations or texts are not being adopted as frequently as between 1960 and 1990.

Consequently, the state *consensus*, in which the resolution is crystallized is arrived at after a long process with several stages, at which the individual consent of the State regarding the resolution is manifested (this consent is specified in the negotiations, deliberations, transactions and consultations regarding the text), and this consent is manifested or exteriorized later in the form of adoption of the norm.

In my opinion, the classical manifestation of the ICJ in its advisory opinion on *the Legal consequences for States of the Continued Presence of South Africa in Namibia (South-West Africa) notwithstanding Security Council Resolution 276 (1970)* in the sense that, "an international instrument has to be interpreted and applied within the framework of the entire legal system prevailing at the time of the interpretation",[81] backs the position I have adopted as regards the legal force of the resolutions of the General Assembly. At the present time, the relevance of the General Assembly is considerably greater than when the Charter was drafted. The ideological context has also been modified and facilitates the conclusion of norms that express the general consensus of the Member States. Finally, the process for the drafting of the resolution is also different from the process at the time the Charter was drawn up. In short, International Society has changed radically. All these changes affect the legal force of the resolutions of the General Assembly and their study cannot be addressed using the schemes of 1945. When the resolution is adopted, it has already passed through the filter of negotiation. It has been the subject of transactions, deliberations and consultations. The final text faithfully reflects the will of the State.

Therefore, the determining factor is not the denomination the institutional norm receives but the attitude of the States with regard to it. This attitude may appear as the manifestation of the *opinio iuris* concerning the norm (or the set of norms) in question, and may be considered as from then independent of the other provisions, especially those of an institutional nature, to which it is submitted at the conventional level of the Charter.[82]

Finally, the resolutions of the General Assembly have legal effects. They are norms of international law.[83] Whether they have obligatory legal force as regards the specific recipient involved is something that must be analysed case by case based on the criteria examined above.

---

[81] ICJ, *Reports 1971*, 31.

[82] Cf. ICJ, *Military and Paramilitary Activities in and against Nicaragua*, *Reports1986*, para. 188.

[83] According to Virally, the resolutions of the International Organisations "are the expression of a political agreement made between states which have participated in its adoption. Insofar as they share specific commitments for the states, these commitments must be considered as politically binding the states which have accepted them, and they do not have a value inferior to those the states assume in other actions apart from the institutions of the international organisations or at conferences convened to adopt an agreement" ("Résolution . . .", *op. cit.*, 305 et seq.). However as P. M. Dupuy points out, "the nature and the intensity of the relations maintained between the two regulation orders, the political order and the legal order" remain to be known. (*Droit. . .*, *op. cit.*, 281).

An additional reflection should be added: the role played by the resolutions of the General Assembly of the United Nations in the contemporary international community. As we have stated above, practically all the States which make up this world or universal community participate in the General Assembly and make pronouncements on questions and problems, which are classical or new. Thus, analysis of the Charter, once more than 65 years have elapsed since it came into force, with schemes that lead to literal interpretations of the Charter in relation to the resolutions of the General Assembly, does not allow the role that this institution and its norms play in the International Community at the beginning of the XXI century to be addressed satisfactorily. Following this line of thought, it should be remembered that questions not laid down in the Charter or only listed in it have been dealt with and developed later based on resolutions adopted by the General Assembly. This is the case, for example, of the sectors of the international legal system concerning the international protection of the environment and human rights, whose first norms were the resolutions of the General Assembly.[84]

The same evolutionary nature of the international legal system positively affects the relevance of the resolutions of the General Assembly as concerns the new problems confronting the International Community and which are the subject of attention of this legal system require responses in accordance with this evolution and one of the characteristics of this evolution is the fundamental role played by the international organizations in general and the UN in particular, as well as the institutional norms they draw up. Consequently, the process for forming the international norms cannot be addressed exclusively from the classical perspective, reduced to conventional and customary norms, but the evolution I have described must also include the growing relevance of the institutional norms within this system. Otherwise, both the study of the process of formation of international norms and the phenomenon of the International Organizations will be incomplete as it ignores a reality that is more and more established as a consequence of the progressive institutionalization of the International Community. This institutionalization is characterized by the negotiation, discussion, deliberation, transaction and flexibility at the time the decisions are taken or the norms are drafted.

In my opinion, it is in this context and in the light of the criteria just exposed that the recent attention of International Law to victims shall take place. Like before in other sectors of International Law, the first international norms related to the different categories of victims have now come into existence with an institutional legal nature. Likewise, as also before in other sectors of international norms, these

[84] For example, the 1972 Declaration of Stockholm, the Universal Declaration of Human Rights of December 10, 1948, the Declaration on Protection Against Torture or Cruel, Inhuman or Degrading Treatment or Punishment of December 9, 1975, etc As regards the Human Rights sector cf. Kiss (1988), 51 et seq. The same can be said as regards the principle of the freedom of movement of people.

international norms are followed before or later by international treaties. This is the case of international norms on victims of crime (in the frame both of the UN and of the Council of Europe)[85] and on victims of enforced disappearances (in the frame both of the UN and of the OAS).[86] As I have pointed out, this is the itinerary followed in the past by different international treaties on human rights, among them, for example, those related to the fight against racial discrimination,[87] the fight against discrimination against women,[88] the fight against torture[89] and the protection of the child.[90]

Characteristics of the Rights of Victims Recognized by International Norms

The Majority Are Rights Already in Force in International Law of Human Rights

As we will see in the following pages,[91] most of the rights forming part of the international legal statute of victims are rights currently in force in international law of human rights. They are, therefore, rights already consolidated. Together with them international norms related to the different categories of victims include other

[85] Due to the characteristics of the law of the EU (specially the binding nature of the principal legal acts) in the frame of the EU it is not necessary that the institutional norm become followed by an international treaty.

[86] So, the Declaration on the Protection of All Persons from Enforced Disappearance adopted by A/RES/47/133 of 18 December 1992 was followed by the International Convention for the Protection of All Persons from Enforced Disappearance adopted on 20 December 2006 by A/RES/61/177.

[87] So, the Declaration on the Elimination of All Forms of Racial Discrimination adopted by A/RES/1904 (XVIII) of 20 November was followed by the International Convention on the Elimination of All Forms of Racial Discrimination adopted and opened for signature by A/RES/2106 (XX) of 20 December 1965.

[88] So, the Declaration on the Elimination of Discrimination against Women adopted by A/RES/2263 (XXII) was followed by the Convention on the Elimination of All Forms of Discrimination against Women adopted on 18 December 1979.

[89] So, the Declaration on the Protection of All Persons from being subjected to Torture and Other Cruel, Inhuman or Degrading Treatment or Punishment adopted by A/RES/3452 (XXX) of 9 December 1975 was followed by the Convention Against Torture and Other Cruel, Inhuman or Degrading Treatment or Punishment of 10 December 1984.

[90] So, the Declaration of the Rights of the Child adopted by the General Assembly on 20 November 1959 was followed by the Convention on the Rights of the Child adopted and opened for signature, ratification and accession on 20 November 1989 by A/RES/44/25.

[91] In concrete, in Chapter VI of the present work.

rights closely linked to the condition of victim. These are rights that do not appear in international treaties on human rights in force before such international norms on victims. The reason for it is nothing else but the recent attention paid by International Law to victims as opposed to the protection of the individual already existent in International Law of human rights.[92] In consequence, general international treaties of human rights do not echo a problem—that of victims—that only a few years ago received the attention of States in the field of law. On the contrary, the most recent treaties of human rights proclaim new rights in favour of victims. There is the case, for example, of victims, right to a prompt and effective investigation as well as to reparation that is envisaged by the *UN Convention Against Torture and Other Cruel, Inhuman or Degrading Treatment or Punishment* of 10 December 1984.[93] It is also the case of other international treaties of human rights containing references to certain forms of reparation linked to the object and purpose pursued by the treaty.[94]

The fact that most of the victim's rights are rights already in force is a reality that international norms on victims state and underline. So, for example, the General Assembly Resolution 60/147 of 16 December 2005 adopting the *Basic principles and guidelines of the right to a remedy and reparation for victims of gross violations of international human rights law and serious violations of International Humanitarian Law*[95] that were previously adopted by the UN Commission on Human Rights on 19 April 2005, by Resolution 2005/35, expressly states in its preamble that these basic principles and guidelines do not entail new international or domestic legal obligations but identify mechanisms, modalities, procedures and methods for the implementation of *existing legal obligations* under International Human Rights Law and International Humanitarian Law.[96]

---

[92] When I say "general", I refer to the treaties, both at the universal and regional level, claiming a catalogue of rights and freedoms. It is the case, for example, of the two international Covenants of the United Nations of 1966, as well as of the regional conventions: European (1950), American (1966) and African (1980).

[93] Due to the high number of ratifications, Bottigliero considers that the Torture Convention forms one of the pillars in the codification of the fundamental principle of victims' right to redress for human rights violations (Bottigliero (2004), 123).

[94] So, Article 39 of UN Convention on the Rights of the Child of 20 November 1989: "States Parties shall take all appropriate measures to promote physical and psychological recovery and social reintegration of a child victim of: any form of neglect, exploitation, or abuse; torture or any other form of cruel, inhuman or degrading treatment or punishment; or armed conflicts. Such recovery and reintegration shall take place in an environment which fosters the health, self-respect and dignity of the child".

[95] UN E/CN.4/2005/L.10/Add. 11. It was adopted by a recorded vote of 40 to none, with 13 abstentions.

[96] Italics are mine.

In the opinion of Tomuschat, these Basic principles and guidelines shall be carefully handled because principles and rules of positive International Law stand side by side with propositions of a purely hortatory character.[97] According to him, the title of such Principles in itself makes it clear that it is not its intent to codify positive law but to enunciate recommendations as the language used by it also shows.[98]

Nevertheless, a detail examination of the General Assembly Resolution 60/147 allows the conclusion that it has binding legal effects in most of its content. So, first and as we have seen, its preamble expressly states that it does not do anything other than identifying mechanisms, modalities, procedures and methods for the implementation of *existing legal obligations* under International Human Rights Law and International Humanitarian Law. Second, it shall be added that hortatory language is only used in Principe 18 related to reparation for victims:

> 18. In accordance with domestic law and international law, and taking account of individual circumstances, victims of gross violations of international human rights law and serious violations of international humanitarian law should, as appropriate and proportional to the gravity of the violation and the circumstances of each case, be provided with full and effective reparation, as laid out in principles 19 to 23, which include the following forms: restitution, compensation, rehabilitation, satisfaction and guarantees of non-repetition.

All other principles (26) either use a clearly binding language or lean on international norms already in force. So, it is possible to conclude that hortatory language is the exception and binding language the general rule.

Therefore, it is also possible to conclude that with regard to the majority of the rights belonging to the international legal statute of victims we are confronted by fundamental rights of the person. That is rights that international treaties of human rights both of a general and of a regional character state with regard to "everyone". Rights, too, to which victims are entitled in their condition as persons. That is, independent of its possible ulterior condition as victim. Rights, at least, on the charge of States that these last must guarantee and make sure that they become effective.

In other words, what international norms related to victims make is nothing other than reiterating such rights and particularizing them with regard to the victims.[99]

It must be remembered that most of these victim's rights are also rights already in force in international law of human rights. Rights that international norms proclaim with regard to victims but that, at the same time, are basic rights of the person. Rights at least that independent of their conventional legal nature because of being stated in treaties also bind States because of its customary legal nature: they are customary norms.

---

[97] Cf. Tomuschat (2007), 572.

[98] Cf. Tomuschat (2009), 11.

[99] Consequently, they are not rights of *lege ferenda* but *lex data*.

They Are Also Rights Which Are Interpreted by International Bodies Under International Treaties of Human Rights

Other characteristic rights victims have is that, due to the link with the International Law of Human Rights, the majority are rights which are interpreted and developed by the international bodies envisaged in international treaties on human rights both of a general and regional scope. This is the case, for example, in the general or universal system of the interpretation developed by the Human Rights Committee with regard to the International Covenant on Civil and Political Rights of 16 December 1966 through its observations, recommendations and general comments on the different articles of the Covenant.

With regard to such an interpretation a doctrinal sector considers that it is not binding on States, for example Tomuschat who underlines that such international bodies "have not been invested with powers to make binding interpretations of the instruments committed to their care". This is why its practice would lack binding authoritativeness. Nevertheless, he adds that this observation "does not detract from the enormous factual weight of the views expressed by the treaty bodies" because these bodies are composed of leading experts, "even *the* leading experts of the subject-matter concerned".[100] Despite it, he considers that interpretation of a conventional text "cannot lightly construe duties of States where none have been explicitly laid down".[101]

In my opinion that statement forgets that it is the First Optional Protocol to the Covenant itself that gives the Committee the competence to examine individual complaints with regard to alleged violations of the Covenant by States parties to the Protocol. Second, it also forgets that States having accepted the competence of the Human Rights Committee have done it through a formal act as relevant as the ratification of the First Optional Protocol. Consequently, those States are obliged to accept and follow the decisions the Human Rights Committee takes with regard to them.

A similar conclusion concerns the decisions of all international treaty bodies on human rights whose competence has been accepted by the concerned States and the treaties on human rights envisaging such bodies state it clearly. In other words, the State party to the treaty that accepts the competence of the treaty body envisaged in it clearly knows that it will be bound by the decisions of the treaty body and that such decisions have legal effects. The most important is the obligation on the charge of the concerned State to restore or to correct the right or freedom the breach of which has been declared by the treaty body in question.

Therefore when States accept the competence of such treaty bodies—which they do freely and voluntary—they cannot later say that the decisions of the treaty body

[100] Tomuschat, "Reparation in Favour of Individual Victims of Gross Violations of Human Rights and International Humanitarian Law", *op. cit.*, 325.

[101] *Ibid.*, 338.

deriving from the competence the treaty gives to it and that the concerned States have accepted do not have legal effects. Such a position is not in conformance with the duty of the States to comply fully and in good faith with its international obligations. On the contrary, such a position implies to accept that it is possible to be bound by a treaty and to defeat, in a certain way, its object and purpose later.

It must also be added that according to article 2.2 of the International Covenant on Civil and Political Rights of 16 December 1966 the State Parties to it undertake to take the necessary steps, in accordance with its constitutional processes and with the provisions of the Covenant, to adopt such laws or other measures as may be necessary to give effect to the rights recognized in the Covenant. Therefore when the Human Rights Committee declares a breach by a State party of a right or a freedom of the Covenant, it also obliges the concerned State to correct such breach. If it would not be so and if the concerned State would not be compelled to comply with and to follow the decisions of the Human Rights Committee, then, the decisions of the Human Rights Committee would lack legal effect and the fact of having accepted expressly its competence through the ratification of the First Optional Protocol would not make any sense. In all cases where there are decisions declaring a breach of the Covenant, this is a breach that was not appreciated before in domestic law. On the occasion of the exhaustion of all available domestic remedies by the concerned individual and as a consequence of it, leads to the lack of effect of the concerned provision of the Covenant.[102]

Those who state that the decisions of the Human Rights Committee lack binding legal effects on the concerned State also forget that the absence of formalism that characterizes international law becomes manifest in international law of human rights in the fact that the treaty bodies established by international treaties on human rights are those that interpret such treaties and those that on the basis of such

[102] In the same line, Article 14 of the Convention Against Torture and Other Cruel, Inhuman or Degrading Treatment and Punishment of 10 December 1984 obliges States Parties to ensure in their legal systems that the victim of an act of torture obtains redress and has an enforceable right to fair and adequate compensation, "including the means for as full rehabilitation as possible". See the recognizing of the competence of the Committee against Torture and Article 22.7. Also, Article 6 of the Convention on the Elimination of All Forms of Racial Discrimination of 21 December 1965, linked to the recognizing of the competence of the Committee on the Elimination of Racial Discrimination; Articles 7.4 and 7.5 of the Convention on the Elimination of Discrimination against Women of 18 December 1979, linked to the optional character of the 1999 Protocol to the Convention which envisages the recognizing of the competence of the Committee on the Elimination of Discrimination against Women and the decisions of the Committee declaring the violation of rights protected under the Convention. Last but not least, see also Article 4.1.a) of the Convention on the Rights of Persons with disability of 13 December 2006, linked to the recognizing of the competence of the Committee on the Rights of Persons with Disabilities which is provided in Article 1 of the Optional Protocol to that Convention, to Article 3 of the Optional Protocol (which obliges the concerned State Party to submit to the Committee written explanations or statements clarifying the matter and the remedy, if any, that may have been taken by that State) and to Article 5 of the Optional Protocol (which provides that, after examining a communication sent to it in the frame of this Protocol, the Committee shall forward its suggestions and recommendations, if any, to the State Party concerned and to the petitioner).

interpretation decide in concrete case if States Parties have or have not breached a provision of the treaty.

A similar conclusion is arrived at in the case of reports States Parties have to submit to the treaty bodies on the measures they have taken to give effect to their undertakings under the concrete convention. In these cases too, it is the treaty body that analyses the report submitted by the State Party and that through its own interpretation of the concerned convention concludes that the measures taken by such State Party to the convention are or are not in conformity with the obligations such State has undertaken with regard to it.

So, both in the case of reports States Parties have to submit to the treaty bodies in execution of the obligation they have freely and voluntary undertaken at the moment of becoming Parties to the treaty and of communications from or on behalf of individuals subject to its jurisdiction who claim to be victims of a violation by a State Party of the provisions of the concerned treaty, the treaty body envisaged by that treaty is *de facto* the body that interprets an interpretation which is imposed on State Parties. Moreover, the treaty body doesn't consider that the State Party has fulfilled its obligations to the treaty until the State Party undertakes to fulfil the general comments on the report and the recommendations the treaty body has made.[103]

In this context, it must be remembered that the treaty bodies themselves underline the binding nature of their decisions to the State Parties. This is the case of the Human Rights Committee which in its General Comment No. 3 on Article 2 of the International Covenant on Civil and Political Rights (implementation at the national level), of 29 July 1981, stated that the obligation under the Covenant is not confined to the respect of human rights, but that States Parties have also undertaken to ensure the enjoyment of these rights to all individuals under their jurisdiction. Consequently "all administrative and judicial authorities should be aware of the obligations which the State party has assumed under the Covenant".

Later, in its General Comment No. 31 of 29 March 2004, on the Nature of the General Legal Obligation Imposed on States Parties to the Covenant, the Human Rights Committee stated that every State Party to the Covenant has a legal interest in the performance by every other State Party of its obligations. This is so because it follows from the fact that the "rules concerning the basic rights of the human person' are *erga omnes* obligations" and because, "as indicated in the fourth preambular paragraph of the Covenant, there is a United Nations Charter obligation to promote universal respect for, and observance of, human rights and fundamental freedoms".[104] Next, the Human Rights Committee adds that Article 2 of the Covenant defines the scope of the legal obligations undertaken by States Parties to the Covenant. So, "a general obligation is imposed on States Parties to respect the

[103] Despite its name of "recommendations", they have legal effects on State Parties to the treaty. About this question, see Fernández de Casadevante Romani (2011).

[104] See points 2 and 3 of General Comment No. 31 of 29 March 2004. It replaces the former General Comment of 29 July 1981.

Covenant rights and to ensure them to all individuals in their territory and subject to their jurisdiction".[105] Last but not least the Committee remind State Parties that the obligations of the Covenant in general and Article 2 in particular are binding on every State Party as a whole. This means that "all branches of government (executive, legislative and judicial), and other public or governmental authorities, at whatever level—national, regional or local—are in a position to engage the responsibility of the State Party".[106]

Consequently, and pursuant to the principle articulated in Article 26 of the Vienna Convention on the Law of Treaties, "States Parties are required to give effect to the obligations under the Covenant in good faith".[107] And this although Article 2, paragraph 2, allows States Parties to give effect to Covenant rights in accordance with domestic constitutional processes, because the same principle operates so as to prevent States parties from invoking provisions of the constitutional law or other aspects of domestic law to justify a failure to perform or give effect to obligations under the treaty. This is why it should be remembered that State Parties, obligation to fulfil the decisions of the Committee also appertain to the set of obligations contained in Article 2 of the Covenant.

In order to reinforce the fulfilment of State Parties, obligation to carry out the concluding observations of the Human Rights Committee, the Committee established in 1990 a follow-up procedure. For this purpose and to enable the Committee to take further action, the Committee also appointed a special rapporteur charged with the task of reporting to the Committee. This special rapporteur should report with regard to the information received from the State Party (within a specified deadline) as to the steps taken, if any, to meet the recommendations of the Committee.[108]

In this context, the interpretative task of the Human Rights Committee has covered several articles of the Covenant, for example, Article 14 (related to the equality of all persons before the courts and tribunals as well as to the right of everyone to be entitled to a fair and public hearing by a competent, independent and impartial tribunal established by law) with regard to which the Human Rights Committee has stated that its object is to ensure the proper administration of justice, and to this end uphold a series of individual rights such as equality before the courts and tribunals and the right to a fair and public hearing by a competent, independent and impartial tribunal established by law.

---

[105] *Ibid.*, point 3.

[106] *Ibid.*

[107] *Ibid.*

[108] This Special Rapporteur began its work on March 2001, since the 71st period of session of the Human Rights Committee. This mechanism makes clear the binding effects of Humans Rights Committee decisions Cf. UN, Reports of the Human Rights, Volume II, Eighty-eighth session (16 October–3 November 2006), A/62/40 (volume II); Volume I, Eighty-nine session (12–30 March de 2007), A/62/40 (volume I); Volume I, 90 session (9–27 July 2007), A/62/40 (volume I).

It is also the case of the right to an effective remedy which, according to the interpretation made by the Human Rights Committee, obliges the States to effectively comply with its undertakings under the treaty and to ensure that individuals also have accessible and effective remedies to vindicate those rights.[109]

As I have stated, the interpretation of rights contained in the different treaties on human rights also has a place in the regional systems of protection of human rights. Here, I will refer to the *European and American regional systems* because the case law on the matter is more abundant here than in the African system. For example, the jurisprudence the *ECHR* bases the right to medical assistance on Articles 2 (right to life) and 3 (prohibition of torture) of the European Convention for the Protection of Human Rights and Fundamental Freedoms of 4 November 1950. From this perspective, the ECHR has stated that an issue may arise under Article 2 of the Convention (right to life), where it is shown that the authorities of a Contracting State put an individual's life at risk through the denial of health care that they have undertaken to make available to the population at large. It is the opinion of the Court that Article 2 paragraph 1 of the European Convention enjoins the State not only to refrain from the intentional and unlawful taking of life, but also to take appropriate steps to safeguard the lives of those within its jurisdiction.[110]

But prior to this case law, the European Commission of Human Rights had already recognized the existence of a positive obligation deriving from Article 3 of the Convention (prohibition of torture) according to which States are in certain circumstances under the obligation to make available immediate medical care.[111]

---

[109] Cf. Human Rights Committee, General Comment No. 31, adopted on 29 March 2004, para. 15 (CCPR/C/21/Rev.1/Add. 13), 26 May 2004.

[110] Cf. ECHR, *Case of Cyprus v. Turkey*, Application no. 25781/94, Judgement of 10 May 2001, para. 219. In this judgement, the ECHR refers to the *Case L.C.B. v. the United Kingdom*, Judgement of 9 June 1998, *Reports* 1998-III, p. 1403, § 36). This jurisprudence is reiterated in the *Case Berktay v. Turkey*, Judgement of the 1st March 2001 (see para. 154) and in its decision on the admissibility in the *Case Nitecki v. Poland*, of 21 Mach 2002 (Application No. 65653/01).

[111] So, for example in the *Case Hurtado v. Switzerland* in which the European Commission of Human Rights unanimously expressed the view that Article 3 of the Convention (prohibition of torture) had been violated, in particular inasmuch as the applicant was not examined by a doctor until 8 days after his arrest. This case concluded with a friendly settlement and the ECHR struck it off list through Judgement of 28 January 1994. See also the *Case McGlinchey and Others v. The United Kingdom*, Judgement of 29 April 2003, in which medical assistance is analysed in the context of Article 3 (prohibition of torture) with regard to the conditions in which a person is detained. The ECHR stated that under this provision "the State must ensure that a person is detained in conditions which are compatible with respect for her human dignity, that the manner and method of the execution of the measure do not subject her to distress or hardship of an intensity exceeding the unavoidable level of suffering inherent in detention and that, given the practical demands of imprisonment, her health and well-being are adequately secured by, among other things, providing her with the requisite medical assistance (see, *mutatis mutandis*, *Aerts v. Belgium*, judgment of 30 July 1998, *Reports* 1998-V, p. 1966, §§ 64 et seq., and *Kudła v. Poland* [GC], no. 30210/96, § 94, ECHR 2000-XI)" (*Application no. 50390/99*, Judgement of 29 April 2003, para. 46).

Like in the universal system of the UN and in the European regional system, in the *American regional system* too, the jurisprudence of the Inter-American Court of Human Rights (I/ACHR) in the frame of the American Convention of Human Rights, of 22 November 1969, has contributed to the interpretation and systematization of the rights envisaged in it. With regard to victims, it is a case, for example, of its interpretation and development of the *right of access to justice* according to which the right to justice is limited not only to the formal institution of domestic proceedings, but also involves the assurance within reasonable time of the right of alleged victims or their relatives to have every necessary step taken to know the truth and punish those responsible for the events.[112] Moreover, the I/ACHR concludes that the access to justice is a peremptory norm of international law (*jus cogens*).[113]

It is also a case of its interpretation of the States' *duty to investigate* human rights violations of the American Convention *and to prosecute and punish* those responsible; duty closely linked both to the rights of victims of such violations, or their relatives, to be heard and to participate in the procedures (with the view of clearing up of the facts and the punishment of those responsible as well as with the view of obtaining reparation) and to the right to a prompt remedy or to any effective remedy before the competent judges or courts.

Last but not least, with regard to the *scope* that *Article 63, paragraph 1* of the American Convention recognizes as the right of victims of violations of it[114] the I/ACHR has underlined several conclusions. On the one hand, it has stated that it is a principle of international law, which jurisprudence has considered "even a general concept of law," that every violation of an international obligation which results in harm creates a duty to make adequate reparation.[115] On the other hand, the I/ACHR has also specified the content reparation has its modalities as well as the damages to be repaired. Third, it has also declared the inadmissibility of all amnesty provisions, provisions on prescription as well as the establishment of measures designed to eliminate responsibility "because they are intended to prevent the investigation and punishment of those responsible for serious human rights violations such as torture, extrajudicial, summary or arbitrary execution and forced disappearance, all of them prohibited because they violate non-derogable rights recognized by international

[112] Cf. ICHR, I/A Court H.R., *Case of La Cantuta v. Peru.* Merits, Reparations and Costs. Judgement of November 29, 2006, Series C No. 162, para. 149.

[113] Cf. *ibid.*, para. 160.

[114] It states: "1. If the Court finds that there has been a violation of a right or freedom protected by this Convention, the Court shall rule that the injured party be ensured the enjoyment of his right or freedom that was violated. It shall also rule, if appropriate, that the consequences of the measure or situation that constituted the breach of such right or freedom be remedied and that fair compensation be paid to the injured party."

[115] I/A Court H.R., *Case of Velásquez-Rodríguez v. Honduras*. Reparations and Costs. Judgement of July 21, 1989. Series C No. 7, para. 25.

human rights law".[116] Moreover, the I/ACHR has stated that certain violations of human rights like extrajudicial executions and forced disappearances are *crimes against humanity* "that cannot go unpunished, are non-extinguishable and cannot be the subject-matter of amnesty".[117]

They Are Rights That Are Interrelated and That Have Links Between Each Other

At least, before analysing the catalogue of rights that are part of the international legal statute of victims, I would like to underline the existence of links between the different rights. It is a link that has been pointed out by the different international treaty bodies on human rights through their interpretation of the treaties over which they have competence. Such an appointment has been done both on the occasion of the application of the treaty to the concrete case and on the occasion of the Observations and General Comments that such international treaty bodies belonging to the UN system of protection of human rights make with regard to their respective treaties.[118]

This fact should not be a surprise because most of the rights of the different categories of victims that international norms recognize are, as I have highlighted, rights that international treaties on human rights recognize as due "to everyone" and that are based on the human being's dignity. But the international treaty bodies do not only underline the links existing between the different rights and highlight that most of them are entwined but also draw the conclusion from this fact that the violation of a certain right entails that of other rights to which the first is linked.

Without pretensions of completeness because in the next pages, I will discuss the catalogue of rights that constitutes part of the international legal statute of victims, here I will only quote some examples of the links I have just mentioned. It is a case of the links underlined by the international treaty bodies on human rights between *the right of effective access to justice, the right of investigation and the right to reparation*. According to this interpretation, the right of effective access to the law and to justice entails the right of access to competent courts, through effective remedies, to bring an action to attack the violation the victim has suffered. However, the effective character of the remedies at the disposal of the victim is in turn closely linked to the effectiveness of the investigation carried out with regard to the factual origin of the concerned violation. Yes, it is evident that without an efficient investigation of such facts (at the same time such an attitude would also give place

[116] So in the *Case of Barrios Altos v. Peru*, Judgement of 14 March 2001, para. 41 (cf. I/A Court H. R. *Case of Barrios Altos v. Peru*, Merits. Judgment March 14, 2001. Series C No. 75, para. 41).

[117] So in the *Case of La Cantuta v. Peru*. Merits, Reparations and Costs. Judgement of November 29, 2006 ((I/A Court H.R., Series C No. 162, para. 225).

[118] Related to Spain, see Fernández de Casadevante Romani (2010).

to the violation of the obligation of investigation on the charge of State) both the right to effective access to justice and the right of victims to reparation would also be violated. In the first case, that is the right to effective access to justice, because access to justice in such conditions would neither be useful nor be effective. Moreover, as a consequence of the absence of an effective investigation the existent remedies at the disposal of the victim to attack the concerned violation would not be effective either. In such a situation, the right of victims to reparation would also be violated because without a prompt and effective investigation there is no place for reparation.[119]

As in the case of the right to effective access to law and justice in the case of the right to administration of justice—that is the right to a fair and public hearing within a reasonable time by an independent and impartial tribunal established by law—the requirement to obtain a judgement of a competent court "within a reasonable time" derives from the human right to a fair trial. Consequently, its violation entails that of the other.

A third example of the links I refer to here is that existing between the *right to the protection of the dignity and security of victims and the right to effective access to law and justice*, particularly in the different steps of the judicial proceeding in which it takes place. Here, the charge is on the States for the adoption of measures for protection of the identity of the victim, ensuring a specific treatment to victims who are particularly vulnerable or protecting them when they have the status of witnesses to the proceedings.

The *right to information* is also linked *to the right to effective access to law and justice*. With regard to victims, the right to information does not have the wide content it has in international treaties on human rights concretized in the freedom of expression and in the freedom to hold ideas and opinions and to receive and impart information and ideas without interference by public authority and regardless of frontiers. No, with regard to victims, the right to information concerns the proceedings. That is the obligation on the charge of the State to inform victims of every question related to the proceedings, about the state of investigations, the way victims can benefit from legal aid, the final decision concerning prosecution, the court's sentence, the date and place of the hearings, the conditions under which victims may acquaint themselves with the decisions handed down, the moment in which the person sentenced for the offence is released, etc.

With regard to the different categories of victims, the right to information is also concretized in the obligation on the charge of State to set up appropriate contact points for the victims, concerning their rights in particular, the existence of victims

[119] Such a construction is present in the jurisprudence both of the ECHR and of the I/ACHR. See 137 et seq. of the present work.

support bodies, the possibility of obtaining assistance, practical and legal advice as well as redress or compensation.[120]

In the case of enforced disappearances, the right to information implies in certain circumstances the right of the relatives of an enforced person to be informed by the State about the investigations and about the whereabouts of the concerned victim.

Last but not least and without pretending to exhaust all the examples present, a last example can be quoted. It is a case of the links existing between *the right to truth and the obligation on the charge of States to manage effective investigations* of gross violations of international human rights and of serious violations of international humanitarian law as well as with State's obligation to ensure effective remedies and redress. At the same time, the right to truth is related to the rule of law and the principles of transparency, responsibility, and good management of public affairs in a democratic society, as well as with the right to an effective remedy, the right to legal and judicial protection, the right to family life, the right to an effective investigation, the right to be heard by a competent, independent and impartial court, the right to reparation, the freedom of expression (which includes the right to obtain and to impart information),[121] the right to memory (which is linked to the right to dignity), as well as to the right to the protection of private and family life (which is linked to the right to an effective remedy that victims can exercise when their right to private and family life has been violated).

References

Abbot KW, Snidal D (2000) Hard and soft law in International Governance. Int Organ 54 (3):421–456

Amerasinghe CF (1994) Interpretation of texts in Open International Organizations. Br Yearb Int Law:175

Barberis J (1994) Formación del derecho internacional, ed. Abaco de Rodolfo De Palma, Buenos Aires

Blokker N (1999) Decisions of international organizations: the case of the european union. NY Int Law XXX:45

Bottigliero I (2004) Redress for victims of crimes under international law. M. Nijhoff, Leiden

Carrillo Salcedo JA (1993) Algunas Reflexiones sobre el valor jurídico de la Declaración Universal de Derechos Humanos. In the collective work, Hacia un nuevo orden internacional y europeo. Homenaje al Profesor M. Díez de Velasco, Tecnos, Madrid

Castañeda J (1970-I) Valeur juridique des résolutions des Nations Unies. HR 129:171

Fernández de Casadevante Romani C (coord.) (2010) España y los órganos internacionales de control en materia de derechos humanos

Fernández de Casadevante Romani C (dir) (2011) Derecho Internacional de los Derechos Humanos

[120] International norms on victims recognize the right of victims not to receive such information unless such communication thereof is compulsory under the terms of the relevant criminal proceedings. See 194 et seq. of the present work.

[121] See *in extenso* 239 et seq. of the present work.

IIL (1987) Yearbook of the Institute of International Law vol. 62-II
Jacque JP (388) Acte et norme en Droit International Public. R des C 227:388
Jiménez de Aréchaga E (1978-I) General course in public international law. HR 159:31
Kiss A Ch (1988) Le rôle de la Déclaration universelle des droits de l'homme dans le développement du droit international. Bulletin des Droits de l'Homme, éd spéciale, Nations Unies, New York
Maluwa T (2000) International law-making in the organization of African unity: an overview. Rev Afr DI Comp 12(2):201
Roucunas E (1987-VI) Engagements parallèles et contradictoire. R des C VI 206:9
Sepulveda C (1990) Methods and procedures for the creation of legal norms in the international system of states: an inquiry into the progressive development of international law in the present era. German Yearb Int Law 33:444
Tomuschat C (2007) Reparation in favour of individual victims of gross violations of human rights and international humanitarian law. In the collective work, Promoting justice, human rights and conflict resolution through international law. Liber Amicorum Lucius Caflish, p 572.
Tomuschat C (2009) La protection internationale des droits des victimes. In: Flauss J-F (ed) La protection internationale des droits de l'homme et les droits des victimes, p 11
Vallat FA (1959-II) The competence of the United Nations General Assembly. R des C 97:225
Virally M (1984) Résolution et Accord International, in the collective work Essays in International Law in Honour of Judge Manfred Lachs. Nijhoff, The Hague
Zappalá S (2009) The rights of victims of terrorism: the teaching of international law. In: the collective work, Flauss J-F (ed) La protection internationale des droits de l'homme et les droits des victimes. Bruylant, Bruxelles

The Catalogue of Rights Afforded to Victims by International Norms

Right of Emergency Assistance

In contrast to other rights found in the international norms related to the different categories of victims, which are as stated earlier, rights still in force in the international law of human rights, both the right of emergency assistance and the right of continuing assistance (which I will analyze later) are rights closely linked with the condition of being a victim. This is why they are not present in international treaties on human rights. This is why, too, they are present in international norms on victims.

This is a case of *norms of a universal or general character* like the *Declaration of Basic Principles of Justice for Victims of Crime and Abuse of Power* adopted on 29 November 1985 by the General Assembly Resolution 40/34. With regard to the question I am treating now, it refers to the material, medical, psychological and social assistance victims may receive, but it does not distinguish between the types of assistance. It states in paragraphs Nr. 14 and 15 related to "assistance":

> 14. Victims should receive the necessary material, medical, psychological and social assistance through governmental, voluntary, community-based and indigenous means.
>
> 15. Victims should be informed of the availability of health and social services and other relevant assistance and be readily afforded access to them.[1]

In the *European regional system*, the right to emergency assistance—related to crime victims—is formulated in paragraph 4 of Recommendation No. R (87) 21

[1] And paragraph Nr. 17 adds: "17. In providing services and assistance to victims, attention should be given to those who have special needs because of the nature of the harm inflicted or because of factors such as those mentioned in paragraph 3 above." Paragraph 3 is related to non-discrimination: "3. The provisions contained herein shall be applicable to all, without distinction of any kind, such as race, colour, sex, age, language, religion, nationality, political or other opinion, cultural beliefs or practices, property, birth or family status, ethnic or social origin, and disability".

C. Fernández de Casadevante Romani, *International Law of Victims*,
DOI 10.1007/978-3-642-28140-2_6, © Springer-Verlag Berlin Heidelberg 2012

On Assistance to Victims and the Prevention of Victimisation adopted by the Committee of Ministers on 17 September 1987. In this paragraph, the Committee of Ministers recommends that the governments of Member States "ensure that victims and their families, especially those who are most vulnerable, receive in particular: emergency help to meet immediate needs, including protection against retaliation by the offender".[2] This recommendation was brought up and substituted in 2006 by Recommendation (2006) 8 *On Assistance to Crime Victims* adopted by the Committee of Ministers on 14 June 2006.[3] On point 3.1, this Recommendation underlines that States "should identify and support measures to alleviate the negative effects of crime and to undertake that victims are assisted in all aspects of their rehabilitation, in the community, at home and in the workplace". Later, point 3.2, states:

> The assistance available should include the provision of medical care, material support and psychological health services as well as social care and counselling. These services should be provided free of charge at least in the immediate aftermath of the crime.

With regard to *victims of terrorism*, the right of *emergency assistance* is drawn up in the *Guidelines on the Protection of Victims of Terrorist Acts* adopted by the Committee of Ministers on 2 March 2005:

> In order to cover the immediate needs of the victims, states should ensure that appropriate (medical, psychological, social and material) emergency assistance is available free of charge to victims of terrorist acts; they should also facilitate access to spiritual assistance for victims at their request.[4]

Last but not least, the right to medical assistance is also founded on the jurisprudence of the ECHR; jurisprudence binding the 47 Member States of the Council of Europe. Although this jurisprudence is related to violations of the European Convention for the Protection of Human Rights and Fundamental Freedoms of 4 November 1950 attributed to States Parties what is important of it is that it states the obligations on the charge of States Parties; violations too engaging the international responsibility of the State. But the importance of this

---

[2] This Recommendation completes both the European Convention on the Compensation of Victims of Violent Crimes, of 24 November 1983, and Recommendation No. R (85) 11 *On the Position of the Victim in the Framework of Criminal Law and Procedure* (see both in Conseil de l'Europe, *Soutien et aide aux victimes*, 2006, 9 et seq., 181 et seq. and 185 et seq.). In Spanish in Fernández de Casadevante Romani C, Mayordomo Rodrigo V (2011) *Código de normas internacionales relativas a las víctimas*, Tecnos, Madrid.

[3] The aim of this Recommendation is to update Recommendation No. R (87) 21 *On Assistance to victims and the Prevention of victimisation* in the line of the "significant developments have occurred in the field of assistance to victims including developments in national legislation and practice, a better understanding of the victims' needs and new research". Also, to aid Member States to prevent repeat victimization in particular for victims belonging to vulnerable groups. At least, to guide Member States in their internal legislation and practice by the principles set out in the appendix to this recommendation.

[4] On point II.

jurisprudence grows because European international norms on victims take this jurisprudence into account. This is a case of the *Guidelines on the Protection of Victims of Terrorist Acts* adopted by the Committee of Ministers on 2 March 2005, which bases the right to medical assistance on Article 2 (right to life) and on Article 3 (prohibition of torture) of the European Convention for the Protection of Human Rights and Fundamental Freedoms of 4 November 1950 as it is interpreted by the ECHR. For example, the case of the Judgement of the ECHR of 10 May 2001 in *Case Cyprus v. Turkey* in which with regard to Article 2 the ECHR states:

> 219. The Court observes that an issue may arise under Article 2 of the Convention where it is shown that the authorities of a Contracting State put an individual's life at risk through the denial of health care which they have undertaken to make available to the population generally. It notes in this connection that Article 2 § 1 of the Convention enjoins the State not only to refrain from the intentional and unlawful taking of life, but also to take appropriate steps to safeguard the lives of those within its jurisdiction (see the *L.C.B. v. the United Kingdom* judgment of 9 June 1998, *Reports* 1998-III, p. 1403, § 36).[5]

As underlined by the Committee of Ministers in its *Guidelines on the Protection of Victims of Terrorist Acts*, the European Commission of Human Rights also recognized the existence of a positive obligation deriving from Article 3 of the Convention according to which States are obliged under certain particular circumstances to give immediate medical treatment. The Guidelines quote, as an example, the case *Hurtado v. Switzerland* where the Commission unanimously expressed the view that Article 3 of the Convention had been violated, in particular inasmuch as the applicant was not examined by a doctor until 8 days after his arrest.[6]

[5] ECHR, Judgement of 10 May 2001, par. 219. This jurisprudence of Article 2 is repeated in the *case Berktay v. Turkey*, Judgement of the 1st March 2001 (on par. 154) as well as in the decision on admissibility in the case *Nitecki v. Poland*, Judgement of 21 March 2002 (application No. 65653/01). The existence of a positive obligation deriving from Article 3 had been recognized earlier by the European Commission of Human Rights. According to it, States have under certain particular circumstances the obligation to give immediate medical treatment.

[6] This case did not arrive at the ECHR because of the friendly settlement concluded between the Government of Switzerland and the applicant. Consequently, the Court decided to strike the case out of the list by Judgement of 28 January 1994.

Another example is the case *McGlinchey v. United Kingdom*, Judgement of 29 April 2003. This case is related to the conditions of imprisonment of an individual. According to the interpretation of the ECHR, under Article 3 the State "must ensure that a person is detained in conditions which are compatible with respect for her human dignity, that the manner and method of the execution of the measure do not subject her to distress or hardship of an intensity exceeding the unavoidable level of suffering inherent in detention and that, given the practical demands of imprisonment, her health and well-being are adequately secured by, among other things, providing her with the requisite medical assistance (see, *mutatis mutandis*, *Aerts v. Belgium*, judgment of 30 July 1998, *Reports* 1998-V, p. 1966, §§ 64 et seq., and *Kudła v. Poland* [GC], no. 30210/96, § 94, ECHR 2000-XI)" (para. 46).

Right of Continuing Assistance

The right of continuing assistance is another of the fundamental rights of victims whose effectiveness should be guaranteed.[7]

As we have seen, *in the frame of the UN* point 14 of the *Declaration of Basic Principles of Justice for Victims of Crime and Abuse of Power* adopted by the General Assembly resolution 40/34 of 29 November 1985, refers in general to material, medical, psychological and social assistance that victims of crime and victims of abuse of power shall receive.[8]

Outside the universal system, it is in the *European regional system* where this right has been drawn up and widely developed with regard to both victims of crime and, more recently, victims of terrorism. With regard to the first, this right is drawn up in paragraph 4 of Recommendation No. R (87) 21 of the Committee of Ministers of the Council of Europe of 17 September 1987 on *Assistance to Victims and the Prevention of Victimisation*[9], which recommends that governments of Member states ensure "that victims and their families, especially those who are most vulnerable, receive in particular (. . .) continuing medical, psychological, social and material help".

This Recommendation, as said, was updated and substituted by Recommendation No. R (2006) 8 of the Committee of Ministers of the Council of Europe of 14 June 2006 on *Assistance to Crime Victims*, which in points Nr. 3.1 and 3.2 states:

> 3.1. States should identify and support measures to alleviate the negative effects of crime and to undertake that victims are assisted in all aspects of their rehabilitation, in the community, at home and in the workplace.
>
> 3.2. The assistance available should include the provision of medical care, material support and psychological health services as well as social care and counselling. These services should be provided free of charge at least in the immediate aftermath of the crime.

This same Recommendation, in the point related to assistance of victims, adds that victims should be protected as far as possible from secondary victimization

---

[7] Cf. Sanz Hermida, *op. cit.*, 69 et seq.

[8] Without relationship with victims, Article 12 of the *International Covenant on Economic, Social and Cultural Rights* of 16 December 1966 recognizes the more general right of everyone to the enjoyment of the highest attainable standard of physical and mental health. According to it: "1. The States Parties to the present Covenant recognize the right of everyone to the enjoyment of the highest attainable standard of physical and mental health. 2. The steps to be taken by the States Parties to the present Covenant to achieve the full realization of this right shall include those necessary for: (a) The provision for the reduction of the stillbirth-rate and of infant mortality and for the healthy development of the child; (b) The improvement of all aspects of environmental and industrial hygiene; (c) The prevention, treatment and control of epidemic, endemic, occupational and other diseases; (d) The creation of conditions which would assure to all medical service and medical attention in the event of sickness."

[9] Without relationship with victims, the *European Social Charter* envisages the right to social and medical assistance (on Article 11) as well as the right to benefit from social welfare services (on Article 14). Despite its general character, the Committee of Ministers quote it in its *Guidelines on the Protection of Victims of Terrorist Acts* to support on it the right of victims to continuing assistance.

(point Nr. 3.3). But States should also ensure that victims who are particularly vulnerable, "either through their personal characteristics or through the circumstances of the crime", can benefit from special measures best suited to their situation. Finally point Nr. 3.5 it states that wherever possible, assistance should be provided in a language understood by the victim.

Related to the right of continuing assistance, point Nr. 5 of Recommendation No. R (2006) 8 envisages victim support services and encourages States both to provide or promote dedicated services for the support of victims and to encourage the work of non-governmental organizations in assisting victims (point Nr. 5.1).

According to point Nr. 5.2, such services should be easily accessible. It should also provide victims with free emotional, social and material support before, during and after the investigation and legal proceedings; be fully competent to deal with the problems faced by the victims they serve; provide victims with information on their rights and on the services available; refer victims to other services when necessary; and respect confidentiality when providing services.

With regard to victim support services, points Nr. 5.3 and 5.4 of Recommendation No. R (2006) 8 encourage States both to support the setting up or the maintenance of specialized centres for victims of crimes such as sexual and domestic violence and to facilitate access to these centres and to consider it necessary to encourage the establishment or maintenance of specialized centres for victims of crimes of mass victimization, including terrorism (point Nr. 5.5).

Last but not least, for the coordination of services for victims, it asks States to take steps to ensure that the work of services offering assistance to victims is coordinated and that a comprehensive range of services is available and accessible. Also, that standard of good practice for services offering help to victims are prepared and maintained, that appropriate training is provided and coordinated and that services are accessible to the government for consultation on proposed policies and legislation. To achieve it, the required coordination could be provided by a single national organization or by some other means.

With regard to *victims of terrorism*, the *Guidelines on the Protection of Victims of Terrorist Acts* adopted by the Committee of Ministers of the Council of Europe draws up the right of continuing assistance in the following terms:

1. States should provide for appropriate continuing medical, psychological, social and material assistance for victims of terrorist acts.
2. If the victim does not normally reside on the territory of the state where the terrorist act occurred, that state should cooperate with the state of residence in ensuring that the victim receives such assistance.[10]

The Committee of Ministers of the Council of Europe bases this right on the decision of the ECHR in the *case Larioshina v. Russia* of 23 April 2002 by which it declares inadmissible the concrete application. Here, the Court considers that a complaint about a wholly insufficient amount of pension and the other social

---

[10] On Part III, entitled "Continuing assistance".

benefits may, in principle, raise an issue under Article 3 of the Convention, which prohibits inhuman or degrading treatment.[11]

In conclusion, the scope and the extent of the assistance given to victims, which is envisaged by international norms, concern the following types. On the one hand, *legal assistance* to give victims information about the legal facilities offered by the legal order of the concerned State. On the other hand, *integral assistance*, which covers both legal advice, medical attention, psychological attention and other attention needed by victims. Finally, it also covers *specialized assistance* for victims of certain crimes or for certain groups of victims.[12]

Right to Investigation and to Prosecution

In International Law on human rights, there are no doubts about the States' obligation to effectively investigate human rights violations. In this respect, the position of international bodies on the matter is clear as it is shown by the case-law of the Committee of Human Rights and the jurisprudence both of the ECHR and of the Inter-American Court of Human Rights. The analysis of that case-law and jurisprudence shows that this obligation of investigation has a double content. On the one hand, it is a measure of the redress that is due to the victim and to his relatives for the violation committed. On the other hand, it is a preventive measure for future violations.

However, there is no similar consensus on the configuration of punishment as a measure as part of the individual protection of human rights.[13] In other words, while the obligation the States have to investigate violations of human rights is clear and indisputable, it is not so clear that States also have the obligation to prosecute and to punish the perpetrator of the violation as an element that is part of the individual right of the victim to be protected.[14]

---

[11] Because such an insufficiency constitutes an inhuman or degrading treatment. However, on the basis of the material in its possession, the Court finds no indication that the amount of the applicant's pension and the additional social benefits has caused such damage to her physical or mental health capable of attaining the minimum level of severity falling within the ambit of Article 3 of the Convention.

[12] Cf. Sanz Hermida, *op. cit.*, 142–147.

[13] About this question cf. Seibert-Fohr (2009), 189–227.

[14] In International Law on human rights some treaties contain such an obligation, for example, UN *Convention Against Torture and Other Cruel, Inhuman or Degrading Treatment and Punishment* of 10 December 1984. Also, *the Convention for the Protection of All Person from Enforced Disappearance* of 6 February 2007. In the field of institutional norms, the UN *Declaration on the Protection of All Persons from Enforced Disappearance* adopted by A/RES/47/133 of 18 December 1992 and the General Assembly Resolution 60/147 adopted on 16 December 2005 through which the *Basic principles and guidelines of the right to a remedy and reparation for victims of gross violations of international human rights law and serious violations of International Humanitarian Law* adopted by the UN Commission on Human Rights on 19 April 2005 by Resolution 2005/35 were adopted.

However, as underlined by Tomuschat, since the competent international tribunals on human rights (the ECHR and the Inter-American CHR) have embraced the view that in instances of grave attacks against the life, physical integrity and freedom of the victims the duty to protect and ensure human rights entails a duty to punish the responsible perpetrators, "that proposition seems by now to have acquired sufficiently broad foundational stand as a rule of applicable positive law."[15]

On the one hand, the right of investigation and the correspondent obligation on the charge of States to achieve it is drawn up both in international norms on the different categories of victims and in international treaties of human rights. On the other hand, as we have seen in the preceding pages of the present work and like other rights, the right of investigation is also linked with other rights of victims, with the right to justice and with the right to redress, this last, understood in its wide sense: compen sation and other means of redress. As already stated, it is a right that on its reverse has on the charge of the State the obligation to effectively investigate the facts giving place to the violation of the right or to the concrete victimizer act. An investigation, too, that shall fulfil certain characteristics to be in accord with the international standards that international bodies on the protection of human rights require.

With regard to the *international norms related to the different categories of victims*, and in the general or universal frame of the UN, the right of investigation—linked with State's obligation to prosecute—is established in General Assembly Resolution 60/147 of 16 December 2005 through which the *Basic principles and guidelines of the right to a remedy and reparation for victims of gross violations of international human rights law and serious violations of International Humanitarian Law,* adopted before by the UN Commission on Human Rights on 19 April 2005 by Resolution 2005/35 were adopted. Point Nr. II.3, paragraph b) clearly states the obligation on the charge of States to investigate violations. Point Nr. III.4 adds that "if there is sufficient evidence", States also have the duty to submit to prosecution the person allegedly responsible for the violations and, if found guilty, the duty to punish her or him.[16]

---

[15] Tomuschat (2002), 325. In the opinion of this author, the acceptance of a general duty to prosecute authors of grave crimes involved in human rights violations does not solve all the problems "because such a duty to punish is limited to acts and events that have occured under the territorial jurisdiction of the State concerned" (*ibid.*, 326). "That is, where it enjoys the monopoly of employing force. With regard to crimes committed outside their borders, no customary rules involving a duty to act exist" (*ibid.*, 343).

[16] Point Nr. III.4 states: "4. In cases of gross violations of international human rights law and serious violations of international humanitarian law constituting crimes under international law, States have the duty to investigate and, if there is sufficient evidence, the duty to submit to prosecution the person allegedly responsible for the violations and, if found guilty, the duty to punish her or him. Moreover, in these cases, States should, in accordance with international law, cooperate with one another and assist international judicial organs competent in the investigation and prosecution of these violations."

Later, the obligation of investigation—linked with the obligation to punish—is envisaged in Articles 13 and 14 of the *Declaration on the Protection of All Persons from Enforced Disappearance* adopted by the General Assembly of the United Nations in its resolution A/RES/47/133 of 18 December 1992. According to Article 13, paragraph 2, States shall ensure that the competent authority shall have the necessary powers and resources to conduct the investigation effectively, including powers to compel attendance of witnesses and production of relevant documents and to make immediate on-site visits. Article 14 asks States to take any lawful and appropriate action available to them to bring to justice all persons presumed responsible for an act of enforced disappearance, who are found to be within their jurisdiction or under their control.

The UN *International Convention for the Protection of All Persons from Enforced Disappearance* of 20 December 2006 follows the way marked by the preceding Declaration. So, Article 3 obliges States Parties to take appropriate measures to investigate acts of enforced disappearance committed "by persons or groups of persons acting without the authorization, support or acquiescence of the State and to bring those responsible to justice." For the prosecution of this crime, Article 9 obliges States Parties to take the necessary measures to establish its competence to exercise jurisdiction over the offence of enforced disappearance.

At least, in the frame of International Criminal Law (ICC), the *Statute of the International Criminal Court* envisages the Prosecutor as the organ charged with the investigation. It is an organ acting independently as a separated organ of the Court.

The Statute envisages two types of investigation: preliminary investigation (which is the object of Article 15) and specific investigation with the aim of a possible indictment or prosecution of perpetrators of the crimes under the jurisdiction of the Court (which is the object of Article 57).

With regard to the *preliminary investigation*, and according to Article 15.1, the Prosecutor may initiate investigations *proprio motu* on the basis of information on crimes within the jurisdiction of the Court, but it is the Pre-Trial Chamber which authorizes the Prosecutor to commence the investigation. It is the responsibility of the Prosecutor if he concludes that there is a reasonable basis to proceed with an investigation to submit to the Pre-Trial Chamber a request for authorization of an investigation, together with any supporting material collected.

With regard to the *specific investigation* linked with the possible indictment or prosecution of the perpetrators of crimes under the jurisdiction of the Court, and according to Article 53 of the Statute, the Prosecutor—after having evaluated the information made available to him—shall initiate an investigation unless he determines that there is no reasonable basis to proceed under this Statute. If the Prosecutor determines that there is no reasonable basis to proceed, then he shall inform the Pre-Trial Chamber and the State which have referred the situation to him or the Security Council if it has referred the situation to him. Nevertheless, the decision of the Prosecutor not to proceed may be reviewed by the Pre-Trial

Chamber at the request of the State, which has referred the situation to the Prosecutor.[17]

As stated earlier when I have referred to the victims of violations of International Criminal Law, the Statute of the ICC envisages the intervention of victims on the occasion of the preliminary investigation. This intervention takes place when the Pre-Trial Chamber, upon examination of the request and the supporting material (which includes observations presented by victims), considers that there is a reasonable basis to proceed with an investigation and that the case appears to fall within the jurisdiction of the Court. In that case, it shall authorize the commencement of the investigation.[18]

In this context, Rule 50 states that the Prosecutor, when he or she intends to seek authorization from the Pre-Trial Chamber to initiate an investigation pursuant to Article 15, paragraph 3, shall inform the victims, known to him or her or to the Victims and Witnesses Unit, or their legal representatives, "unless the Prosecutor decides that doing so would pose a danger to the integrity of the investigation or the life or well-being of victims and witnesses".[19] That information once given by the Prosecutor to the victims, the victims may make representations in writing to the Pre-Trial Chamber. Victims may also participate when the Pre-Trial Chamber decides on the procedure to be followed because according to Rule 50, paragraph 4, it is at this occasion that the Pre-Trial Chamber may request additional information from the Prosecutor and from any of the victims who have made representations, and, if it considers it appropriate, may hold a hearing.[20]

At least the Pre-Trial Chamber shall issue its decision, including its reasons, as to whether to authorize the commencement of the investigation with respect "to all or any part" of the request by the Prosecutor. Notice of this decision of the Chamber shall be given to victims who have made representations.[21]

With regard to victims, in the *European regional system* the right of investigation and prosecution is drawn up in the *Guidelines on the Protection of Victims of Terrorist Acts* adopted by the Committee of Ministers of the Council of Europe on 2 March 2005. According to it:

1. Where there have been victims of terrorist acts, states must launch an effective official investigation into those acts.
2. In this framework, special attention must be paid to victims without it being necessary for them to have made a formal complaint.
3. In cases where, as a result of an investigation, it is decided not to take action to prosecute a suspected perpetrator of a terrorist act, states should allow victims to ask for this decision to be re-examined by a competent authority.

---

[17] Cf. Article 53. Part V of the Statute concerns investigation and prosecution. With regard to the first, see also Articles 54–57 of the Statute.

[18] Cf. Article 15, paragraph 3.

[19] Rule 50 of the Rules of Procedure and Evidence of the ICC.

[20] Rule 50.4.

[21] Rule 50.5.

Apart from the international norms on victims in *International Law of human rights*, the States' obligation to investigate and to prosecute those responsible for the violations of human rights is implicit, in the UN system, in Article 7 of the *International Covenant on Civil and Political Rights* of 16 December 1966[22] and so it is underlined by the Committee of Human Rights of the Covenant.[23]

The obligation to investigate is drawn up later, but here expressed and linked with the obligation of prosecution, in Article 6, paragraphs 1 and 2 of the UN *Convention Against Torture and Other Cruel, Inhuman or Degrading Treatment and Punishment* of 10 December 1984. While Article 6, paragraph 2 states that States Parties shall immediately make a preliminary inquiry into the facts, Article 6, paragraph 1 obliges States Parties in whose territory a person alleged to have committed any act of torture is present to take the person into custody or to take other legal measures to ensure the person's presence.

In the *European and American regional systems*, the obligation States have to investigate is linked both with the general obligation on the charge of States according to which the rights and freedoms of both conventions shall be *effective* and with the exercise and effectiveness of concrete rights, for example the right to justice and the right to an effective remedy. This is what derives from the jurisprudence both of the ECHR and the Inter-American CHR.[24]

In the *African regional system*, on the contrary, there does not exist any jurisprudence on the matter. It is not strange because the first general international treaty

---

[22] It has been underlined so by the Human Rights Committee in the interpretation it has given of Article 7 of the *International Covenant on Civil and Political Rights* of 16 December 1966 concretely in its General Comment No. 20 on Article 7 (forty-fourth session, 1992) where it stated that complaints must be investigated promptly and impartially by competent authorities so as to make the remedy effective. In the opinion of Ch. Tomuschat, the first case where the Committee went beyond its standard formula is that of *Dermit Barbato*, who died while being imprisoned (cf. Tomuschat (2002), 320 et seq.). In this case, the Committee states Uruguay's obligation not only to take effective steps to establish the facts of Hugo Dermit's death but, too, "to bring to justice any persons found to be responsible for his death and to pay appropriate compensation to his familiy"(cf. Selected Decisions II, 116, para. 11. In the same line, the pronouncements of the Committee in its Views of 24 July 1984 (case *Muteba v. Zaire*, Selected Decisions II, 160, para. 13) and of 4 April 1985 (case *Surinam*, *ibid.*, 176, para. 16).

[23] In the opinion of Tomuschat, it is a firmly settled jurisprudence but related to grave violations of human rights. In the same line, the Committee Against Torture created by the UN Convention Against Torture and Other Cruel, Inhuman or Degrading Treatment and Punishment of 10 December 1984 has declared that national amnesties cannot avoid the duty to prosecute. In this Convention, the duty to prosecute is envisaged in Articles 4–6 (cf. Tomuschat, "The duty to…", *op. cit.*, 323).

[24] In the opinion of Tomuschat, "since the competent international tribunals (ECHR and I/ACHR have also embraced the view that in instances of grave attacks against the life, physical integrity and freedom of the victims the duty to protect entails a duty to punish the responsible perpetrator, that proposition seems by now to have acquired sufficiently broad foundations to stand as a rule of applicable positive law" (*ibid.*, 325).

of human rights in this regional system is very recent.[25] Also both the techniques and the organs of control have a very different configuration from those existent in the European and American regional systems. So, for example, Article 55 paragraph 1 of the *African Charter on Human and People's Rights* speaks of "communications other than those of States Parties" to the Charter but it does not define them. In the same line, another example can be quoted. It is the African Commission on Human and People's Rights which indicates the individual communications that should be considered by the Commission. Another example is also the fact that until recently no international tribunal on the matter existed in this regional system. This gap was covered by the Protocol of 10 June 1998 creating the *African Court on Human and People's Rights*.[26]

Right to an Official Effective Investigation

The obligation of investigation once stated, the different international norms on victims and on human rights specify the characteristics an investigation shall fulfil to be consistent with international standards. It shall be prompt, rapid, effective, exhaustive and impartial.

With regard to victims, such standards have been underlined in the *general or universal system of the UN* by the General Assembly Resolution 60/147 adopted on 16 December 2005 through which the *Basic principles and guidelines of the right to a remedy and reparation for victims of gross violations of international human rights law and serious violations of International Humanitarian Law* adopted by the UN Commission on Human Rights on 19 April 2005, by Resolution 2005/35, have been adopted. According to point Nr. II.3, paragraph b) of it, investigation shall be effective, prompt, thorough and impartial[27] and on point Nr. III.4 other duties such as those concerning the duty to submit to prosecution the person allegedly responsible for the violations and, if found guilty, the duty to punish her or him are added to the duty of investigation.[28]

---

[25] The African Charter of Human and People's Rights was approved on 27 July 1981. Into force: the 21 October 1986. I say "general" because it contains a general catalogue of rights and freedoms.

[26] It entered into force on 20 January 2004. It is actually ratified by 26 States. About the African regional system vid. Heins and Killander (2009), 858–898; Mutua (2009), 899–924, respectively. Also my Chapter "El sistema regional africano", in *Derecho Internacional de los Derechos Humanos*, *op. cit.*, 277 et seq.

[27] According to it, States shall: "(*b*) Investigate violations effectively, promptly, thoroughly and impartially and, where appropriate, take action against those allegedly responsible in accordance with domestic and international law".

[28] Point Nr. III.4 states: "4. In cases of gross violations of international human rights law and serious violations of international humanitarian law constituting crimes under international law, States have the duty to investigate and, if there is sufficient evidence, the duty to submit to prosecution the person allegedly responsible for the violations and, if found guilty, the duty to punish her or him. Moreover, in these cases, States should, in accordance with international law,

Similar statements are present with regard to victims of enforced disappearance both in the *Declaration on the Protection of All Persons from Enforced Disappearance* adopted by the General Assembly of the United Nations in its resolution A/RES/47/133 of 18 December 1992 and in the *International Convention for the Protection of All Persons from Enforced Disappearance* of 20 December 2006 adopted by resolution A/RES/61/177 of the General Assembly. The first in Article 13 states that investigation shall be exhaustive and impartial; obligation which exists until the fate of the victim of enforced disappearance remains unclarified.[29] The second follows its trail and in Article 12, paragraph 2, specifies that investigation shall be "exhaustive and impartial"; duty which persists "even if there has been no formal complaint" where there are reasonable grounds for believing that a person has been subjected to enforced disappearance.[30]

With regard to *victims of violations of International Criminal Law*, as we have seen, the Statute of the ICC shapes the Prosecutor as the organ charged with the investigation. So, in contrast to other international norms both on victims and on International Law of human rights, the Statute of the ICC—an international treaty—does not impose upon States a duty of investigation on the charge of States under the control or under the jurisdiction of which the criminal fact under the jurisdiction of the ICC has been committed but gives the competence to the Prosecutor as an independent and separate organ of the Court. In other words, in

cooperate with one another and assist international judicial organs competent in the investigation and prosecution of these violations."

[29] Article 13 states: "1. Each State shall ensure that any person having knowledge or a legitimate interest who alleges that a person has been subjected to enforced disappearance has the right to complain to a competent and independent State authority and to have that complaint promptly, thoroughly and impartially investigated by that authority. Whenever there are reasonable grounds to believe that an enforced disappearance has been committed, the State shall promptly refer the matter to that authority for such an investigation, even if there has been no formal complaint. No measure shall be taken to curtail or impede the investigation. 2. Each State shall ensure that the competent authority shall have the necessary powers and resources to conduct the investigation effectively, including powers to compel attendance of witnesses and production of relevant documents and to make immediate on-site visits. 3. Steps shall be taken to ensure that all involved in the investigation, including the complainant, counsel, witnesses and those conducting the investigation, are protected against ill-treatment, intimidation or reprisal. 4. The findings of such an investigation shall be made available upon request to all persons concerned, unless doing so would jeopardize an ongoing criminal investigation. 5. Steps shall be taken to ensure that any ill-treatment, intimidation or reprisal or any other form of interference on the occasion of the lodging of a complaint or during the investigation procedure is appropriately punished. 6. An investigation, in accordance with the procedures described above, should be able to be conducted for as long as the fate of the victim of enforced disappearance remains un-clarified."

[30] And Article 24, paragraph 6 adds: "6. Without prejudice to the obligation to continue the investigation until the fate of the disappeared person has been clarified, each State Party shall take appropriate steps with regard to the legal situation of disappeared persons whose fate has not been clarified and that of their relatives, in fields such as social welfare, financial matters, family law and property rights".

the Statute the investigation takes place in the context of judicial procedures and by judicial organs.

This is why in the Statute there are no references to the characteristics of the investigation. In effect, the ICC being an independent international judicial organ not linked with any State, it is presupposed that both the preliminary investigation (of Article 15, paragraph 3) and specific investigation with the aim of a possible indictment or prosecution of perpetrators of crimes under the jurisdiction of the Court (of Article 57) will be developed according to the required international standards of impartiality, promptness, effectiveness and exhaustiveness.

In the conventional field of *international treaties on human rights* and inside the UN system, the duty to investigate is implicit on Article 7 of the *International Covenant on Civil and Political Rights* of 16 December 1966[31], and it has been underlined so by the Human Rights Committee in the interpretation of that article in its General Observation No. 20 (Forty-fourth session, 1992), where it stated that complaints must be investigated promptly and impartially by competent authorities so as to make the remedy effective.[32] If not, the right to a remedy lacks effectiveness and gives place to another violation of the Covenant. It is a violation which is independent of the violation of the duty to investigate.

As examples of it, one can quote the statements of the *Human Rights Committee* in *Rodriguez v. Uruguay*[33]and in *Blanco v. Nicaragua*[34] where it specifies that the obligation States have to investigate falls under the State Party's obligation to grant an effective remedy circumstance, which is lacking when allegations of human rights violations fail to be investigated promptly and impartially by competent authorities. In the same line, the Human Rights Committee holds that "purely disciplinary and administrative remedies cannot be deemed to constitute adequate and effective remedies within the meaning of Article 2(3), of the Covenant, in the event of particularly serious violations of human rights, notably in the event of an alleged violation of the right to life".[35]

With regard to amnesties that some States have granted in respect of acts of torture the Human Rights Committee has stressed that such amnesties are incompatible with the duty of States to investigate and that they affect victims' right to a remedy. This Committee states that:

> Amnesties are generally incompatible with the duty of States to investigate such acts; to guarantee freedom from such acts within their jurisdiction; and to ensure that they do not

[31] Which states: "No one shall be subjected to torture or to cruel, inhuman or degrading treatment or punishment. In particular, no one shall be subjected without his free consent to medical or scientific experimentation."

[32] Cf. ONU, HRI/GEN/1/Rev. 7, 161, para. 14.

[33] Cf. Comm. No. 322/1988, CCPR/C/51/D/322/1988, U.N. GAOR, Hum. Rts. Comm., U.N. Doc. CCPR/C/51/D/322/1988, paras 12.3 and 12.4 (1994).

[34] Comm. No. 328/1988, CCPR/C/51/D/328/1988.

[35] Cf. *Bautista de Arellana v. Colombia*, Comm. No. 563/1993, U.N. GAOR, Hum. Rts. Comm., U.N. Doc. CCPR/C/55/D/563/1993, para. 10.

> occur in the future. States may not deprive individuals of the right to an effective remedy, including compensation and such full rehabilitation as may be possible.[36]

As already stated, the UN *Convention Against Torture and Other Cruel, Inhuman or Degrading Treatment and Punishment* of 10 December 1984 also envisages the right to an effective investigation. Moreover, here this obligation is a consequence of the more wide duty that States have "to establish its jurisdiction" over the offences of torture, over all attempt to commit torture and over an act by any person which constitutes complicity or participation in torture.[37] This is why article 6, paragraph 2, establishes upon States Parties the obligation to "immediately make a preliminary inquiry into the facts"; an obligation that is completed with the other imposed by Article 6, paragraph 4, according to which the State, which makes the preliminary inquiry, shall promptly report its findings to the said States and shall indicate whether it intends to exercise jurisdiction.

In the *European regional system*, the obligation on the charge of States to open an effective official investigation when a terrorist act has caused victims is foreseen in the *Guidelines on the Protection of Victims of Terrorist Acts* adopted by the Committee of Ministers of the Council of Europe on 2 March 2005,[38] which bases it upon the jurisprudence of the ECHR. As a concrete instance the *case Ulku Ekinci v. Turkey*, Judgement of 16 July 2002 where the Court held that an official investigation must be launched when individuals have been killed as a result of the use of force and that this obligation is not confined to cases where it has been established that the killing was caused by an agent of the State. In this case, the ECHR recalled that according to its jurisprudence, the obligation to protect the right to life under Article 2, read in conjunction with the State's general duty under Article 1 to secure to everyone within its jurisdiction the rights and freedoms defined in the Convention, requires by implication:

> 144 ... that there should be some form of effective official investigation when individuals have been killed as a result of the use of force. This obligation is not confined to cases where it has been established that the killing was caused by an agent of the State. Nor is it decisive whether members of the deceased's family or others have lodged a formal complaint about the killing with the competent investigation authority. The mere fact that the authorities were informed of the killing of the applicant's husband gave rise *ipso facto* to an obligation under Article 2 of the Convention to carry out an effective investigation into the circumstances surrounding the death (cf. *Tanrıkulu v. Turkey* [GC], no. 23763/94, §§ 101 and 103, ECHR 1999-IV). The nature and degree of scrutiny which satisfies the minimum threshold of an investigation's effectiveness depends on the circumstances of each particular case. It must be assessed on the basis of all relevant facts and with regard to the practical realities of investigation work (cf. *Velikova v. Bulgaria*, no. 41488/98, § 80, ECHR 2000-VI).[39]

---

[36] General Comment No. 20 (forty-fourth session, 1992), ONU, HRI/GEN/1/Rev. 7, 161, para. 15.

[37] Cf. Articles 4 and 5.

[38] Which say: "1. Where there have been victims of terrorist acts, states must launch an effective official investigation into those acts."

[39] ECHR, Judgement of 16 July 2002, para. 144.

Also in *case Tepe v. Turkey* where the ECHR states that:

> due to the fundamental importance of the right to the protection of human life, article 13—of the European Convention on human rights and fundamental freedoms—demands not only the payment of a compensation where appropriate, but also a meticulous and effective investigation aimed at leading to the identification and punishment of those responsible for having deprived someone of life, including an effective access of the applicant to the investigation procedure (vid. *Kaya*,. . ., pp. 330–31, para. 107).[40]

Therefore, the State's duty to launch an effective investigation is linked to Article 2 of the Convention which implies and requires it to carry out an effective investigation when the use of force has led to the death of a man:

> The obligation to protect the right to life under article 2 of the Convention, combined with the general duty which is incumbent on the State by virtue of article 1 of the Convention "to recognize any person under their jurisdiction the rights and freedoms defined in the Convention", implies and requires to carry out an effective investigation when the use of force has led to the death of a man (see, *mutatus mutandis*, the judgements McCann and Others. . ., p. 48, para. 161 and Kaya just quoted, p. 324, para 86).[41]

But the ECHR does not limit itself to affirm the right of the victim to an effective investigation including the effective access of the applicant to the procedure of investigation but it has also specified that the investigation must fulfil the following characteristics: it must be prompt, diligent, complete and it should lead to the identification, arrest and punishment of those responsible. So, for example, in the *case Finucane v. United Kingdom*:

> 70. A requirement of promptness and reasonable expedition is implicit in this context (see *Yaşa v. Turkey*, judgment of 2 September 1998, *Reports* 1998-VI, pp. 2439-40, §§ 102-04; *Çakıcı v. Turkey* [GC], no. 23657/94, §§ 80, 87 and 106, ECHR 1999-IV; *Tanrıkulu*, cited above, § 109; and *Mahmut Kaya v. Turkey*, no. 22535/93, §§ 106-07, ECHR 2000-III). While there may be obstacles or difficulties which prevent progress in an investigation in a particular situation, a prompt response by the authorities in investigating a use of lethal force may generally be regarded as essential in maintaining public confidence in their adherence to the rule of law and in preventing any appearance of collusion in or tolerance of unlawful acts (see, for example, *Hugh Jordan*, cited above, §§ 108, 136-40).[42]

On the other hand, the lack of an effective investigation has effects on the prescription of the offence. In such situations, the ECHR "cannot accept that an

---

[40] ECHR, Judgement of 9 May 2003, para. 195. The original is in French. The translation to English is mine. When no effective criminal investigation can be considered to have been carried out in accordance with Article 13 the ECHR finds that any other remedies, including a claim for damages, "are theoretical and illusory, and not capable of affording redress to the applicant" (*Case Carabulea v. Romania*, Judgement of 13 July 2010, para. 166).

[41] *Case Yasa v. Turkey*, Judgement of 2 September 1998, para. 98.

[42] ECHR, Judgement of the 1st July 2003, para. 70. Cf. also *Case Association 21 December 1989 and Others v. Romania (GC)*, Judgement of 24 May 2011, para. 133; *Case McKerr v. United Kingdom*, Judgement of 4 May 2001, para. 121 and *Case Yasa v. Turkey*, Judgement of 2 September 1998, para. 74.

investigation is effective when the same effect is the prescription of criminal liability, when the authorities have remained inactive." (*Case Association 21 December 1989 and Others v. Romania (GC)*, Judgement of 24 May 2011). That is, such a prescription is null and void and without effect.[43]

Linked to the right to life, the State's obligation to investigate effectively does not allow exceptions or derogations. Consequently, the State may not invoke shortcomings or deficiencies of any kind to justify the lack of invesigation or that the practiced investigation has been poor or inadequate.[44]

Finally, it is said that the ECHR does not have an independent right to have third parties prosecuted or sentenced for a criminal offence. On the contrary, the Court states that such a right must be indissociable from the victim's exercise of a right to bring civil proceedings in domestic law, even if only to secure symbolic reparation or to protect a civil right. As a concrete instance, the Great Chamber in the *case Perez v. France*, Judgement of 12 February 2004 quoted by the *Guidelines on the Protection of Victims of Terrorist Acts* adopted by the Committee of Ministers of the Council of Europe on 2 March 2005, states that:

> 70. The Court considers that in such cases the applicability of Article 6 has reached its limits. It notes that the Convention does not confer any right, as demanded by the applicant, to "private revenge" or to an *actio popularis*. Thus, the right to have third parties prosecuted or sentenced for a criminal offence cannot be asserted independently: it must be indissociable from the victim's exercise of a right to bring civil proceedings in domestic law, even if only to secure symbolic reparation or to protect a civil right such as the right to a "good reputation" (see *Golder v. the United Kingdom*, judgment of 21 February 1975, Series A no. 18, p. 13, § 27; *Helmers*, cited above, p. 14, § 27; and *Tolstoy Miloslavsky v. the United Kingdom*, judgment of 13 July 1995, Series A no. 316-B, p. 78, § 58).

In the *American regional system*, the obligation of investigation is drawn up in Article 8 of the *Inter-American Convention to Prevent and Punish Torture* of 9 December 1985 according to which if there is an accusation or well-grounded reason to believe that an act of torture has been committed within their jurisdiction, the States Parties shall guarantee "that their respective authorities will proceed properly and immediately to conduct an investigation into the case and to initiate, whenever appropriate, the corresponding criminal process."

Inside the American Convention on Human Rights, the obligation of investigation—which is not expressly specified in it—has been asserted and developed through the case-law of the I/ACHR. With regard to it, this Court has declared, first, that it is the States' obligation to investigate every situation involving a violation of the rights protected by the American Convention. A consequence of it is that if the State apparatus acts in such a way that the violation goes unpunished and the victim's full enjoyment of such rights is not restored as soon as possible, the State has failed to comply with its duty to ensure the free and full exercise of those

[43] The original text of this Judgement is in French. The translation to English is mine.

[44] Cf., for example, *Case Yasa v. Turkey*, Judgement of 2 September 1998, para. 103; *Case Issayeva and Others v. Russia*, Judgement of 24 February 205, para. 219.

rights to the persons within its jurisdiction. On the other hand, the same is true when the State allows private persons or groups to act freely and with impunity to the detriment of the rights recognized by the Convention.[45]

Second, in certain circumstances, it may be difficult to investigate acts that violate an individual's rights but the duty to investigate being an obligation of means, it must be undertaken in a serious manner and not as a mere formality preordained to be ineffective. So,

> 177. . ..it must be undertaken in a serious manner and not as a mere formality preordained to be ineffective. An investigation must have an objective and be assumed by the State as its own legal duty, not as a step taken by private interests that depends upon the initiative of the victim or his family or upon their offer of proof, without an effective search for the truth by the government. This is true regardless of what agent is eventually found responsible for the violation. Where the acts of private parties that violate the Convention are not seriously investigated, those parties are aided in a sense by the government, thereby making the State responsible on the international plane.[46]

But at the same time the State is required to guarantee to the victims' next of kin full access and procedural capacity at all stages of and before all courts involved in such investigations and proceedings, pursuant to the domestic law and the provisions of the American Convention.[47]

Third, the I/ACHR specifies that the investigation must be rapid and exhaustive. That is, according to the international standards on the matter, we have examined both the European regional system and the general or universal system of the UN:

> 149. As regards the length of investigations and trials, this Court has stated that the right to justice is not limited to the formal institution of domestic proceedings, but it also involves the assurance within reasonable time of the right of alleged victims or their relatives to have every necessary step taken to know the truth and punish those responsible for the events.[48]

Fourth, the I/ACHR has manifested on several occasions that it is not enough to investigate to punish those responsible but that all efforts should be oriented towards the reparation of the victim. In this sense:

---

[45] I/ACHR, *Case Velasquez Rodriguez*, Judgement of 29 July 1988, para. 176. Moreover, "the State has a legal duty to take reasonable steps to prevent human rights violations and to use the means at its disposal to carry out a serious investigation of violations committed within its jurisdiction, to identify those responsible, to impose the appropriate punishment and to ensure the victim adequate compensation." (*ibid.*, para. 174).

[46] *Ibid.*, párr. 177. *Cf. Case of Montero-Aranguren et al. (Detention Center of Catia), supra* note 97, para. 139; *Case of Baldeón-García, supra* note 163, para. 199; and *Case of Blanco-Romero et al., supra* note 100, para. 97.

[47] I/ACHR, *Case La Cantuta vs. Perú*, Judgment of 29 November 2006, para. 228. *Cf.* also *Case of Montero-Aranguren et al. (Detention Center of Catia), supra* note 97, para. 139; *Case of Baldeón-García, supra* note 163, para. 199; and *Case of Blanco-Romero et al., supra* note 100, para. 97.

[48] I/ACHR, *Case La Cantuta vs. Perú*, Judgment of 29 November 2006, para. 149. In this Judgement, the I/ACHR quoted its jurisprudence on the following cases: *Case of the "Mapiripan Massacre", supra* note 2, para. 216; *Case of the Serrano-Cruz Sisters, supra* note 98, para. 66, and *Case of 19 Tradesmen, supra* note 110, para. 188.

> 174. The State has a legal duty to take reasonable steps to prevent human rights violations and to use the means at its disposal to carry out a serious investigation of violations committed within its jurisdiction, to identify those responsible, to impose the appropriate punishment and to ensure the victim adequate compensation.[49]

Finally, the logical consequence of this case-law building is the non-compatibility of amnesty provisions that is similar to the American Convention on Human Rights. Such an important statement was made for the first time by the I/ACHR in its Judgement of 14 March 2001 in the *Case of Barrios Altos v. Peru (Merits)*. Here,

> 41. This Court considers that all amnesty provisions, provisions on prescription and the establishment of measures designed to eliminate responsibility are inadmissible, because they are intended to prevent the investigation and punishment of those responsible for serious human rights violations such as torture, extrajudicial, summary or arbitrary execution and forced disappearance, all of them prohibited because they violate non-derogable rights recognized by international human rights law.[50]

In consequence, the States resorting to such laws act in violation of the American Convention on Human Rights. In this sense, it is the opinion of the I/ACHR that:

> 43. . . .Self-amnesty laws lead to the defenselessness of victims and perpetuate impunity; therefore, they are manifestly incompatible with the aims and spirit of the Convention. This type of law precludes the identification of the individuals who are responsible for human rights violations, because it obstructs the investigation and access to justice and prevents the victims and their next of kin from knowing the truth and receiving the corresponding reparation.
>
> 44. Owing to the manifest incompatibility of self-amnesty laws and the American Convention on Human Rights, the said laws lack legal effect and may not continue to obstruct the investigation of the grounds on which this case is based or the identification and punishment of those responsible, nor can they have the same or a similar impact with regard to other cases that have occurred in Peru, where the rights established in the American Convention have been violated.[51]

The Role of Victims Regardless of Whether They Have Filed an Official Complaint or Not

Another characteristic of the obligation of investigation is that it exists independent of the fact that victims have or have not filed a formal complaint.

On this question Article 12, paragraph 2 of the *UN International Convention for the Protection of All Persons from Enforced Disappearance* of 20 December 2006

---

[49] I/ACHR, *Case Velasquez Rodriguez*, Judgement of 29 July 1988, para. 174. Cf. also the *Case of the "Street Children" (Villagrán Morales et al.) vs. Guatemala*, Judgement of 19 November 1999, Merits, para. 226 (Series C, No. 63). In this judgement, the I/ACHR quotes its Judgements on the following cases: *Case Godínez Cruz*, para. 188 and *Case Velásquez Rodríguez*, para. 177.

[50] I/ACHR, *Case Barrios Altos vs. Perú (Merits)*, Judgement of 14 March 2001, para. 41.

[51] *Ibid.*

states that where there are reasonable grounds for believing that a person has been subjected to enforced disappearance, an investigation shall be undertaken even if there has been no formal complaint. On this matter, this Convention follows the wake marked by the *Declaration on the Protection of All Persons from Enforced Disappearance* adopted by the General Assembly of the United Nations in its resolution A/RES/47/133 of 18 December 1992.[52]

In the case of the *ICC*, the fact that the competence of investigation is attributed to the Prosecutor, who can initiate it on his own, has as a consequence the position where Prosecutor can act even without a complaint from the victims. Moreover, both situations whether with a complaint from the victims or without the participation of the victims are envisaged—as seen—in Article 15 of the Statute and in Rule 50 of the Rules of Procedure and Evidence because victims can present observations to the Pre-Trial Chamber before it decides if it authorizes the Prosecutor to initiate the investigation or not.

In the *European regional system*, and inside the *European Union*, according to Article 10, paragraph 1 of Council Framework Decision (2002/475/JHA) of 13 June 2002, on combating terrorism,[53] the obligation of investigation on the charge of Member States is not dependent on a report or accusation made by the victim. Under the title "Protection of, and assistance to, victims" paragraph 1 asserts:

> 1. Member States shall ensure that investigations into, or prosecution of, offences covered by this Framework Decision are not dependent on a report or accusation made by a person subjected to the offence, at least if the acts were committed on the territory of the Member State.

In the frame of the *Council of Europe*, the *Guidelines on the Protection of Victims of Terrorist Acts* adopted by the Committee of Ministers of the Council of Europe on 2 March 2005 contains a similar provision:

> 2. In this framework –that is, that of the obligations States have to launch an effective official investigation where there have been victims of terrorist acts- special attention must be paid to victims without it being necessary for them to have made a formal complaint.

But the *Guidelines on the Protection of Victims of Terrorist Acts* does not solely base this obligation on Article 10, paragraph 1, of Council Framework Decision (2002/475/JHA). It also quotes jurisprudence of the ICHR. According to it, the authorities must open an investigation of their own motion and as soon as the case comes to their attention. In other words, the initiative is with the State independent of what the relatives of the victim do. On this question, the opinion of the ECHR is very clear. So, the authorities cannot leave it to the initiative of the deceased's next of kin either to lodge a formal complaint or to take responsibility for any investigative procedure. This is why the victim's next of kin must be involved in the procedure to the extent necessary to safeguard their legitimate interests. If not, such an investigation will not be "effective".

---

[52] Which contain the same obligation on Article 13, paragraph 1.

[53] *OJEC* L 164, of 22 June 2002.

Such an interpretation is given by the ECHR in the *case Slimani v. France*, where it states:

> 32. (...) there must be a sufficient element of public scrutiny of the investigation or its results to secure accountability in practice as well as in theory. It has specified that although the degree of public scrutiny required may vary from case to case the next-of-kin of the victim must in all cases be involved in the procedure to the extent necessary to safeguard their legitimate interests (see, *inter alia*, *Hugh Jordan v. the United Kingdom*, no. 24746/94, § 109, 4 May 2001; *McKerr*, § 115; and *Paul and Audrey Edwards*, § 73). It considers that this must be the case where a person dies while in the custody of authorities...
>
> 47. Nevertheless, as the Court has already stressed, whenever a person in detention dies in suspicious circumstances, Article 2 requires the authorities to conduct an "effective and official investigation" of their own motion as soon as the case comes to their attention to enable the causes of death to be established and anyone responsible for the death to be identified and punished. The authorities cannot leave it to the initiative of the deceased's next-of-kin either to lodge a formal complaint or to take responsibility for any investigative procedure. To that should be added that such an investigation cannot be described as "effective" unless, among other things, the victim's next-of-kin are involved in the procedure to the extent necessary to safeguard their legitimate interests (see paragraphs 29–32 above).
>
> In the Court's opinion, requiring a deceased's next-of-kin to lodge a criminal complaint together with an application to join the proceedings as a civil party if they wish to be involved in the investigation proceedings contravenes these principles. It considers that as soon as the authorities become aware of a death in suspicious circumstances, they should carry out an investigation of their own motion in which the deceased's next-of-kin should automatically be involved.[54]

The Committee of Ministers also quotes the *case McKerr v. United Kingdom*. Here, the ECHR states:

> 148. In this case, it may be observed that the lack of access to the witness statements was the reason for several long adjournments in the inquest. This contributed significantly to prolonging the proceedings. The Court considers this further in the context of the delay (see paragraph 152 below). The previous inability of the applicant's family to have access to witness statements before the appearance of the witness must also be regarded as having placed them at a disadvantage in terms of preparation and ability to participate in questioning. This contrasts strikingly with the position of the RUC who had the resources to provide for legal representation and full access to relevant documents. The Court considers that the right of the family of the deceased whose death is under investigation to participate in the proceedings requires that the procedures adopted ensure the requisite protection of their interests, which may be in direct conflict with those of the police or security forces implicated in the events. The Court is not persuaded that the applicant's interests as next-of-kin were fairly or adequately protected in this respect.
>
> 159. It is not for this Court to specify in any detail which procedures the authorities should adopt in providing for the proper examination of the circumstances of a killing by State agents. While reference has been made, for example, to the Scottish model of inquiry conducted by a judge of criminal jurisdiction, there is no reason to assume that this may be the only method available. Nor can it be said that there should be one unified procedure satisfying all requirements. If the aims of fact-finding, criminal investigation and prosecution are carried out by or shared between several authorities, as in Northern Ireland, the

[54] ECHR, Judgement of 27 July 2004, para. 47.

Court considers that the requirements of Article 2 may nonetheless be satisfied if, while seeking to take into account other legitimate interests such as national security or the protection of material relevant to other investigations, the various procedures provide for the necessary safeguards in an accessible and effective manner. In the present case, the available procedures have not struck the right balance.

160. The Court would observe that the shortcomings in transparency and effectiveness identified above run counter to the purpose identified by the domestic courts of allaying suspicions and rumour. Proper procedures for ensuring the accountability of agents of the State are indispensable in maintaining public confidence and meeting the legitimate concerns that might arise from the use of lethal force. A lack of such procedures will only add fuel to fears of sinister motivations, as is illustrated, *inter alia*, by the submissions made by the applicant concerning the alleged shoot-to-kill policy.[55]

In the *American regional system*, the State's investigation on their own motion is envisaged in Article 8 of the *Inter-American Convention to Prevent and Punish Torture* of 9 December 1985 according to which if there is an accusation or well-grounded reason to believe that an act of torture has been committed within their jurisdiction, the States Parties shall guarantee that their respective authorities will proceed "properly and immediately" to conduct an investigation into the case and to initiate, whenever appropriate, the corresponding criminal process.

Victims' Right to Ask for the Re-examination of the State's Decision Not to Take Action to Prosecute a Suspected Perpetrator of a Victimizer Act

In the *European regional system*, this right is drawn up in the *Guidelines on the Protection of Victims of Terrorist Acts* adopted by the Committee of Ministers of the Council of Europe in the following terms:

3. In cases where, as a result of an investigation, it is decided not to take action to prosecute a suspected perpetrator of a terrorist act, states should allow victims to ask for this decision to be re-examined by a competent authority.

The right of victims to ask for the re-examination, by a competent authority, of the State's decision not to take action to prosecute a suspected perpetrator of a terrorist act—for example due to lack of proofs—was envisaged earlier in Recommendation No. R (85) 11 of the Committee of Ministers of the Council of Europe *On the Position of the Victim in the Framework of Criminal Law and Procedure* adopted on 28 June 1985, whose paragraph 7 states:

7. The victim should have the right to ask for a review by a competent authority of a decision not to prosecute, or the right to institute private proceedings;

[55] ECHR, Judgement of 4 May 2011.

The *Guidelines on the Protection of Victims of Terrorist Acts* adopted by the Committee of Ministers of the Council of Europe also bases this right on the jurisprudence of the ECHR. As a concrete instance this emerged in the *case Finucane v. United Kingdom*, where the Court asserted the victim's right to the scrutinize the investigation or its results. In this sense, it states:

> 71. For the same reasons, there must be a sufficient element of public scrutiny of the investigation or its results to secure accountability in practice as well as in theory. The degree of public scrutiny required may well vary from case to case. In all cases, however, the next-of-kin of the victim must be involved in the procedure to the extent necessary to safeguard his or her legitimate interests (see *Güleç*, cited above, p. 1733, § 82; *Oğur*, cited above, § 92; *Gül*, cited above, § 93; and the recent Northern Irish cases, for example *McKerr*, cited above, § 148).[56]

With regard to the *European Union*, a recent Commission Staff Working Paper on the matter underlines that "although a majority of Member States have an institutionalised right to review of decision not to prosecute in place, in six Member States the victim has no right to such review. At the same time, in three Member States no information is provided to victims concerning the decision to prosecute and in seven Member States only information on negative decisions is provided"[57]

In the frame of *International Criminal Law*, the Statute of the ICC gives to the Prosecutor the competence to initiate an investigation on his own motion or at the instance of a State Party to the Statute or of the Security Council. As seen, and to these effects, victims can send to the Prosecutor the information they consider pertinent. As for the Prosecutor, he has two options: either he concludes that there is a reasonable basis to proceed with an investigation—and in this case he shall submit to the Pre-Trial Chamber a request for authorization of an investigation—or he concludes the contrary. In this last case, Article 15 paragraph 6 of the Statute states that the Prosecutor shall inform this refusal to those who provided the information. Nevertheless, this refusal does not preclude the Prosecutor from considering further information submitted to him regarding the same situation "in the light of new facts or evidence."[58]

The same situation exists with regard to the Pre-Trial Chamber because it is this organ that authorizes the Prosecutor to commence the investigation once he concludes that there is a reasonable basis to proceed with it. If the Pre-Trial Chamber does not authorize the investigation, Article 15, paragraph 5 declares

[56] ECHR, Judgement of the 1st July 2003, para. 71.

[57] European Commission, Commission Staff Working Paper, Impact Assessment Accompanying the document "Communication from the Commission to the European Parliament, the Council, The European economic and social Committee and the Committee of Regions", Proposal for a DIRECTIVE OF THE EUROPEAN PARLIAMENT AND OF THE COUNCIL establishing minimum standards on the rights, support and protection of victims of crime, SEC(2011) 580 final, Brussels, 18.5.2011), 12 et seq.

[58] Art. 15.6 *in fine*.

that this refusal "shall not preclude the presentation of a subsequent request by the Prosecutor based on new facts or evidence regarding the same situation."

In consequence, the Statute does not configure a right of reconsideration in favour of those who inform the Prosecutor, but it envisages the possibility that the Prosecutor considers further information submitted to him regarding the same situation in the light of new facts or evidence.

The Right of Effective Access to the Law and to Justice

In the past, one of the important problems crime victims have encountered in some national legal orders has been that of access to justice to achieve the adequate protection of their rights.[59]

In the frame of International Law, some international norms on victims make a distinction between the "right to the administration of justice" and the "right to effective access to law and to justice". According to them, on the one hand, the content of the "right to the administration of justice" concerns the right to a fear and public hearing, by an independent and impartial tribunal established by law. In other words, it concerns a fundamental human right that international treaties on the matter declare "to everyone".

On the other hand, the "right of effective access to law and to justice" concerns both the right to a prompt and effective remedy, the participation of victims in criminal and in civil proceedings as well as the right to a judicial resolution within a reasonable time.

In the *general or universal system of the UN* and with regard to victims, the right of effective access to law and to justice is envisaged in the first international norm on victims of this international organization. That is on paragraph 6 of the *Declaration of Basic Principles of Justice for Victims of Crime and Abuse of Power* adopted by the General Assembly resolution 40/34 of 29 November 1985, which states:

> 6. The responsiveness of judicial and administrative processes to the needs of victims should be facilitated by:
> (a) Informing victims of their role and the scope, timing and progress of the proceedings and of the disposition of their cases, especially where serious crimes are involved and where they have requested such information;
> (b) Allowing the views and concerns of victims to be presented and considered at appropriate stages of the proceedings where their personal interests are affected, without prejudice to the accused and consistent with the relevant national criminal justice system;

[59] Sanz Hermida, *op. cit.*, 58 et seq. It is a problem which has different profiles depending on the fact that the access concerns civil or criminal jurisdictional organs. The first to claim for restitution or compensation of the prejudices suffered. The second to actively participate in the criminal proceedings or to have only a knowledge of the development of the indictment and the result of it or to participate in it as witnesses.

(c) Providing proper assistance to victims throughout the legal process;
(d) Taking measures to minimize inconvenience to victims, protect their privacy, when necessary, and ensure their safety, as well as that of their families and witnesses on their behalf, from intimidation and retaliation;
(e) Avoiding unnecessary delay in the disposition of cases and the execution of orders or decrees granting awards to victims.

In 1992, this right was also drawn up on Article 9 of the *Declaration on the Protection of All Persons from Enforced Disappearance* adopted by the General Assembly of the United Nations in its resolution A/RES/47/133 of 18 December 1992:

1. The right to a prompt and effective judicial remedy as a means of determining the whereabouts or state of health of persons deprived of their liberty and/or identifying the authority ordering or carrying out the deprivation of liberty is required to prevent enforced disappearances under all circumstances, including those referred to in article 7 above.
2. In such proceedings, competent national authorities shall have access to all places where persons deprived of their liberty are being held and to each part of those places, as well as to any place in which there are grounds to believe that such persons may be found.
3. Any other competent authority entitled under the law of the State or by any international legal instrument to which the State is a party may also have access to such places.[60]

But the international norm that most widely describes this right and also follows the line of the two Declarations just examined is the General Assembly Resolution 60/147 adopted on 16 December 2005 through which the *Basic principles and guidelines of the right to a remedy and reparation for victims of gross violations of international human rights law and serious violations of International Humanitarian Law* adopted by the UN Commission on Human Rights on 19 April 2005, by Resolution 2005/35, have been adopted. This resolution devotes three paragraphs to this obligation: scope of the obligation to respect, ensure respect for and implement international human rights law and international humanitarian law (Principle II, point 3); victim's right to remedies (Principle VII, point 11) and access to justice (Principle VIII, points 12, 13 and 14).

Concerning the *scope of the obligation to respect, ensure respect for and implement international human rights law and international humanitarian law* point 3 of Principle II specifies that it include the duty "to provide effective remedies to victims".[61]

[60] Article 7 says: "No circumstances whatsoever, whether a threat of war, a state of war, internal political instability or any other public emergency, may be invoked to justify enforced disappearances."

[61] Together with the following duties: "(*a*) Take appropriate legislative and administrative and other appropriate measures to prevent violations; (*b*) Investigate violations effectively, promptly, thoroughly and impartially and, where appropriate, take action against those allegedly responsible in accordance with domestic and international law; provide those who claim to be victims of a human rights or humanitarian law violation with equal and effective access to justice, as described below, irrespective of who may ultimately be the bearer of responsibility for the violation".

With regard to the *access to justice* remedies shall be "adequate, effective and prompt" and it "should include all available and appropriate international processes in which a person may have legal standing" and "should be without prejudice to any other domestic remedies".[62] At least, the access to an effective judicial remedy shall be not only equal but "as provided for under international law."[63]

With the aim to assure the equal access of victims of gross violations of international human rights law and serious violations of International Humanitarian Law to an effective judicial remedy Principle VIII (access to justice) imposes upon the States the following duties:

> 12. A victim of a gross violation of international human rights law or of a serious violation of international humanitarian law shall have equal access to an effective judicial remedy as provided for under international law. Other remedies available to the victim include access to administrative and other bodies, as well as mechanisms, modalities and proceedings conducted in accordance with domestic law. Obligations arising under international law to secure the right to access justice and fair and impartial proceedings shall be reflected in domestic laws. To that end, States should:
> (a) Disseminate, through public and private mechanisms, information about all available remedies for gross violations of international human rights law and serious violations of international humanitarian law;
> (b) Take measures to minimize the inconvenience to victims and their representatives, protect against unlawful interference with their privacy as appropriate and ensure their safety from intimidation and retaliation, as well as that of their families and witnesses, before, during and after judicial, administrative, or other proceedings that affect the interests of victims;
> (c) Provide proper assistance to victims seeking access to justice;
> (d) Make available all appropriate legal, diplomatic and consular means to ensure that victims can exercise their rights to remedy for gross violations of international human rights law or serious violations of international humanitarian law.

In contrast to the preceding rights what Principle VII, entitled "Victim's right to remedies", does is to list several rights of victims that are asserted in its condition of "remedies for gross violations of international human rights law and serious violations of international humanitarian law" adding that it is "as provided for under international law". These rights are the following: the right to equal and effective access to law and justice; the right to an adequate, effective and prompt reparation for harm suffered; and the right of access to relevant information concerning violations and reparation mechanisms.

---

[62] Principle VIII, point 14. Related to it, point 13 makes reference to the development of "procedures to allow groups of victims to present claims for reparation and to receive reparation, as appropriate."

[63] *Ibid.*, point 12. Due to the content of the resolution, one can suppose that the equal access from which this point speaks shall be understood as related to all victims. Point 12 adds: "Other remedies available to the victim include access to administrative and other bodies, as well as mechanisms, modalities and proceedings conducted in accordance with domestic law. Obligations arising under international law to secure the right to access justice and fair and impartial proceedings shall be reflected in domestic laws."

The way described here—exclusively based upon institutional norms on victims—finally ended in 2006 with an international treaty: the *International Convention for the Protection of All Persons from Enforced Disappearance* of 20 December 2006 adopted by resolution A/RES/61/177 of the General Assembly,[64] Article 17 paragraph 2.f) of which states the right of effective access and the right of access to justice. According to it and without the prejudice to other international obligations of the States Parties, each State Party shall, in its legislation:

> (f) Guarantee that any person deprived of liberty or, in the case of a suspected enforced disappearance, since the person deprived of liberty is not able to exercise this right, any persons with a legitimate interest, such as relatives of the person deprived of liberty, their representatives or their counsel, shall, in all circumstances, be entitled to take proceedings before a court, in order that the court may decide without delay on the lawfulness of the deprivation of liberty and order the person's release if such deprivation of liberty is not lawful.

This Convention also envisages the possibility that States Parties apply a statute of limitations in respect of enforced disappearance. In such a case, and according to Article 8, paragraph 2, the States Parties shall guarantee the right of victims of enforced disappearance to an effective remedy during the term of limitation.[65]

In the frame of *International Criminal Law*, the visibility of victims in the criminal proceedings has been recently confronted by the *ICC' Statute*. That is an international treaty allowing victims to *participate in an active manner in the proceedings*. So, according to Article 68, paragraph 3, of the Statute the Court—at stages of the proceedings determined to be appropriate by the Court and in a manner which is not prejudicial to or inconsistent with the rights of the accused and a fair and impartial trial—shall permit that views and concerns of victims be presented and considered where the personal interests of the victims are affected. In such cases, the views and concerns may be presented by the legal representatives of the victims where the Court considers it appropriate, in accordance with the Rules of Procedure and Evidence.

On the contrary, and according to Rule 89, victims (as well as persons acting with the consent of the victim, or persons acting on behalf of a victim, in the case of a victim who is a child or, when necessary, a victim who is disabled) shall make a written application to the Registrar, who shall transmit the application to the relevant Chamber.[66]

Victims are free to choose a *legal representative* but where there are a number of victims it is possible for the Chamber to request victims to choose a common legal representative or representatives for the purposes of ensuring the effectiveness of the

---

[64] Into force on 23 December 2010.

[65] This provision is contradictory to Article 5 that states that the widespread or systematic practice of enforced disappearance constitutes a crime against humanity, because crimes against humanity do not have limitation of time to be prosecuted. Article 5 says: "The widespread or systematic practice of enforced disappearance constitutes a crime against humanity as defined in applicable international law and shall attract the consequences provided for under such applicable international law".

[66] Cf. Rule 89, paragraphs 1 and 3.

proceedings. On the one hand, if the victims are unable to choose a common legal representative or representatives within a time limit that the Chamber may decide, then the Chamber may request the Registrar to choose one or more common legal representatives. On the other hand, if a victim or group of victims lacks the necessary means to pay for a common legal representative chosen by the Court, then it may receive assistance from the Registry, including, as appropriate, financial assistance.[67]

The victim and his or her legal representative attend and participate in the proceedings. This includes the questioning of witnesses, experts or the accused, which shall be requested through an application made to the Chamber.[68] On the same lines, both the victims and the legal representatives will be notified of all proceedings before the Court. So, and in order that victims can ask for authorization to participate in the proceedings as envisaged in Rule 89 (related to the request of victims for participating in the proceedings), the Court shall notify them concerning the decision of the Prosecutor not to initiate an investigation or not to prosecute pursuant to Article 53. Such a notification shall be given to the victims or their legal representatives who have already participated in the proceedings or, as far as possible, to those who have communicated with the Court in respect of the situation or case in question.[69]

For his part, the Secretary of the ICC shall notify to the victims and their legal representatives all proceedings before the Court, which includes the dates of hearing and any postponements thereof, and the date of delivery of the decision as well as requests, submissions, motions and other documents relating to such requests, submissions or motions.

With respect to the Chambers, Rule 93 authorizes them to seek the views of the victims or their legal representatives participating as well as of other victims over any question as appropriate.

In contrast to the Statute of the ICC, the *Statutes of the International Criminal Courts* for the *former Yugoslavia* and for *Rwanda* gave to victims a much more reduced prominence because they only envisaged their participation as witnesses of the Prosecutor without the possibility of obtaining any compensation from these courts. The explication of this limited approach is owing to the fact that the foundation and the description of the statute of the victim took place in the frame of the Prosecutor's statute because it was this one who lead public action with the aim of defending public international order and the repression of crime.[70] The consequence of it is that both statutes have built a system of measures of protection of victims in their condition of victims but have not envisaged any particular statute of the victim. This is why it rests with the Prosecutor to direct public international action and victims cannot constitute themselves as a civil party in the proceedings.

---

[67] Cf. Rule 90.

[68] Cf. Rule 91.3.

[69] Cf. Rule 92.2.

[70] Jorda, "L'accès des victimes à la justice pénale internationale", in *Terrorisme, victimes et. . ., op. cit.*, 363. Cf. also C. Tournaye, "L'apport des Tribunaux *as hoc* pour la repression du terrorisme", *ibid.*, 416–430.

Being only conceived as witnesses victims cannot participate for themselves in the proceedings. In this context, victims had to swear before testifying, they could only speak in the frame of the questionings, they do not have access to the elements of proof, they can only assist in the questioning of other witnesses from the banks reserved to the public and they cannot obtain compensation for the prejudice suffered.

It should be remembered that this conception is justified on the basis of three reasons. On the one hand, the fact that the proceeding chosen by the statutes of both Courts is an accusatory one. That is a proceeding that confronts the accused (with aims for a repressive finality) and the defence under the arbitral look of the judge.

Second, the repressive imperatives inherent to an international criminal justice case where the objective is to look for the offender, to investigate, to take the offender before the court and once there to punish or to absolve him. Finally, the human rights protection of the accused that in the moment of the drafting of these statutes opined that the intervention of the victim could make difficult the celerity of the proceedings.

This is why some authors consider that giving power to the victims to initiate proceedings would have constituted a threat to the discretionary power of the Prosecutor. A discretion that is already greater in courts like those for the *former Yugoslavia* and for *Rwanda* that possess limited time so that they have to work without any delay between their work and the commission of the facts they have to judge.

But there was also another difficulty in giving victims a more active role. The fact that both war crimes and crimes against humanity are crimes on a huge scale that concern a large number of victims and that they are committed in a specific context and with very strong passionate dimensions.

In the opinion of the former president of the *International Criminal Court* for the *former Yugoslavia*, Jorda, the situation just described has an advantage: the celerity of the proceedings as a consequence of the non-existence of a third actor (the victim) on it. On the other hand, he considers that being an accusatory proceeding, it is very difficult to situate on it the place of the victim. But it also has a disadvantage that is determined by the fact that the interests of the Prosecutor in the proceedings are not necessarily those of victims. In both Courts, the Prosecutor is not the guardian of public international order but his aim is the winning of the process and from this perspective the interference of a victim's lawyer or his constitution as a civil party in the proceedings would notably have a bearing upon the development of the process. This is why even in the condition of witness the victim is only called to appear in court when his testimony will exactly confirm the thesis the accusation pretends to demonstrate.[71]

[71] Cf. *ibid.*, 362–365.

In the *regional system* and with regard to victims, the right to an effective access to justice is solely envisaged in the *European system* and this in the frame of the Council of Europe and of the European Union.

With respect to the *Council of Europe*, this right is drawn up both in several recommendations of the Committee of Ministers on victims of crime and in the *Guidelines on the Protection of Victims of Terrorist Acts* that asserts that States should ensure that the position of victims of terrorist acts is adequately recognized in criminal proceedings. In the frame of the *European Union*, this right is expressly envisaged on *Council Framework Decision 2001/220/JHA* of 15 March 2001 related to the standing of victims in criminal proceedings.

With regard to *victims of crime*, the different scales of this right have been progressively treated by the Committee of Ministers through a set of recommendations.[72] It is the case in the following: *Recommendation No. R (81) 7* of 14 May 1981, *On Measures facilitating Access to Justice* the principles of which are also applicable to victims of terrorism[73]; *Recommendation No. R (83)7*, of 23 June 1983 *On Participation of the Public in Crime Policy*[74]; *Recommendation No. R (85) 11* of 28 June 1985, *On the Position of the Victim in the Framework of Criminal Law and Procedure*[75]; *Recommendation No. R (87) 21* of 17 September 1987, *On Assistance to Victims and Prevention of Victimisation*[76] and, finally, *Recommendation No. R (93) 1*, of 8 January 1993 *On Effective Access to the Law and to Justice For the Very Poor*.

---

[72] Recommendations that are used by the ECHR in its jurisprudence. So, for example, in the *Case Pérez v. France (GC)*, judgement of 12 February 2004. See page 156 of the present work.

[73] This Recommendation declares that States "should take all necessary steps to inform the public on the means open to an individual to assert his rights before courts and to make judicial proceedings, relating to civil, commercial, administrative, social or fiscal matters simple, speedy and inexpensive." To this end, this Recommendation asserts that States should have particular regard to the following principles: "1. Appropriate measures should be taken to inform the public of the location and competence of the courts and the way in which proceedings are commenced or defended before those courts. 2. General information should be available from the court or a competent body or service on the following items:—procedural requirements provided that this information does not involve giving legal advice concerning the substance of the case;—the way in which, and the time within which, a decision can be challenged, the rules of procedure and any required documents to this effect;—methods by which a decision might be enforced, and if possible, the costs involved."

[74] Paragraph 29 of which (inside point "D. A crime policy taking account of the victims' interests") refers to "Establishing an efficient system of legal aid for victims so that they may have access to justice in all circumstances."

[75] Point 9 of it (entitled "D. Court proceedings") states: "The victim should be informed of: the date and place of a hearing concerning an offence which caused him suffering; his opportunities of obtaining restitution and compensation within the criminal justice process, legal assistance and advice; how he can find out the outcome of the case;"

[76] Paragraph 4 of it specifies that the States shall take measures to ensure that victims and their families, especially those who are most vulnerable, receive in particular "assistance during the criminal process, with due respect to the defence;"

All these recommendations recognize the place of victims in criminal proceedings.

More recently, and on the same lines *Recommendation (2006) 8*, of 14 June 2006, *On Assistance to Crime Victims* expressly contains this right under the title "Right to effective access to other remedies". According to it:

> 7.1. Victims may need to seek civil remedies to protect their rights following a crime. States should therefore take the necessary steps to ensure that victims have effective access to all civil remedies, and within a reasonable time, through:
> – the right of access to competent courts; and
> – legal aid in appropriate cases.
>
> 7.2. States should institute procedures for victims to claim compensation from the offender in the context of criminal proceedings. Advice and support should also be provided to victims in making these claims and in enforcing any payments awarded.

Also in the Council of Europe but directly linked with *victims of terrorism*, the right to effective access to justice is specified in the *Guidelines on the Protection of Victims of Terrorist Acts* and this with a double scale: on the one hand with regard to the participation of victims in criminal proceedings[77] and on the other hand in relationship to the victims' right of access to competent courts in order to bring a civil action in support of their rights.[78]

Like in the case of the rights just examined with regard to the right of effective access to the law and to justice, the *Guidelines on the Protection of Victims of Terrorist Acts* adopted by the Committee of Ministers also refers to the jurisprudence of the ECHR. A concrete instance is the Judgement of the Great Chamber in the *case Perez v. France*, of 12 February 2004 where the ECHR states the following:

> 70. The Court considers that in such cases the applicability of Article 6 has reached its limits. It notes that the Convention does not confer any right, as demanded by the applicant, to "private revenge" or to an *actio popularis*. Thus, the right to have third parties prosecuted or sentenced for a criminal offence cannot be asserted independently: it must be indissociable from the victim's exercise of a right to bring civil proceedings in domestic law, even if only to secure symbolic reparation or to protect a civil right such as the right to a "good reputation" (see *Golder v. the United Kingdom*, judgment of 21 February 1975, Series A no. 18, p. 13, § 27; *Helmers*, cited above, p. 14, § 27; and *Tolstoy Miloslavsky v. the United Kingdom*, judgment of 13 July 1995, Series A no. 316-B, p. 78, § 58).
>
> (...)

[77] In the following terms: "1. States should, in accordance with their national legislation, strive to bring individuals suspected of terrorist acts to justice and obtain a decision from a competent tribunal within a reasonable time. 2. States should ensure that the position of victims of terrorist acts is adequately recognised in criminal proceedings."

[78] In the following terms: "States should provide effective access to the law and to justice for victims of terrorist acts by providing: (i) the right of access to competent courts in order to bring a civil action in support of their rights, and (ii) legal aid in appropriate cases".

72. Such an approach is consistent with the need to safeguard victims' rights and their proper place in criminal proceedings. Simply because the requirements inherent in the concept of a "fair trial" are not necessarily the same in disputes about civil rights and obligations as they are in cases involving criminal trials, as evidenced by the fact that for civil disputes there are no detailed provisions similar to those in Article 6 §§ 2 and 3 (see *Dombo Beheer B.V. v. the Netherlands*, judgment of 27 October 1993, Series A no. 274, p. 19, § 32) does not mean that the Court can ignore the plight of victims and downgrade their rights. In any event, the Code of Criminal Procedure, in a preliminary Article introduced by law no. 2000-516 of 15 June 2000, expressly sets out certain principles fundamental to criminal trials, including "a balance between the rights of the parties" and that the "rights [of victims shall be] safeguarded" (see paragraph 19 above). Lastly, the Court draws attention for information to the text of Recommendations Nos. R (83) 7, R (85) 11 and R (87) 21 of the Committee of Ministers (see paragraphs 26-28 above), which clearly specify the rights which victims may assert in the context of criminal law and procedure.

With respect to the *European Union*, the right of effective access to the law and to justice is firmly ruled on in *Council Framework Decision 2001/220/JHA* of 15 March 2001 related to the standing of victims in criminal proceedings. As Article 2, paragraph 1 of it states, this Framework Decision obliges Member States to ensure that victims have a real and appropriate role in the criminal proceedings.[79] To this effect, they should continue to make every effort to ensure that victims are treated with due respect for the dignity of the individual during proceedings and shall recognize the rights and legitimate interests of victims with particular reference to criminal proceedings. Consequently, the States shall safeguard the possibility for victims to be heard during the proceedings and to supply evidence, and it also shall take appropriate measures to ensure that its authorities question victims only insofar as necessary for the purpose of criminal proceedings.[80]

In keeping with what is specified in the preceding articles, Article 4 refers to the access to information that Member States shall ensure to victims "as from their first

[79] The reality is different. So, only in a few Member States do victims have easy access to a range of information regarding available support, legal advice and aid and essential issues concerning the criminal proceedings, including the decision to prosecute, the court date and positive or negative court decisions (cf. European Commission, Commission Staff Working Paper, Impact Assessment Accompanying the document "Communication from the Commission to the European Parliament, the Council, The European economic and social Committee and the Committee of Regions", Proposal for a DIRECTIVE OF THE EUROPEAN PARLIAMENT AND OF THE COUNCIL establishing minimum standards on the rights, support and protection of victims of crime, SEC (2011) 580 final, Brussels, 18.5.2011).

[80] See Article 3. In the European Union, victims are not always able to attend trial "because the availability of reimbursement of victims' expenses to get there is in most Member States inadequate or victims are not informed about such a right" (European Commission, Commission Staff Working Paper, Impact Assessment *Accompanying the document* "Communication from the Commission to the European Parliament, the Council, The European economic and social Committee and the Committee of Regions", Proposal for a DIRECTIVE OF THE EUROPEAN PARLIAMENT AND OF THE COUNCIL establishing minimum standards on the rights, support and protection of victims of crime, SEC(2011) 580 final, Brussels, 18.5.2011), 12.

contact with law enforcement agencies"[81] while Article 6 is dedicated to the specific assistance to the victim.[82]

Finally from a transfrontier perspective, Article 11 specifies that Member States shall ensure that its competent authorities "can take appropriate measures to minimize the difficulties faced where the victim is a resident of a State other than the one where the offence has occurred, particularly with regard to the organisation of the proceedings".

Nevertheless in Council Framework Decision 202/220/JHA, there is no express reference to the need that Member States envisage in their national legal systems the intervention of victims as a part in the criminal process. This question is left to the national legislatives.[83]

In the *American regional system* and with regard to victims of enforced disappearance what exists is the possibility for victims to claim before treaty bodies once domestic remedies are exhausted. It is not an innovation because this possibility was already ruled in 1969 in the American Convention on Human Rights and is compulsory on States Parties with regard to individual complaints before the Inter-

---

[81] Article 4.1.f). It concerns a very wide information that shall include at least: "(a) the type of services or organisations to which they can turn for support; (b) the type of support which they can obtain; (c) where and how they can report an offence; (d) procedures following such a report and their role in connection with such procedures; (e) how and under what conditions they can obtain protection; (f) to what extent and on what terms they have access to: (i) legal advice or (ii) legal aid, or (iii) any other sort of advice, if, in the cases envisaged in point (i) and (ii), they are entitled to receive it; (g) requirements for them to be entitled to compensation; (h) if they are resident in another State, any special arrangements available to them in order to protect their interests." Member States, too, shall ensure "that victims who have expressed a wish to this effect are kept informed of: (a) the outcome of their complaint; (b) relevant factors enabling them, in the event of prosecution, to know the conduct of the criminal proceedings regarding the person prosecuted for offences concerning them, except in exceptional cases where the proper handling of the case may be adversely affected; (c) the court's sentence." (Article 4 paragraphs 1 and 2). Cf. also Articles 6 and 8.

[82] According to it: "Each Member State shall ensure that victims have access to advice as referred to in Article 4(1)(f) (iii), provided free of charge where warranted, concerning their role in the proceedings and, where appropriate, legal aid as referred to in Article 4(1)(f) (ii), when it is possible for them to have the status of parties to criminal proceedings".

[83] Article 3 of this Framework Decision only contains some general provisions charging Member States with the obligation to safeguard the possibility for victims to be heard during proceedings and to supply evidence as well as to take appropriate measures to ensure that its authorities question victims only insofar as necessary for the purpose of criminal proceedings. About this questions, cf. Sanz Hermida, *op. cit.*, 60–62.

In this regard, "from studies and surveys throughout Europe, it appears that victims are often ignored or are not sufficiently provided with information about the judicial process. For this basic need to be met, the prerequisite is that a victim's needs are clearly identified and catered for." (European Commission, Commission Staff Working Paper, Impact Assessment *Accompanying the document* "Communication from the Commission to the European Parliament, the Council, The European economic and social Committee and the Committee of Regions", Proposal for a DIRECTIVE OF THE EUROPEAN PARLIAMENT AND OF THE COUNCIL establishing minimum standards on the rights, support and protection of victims of crime, SEC(2011) 580 final, Brussels, 18.5.2011), 9.

American Commission of Human Rights. In fact what the *Inter-American Convention on Forced Disappearance of Persons* of 9 July 1994 does on the matter is to forward States Parties to the American Convention of Human Rights. So Article XIII states:

> For the purposes of this Convention, the processing of petitions or communications presented to the Inter-American Commission on Human Rights alleging the forced disappearance of persons shall be subject to the procedures established in the American Convention on Human Rights and to the Statue and Regulations of the Inter-American Commission on Human Rights and to the Statute and Rules of Procedure of the Inter-American Court of Human Rights, including the provisions on precautionary measures.[84]

But the fact that this right of effective access to the law and to justice with regard to victims is only envisaged in the European regional system is not so relevant as it could be argued that it is a *fundamental human right* integrated into the right to a fair trial declared in all international treaties on human rights—both of the general or universal and of the regional systems—and applicable "to everyone."[85] In consequence, its specification or not with regard to victims is not of importance because "everyone"—and victims too—is entitled to it.

With regard to the way in which those treaties on human rights declare this right and in respect of the UN *general or universal system*, a reference to the General Comments of the Human Rights Committee on the *International Covenant on Civil and Political Rights* of 16 December 1966 is necessary. As already stated, these General Comments constitute the interpretation the Human Rights Committee—the Covenant's treaty body—makes of it. It is also an interpretation linking the States Parties. It should be added that this Covenant is an international treaty actually ratified by almost all of the States of the International Community[86] and that its norms have both a conventional and a customary legal nature.

With respect to Covenant's Article 14 which stresses the equality of all persons "before the courts and tribunals" and declares the right of everybody to a fair and public hearing by a competent, independent and impartial tribunal established by law "in the determination of any criminal charge against him, or of his rights and

[84] Adding Article XIV: "Without prejudice to the provisions of the preceding article, when the Inter-American Commission on Human Rights receives a petition or communication regarding an alleged forced disappearance, its Executive Secretariat shall urgently and confidentially address the respective government, and shall request that government to provide as soon as possible information as to the whereabouts of the allegedly disappeared person together with any other information it considers pertinent, and such request shall be without prejudice as to the admissibility of the petition."

[85] Cf. Article 14 of the International Covenant on Civil and Political Rights of 16 December 1966; Article 13 of the European Convention for the Protection of Human Rights and Fundamental Freedoms of 4 November 1950; Article 25 of the American Convention of Human Rights of 22 November 1969 and Article 7 of the African Charter of Human and People's Rights of 27 June 1981. Since 1948, it is envisaged in Article 8 of the Universal Declaration of Human Rights of 10 December. According to Article 8: "Everyone has the right to an effective remedy by the competent national tribunals for acts violating the fundamental rights granted him by the constitution or by law".

[86] Actually 167 State Parties.

obligations in a suit at law", the Human Rights Committee in 1984 stated that the aim of all these provisions is:

> to ensure that equality before the courts, including equal access to courts, fair and public hearings and competence, impartiality and independence of the judiciary are established by law and guaranteed in practice. In particular, States parties should specify the relevant constitutional and legislative texts which provide for the establishment of the courts and ensure that they are independent, impartial and competent, in particular with regard to the manner in which judges are appointed, the qualifications for appointment, and the duration of their terms of office; the condition governing promotion, transfer and cessation of their functions and the actual independence of the judiciary from the executive branch and the legislative.[87]

From a *general perspective*, the effective access to the law and to justice (specified in the right to an effective judicial remedy) is an obligation on the charge of the States Parties to *international treaties of human rights*. Moreover with independence of its existence as a specific right of everyone in a concrete case, the right to an effective judicial remedy is, at the same time, the *conditio sine qua non* to make effective the rights those international treaties of human rights declare.

This fact has also been expressly declared by the Human Rights Committee on the occasion of its interpretation of Article 2, paragraph 3 of the *International Covenant on Civil and Political Rights*.[88] From this interpretation, two obligations on the charge of the States Parties derive.[89] On the one hand, the States Parties are obliged to effectively protect the rights of the Covenant. On the other hand, States Parties must ensure that individuals also have accessible and effective remedies to vindicate those rights; remedies that "should be appropriately adapted so as to take account of the special vulnerability of certain categories of person, including in particular children."[90] At the same time, the Human Rights Committee notes that "the enjoyment of the rights recognized under the Covenant can be effectively

[87] UN. *CCPR General Comment No. 13. (General Comments), 13/04/1984*. It adds that the provisions of Article 14 apply to all courts and tribunals within the scope of that article whether ordinary or specialized (*ibid.*, para. 4).

[88] Article 2, paragraph 3 states: "Each State Party to the present Covenant undertakes: (a) To ensure that any person whose rights or freedoms as herein recognized are violated shall have an effective remedy, notwithstanding that the violation has been committed by persons acting in an official capacity; (b) To ensure that any person claiming such a remedy shall have his right thereto determined by competent judicial, administrative or legislative authorities, or by any other competent authority provided for by the legal system of the State, and to develop the possibilities of judicial remedy; (c) To ensure that the competent authorities shall enforce such remedies when granted."

[89] Interpretation contained in *General Comment No. 31 (80)*: "The nature of the general legal obligation imposed on State parties", adopted on 29 March 2004 (2187th meeting), CCPR/C/21/Rev.1/Add. 13, 26 May 2004.

[90] *Ibid.*, para. 15. This express quotation does not exclude other categories of special vulnerability persons like, for example, victims of gross violations of international human rights law, victims of serious violations of International Humanitarian Law, victims of violations of International Criminal Law or victims of terrorism.

assured by the judiciary in many different ways, including direct applicability of the Covenant, application of comparable constitutional or other provisions of law, or the interpretive effect of the Covenant in the application of national law. Administrative mechanisms are particularly required to give effect to the general obligation to investigate allegations of violations promptly, thoroughly and effectively through independent and impartial bodies."[91]

Like the preceding rights, the right of effective access to the law and to justice *is also with other human rights.* So also with the obligation of investigation that the States have and with the victim's right to redress. In respect to the obligation of investigation, the Human Rights Committee states that complaints "must be investigated promptly and impartially by competent authorities so as to make the remedy effective."[92] This is why the reports that the States Parties have to present regularly to the Committee "should provide specific information on the remedies available to victims of maltreatment and the procedure that complainants must follow, and statistics on the number of complaints and how they have been dealt with."[93]

At the same time, the right to an effective remedy *is linked* with the obligation on the charge of States Parties to investigate any violation of the Covenant. In this sense, the Human Rights Committee declares that where the investigations reveal violations of certain Covenant rights, "States Parties must ensure that those responsible are brought to justice. As with failure to investigate, failure to bring to justice perpetrators of such violations could in and of itself give rise to a separate breach of the Covenant."[94]

According to the Human Rights Committee, these obligations arise "notably in respect of those violations recognized as criminal under either domestic or international law, such as torture and similar cruel, inhuman and degrading treatment (Article 7), summary and arbitrary killing (Article 6) and enforced disappearance (Articles 7 and 9 and, frequently, Article 6). Indeed, the problem of impunity for these violations, a matter of sustained concern for the Committee, may well be an important contributing element in the recurrence of the violations. When committed as part of a widespread or systematic attack on a civilian population, these violations of the Covenant are crimes against humanity (see Rome Statute of the International Criminal Court, Article 7)."[95] This is why the Committee considers that amnesties granted by certain States to acts of torture "are generally incompatible with the duty of States to investigate such acts; to guarantee freedom from such acts within their jurisdiction; and to ensure that they do not occur in the future.

---

[91] *Ibid.*

[92] UN CCPR, *General Comment No.20 44,* Replaces general comment 7concerning prohibition of torture and cruel treatment or punishment (Art. 7), forty-fourth session 1992, 10/03/1992, para. 14.

[93] *Ibid.*

[94] UN CCPR, *CCPR General Comment No. 31 (80).* "The nature of the general legal obligation imposed on State parties", adopted on 29 March 2004 (2187th meeting), CCPR/C/21/Rev.1/Add. 13, 26 May 2004, para. 18.

[95] *Ibid.*

States may not deprive individuals of the right to an effective remedy, including compensation and such full rehabilitation as may be possible".[96]

At least and with respect to the right to reparation, according to the interpretation of the *International Covenant on Civil and Political Rights* by the Human Rights Committee, Article 2, paragraph 3, requires that the States Parties make reparation to individuals whose Covenant rights have been violated. Consequently, "without reparation to individuals whose Covenant rights have been violated, the obligation to provide an effective remedy, which is central to the efficacy of Article 2, paragraph 3, is not discharged."[97]

At the same time, and from another perspective, without an effective remedy no reparation is possible. First, because without an effective remedy it is not possible to attack the lack of investigation or an investigation that does not respond to the international standards of seriousness, impartiality, celerity and effectiveness. On the other hand, because without investigation or with an investigation that does not respond to the international standards quoted above and without effective remedies to attack it, reparation due to the victim is not possible because it depends on the fact that both the investigation of the facts and the remedies at the disposal of the victim are not polluted.

In conclusion, as a consequence of the links existing between the three rights the violation of one of them entails that of the others.

In the frame of the *European Union*, the right to an effective remedy—linked with the right to a fair trail—is specified in Article 47 of the *Charter of Fundamental Rights of the European Union*. Article 47 states:

> Everyone whose rights and freedoms guaranteed by the law of the Union are violated has the right to an effective remedy before a tribunal in compliance with the conditions laid down in this Article.
>
> Everyone is entitled to a fair and public hearing within a reasonable time by an independent and impartial tribunal previously established by law. Everyone shall have the possibility of being advised, defended and represented.
>
> Legal aid shall be made available to those who lack sufficient resources in so far as such aid is necessary to ensure effective access to justice.[98]

---

[96] UN CCPR, *General Comment No.20 44,* Replaces general comment 7concerning prohibition of torture and cruel treatment or punishment (Art. 7), forty-fourth session 1992, 10/03/1992, para. 15.

[97] UN CCPR, *CCPR General Comment No. 31 (80).* "The nature of the general legal obligation imposed on State parties", adopted on 29 March 2004 (2187th meeting), CCPR/C/21/Rev.1/Add. 13, 26 May 2004, para. 16. Article 2, paragraph 3 of the Convenant states: "3. Each State Party to the present Covenant undertakes: (a) To ensure that any person whose rights or freedoms as herein recognized are violated shall have an effective remedy, notwithstanding that the violation has been committed by persons acting in an official capacity; (b) To ensure that any person claiming such a remedy shall have his right thereto determined by competent judicial, administrative or legislative authorities, or by any other competent authority provided for by the legal system of the State, and to develop the possibilities of judicial remedy; (c) To ensure that the competent authorities shall enforce such remedies when granted."

[98] According to Article 6, paragraph 1, of the Treaty of Lisbon the Charter of fundamental Rights of the European Union "the Charter of Fundamental Rights of the European Union of 7 December 2000, as adapted at Strasbourg, on 12 December 2007, which shall have the same legal value as the Treaties". Cf. López Escudero (2008), 740.

As can be appreciated, the first paragraph concerns the right to an effective remedy and is based upon Article 13 of the European Convention for the Protection of Human Rights and Fundamental Freedoms. Nevertheless, according to the *Explanations relating to the Charter of Fundamental Rights of the European Union*, "in Community law the protection is more extensive since it guarantees the right to an effective remedy before a court."[99] Later, it adds:

> The Court of Justice enshrined the principle in its judgment of 15 May 1986 (Case 222/84 Johnston [1986] ECR 1651; see also judgment of 15 October 1987, Case 222/86 Heylens [1987] ECR 4097 and judgment of 3 December 1992, Case C-97/91 Borelli [1992] ECR I-6313. According to the Court, this principle also applies to the Member States when they are implementing Community law. The inclusion of this precedent in the Charter is not intended to change the appeal system laid down by the Treaties, and particularly the rules relating to admissibility. This principle is therefore to be implemented according to the procedures laid down in the Treaties. It applies to the institutions of the Union and of Member States when they are implementing Union law and does so for all rights guaranteed by Union law.[100]

Moreover, Article 47 of the Charter is based on Articles 6.1 and 13 of the European Convention on Human Rights, November 4, 1950, "but its scope is broader because it applies to anyone who wants to enforce a right under the regulations of the European Union before the Court of Justice of the European Communities (...) (with all its instances) or before national judges. This right to effective judicial protection requires both the institutions and bodies of the Union and the Member States".[101]

Apart from its conventional nature and according to a firm jurisprudence of the CJEU in the frame of European community law, the principle of an effective remedy is also a general principle of Community law "which underlines the constitutional traditions common to the Member States and that is also laid down in Articles 6 and 13 of the European Convention for the Protection of Human Rights and Fundamental Freedoms of 4 November 1950".[102] This jurisprudence also underlines the fact that this general principle has also been reaffirmed by Article 47 of the *Charter of Fundamental Rights of the European Union.*[103]

But the CJEU has also specified that according to the principle of cooperation laid down in the old Article 10 of ECT (actually in Article 4, paragraph 3 of the EUT), it is for the Member States to ensure judicial protection of an individual's

---

[99] *Explanations relating to the Charter of Fundamental Rights of the European Union* (*OJ* C 303, 14 December 2007).

[100] *Ibid.*

[101] *Ibid.*, 743.

[102] ECEC, Judgement of 15 May 1986, *Johnston*, 222/84, [1986] ECR 1651, paras. 18 and 19. Cf. also Judgement of 15 October 1987, *Heylens and others*, 222/86, [1987] ECR 4097, para. 14; Judgement of 27 November 2001, *Commission/Austria*, C-424/99, [2001] ECR I-9285, para. 45; Judgement of 25 July de 2002, *Unión de Pequeños Agricultores/Council*, Case C-50/00, [2002] ECR I-6677, para. 39; Judgement of 19 June 2003, *Eribrand*, Case C-467/01, [2003] ECR I-6471, para. 61.

[103] Cf. ECEC, Judgement of 13 May 2007, *Unibet (London) Ltd. And Unibet (International) v. Justitiekanslern*, Case C-432/05, para. 37.

rights under Community law. This is why in the absence of Community rules governing the matter, "it is for the domestic legal system of each Member State to designate the courts and tribunals having jurisdiction and to lay down the detailed procedural rules governing actions for safeguarding rights which individuals derive from Community law".[104]

Besides the right to an effective remedy (Article 47, paragraph 1), Article 47, paragraph 2 of the Charter includes the right to a fair trail; right concretized both in the right to a fair and public hearing within a reasonable time and by an independent and impartial tribunal previously established by law.[105]

The *Explanations relating to the Charter of Fundamental Rights of the European Union* specify that Article 47 of the Charter is based upon Article 6, of the European Convention for the Protection of Human Rights and Fundamental Freedoms adding that "in Community law, the right to a fair hearing is not confined to disputes relating to civil law rights and obligations."[106] This means that the right to a fair trail is regulated in Article 47 with a general scope and not limited to civil and criminal scopes as is the case of Article 6, paragraph 1, of the European Convention for the Protection of Human Rights and Fundamental Freedoms. Consequently, Article 47 of the Charter also covers administrative proceedings but always within the scope of the application of the European Charter of Fundamental Rights; a scope which according to Article 51 of the Charter is limited to the implementation of Union law.[107] Except for this difference concerning the scope of application, the guarantees of Article 47, paragraph 2, are applied in a similar manner as Article 6, paragraph 1 and Article 13 of the European Convention for the Protection of Human Rights and Fundamental Freedoms.[108]

In conclusion, the guarantee of the right to an effective remedy is applicable with regard to any right recognized as due to an individual by a norm of the European Union.[109]

Like the right to an effective remedy, the right to a fair trial has a conventional legal nature and at the same time it is a *general principle of Community law* as it has

[104] Cf. *ibid.*, paras. 38 and 39.

[105] Article 47, paragraph 2 says: "Everyone is entitled to a fair and public hearing within a reasonable time by an independent and impartial tribunal previously established by law. Everyone shall have the possibility of being advised, defended and represented."

[106] Just quoted. It adds: "That is one of the consequences of the fact that the Community is a community based on the rule of law as stated by the Court in Case 294/83, "Les Verts" v. European Parliament (judgment of 23 April 1986, [1988] ECR 1339). Nevertheless, in all respects other than their scope, the guarantees afforded by the ECHR apply in a similar way to the Union."

[107] Article 51 states: "1. The provisions of this Charter are addressed to the institutions and bodies of the Union with due regard for the principle of subsidiarity and to the Member States only when they are implementing Union law. They shall therefore respect the rights, observe the principles and promote the application thereof in accordance with their respective powers. 2. This Charter does not establish any new power or task for the Community or the Union, or modify powers and tasks defined by the Treaties."

[108] Cf. López Escudero, "Artículo 47...", *op. cit.*, 750.

[109] *Ibid.*

been asserted by the jurisprudence of the CJEU.[110] In addition and on the lines of its jurisprudence on human rights, the CJEU has declared that the general principle of Community law that everyone is entitled to a fair legal process is inspired by the fundamental rights, which form an integral part of the general principles of Community law "which the Court of Justice enforces, drawing inspiration from the constitutional traditions common to the Member States and from the guidelines supplied, in particular, by the European Convention for the Protection of Human Rights and Fundamental Freedoms, signed in Rome on 4 November 1950."[111]

So, it is possible to conclude that the right to an effective remedy as such is a safeguard on Article 6 of the European Convention for the Protection of Human Rights and Fundamental Freedoms is a fundamental right that the European Union respects as a general principle in virtue of Article 6, paragraph 2 of the EU Treaty.[112]

Regarding the content of this right, according to both Article 6, paragraph 1, of the European Convention for the Protection of Human Rights and Fundamental Freedoms and to the jurisprudence of the ECHR,[113] the right to an effective remedy comprehends a group of procedural guarantees. It is a case of the right of access to a tribunal, the principle of equality of arms in the procedure, the right to an independent and impartial tribunal, the publicity and celerity of the proceedings and the right to the execution of judiciary decisions.[114]

With regard to the most recent jurisprudence of the ECHR, in the *case Büyükdag c. Turquía*, Judgement of 21 December 2000, the Court states that the effectiveness required by Article 13 of the European Convention for the Protection of Human Rights and Fundamental Freedoms must be both in practice and in law. In law,

---

[110] According to this jurisprudence: "The general principle of Community law that everyone is entitled to fair legal process, which is inspired by those fundamental rights (see in particular Opinion 2/94 [1996] ECR I-1759, paragraph 33, and judgement in Case C-299/95 Kremzow [1997] ECR I-2629, paragraph 14), and in particular the right to legal process within a reasonable period, is applicable in the context of proceedings brought against a Commission decision imposing fines on an undertaking for infringement of competition law." (Judgement of 17 December 1998, *Baustahlgewebe/Comisión*, C-185/95, P, (1998) ECR I-8417, para. 21). Cf. also, Judgement of 11 January 2000, *Netherlands and Van der Wal/Commission*, C-174/98 P and C-189/98 P, *Rec.*, p. I-1, para. 17 and Judgement of 2 May 2006, *Eurofood IFSC Ltd.*, C-341/04, (2004) ECRI-3813, para. 65.

[111] ECEC, Judgement of 2 May 2006, *Eurofood IFSC Ltd.*. Cf. also Judgement of 25 January 2007, *Salzgitter Mannesmann/Commission*, C-411/04 P, para. 41.

[112] Cf. in this sense the Judgement of 27 June 2007, *Ordre des barreaux francophines et germanophone*, C-305/05, para 29. Also, M. López Escudero, "Artículo 47. Derecho a la tutela judicial efectiva y a un juez imparcial", *op. cit*, 751.

[113] Cf., between others the following cases: *case Golder v.United Kingdom*, Judgement of 21 February 1975, Serie A núm. 18, paras. 26–40; *case Campbell y Fell v.United Kingdom*, Judgement of 28 June 1984, Serie A, núm. 80, paras. 97–113; and *case Borgers v. Belgium*, Judgement of 30 October 1991, Serie A, No.. 214-B, para. 24.

[114] Cf. López Escudero, "Artículo 47. Derecho a la tutela judicial efectiva y a un juez imparcial", *op. cit.*, 751.

it means that the exercise of this right must not be unjustifiably hindered by the acts or the omissions of the authorities of the respondent State.[115]

Earlier, in the *Case Leander v. Sweden* the ECHR listed the general principles of relevance for the interpretation of Article 13 of the European Convention of Human Rights and fundamental Freedoms:

(a) where an individual has an arguable claim to be the victim of a violation of the rights set forth in the Convention, he should have a remedy before a national authority in order both to have his claim decided and, if appropriate, to obtain redress (see, inter alia, the above-mentioned Silver and 0thers judgment, Series A no. 61, p. 42, § 113);
(b) the authority referred to in Article 13 (art. 13) need not be a judicial authority but, if it is not, the powers and the guarantees which it affords are relevant in determining whether the remedy before it is effective (ibid.);
(c) although no single remedy may itself entirely satisfy the requirements of Article 13 (art. 13), the aggregate of remedies provided for under domestic law may do so (ibid.);
(d) Article 13 (art. 13) does not guarantee a remedy allowing a Contracting State's laws as such to be challenged before a national authority on the ground of being contrary to the Convention or equivalent domestic norms (see the James and Others judgment of 21 February 1986, Series A no. 98, p. 47, § 85).[116]

Reference should at least be made to the evolution of the jurisprudence of the ECHR on the right to an effective remedy linked with Article 13 of the European Convention; an evolution which is present in the *case Kudla v. Poland*, Judgement of 26 October 2000. Here, the ECHR recalls that in many previous cases in which it had found a violation of Article 6 § 1, it did not consider it necessary to also rule on an accompanying complaint made under Article 13. In other words, Article 6, paragraph 1 was deemed to constitute a *lex specialis* in relation to Article 13. However, in the *case Kudla v. Poland*, the ECHR changed its criteria and stated:

> 146. ...Thus, where the Convention right asserted by the individual is a "civil right" recognised under domestic law—such as the right of property—the protection afforded by Article 6 § 1 will also be available (see, for example, the Sporrong and Lönnroth v. Sweden judgment of 23 September 1982, Series A no. 52, pp. 31–32, § 88). In such circumstances the safeguards of Article 6 § 1, implying the full panoply of a judicial procedure, are stricter than, and absorb, those of Article 13 (see, for example, the Brualla Gómez de la Torre judgment cited above, p. 2957, § 41).

---

[115] In this case, violation of Article 13 occurs because of the inadequacy of the official investigation concerning the death of the applicant's brother. As stated in paragraph 106: "The scope of the obligation under Article 13 varies depending on the nature of the applicant's complaint under the Convention. Nevertheless, the remedy required by Article 13 must be "effective" in practice as well as in law, in particular in the sense that its exercise must not be unjustifiably hindered by the acts or the omissions of the authorities of the respondent State (see the above-mentioned Aksoy judgment, p. 2286, § 95; the above-mentioned Aydın judgment, pp. 1895–96, § 103; and the above-mentioned Menteş judgment, pp. 2715–16, § 89)." (ECHR, *Case Kaya v. Turkey*, Judgement of 19 February 1998). "Consequently, the Court finds that the applicant has been denied an effective remedy in respect of the death of his brother and has thereby been denied access to any other available remedies at his disposal, including a claim for compensation and concludes violation of Article 13 of the Convention" (*Case Carabulea v. Romania*, judgement of 13 July 2010, para. 167).

[116] ECHR, Judgement of 26 March 1987, Series A nº 116, 29 et seq. para. 77.

The Court has applied a similar logic in cases where the applicant's grievance has been directed at the adequacy of an existing appellate or cassation procedure coming within the ambit of both Article 6 § 1 under its "criminal" head and Article 13 (see the Kamasinski v. Austria judgment of 19 December 1989, Series A no. 168, pp. 45–46, § 110—in relation to nullity proceedings before the Supreme Court).

In such cases there is no legal interest in re-examining the same subject matter of complaint under the less stringent requirements of Article 13.

147. There is, however, no overlap and hence no absorption where, as in the present case, the alleged Convention violation that the individual wishes to bring before a "national authority" is a violation of the right to trial within a reasonable time, contrary to Article 6 § 1. The question of whether the applicant in a given case did benefit from trial within a reasonable time in the determination of civil rights and obligations or a criminal charge is a separate legal issue from that of whether there was available to the applicant under domestic law an effective remedy to ventilate a complaint on that ground. In the present case the issue to be determined before the Article 6 § 1 "tribunals" was the criminal charges brought against the applicant, whereas the complaint that he wanted to have examined by a "national authority" for the purposes of Article 13 was the separate one of the unreasonable length of the proceedings.

In comparable cases in the past, the Court has nonetheless declined to rule on an accompanying complaint of the absence of an effective remedy as guaranteed by Article 13, considering it unnecessary in view of its prior finding of a breach of the "reasonable time" requirement laid down in Article 6 § 1 (see, among other examples, the judgments cited above: Pizzetti, p. 37, § 21; *Bouilly*, § 27; and *Giuseppe Tripodi*, § 15).

148. In the Court's view, the time has come to review its case-law in the light of the continuing accumulation of applications before it in which the only, or principal, allegation is that of a failure to ensure a hearing within a reasonable time in breach of Article 6 § 1.

The growing frequency with which violations in this regard are being found has recently led the Court to draw attention to "the important danger" that exists for the rule of law within national legal orders when "excessive delays in the administration of justice" occur "in respect of which litigants have no domestic remedy" (see, for example, *Bottazzi v. Italy* [GC], no. 34884/97, § 22, ECHR 1999-V; *Di Mauro v. Italy* [GC], no. 34256/96, § 23, ECHR 1999-V; *A.P. v. Italy* [GC], no. 35265/97, § 18, 28 July 1999, unreported; and *Ferrari v. Italy* [GC], no. 33440/96, § 21, 28 July 1999, unreported).

149. Against this background, the Court now perceives the need to examine the applicant's complaint under Article 13 taken separately, notwithstanding its earlier finding of a violation of Article 6 § 1 for failure to try him within a reasonable time.

(...)

152. On the contrary, the place of Article 13 in the scheme of human rights protection set up by the Convention would argue in favour of implied restrictions of Article 13 being kept to a minimum.

By virtue of Article 1 (which provides: "The High Contracting Parties shall secure to everyone within their jurisdiction the rights and freedoms defined in Section I of this Convention"), the primary responsibility for implementing and enforcing the guaranteed rights and freedoms is laid on the national authorities. The machinery of complaint to the Court is thus subsidiary to national systems safeguarding human rights. This subsidiary character is articulated in Articles 13 and 35 § 1 of the Convention.

The purpose of Article 35 § 1, which sets out the rule on exhaustion of domestic remedies, is to afford the Contracting States the opportunity of preventing or putting right the violations alleged against them before those allegations are submitted to the Court (see, as a recent authority, *Selmouni v. France* [GC], no. 25803/94, § 74, ECHR 1999-V). The rule in Article 35 § 1 is based on the assumption, reflected in Article 13 (with which it has a close affinity), that there is an effective domestic remedy available in respect of the alleged breach of an individual's Convention rights (ibid.).

In that way, Article 13, giving direct expression to the States' obligation to protect human rights first and foremost within their own legal system, establishes an additional guarantee for an individual in order to ensure that he or she effectively enjoys those rights. The object of Article 13, as emerges from the *travaux préparatoires* (see the *Collected Edition of the "Travaux Préparatoires" of the European Convention on Human Rights*, vol. II, pp. 485 and 490, and vol. III, p. 651), is to provide a means whereby individuals can obtain relief at national level for violations of their Convention rights before having to set in motion the international machinery of complaint before the Court. From this perspective, the right of an individual to trial within a reasonable time will be less effective if there exists no opportunity to submit the Convention claim first to a national authority; and the requirements of Article 13 are to be seen as reinforcing those of Article 6 § 1, rather than being absorbed by the general obligation imposed by that Article not to subject individuals to inordinate delays in legal proceedings.

(....)

156. In view of the foregoing considerations, the Court considers that the correct interpretation of Article 13 is that that provision guarantees an effective remedy before a national authority for an alleged breach of the requirement under Article 6 § 1 to hear a case within a reasonable time.[117]

With respect to the international treaties on human rights quoted above, several reflections are called for. First, all these treaties are earlier to the new developments in International Law's procedure of humanization, which expressly recognizes victims. This is why such treaties on human rights do not contain any reference to victims' rights. In any case, most of victims' rights are rights that International Law of human rights recognizes as due to "everyone". From this perspective, victims as "everyone" are entitled to them. This is precisely the case of the right of effective access to the law and to justice, which is recognized as due to "everyone" independent of the fulfilment or not of the condition of being a victim.

Second, it should also be remembered that human rights have been developed through international jurisprudence of the different existent treaty bodies in the frame of the respective treaties; jurisprudence which, as we have seen, have specified such rights.

The Right to a Judicial Resolution Within a Reasonable Delay

The right to an effective access to justice is also concretized in the right to obtain a judicial resolution "in a reasonable delay". On the lines of what I have written before, it should be remembered that although international norms on victims refer to it the fact is that this right is part of the human right to a fair trial declared by international treaties of human rights.

[117] ECHR, Judgement of 26 October 2000, paras. 146–149, 152 and 156.

With regard to victims and in the frame of the *UN general or universal system*, this right is specified in the *Declaration of Basic Principles of Justice for Victims of Crime and Abuse of Power* adopted by the General Assembly resolution 40/34 of 29 November 1985, which states that the States shall facilitate the responsiveness of judicial and administrative processes to the needs of victims "avoiding unnecessary delay in the disposition of cases and the execution of orders or decrees granting awards to victims."[118]

In the *European regional frame*, the requirement of a "reasonable delay" is present in different recommendations of the Committee of Ministers of the Council of Europe. This is the case, for example, in *Recommendation No. R (81) 7* of 14 May 1981 *On Measures Facilitating Access to Justice* the principles of which are also applicable to victims of terrorist acts. So, in paragraph C—related to the acceleration of judicial proceedings—point 8 stresses that

> 8. All measures should be taken to minimise the time to reach a determination of the issues. To this end steps should be taken to eliminate archaic procedures which fulfil no useful purpose, to ensure that the courts are adequately staffed and they operate efficiently, and to adopt procedures which will enable the court to follow the action from an early stage.

Later, the right to obtain a judicial resolution "in a reasonable delay" is repeated in other recommendations of the Committee of Ministers. These are the cases both in *Recommendation No. R (83) 7*, of 23 June 1983, *On Participation of the Public in Crime Policy* and in *Recommendation No. R (85) 11*, of 28 June 1985, *On the Position of the Victim in the Framework of Criminal Law and Procedure*, as well as more recently also in point 7.1 of *Recommendation No. R (2006) 8*, of 14 June 2006, *On Assistance to Crime Victims* we have examined on preceding pages.[119]

With respect to the reasonable character of the delay, as I have stated before, it has been specified in International law of human rights through the jurisprudence of treaty bodies on the matter. This is the case both in the ECHR and of the Inter-American Court of Human Rights. According to this jurisprudence, the reasonableness of the length of proceedings must be assessed in each case according to the following criteria: the particular circumstances of the case, the complexity of the factual or legal issues raised by the case as well as both the conduct of the applicants and the competent authorities. On the other hand, the reasonable character of the delay is a requirement concerning all kind of proceedings: criminal, civil, administrative or other.[120]

---

[118] Paragraph 6.e).

[119] See 154–155 of the present work.

[120] The jurisprudence of the ECHR is built by the following judgements: *case Wemhift*, Judgement of 27 June 1968; *case Neumeister v. Austria*, Judgement of 27 June 1968; *case Ringeisen v. Austria*, Judgement of 16 July 1971; *case König v. Germany*, Judgement of 28 June 1978; *case Buchholz v. Germany*, Judgement of 6 May 1981; *case Foti and Others v. Italy*, Judgement of 10 December 1982; *case Zimmermann and Steiner v. Switzerland*, Judgement of 13 July 1983; *case Lechner and Hess v. Austria*, Judgement of 23 April 1987; *case Capuano v. Italy*, Judgement of 25 June 1987.

As an example of it, the *Guidelines on the Protection of Victims of Terrorist Acts* adopted by the Committee of Ministers of the Council of Europe quotes the Judgement of the ECHR of 8 June 2004 in the *case Mutimara v. France*. Here,

> 69. The Court reminds that the reasonableness of the length of proceedings is to be assessed in the light of the criteria laid down in the Court's case-law, in particular the complexity of the case, the applicant's conduct and that of the competent authorities (see, *Doustaly v. France*, judgement of 22 April 1998, Reports 1998 II, p. 857, par. 39; *Slimane-Kaïd v. France (nº 3)*, nº 45130/98, par. 38, 6 April 2004) and the particular circumstances of the case, required a global evaluation in (*Versini v. France*, judgement of 10 July 2001, No. 40096/98, par. 26; *Slimane-Kaïd*, just quoted).
>
> 70. In this case, the Court verifies that the proceeding started on 1st of August, 1995 (complaint for criminal offence with civil party application lodged by the applicant) is still pending before the examining magistrate. This means a length of eight years and more than eight months today.
>
> 71. According to the Court, the matter was somehow complex. This can be specially proved by looking at numerous international letters of request. Nevertheless, this is not valid in itself to justify the length of the proceeding (. . .)
> 74. Taking into account the circumstances of the case and despite its special features, the Court thinks a global length of almost nine years cannot be considered a 'reasonable' period for criminal information to be still in course.[121]

But as I have just stated what is relevant is the fact that the requirement concerning the obtaining of a decision of a competent court "within a reasonable delay" derives from the human right to an effective remedy declared on international treaties of human rights.[122]

With regard to the *International Covenant on Civil and Political Rights*—an international treaty actually ratified by 167 States—the Human Rights Committee on the occasion of its interpretation of Article 14 has stressed that its provisions:

> are aimed at ensuring the proper administration of justice, and to this end uphold a series of individual rights such as equality before the courts and tribunals and the right to a fair and public hearing by a competent, independent and impartial tribunal established by law.[123]

Subparagraph 3 (c) of Covenant's Article 14 provides that the accused shall be tried without undue delay. According to the criterion of the Human Rights Committee, this guarantee relates "not only to the time by which a trial should commence, but also the time by which it should end and judgement be rendered; all stages must take place 'without undue delay'. To make this right effective,

---

[121] The official version of this judgement of the ECHR is in French. The translation to English is mine.

[122] In Article 14 of the International Covenant on Civil and Political Rights of 16 December 1966; in Article 13 of the European Convention for the Protection of Human Rights and fundamental Freedoms of 4 November 1950; in Article 25 of the American Convention of Human Rights and in Article 7 of the African Charter of Human and People's Rights of 27 June 1981.

[123] UN CCPR, *CCPR General Comment No. 13, Equality before the courts and the right to a fair and public hearing by an independent court established by law (Art. 14)*, !3/04/1984, (twenty-first session, 1984), para. 1. Article 14 declares the right to an effective remedy.

a procedure must be available to ensure that the trial will proceed 'without undue delay', both in the first instance and on appeal."[124]

As stated earlier, international treaties of human rights are prior to the new developments of the process of humanization of International law, which expressly envisages victims. This is why in their provisions no reference is made to victims others than those acquiring this condition as a consequence of the violation of the concerned treaty of human rights by the States Parties to it. In contrast to the International law of victims in the International law of human rights, only the States Parties to those treaties are respondents. Consequently, treaty bodies and techniques of control (reports, communications between the States and communications of individuals against the States Parties) envisaged in such treaties are built from this exclusive perspective. In the International law of human rights, too, "everyone" can become a victim because the rights such as those the general treaties (like the International Covenant on Civil and Political Rights, the European Convention, the American Convention and the African Charter) declare are recognized as due to "everyone".

Contrary to the International law of human rights what international norms on victims introduce as an innovation is the assertion of a catalogue of rights inherent to victims which, at the same time, are obligations on the charge of the States. These are rights that can be invoked when the individuals concerned are immersed in a situation of victimization as a consequence of wrongful behaviours of the States, particulars or groups of particulars. In the last two hypotheses, the State is not liable because it does not breach any international obligation. However, international norms on victims impose on the charge of the State a catalogue of obligations which are, as stated earlier, the reverse of victims' rights that international norms recognize as due to them.

Right to Reparation and Compensation

With regard to this right, the first thing that must be said is that the existence of this international obligation is indisputable. It is a firmly international customary norm that, at the same time, constitutes one of the fundamental principles of International law on the matter of the State's responsibility.[125] On the other hand, all international norms on victims declare the victims' right to redress. However, where unanimity

[124] *Ibid.*, para. 10.

[125] About this question cf. the developments of the I/ACHI in the following cases: *Case Almonacid Arellano and others vs. Chile*, Judgement of 26 September de 2006, par. 135; *Case Montero Aranguren and others v.*, Judgement of 5 July 2006, Series C No. 150, par. 115; *Case Ximenes Lopes v.*, Judgement of 4 de July 2006, Series C No. 149, par. 345.

In the opinion of Tomuschat, the analysis of the practice reveals that a strict rule in accordance with which any violation of human rights would give rise to an obligation to compensate is not acceptable. On these lines, he argues that the simple application by analogy of the regime of the international responsibility of the State should be ruled out (cf. "La protection internationale des droits des victimes", in FLAUSS, J.-F., *La protection internationale des droits de l'homme et les droits des victimes*, 2009, 11).

does not exist is between regional treaties of human rights because—in contrast to the American Convention of 1969 which expressly contemplates compensation—[126] the European Convention on human rights of 1950 only allows the ECHR to agree on a "fair satisfaction". For its part, the African Charter on Human and Peoples' Rights, of 1980, says nothing on this subject.

The reparation for the damage caused to the victim by the breach of an international obligation requires, "wherever possible" full restitution (*restitutio in integrum*). That is, the re-establishment of the situation before the breach. If not possible, the international tribunal can determine a series of measures so that, "as well as ensuring respect for the rights violated, it repairs the consequences which were caused by the violations and establish the payment of compensation as compensation for the damage caused".[127] It must be added, moreover, that the State must take positive measures to ensure that similar harmful acts are not repeated.

Therefore, reparations are measures that tend to do away with the effects of the violations committed.[128] Nevertheless, it should be noted that given the scale of the violence suffered by the victims, full restitution is not always possible.[129] In that regard, as it has been already successful and graphically stated, it is impossible to repair the irreparable[130], in such a way that reparation cannot restore the victim to the position it had before the commission of the crime. There is not, therefore, a "real" reparation, complete, or comprehensive. As Jeangène points out, the damages resulting from gross violations of human rights are, in general, irreparable: "compensate, indemnify, compensate for is the confession of the impossibility to repair, to restore. Try to repair in fact, is to find an equivalent of a reparation that, insofar as such, it is impossible. And the objective of this equivalent is the relief, the consolation of the victim. This means that, reparation *does not repair, it only relieves.* The victim remains victim, even after the repair. Hence, the importance of their rehabilitation".[131]

With regard to its *object*, reparation comprises both *intangible* or *moral harm* and *material damage*. *Material damage* means, the loss or deterioration of victims' revenues, the costs incurred on the occasion of the facts and the consequences of a pecuniary nature which have a causal link with the violations,[132] while *intangible*

---

[126] Due to the wealth of the I/ACHR developments in this matter, I will refer extensively to its jurisprudence in this area. It is a jurisprudence which synthesizes and expresses the existing International law in the field of international redress.

[127] I/ACHR, *Case of Almonacid Arellano and others vs. Chile*, *op. cit.*, para. 136.

[128] Cf. *ibid.*, para. 137.

[129] This is the case of crimes of terrorism, crimes against humanity, war crimes, genocide, forced desappearances, extrajudicial executions and torture.

[130] Cf. Jeangène Vilmer (2009).

[131] *Ibid.*, 7.

[132] Cf. *ibid.*, párr.158. On the same lines cf. *Case Ximenes Lopes vs. Brasil*, *op. cit.*, para. 220; *Case Baldeón García vs. Perú*, para. 183; *Case of Sawhoyamaxa Indigenous Community vs. Paraguay*, Judgement of 29 March 2006, Series C No. 146, párr. 216 y *Case La Cantuta vs. Perú*, Judgement of 29 November 2006, para. 213; *Case Goiburú et alt. v. Paraguay, (Merits, Reparation and Costs)* Judgement of 22 September 2006, Series C No. 153, para. 150; *Case of Montero Aranguren et al.*

or *moral damages* can understand "both the suffering and the afflictions caused the direct victim and their relatives, the erosion of values very significant for the people, as well as alterations, not pecuniary in nature, in the conditions of existence of the victim or his family".[133]

Within this *international obligation of reparation*, and with regard to its forms or modalities it is necessary to distinguish—as do both the more recent international norms relating to the victims and the international jurisprudence on the matter—between *compensation* and *reparation*. Thus, whereas *compensation* is intended to be economic compensation for damage (material and immaterial or moral) caused to the victim,[134] *reparation* has a more broad content that—in addition to the compensation itself,—it also includes other measures as restitution, rehabilitation, satisfaction and guarantees of non-repetition.[135] As repeatedly indicated by both the

---

vs. Venezuela (Detention Center of Catia), op. cit., para. 126, y. *Case Ximenes Lopes vs. Brasil, op. cit.*, para. 220.

[133] I/ACHR, *Case La Cantuta vs. Perú, op. cit.*, para. 216. About this issue and in the same case and paragraph, quoting its judgement on the *Case Goiburú et al.vs. Paraguay*, the I/ACHR adds: "Since accurately quantifying non-pecuniary damage is impossible, such damage can only be compensated, for the purpose of providing comprehensive reparation to the victim, through the payment of such sum of money or the provision of such goods or services of monetary worth as may be determined by the Court, in fairness and at its reasonable judicial discretion, and through public action or works aimed at giving recognition to the victim's human dignity and preventing any further human rights violations." (*ibid.*).

On the same lines cf. *Case of Almonacid Arellano and others v. Chile, op. cit.*, para. 158. Cf. also *Case of Montero Aranguren et al. vs. Venezuela (Detention Center of Catia), op. cit.*, para. 130; *Case of the Ituango Massacres v. Colombia (Preliminary Objections, Merits, Reparations and Costs)*, Judgement of July 1, 2006, para. 383; *Case Baldeón García vs. Perú*, para. 188; *Case Goiburú et alt. v Paraguay, (Merits, Reparation and Costs), op. cit.*, para. 156; *Caso Montero Aranguren y otros (Retén de Catia), op. cit.*, para. 130, and *Case Ximenes Lopes vs. Brasil, op. cit.*, para. 227.

[134] About this issue, the *Basic principles and guidelines of the right to a remedy and reparation for victims of gross violations of international human rights law and serious violations of International Humanitarian Law* adopted by the UN Commission on Human Rights on 19 April 2005, by Resolution 2005/35, and adopted by the UN General Assembly on 16 December 2005 through Resolution 60/147 makes the following enumeration: physical or mental damage; the loss of opportunities, in particular employment, education and social benefits; material damage and loss of earnings, including loss of profits; moral damages; the costs of legal assistance or experts, medicines and medical services and psychological and social services. As stated by Fernández Sola, in the American regional frame the Inter-American Court of Human Rights has presumed the intangible damage that suffering or death of a person brings to their children, spouse or companion, fathers and brothers, so it is not necessary to prove it (cf. *op. cit.*, 411 et seq.).

[135] These forms of reparation are present in the General Assembly Resolution 60/147 adopted on 16 December 2005 through which the *Basic principles and guidelines of the right to a remedy and reparation for victims of gross violations of international human rights law and serious violations of International Humanitarian Law* adopted by the UN Commission on Human Rights on 19 April 2005, by Resolution 2005/35, are adopted. In the opinion of Fernández Sola, the varieties of reparation through satisfaction can be grouped into two categories: the right to justice and the right to the truth. The right to justice and its corollary of punishment to the culprits translates into non-impunity (cf. *ibid.*, 415).

ECHR and the Inter-American Court of Human Rights, the international judgement itself declaring the violation of the treaty is also a form of reparation.[136]

The range of measures which I have just mentioned can be classified into *two groups*. On one side, *individual measures* (restitution, compensation and rehabilitation). On the other side, *collective action* of a symbolic nature (e.g. satisfaction and guarantees of non-repetition) trying to provide moral redress to the victims. It is a case, for example, of the request for forgiveness, for the recognition of the State's responsibility, the restoration of the dignity of victims, the holding of commemorative ceremonies, the erection of monuments or the establishment of national days of remembrance.[137]

Most of the *international norms* that I will discuss in this section relate only to compensation. From this perspective, therefore, they are impregnated with what Cançado Trindade describes as "the logical—or, rather, absence of logic—of the *homo oeconomicus* of our days, for which, in the middle of the new idolatry of the god-market, everything is reduced to the fixing of economic compensation, due to that human relations are commodified".[138] Indeed, compensation alone is not a restorative measure nor is it the first thing the victims want. On the contrary, the first objective and yearning for the victims is for justice, the economic repair being a

[136] A recent example of it with regard to the ECHR is the Judgement of 2 MRCH 2010 (Section IV), *Case Al-Saadoon and Mufdhi v. United Kingdom*– 61498/08. In it, the ECHR concluded that the finding of violation of Articles 3, 13 and 34 with the measure indicated by virtue of Article 46 is possible enough by way of moral damage just satisfaction (cf. ECHR, *Note d'information sur la jurisprudence de la Cour*, No. 128, March, 2010, 14).

With regard to the I/ACHR, for example, the *Case La Cantuta vs. Peru*, where it states: "International courts have repeatedly held that a judgment is, in and of itself, a form of redress. The Court does, however, consider it necessary to order, in fairness, payment of the following sums as compensation for non-pecuniary damage on account of the suffering of the next of kin of the ten victims that were caused to disappear or executed, such next of kin being in turn victims of the breach of the right to humane treatment" (*op.cit.*, para. 219). On the same lines vid. the jurisprudence of ht I/ACHR in the following cases: *Case Goiburú et alt. v. Paraguay, (Merits, Reparation and Costs), op. cit.*,, para. 160; *Case of Almonacid Arellano and others v. Chile, op. cit.*, para. 161; *Case Vargas Areco vs. Paraguay*, para. 150; *Case of the Ituango Massacres v. Colombia, op.cit.*, para. 390, *Case of the Pueblo Bello Massacre v. Colombia Judgment of January 31, 2006 Merits, Reparations and Costs*, para. 258; *Case of the Massacre of La Rochela v. Colombia*, Judgement of 11 May 2007, para. 264.

[137] This division into two groups is contained in the Final report of Joinet to the Sub-Commission for the promotion and protection of human rights (of the UN Human Rights Commission) on the question of the impunity of the perpetrators of violations of human rights entitled: "The Administration of Justice and the Human Rights of Detainees, Question of the Impunity of Perpetrators of Human Rights Violations (Civil and Political)", UN Doc. E/CN.4/Sub.2/1997/20, de 26 de junio de 1997. Cf. the revised Final report of 2nd October 1997, in UN Doc. E/CN.4(/Sub.2/1997/20/Rev.1.

From another perspective, these five forms of reparation may also be classified into forms of *material reparation* (restitution, compensation, rehabilitation), which have a physical existence and forms of *symbolic or moral reparation* (satisfaction, guarantees of non-repetition), because they are more abstract (cf. Jeangène Vilmer (2009), 58–86).

[138] Cited by Garapon in the preface to the work of J-B Jeangène Vilmer, *op. cit.*, p. VIII.

secondary claim. To the extent that, although they have been compensated financially, their legitimate desire for Justice would not be fulfilled unless the perpetrators who were responsible for their victimization are not tried.

As mentioned above, the economic element of compensation is present both in some of the norms specifically relating to some categories of victims and in most of the international human rights treaties. Others, fewer and more recent, opt for a broader perspective of reparation, comprising within it both compensation and reparation.[139]

In relation to the broader perspective of reparation, Bottigliero argues that the recent pronouncements that have taken place in the field of international human rights law relating to torture, forced disappearances and other serious violations of human rights, they have introduced clarity in the applicability and scope of the right of victims to reparation, pointing to a gradual expansion beyond traditional forms of monetary compensation and remedies, to understand also, when appropriate, the legal responsibility of the State of doing justice to the victims by punishing the offender and putting in place mechanisms of investigation or fact-finding.[140]

As I said at the beginning of this section, in the field of *international human rights treaties* only the American Convention of 1969 provides expressly for compensation.[141] The European Convention on human rights of 1950 only allows the ECHR to agree on a "fair satisfaction",[142] whereas the African Charter On Human and Peoples' Rights, in 1980, is silent on this issue.

In the case of the ECHR, the restrictive concept with which is designed reparation in Article 41 of the European Convention on human rights—equitable satisfaction—has led the Court to agree only on financial compensation both for moral damages and material damage (as, for example, the psychological damage of the victim in cases of serious violations of human rights), as well as in order for the payment of costs and the costs of the process. Next to them is the judgement of the Court itself declaring the violation by the State in question of the rights of the claimant.[143]

---

[139] This last concept is present in the UN *Declaration of Basic Principles of Justice for Victims of Crime and Abuse of Power*, of 29 November 1985, in the UN *Declaration on the Protection of All Persons from Enforced Disappearance*, of 18 December 1992, in the General Assembly Resolution 60/147 adopted on 16 December 2005 through which the *Basic principles and guidelines of the right to a remedy and reparation for victims of gross violations of international human rights law and serious violations of International Humanitarian Law* adopted by the UN Commission on Human Rights on 19 April 2005, by Resolution 2005/35, are adopted and in the *International Convention for the Protection of All Persons from Enforced Disappearance*, of 20 December 2006.

[140] Bottigliero, *op. cit.*, p. 111. Cf. in this regard I/ACHR, *Case of the Massacre of La Rochela v. Colombia, Judgement of 11 May 2007*, para. 235.

[141] That has led to an abundant jurisprudence of the I/ACHR with regard to compensation and reparations which I note in this section.

[142] Which makes the ECHR limited exclusively to financial compensation.

[143] Cf. *ut supra*, note 133. However, in view of some "just satisfaction" of Article 41 of the Convention it does not prevent the ECHR from seeking reparation measures other than compensation. It would only be possible with a broader interpretation of Article 41 by the Court.

This restrictive view is also that has done that to date, and so unlike the UN Human Rights Committee and the Inter-American Court of Human Rights, the ECHR not ordered reparations in different forms of compensation. Still more important, the ECHR has not ordered States the amendment or annulment of the national measures that violate the Convention.

However, this strict interpretation has been amended by the own ECHR in its Judgement of 31 October 1995 relapsed in the case *Papamichaloupoulos and other v. Greece*, whereas it authorized itself since then to recommend the adoption of specific measures to the respondent State declared a perpetrator of the violation.[144]

In the view of Bottigliero, the absence of any reference to reparation in international human rights treaties would be due to the fact that the compensation to the victims has been traditionally considered a "secondary law", "a sort of 'extra law'" deriving of the violation of a primary right protected by specific legal provisions. Consequently, it concludes, the right to reparation continues anchored to its indirect connection with the question of compensation.[145]

As I have already pointed out, *as opposed to compensation, reparation* has a wider content comprising a plurality of forms: restitution, compensation,[146] satisfaction, rehabilitation and guarantees of non-repetition and so collected it so much international jurisprudence of universal and regional levels, and most recent international standards relating to the victims.[147]

The *international norm relating to victims* (in reality, a category of them) that most develops and gives more accurately each of these measures is the General Assembly Resolution 60/147 adopted on 16 December 2005 through which the *Basic principles and guidelines of the right to a remedy and reparation for victims of gross violations of international human rights law and serious violations of International Humanitarian Law* adopted by the UN Commission on Human Rights

---

Especially for cases of serious violations of human rights (cf. SHELTON, D., *Remedies in International Human Rights Law*, Oxford University Press, 1999, pp. 148–151). Cf. also Fernández Sola, "El derecho a la reparación de las víctimas...", *op. cit.*, 413 et seq.

[144] Cf. on this issue Bottigliero, *op. cit.*, 152–159.

[145] Cf. Bottigliero, *op. cit.*, 123.

[146] So, the *Basic principles and guidelines of the right to a remedy and reparation for victims of gross violations of international human rights law and serious violations of International Humanitarian Law*, refers to compensation as a form of reparation for any economically assessable damage.

[147] The international norms on victims that gives more information on reparation is General Assembly Resolution 60/147 adopted on 16 December 2005 through which the *Basic principles and guidelines of the right to a remedy and reparation for victims of gross violations of international human rights law and serious violations of International Humanitarian Law* adopted by the UN Commission on Human Rights on 19 April 2005, by Resolution 2005/35, are adopted. In section IX, entitled "Reparation for harm suffered", it concerns both the characteristics and the forms of reparation. Concerning the first, it states that reparation for harm suffered shall be adequate, effective and prompt, the intention being to promote justice by redressing gross violations of international human rights law or serious violations of international humanitarian law. It shall also be proportional to the gravity of the violations and the harm suffered.

on 19 April 2005, by Resolution 2005/35, are adopted. It refers to this question on paragraph IX entitled "Reparation for harm suffered".[148] This paragraph affirms, in general, the characteristics of reparation and its purpose:

> 15. Adequate, effective and prompt reparation is intended to promote justice by redressing gross violations of international human rights law or serious violations of international humanitarian law. Reparation should be proportional to the gravity of the violations and the harm suffered. In accordance with its domestic laws and international legal obligations, a State shall provide reparation to victims for acts or omissions which can be attributed to the State and constitute gross violations of international human rights law or serious violations of international humanitarian law. In cases where a person, a legal person, or other entity is found liable for reparation to a victim, such party should provide reparation to the victim or compensate the State if the State has already provided reparation to the victim.

The fact that this principle referred to domestic law and international obligations of the States leads some to say that there is no general obligation leading the States to reparation and that the existence of an obligation of reparation can only be derived from other additional sources: of the national law or of the principles and rules of international law that need to be identified with regard to the specific case.[149] What I want to point out is that, regardless of the reference to domestic law, this XV principle clearly states the obligation that States have to provide reparation to the victims "for acts or omissions which can be attributed to the State and constitute gross violations of international human rights law or serious violations of international humanitarian law."[150]

With regard to the *forms of reparation*, in accordance with these principles, *restitution* means to restore the victim—whenever possible—to the original situation before the gross violations of international human rights law or serious violations of international humanitarian law occurred, and it includes, "as appropriate: restoration of liberty, enjoyment of human rights, identity, family life and citizenship, return to one's place of residence, restoration of employment and return of property".[151]

---

[148] It is the international norm I use but without forgetting the specifics it contains (as usual) with regard to the category of victims envisaged.

[149] Cf. Tomuschat, "Reparation in Favour of Individual Victims of Gross Violations of Human Rights and International Humanitarian Law", *op. cit.*, 579. In consequence, he states that in matters of reparation these principles and guidelines are not more than guidelines that must be developed by the States (cf. *ibid.*, 576).

[150] The language used in this regard is clear and is not subject to any kind of condition: "States shall provide".

[151] On paragraph 19. In the opinion of J-B. Jeangène Vilmer the first place in which restitution is listed within the different forms of reparation envisaged by General Assembly Resolution 60/147 adopted on 16 December 2005 through which the *Basic principles and guidelines of the right to a remedy and reparation for victims of gross violations of international human rights law and serious violations of International Humanitarian Law* adopted by the UN Commission on Human Rights on 19 April 2005, by Resolution 2005/35, are adopted is not casual. According to him, this fact would show the priority of restitution and that, only when this last is not possible, it could be substituted through compensation (cf. *Réparer l'irréparable, op. cit.*, 58 y s.).

When restitution is materially impossible—what happens in most cases (enforced disappearances, attacks against the life, mutilations, rape, torture, deprivation of liberty, etc.)—reparation by equivalence or compensation takes place. As a result, compensation is *de facto* the most common way to repair. However, it does no repair at all because it is impossible to ascribe to moral damages, a pecuniary equivalent right.

With regard to *rehabilitation*, it generally consists of helping the victims to be reintegrated socially through psychological, medical, legal and social support. Thus, it is expressly stated in paragraph 21 of the above-mentioned principles and guidelines specifying that the rehabilitation should include medical and psychological care as well as legal and social services.[152]

As regards *satisfaction*, paragraph 22 gives to it a very broad content. According to it, satisfaction should include, "where applicable, any or all" of the following measures:

- Effective measures aimed at the cessation of continuing violations;
- Verification of the facts, full and public disclosure of the truth to the extent that such disclosure does not cause further harm or threaten the safety and interests of the victim, the victim's relatives, witnesses, or persons who have intervened to assist the victim or prevent the occurrence of further violations;
- The search for the whereabouts of the disappeared, for the identities of the children abducted, and for the bodies of those killed, and assistance in the recovery, identification and reburial of the bodies in accordance with the expressed or presumed wish of the victims, or the cultural practices of the families and communities;
- An official declaration or a judicial decision restoring the dignity, the reputation and the rights of the victim and of persons closely connected with the victim;
- Public apology, including acknowledgement of the facts and acceptance of responsibility;
- Judicial and administrative sanctions against persons liable for the violations;
- Commemorations and tributes to the victims;
- Inclusion of an accurate account of the violations that occurred in international human rights law and international humanitarian law training and in educational material at all levels.

But satisfaction can also include other measures. It is the case, for example, that either the publication of all or part of the judgement declaring the violation of the concerned treaty by the State[153] or of the Final report of the Commission on the

[152] As emphasized by Jeangène Vilmer, rehabilitation and compensation are interrelated since one can be obtained through the other (cf. *ibid.*, 66).

[153] In the *Case of Almonacid Arellano and others vs. Chile,* "As a measure of satisfaction, the State must publish at least once in the Official Gazette and in another nationwide daily newspaper, the chapter on Proven Facts of this Judgment, without the corresponding footnotes, and the related

truth and reconciliation in the specific case in question.[154] Among the measures of satisfaction, should also be placed acts in relief to the memory of the victims, measures related to the damage caused to the life project of the victims and their families (scholarships for study, employment opportunities, etc.),[155] physical and psychological treatment to the families of the victims;[156] provision to inform family members the places in which are located the remains of the victims[157]; public acts of recognition of responsibility;[158] the implementation of ongoing programs of education in human rights aimed at members of the institutions of the State responsible for the violations of human rights, at all hierarchical levels.[159]

Ultimately, with the measures that constitute the content of this form of reparation which is satisfaction, the aim is to recover the truth about what happened and to determine responsibility. From this point of view, the right to reparation entails the right "to obtain the State investigation, trial and punishment of the guilty parties, i.e. the right to the truth and the right to justice".[160]

Finally, and as satisfaction, *guarantees of non-repetition* also have a very broad content. In accordance with paragraph 23 of the above-mentioned principles and guidelines, the guarantees of non-repetition should include, "where applicable", any or all of the following measures, "which will also contribute to prevention":

- Ensuring effective civilian control of military and security forces;
- Ensuring that all civilian and military proceedings abide by international standards of due process, fairness and impartiality;
- Strengthening the independence of the judiciary;
- Protecting persons in the legal, medical and health care professions, the media and other related professions, and human rights defenders;
- Providing, on a priority and continued basis, human rights and international humanitarian law education to all sectors of society and training for law enforcement officials as well as military and security forces;

---

operative paragraphs." All this, within a period of 6 months following the notification of the judgement (*op. cit*, para. 162).

[154] So, in Perú (cf. *Case La Cantuta vs. Perú, op.cit.*, para. 223).

[155] Cf., I/ACHR, *Case of the Massacre of La Rochela vs. Colombia, op. cit.*, para. 277.

[156] Cf., I/ACHR, *Case La Cantuta vs. Perú, op.cit.*, para. 238; *Case of the Massacre of La Rochela vs. Colombia, op. cit.*, paras. 298–302; *Case of Durand and Ugarte vs. Peru (Reparations and Costs)*, Judgement of 3 December 2001, para. 36 et seq.

[157] So in the American regional frame in the following cases: *Case La Cantuta vs. Perú, op.cit.*, para. 231; *Case of Durand and Ugarte vs. Peru (Reparations and Costs), op.cit.*, para. 39.

[158] Cf. I/ACHR, *Case La Cantuta vs. Perú, op.cit.*, para. 231; *Case Goiburú et alt. v. Paraguay, (Merits, Reparation and Costs), op. cit.*, para. 171; *Case of the 19 Tradesmen vs. Colombia, op. cit.*, para. 265, and *Case Juan Humberto Sánchez vs. Honduras, op. cit.*, para. 187.

[159] Cf. I/ACHR, *Case La Cantuta vs. Perú, op.cit.*, para. 240; *Case of the Massacre of La Rochela vs. Colombia, op. cit.*, para. 303.

[160] Jenagène Vilmer, *Réparer l'irréparable, op. cit.*, 69.

- Promoting the observance of codes of conduct and ethical norms, in particular international standards, by public servants, including law enforcement, correctional, media, medical, psychological, social service and military personnel, as well as by economic enterprises;
- Promoting mechanisms for preventing and monitoring social conflicts and their resolution;
- Reviewing and reforming laws contributing to or allowing gross violations of international human rights law and serious violations of international humanitarian law.[161]

With regard to the *characteristics of the compensation*, international norms relating to the victims require, in general, that the compensation for the damage they have suffered must be "fair", "appropriate", "rapid".[162] When compensation cannot be ensured by other sources,[163] such international norms include subsidiary compensation by the State on whose territory the act of victimization took place. It also requires cooperation between the States when the act that gives rise to compensation has been committed in the territory of a State other than that in which the victim resides.[164] At least, international norms on victims also promoted

[161] To Tomuschat, both satisfaction and guarantees of non-repetition have little to do with reparation (cf. "Reparation in Favour of Individual Victims of Gross Violations of Human Rights and International Humanitarian Law", *op. cit.*, p. 590). In my opinion, it is a strict repair concept because this one is not limited to the material content of the financial compensation.

[162] Cf. point No. 12 of the UN *Declaration of Basic Principles of Justice for Victims of Crime and Abuse of Power*, of 29 November 1985; point No. 20 of the *Basic principles and guidelines of the right to a remedy and reparation for victims of gross violations of international human rights law and serious violations of International Humanitarian Law*, of 19 April 2005; Article 24.4 of the *International Convention for the Protection of All Persons from Enforced Disappearance* of 20 December 2006; and the *Guidelines on the Protection of Victims of Terrorist Acts* adopted by the Committee of Ministers of the Council of Europe on 2 March 2005.

[163] So, for example, the *European Convention on the Compensation of Victims of Violent Crimes*, of 24 November 1983, the exclusive object of which is compensation of victims of violent crimes. The general principle of this convention is the payment of compensation (in this case on the charge of the State on whose territory the crime was committed. According to Article 3 of it: "Compensation shall be paid by the State on whose territory the crime was committed: (a) to nationals of the States party to this Convention; (b) to nationals of all member States of the Council of Europe who are permanent residents in the State on whose territory the crime was committed". On the same lines, Article 2 of *Directive 2004/80/EC*, of 29 April 2004, relating to compensation to crime victims states: "Compensation shall be paid by the competent authority of the Member State on whose territory the crime was committed".

[164] Article 12 of the *European Convention on the Compensation of Victims of Violent Crimes*, of 24 November 1983 provides: "Subject to the application of bilateral or multilateral agreements on mutual assistance concluded between Contracting States, the competent authorities of each Party shall, at the request of the appropriate authorities of any other Party, give the maximum possible assistance in connection with the matters covered by this Convention. To this end, each Contracting State shall designate a central authority to receive, and to take action on, requests for such assistance, and shall inform thereof the Secretary General of the Council of Europe when depositing its instrument of ratification, acceptance, approval or accession."

the creation of specific funds to compensate victims[165] and provide for the adoption of measures other than the compensation.[166]

It can be said, in general, that all these characteristics and conditions are in different international norms to which I will refer in this paragraph.[167]

Also, Article 12.2 of *Directive 2004/80/EC*, of 29 April 2004, relating to compensation to crime victims, states: "All Member States shall ensure that their national rules provide for the existence of a scheme on compensation to victims of violent intentional crimes committed in their respective territories, which guarantees fair and appropriate compensation to victims."

Article 1 of this same Directive states: "Member States shall ensure that where a violent intentional crime has been committed in a Member State other than the Member State where the applicant for compensation is habitually resident, the applicant shall have the right to submit the application to an authority or any other body in the alter Member State." On the same lines, also Article 11 of Council Framework Decisión 2002/220/JHA, of 15 March 2001, also provides that Member States shall ensure that its competent authorities "can take appropriate measures to minimize the difficulties faced where the victim is a resident of a State other than the one where the offence has occurred, particularly with regard to the organization of the proceedings."

On this matter, the judgement of the EUCJ (Second Chamber) of 5 June 2008 declared that "Community law precludes legislation of a Member State which excludes nationals of other Member States who live and work in its territory from the grant of compensation intended to make good losses resulting from offences against the person where the crime in question was not committed in the territory of that State, on the sole ground of their nationality" (Cf. http//:curia.europa.eu., case C-164/07). This judgement is the result of a preliminary ruling on the interpretation of Article 12 EC. The reference was made in the course of proceedings brought by Mr Wood, a British national, against the "Fonds de garantie des victimes des actes de terrorisme et d'autres infractions" (Guarantee Fund for the Victims of Acts of Terrorism and Other Crimes 'Guarantee Fund') concerning the latter's refusal to grant him compensation, on the ground of his nationality, to make good damage caused by a crime committed outside French territory.

[165] Point No. 13 of the UN *Declaration of Basic Principles of Justice for Victims of Crime and Abuse of Power*, of 29 November 1985; Article 8.4 of the *International Convention for the Suppression of the Financing of Terrorism* of 9 December 1999; Resolution 2002/35 of the Commission on Human Rights of 22 April 2002 entitled "Human Rights and Terrorism"; Resolution 2003/37, of 23 April 2003, of the Commission on Human Rights itself; Point No. 10 of Security Council Resolution 1566 (2004) adopted on 8 October 2004; Article 79 of the Statute of the International Criminal Court; the *Guidelines on the Protection of Victims of Terrorist Acts* adopted by the Committee of Ministers of the Council of Europe on 2 March 2005.

[166] For example, the *Guidelines on the Protection of Victims of Terrorist Acts* adopted by the Committee of Ministers of the Council of Europe on 2 March 2005, which referring to compensation assert: "4. Apart from the payment of pecuniary compensation, states are encouraged to consider, depending on the circumstances, taking other measures to mitigate the negative effects of the terrorist act suffered by the victims."

[167] The most relevant are the following: UN *Declaration of Basic Principles of Justice for Victims of Crime and Abuse of Power*, of 29 November 1985; the *Basic principles and guidelines of the right to a remedy and reparation for victims of gross violations of international human rights law and serious violations of International Humanitarian Law*, of 19 April 2005; the *International Convention for the Protection of All Persons from Enforced Disappearance* of 20 December 2006; the *Guidelines on the Protection of Victims of Terrorist Acts* adopted by the Committee of Ministers of the Council of Europe on 2 March 2005. In this same regional frame of the Council of Europe, we also have Recommendation (2006) 8 of the Committee of Ministers of 14 June 2006 concerning the assistance to crime victims which, under the heading entitled "State compensation"

Before proceeding to the consideration of the international norms relating to victims, it is necessary to insist once again on the *link between the different rights*. In the issue I am discussing now, reparation does not exist if previously it has failed to fulfil the obligation to carry out a serious, impartial, prompt and effective investigation. Also, failure to comply with this last obligation entails the violation of the right to an effective remedy and, therefore, too, of the right to compensation and to reparation because without an *effective* remedy neither compensation nor reparation is also possible.[168] This legal interpretation, present for a long time in the jurisprudence of the Inter-American Court of Human Rights permeates, although more recently, the case-law of the ECHR also.[169] Thus, in accordance with the construction of the ECHR, the nature of the right protected in Article 3 of the European Convention on human rights (prohibition of torture) has implications for Article 13 of the same treaty (right to an effective remedy). One of it is that Article 13—without prejudice to any other remedy at the domestic level—imposes upon the States the obligation to carry out an effective investigation of torture. In such cases, Article 13, in addition to the payment of compensation whenever it is appropriate, calls for an effective investigation enabling the identification and punishment of those responsible.[170] Another implication is specified in the fact that this obligation of investigation carried out by the States "is implicit in the notion of 'effective remedy' under Article 13".[171] On another occasion, and in a case of rape, the ECHR stated that Article 13 of the European Convention on human rights along with effective investigation "also implies that the victim be examined by medical professionals competent and independent".[172]

In the frame of the *United Nations*, and with regard to victims, the right to compensation as a result of a crime, a violation of human rights or of an

includes the following aspects: points out that States should adopt a compensation scheme for the victims of crimes committed on their territory, irrespective of the victim's nationality (8.2.); specifies that compensation should be granted without undue delay, at a fair and appropriate level (8.4.); encourages the States to co-operate to enable victims to claim compensation from the State in which the crime occurred by applying to a competent agency in their own country (8.5.); and establishes subsidiary State compensation (but the State compensation should be awarded only to the extent that the damage is not covered by other sources such as the offender, insurance or state funded health and social provisions (8.9.).

[168] So it is noted by the Human Rights Committee of the International Covenant on Civil and Political Rights, of 16 December 1966, in its general comment No. 31, 80 ° session (2004), concerning the Nature of the General Legal Obligation Imposed on the States Parties to the Covenant, adopted at the 2187ª meeting, on 29 March 2004. In accordance with the same "Without reparation to individuals whose Covenant rights have been violated, the obligation to provide an effective remedy, which is central to the efficacy of article 2, paragraph 3, is not discharged" (paragraph 16).

[169] So, for example, in the *case Aksoy v. Turkey*, Judgement of 18 December 1996.

[170] Cf. *ibid*., para. 98.

[171] *Ibid*. Cf. also, ECHR, *Mentes v. Turkey*, Judgement of 27 November 1997.

[172] In the *case Aydin v. Turkey*, Judgement of 25 September 1997. In the *case Salman v. Turkey*, Judgement of 27 July 2000, the investigation and criminal proceedings were declared not effective as a result of the not effective nature of forensic investigations (cf. paragraph 73).

international crime, is regulated in statements by the General Assembly and the Commission on Human Rights and the Security Council, as well as by international treaties adopted within the framework of that international organization.

With regard to the General Assembly, compensation is the object of paragraphs 12 and 13 of the *Declaration of Basic Principles of Justice for Victims of Crime and Abuse of Power*, adopted on 29 November 1985; the first international norm related to victims in the general or universal frame. Paragraph 12 envisages complementary compensation by the State while paragraph 13 encourages the establishment, strengthening and expansion of national funds for compensation to victims:

> 12. When compensation is not fully available from the offender or other sources, States should endeavour to provide financial compensation to:
> (a) Victims who have sustained significant bodily injury or impairment of physical or mental health as a result of serious crimes;
> (b) The family, in particular dependants of persons who have died or become physically or mentally incapacitated as a result of such victimization.
>
> 13. The establishment, strengthening and expansion of national funds for compensation to victims should be encouraged. Where appropriate, other funds may also be established for this purpose, including in those cases where the State of which the victim is a national is not in a position to compensate the victim for the harm.

In 1992, the *Declaration on the Protection of all Persons from Enforced Disappearance* adopted by the General Assembly Resolution 47/133 of 18 December refers to compensation of victims of enforced disappearance in Article 19. According to it, "the victims of acts of enforced disappearance and their family shall obtain redress and shall have the right to adequate compensation, including the means for as complete a rehabilitation as possible. In the event of the death of the victim as a result of an act of enforced disappearance, their dependents shall also be entitled to compensation."

The *International Convention for the Protection of All Persons from Enforced Disappearance* follows the same idea of reparation (which includes restitution, rehabilitation, satisfaction—including restoration of dignity and reputation—and guarantees of non-repetition)[173] and compensation. So, according to Article 24.4:

> 4. Each State Party shall ensure in its legal system that the victims of enforced disappearance have the right to obtain reparation and prompt, fair and adequate compensation.

However, the most relevant international instrument so far on the issue before us—to the extent that it is an international judicial body that ordered the reparation—is the *Statute of the International Criminal Court* (ICC), one of whose most innovative aspects relates to *reparation to victims*, referred to in Article 75. This article not only

---

[173] That is with the broad scope of General Assembly Resolution 60/147, of 16 December 2005, adopting the *Basic principles and guidelines of the right to a remedy and reparation for victims of gross violations of international human rights law and serious violations of International Humanitarian Law*, adopted before by the UN Commission on Human Rights by Resolution 2005/35, of 19 April 2005. Both the Convention and Resolution 60/147 belong to the most recent international norms on victims. This is why it takes into account the broad content of reparation.

provides for compensation to the victims (of its own motion "in exceptional circumstances" or on request), but also instructs the Court to determine the scope and magnitude of the damage, loss or damage caused to the victims or their successors in title indicating to the International Criminal Court the principles on which this last is founded. In addition, the Court may directly issue a decision against the convicted person stating the appropriate remedy to be granted to the victims, including restitution, compensation and rehabilitation.[174]

In addition, and linked with reparation to victims, Article 79 of the Statute provides for the establishment of a Trust Fund for the benefit of victims of crimes and their families within the jurisdiction of the Court, corresponding to the Court order for payment of the same.

As we have seen in the preceding pages of this work, prior to the Statute the only existing international treaty that provided for the compensation of victims is the *European Convention on The Compensation of Victims of Violent Crimes*, of 24 November 1983, therefore, a Treaty with regional scope limited to a particular category of victims: the victims of violent crime. In the Statute of the ICC, however, we have a treaty of general or universal scope that also provides for a particular category of victims: the victims of international crimes or, equivalently, serious violations of international criminal law.[175]

Despite the progress, the existence of limits in the area of reparation to victims should be noted. Thus, the only victims entitled to it are victims who have been the object of a crime within the jurisdiction of the Court, have had a ruling in this Court and have a criminal identified. As a result, if the case is not subject to prosecution by the Court or the criminal does not appear before it, the victim of a crime within the jurisdiction of the ICC may not invoke the right to get reparation. In other words, it is not enough to be a victim to be eligible for

[174] About this issue vid. *in extenso*, Jeangène Vilmer (2009). Article 75 of the Statute of the ICC, dedicated to the reparation of victims, states: "1. The Court shall establish principles relating to reparations to, or in respect of, victims, including restitution, compensation and rehabilitation. On this basis, in its decision the Court may, either upon request or on its own motion in exceptional circumstances, determine the scope and extent of any damage, loss and injury to, or in respect of, victims and will state the principles on which it is acting. 2. The Court may make an order directly against a convicted person specifying appropriate reparations to, or in respect of, victims, including restitution, compensation and rehabilitation. Where appropriate, the Court may order that the award for reparations be made through the Trust Fund provided for in Article 79. 3. Before making an order under this article, the Court may invite and shall take account of representations from or on behalf of the convicted person, victims, other interested persons or interested States. 4. In exercising its power under this article, the Court may, after a person is convicted of a crime within the jurisdiction of the Court, determine whether, in order to give effect to an order which it may make under this article, it is necessary to set up measures under Article 93, paragraph 1. 5. A State Party shall give effect to a decision under this article as if the provisions of Article 109 were applicable to this Article. 6. Nothing in this article shall be interpreted as prejudicing the rights of victims under national or international law."

[175] Concerning reparation in the frame of the ICC vid. *in extenso* J.-P. Jeangène Vilmer, *op. cit.* Specially, 58–87.

compensation by the ICC. On the other hand, it could be compensated by the Fund provided for in the Statute because it is designed with greater scope to the extent that it does not intervene in the Court and that it can be used to provide reparation for the victims of the crimes within the jurisdiction of the Court, although not ruled before her.[176]

In accordance with Article 75.1 of its Statute, the ICC shall establish principles relating to reparations to be granted to the victims or their successors in title. Reparation includes restitution, compensation and rehabilitation. Therefore, the Statute does not provide satisfaction or guarantees of non-repetition as forms of reparation.[177]

On the basis of these principles, the Court, either upon request or on its own motion in exceptional circumstances, may determine in its decision the scope and extent of any damage, loss and injury to or in respect of victims or their successors in title and will state the principles on which it is acting.

Similarly, the Court may make an order directly against the convicted person specifying appropriate reparations to, or in respect of, victims, including restitution, compensation and rehabilitation[178].

But before making an order pursuant to this Article 75, dedicated to reparation to victims, as he points out in Article 75.3, the Court "may invite and shall take account of representations from or on behalf of the convicted person, victims, other interested persons or interested States."

Reparation to the victims is also addressed by the *Rules of Procedure and Evidence of the Court*. The most important notable fact is that the victim can seek redress of any damage, loss or injury suffered,[179] adopting the same following modalities: the return of goods, property or other tangible objects; compensation; or rehabilitation or reparations of other measures.

The evaluation of the reparation is left to the Court. In this regard, Rule 97 provides that "taking into account the scope and extent of any damage, loss or injury, the Court may award reparations on an individualized basis or, where it deems it appropriate, on a collective basis or both." With this aim, and on the request of victims or their legal representatives, or at the request of the convicted person, or on its own motion, the Court may appoint appropriate experts to assist it in determining the scope, extent of any damage, loss and injury to, or in respect of victims and to suggest various options concerning the appropriate types and modalities of reparations. It shall also invite, "as appropriate", victims or their

---

[176] About these questions vid. *ibid.*, 21–43.

[177] GAT has been critized by J.-P- Jeangène Vilmer (cf. *ibid.*, 70–75).

[178] Article 75.2 adds that where appropriate, the Court may order that the award for reparations be made through the Trust Fund provided for in Article 79.

[179] The request for reparations can be made both upon a motion of the victims (article 75 of the Statute) and when the Court acts *ex officio*. It is for the Registrar to take all the necessary measures to give adequate publicity of the reparation proceedings before the Court, "to the extent possible", to other victims, interested persons and interested States (cf. Rule 96.1).

legal representatives, the convicted person as well as interested persons and interested States to make observations on the reports of the experts.[180]

To make effective reparation for victims, Article 79 of the Statute of the International Criminal Court created a *Trust Fund* for the benefit of the victims, fed by grants and public or private endowments.[181]

Individual reparation orders will be issued directly against the convicted person, whose goods will be confiscated at the request of the Pre-Trial Chamber.

With regard to the amount of reparation, it can be paid through the Trust Fund. To this end, the Court may order that the amount of an award for reparation against a convicted person be deposited in the Trust Fund where at the time of making the order it is impossible or impracticable to make individual awards directly to each victim.[182] But the Court may also order that the convicted individual or group pays the amount of reparation through the Trust Fund considering the number of victims and the scope, forms and modalities of reparation as a collective payment may be more advisable or after consultation with the States concerned and the Trust Fund, may order the amount of compensation to be paid through the Trust Fund to an intergovernmental, international or national organization approved by the latter.[183]

Finally, and in accordance with Article 79 of the Statute of the ICC, Rule 98.5 also covers the use of other resources of the Trust Fund for the benefit of the victims.

Ultimately, the way in which the Statute of the Court and, above all, the Rules of Procedure and Evidence provide for the victims represents a notable advance in international law. Its recognition as an actor in the criminal process allowing it to exercise subjective rights is innovative.[184] But the statute of the victim before the International Criminal Court is still more important when, as we have already seen, the statutes of the International Criminal Tribunals for the former Yugoslavia and for Rwanda reserve for victims the role of witness only, lacking, therefore, the possibility of obtaining reparation for the injury suffered.[185]

On the other hand and exclusively related to *the victims of terrorism*, I have already stated that their status in the international legal field is bleak because except for the Guidelines adopted by the Committee of Ministers of the Council of Europe no international norm contemplates them expressly. Within the framework of the UN, they are no more than measures of an aesthetic character. This is the case,

[180] In all these cases, the Court shall respect the rights of victims and the convicted person (cf. Rule 97.3).

[181] According to Article 79: "1. A Trust Fund shall be established by decision of the Assembly of States Parties for the benefit of victims of crimes within the jurisdiction of the Court, and of the families of such victims. 2. The Court may order money and other property collected through fines or forfeiture to be transferred, by order of the Court, to the Trust Fund. 3. The Trust Fund shall be managed according to criteria to be determined by the Assembly of States Parties."

[182] On this question, Rule 98.2 provides that the award for reparations thus deposited in the Trust Fund shall be separated from other resources of the Trust Fund and shall be forwarded to each victim as soon as possible.

[183] Cf. Rules 98.3 and 98.4.

[184] Cf. Ascensio (2009), p. 77 et seq. In particular, 101–103.

[185] Vid. 151–154 of the present work.

since 1994, of General Assembly resolutions related to terrorism addressing the role of the victims of terrorism from a triple perspective:

- Expressing the solidarity of the General Assembly with victims of terrorism;
- Requesting the Secretary-General of the UN to seek the views of Member States on the possible establishment of a United Nations voluntary fund for victims of terrorism; and
- Entrusting to the special rapporteurs, special representatives and working groups of the Commission on Human Rights, as well as the treaty bodies, to provide "appropriate attention, within the framework of their mandates, to the consequences of the acts", "methods and practices of terrorist groups".[186]

Subsequently, compensation for the victims of terrorism is left to the consideration of the States Parties on the *International Convention For The Supression Of The Financing Of Terrorism*, of 9 December 1999,[187] whose Article 8.4 provides that:

> Each State Party shall consider establishing mechanisms whereby the funds derived from the forfeitures referred to in this article are utilized to compensate the victims of offences referred to in article 2, paragraph 1, subparagraph (a) or (b), or their families.[188]

In the framework of the UN, the compensation to the victims of terrorism is part of the object of the *Resolution 2002/25 of the Commission on Human Rights*, of 22 April 2002, entitled "Human Rights and Terrorism". Here, the Commission on Human Rights:

> 11. *Welcomes* the report of the Secretary-General (A/56/190), and invites him to continue to seek the views of Member States on the implications of terrorism in all its forms and manifestations for the full enjoyment of all human rights and fundamental freedoms and on how the needs and concerns of victims of terrorism might be addressed, including through the possible establishment of a voluntary fund for the victims of terrorism, as well as on ways and means to rehabilitate the victims of terrorism and to reintegrate them into society, with a view to incorporating his findings in his reports to the Commission and the General Assembly;.

This issue of the creation of an International Compensation Fund for victims of terrorism—fed by voluntary contributions—is repeated in Resolution 2003/37 of 23

---

186 This is the case of resolutions 49/185 of 23 December 1994; 50/186 of 22 December 1995; 52/133 of 12 December 1997; 54/164 of 17 December 1999; 56/160 of 19 December 2001; 58/174 of 22 December 2003. As I have already criticized in this work, I think that the action of the United Nations as a whole in relation to the victims of terrorism is impoverished. Vid. 61 et seq. of this work.

187 Well, as it can be seen, the effectiveness of this obligation of conventional nature is left in Article 8.4 at the discretion of States Parties. This Treaty currently has 179 States Parties.

188 Paragraphs (a) and (b) of Article 2.1 state: "1. Any person commits an offence within the meaning of this Convention if that person by any means, directly or indirectly, unlawfully and wilfully, provides or collects funds with the intention that they should be used or in the knowledge that they are to be used, in full or in part, in order to carry out: (a) An act which constitutes an offence within the scope of and as defined in one of the treaties listed in the annex; or (b) Any other act intended to cause death or serious bodily injury to a civilian, or to any other person not taking an active part in the hostilities in a situation of armed conflict, when the purpose of such act, by its nature or context, is to intimidate a population, or to compel a Government or an international organization to do or to abstain from doing any act."

April 2003, of the Commission on Human Rights,[189] having been the subject also of several UN Security Council resolutions. Thus, for example, Resolution 1566 (2004) of the Security Council adopted on 8 October 2004, at point 10 states:

> 10. *Requests* further the working group, established under paragraph 9 to consider the possibility of establishing an international fund to compensate victims of terrorist acts and their families, which might be financed through voluntary contributions, which could consist in part of assets seized from terrorist organizations, their members and sponsors, and submit its recommendations to the Council;

With regard to the UN General Assembly, its Resolution 60/147 adopted on 16 December 2005 through which the *Basic principles and guidelines of the right to a remedy and reparation for victims of gross violations of international human rights law and serious violations of International Humanitarian Law* adopted by the UN Commission on Human Rights on 19 April 2005, by Resolution 2005/35, was adopted also envisages compensation for damages suffered by victims as a form of reparation. It does so at point No. 20 (in the paragraph entitled "IX Reparation of harm suffered") that states:

> 20. *Compensation* should be provided for any economically assessable damage, as appropriate and proportional to the gravity of the violation and the circumstances of each case, resulting from gross violations of international human rights law and serious violations of international humanitarian law, such as:
>
> (a) Physical or mental harm;
> (b) Lost opportunities, including employment, education and social benefits;
> (c) Material damages and loss of earnings, including loss of earning potential;
> (d) Moral damage;
> (e) Costs required for legal or expert assistance, medicine and medical services, and psychological and social services.

As we have already seen, in the *European regional system*, the first—and so far only—international treaty which covers compensation to victims is the *European Convention on the Compensation of Victims of Violent Crimes*, of 24 November 1983, with the exclusive objective of compensation of victims of violent crimes.[190] It starts from the general principle according to which "when compensation is not fully available from other sources" the State in the territory of which the crime has been committed shall contribute to compensate. This compensation shall be awarded even if the offender cannot be prosecuted or punished.[191]

As for the beneficiaries of the compensation, it reaches both those who have sustained serious bodily injury or impairment of health directly attributable to an

[189] Which invites the Secretary-General of the United Nations to continue to seek the views of Member States on the implications of terrorism in all its forms and manifestations on the full enjoyment of all human rights and fundamental freedoms, and on possible ways to address the needs and problems of the victims of terrorism, including the possible establishment of a voluntary fund for victims of terrorism, as well as the means to rehabilitate the victims of terrorism and to reintegrate them into society.

[190] Vid. about this issue 20 et seq. of the present work.

[191] Articles 2.1 and 2.2.

intentional crime of violence as well as the dependants of persons who have died as a result of such crime.[192]

A few months later, the Council of Europe once again considered this issue—as well as that relating to the characteristics of the compensation—but this time related to victims of terrorism. The *Guidelines on the Protection of Victims of Terrorist Acts* adopted by the Committee of Ministers of the Council of Europe on 2 March 2005 formulated it as follows:

> 1. Victims of terrorist acts should receive fair, appropriate and timely compensation for the damages which they suffered. When compensation is not available from other sources, in particular through the confiscation of the property of the perpetrators, organisers and sponsors of terrorist acts, the state on the territory of which the terrorist act happened must contribute to the compensation of victims for direct physical or psychological harm, irrespective of their nationality.

Subsequently, the *European Convention on the Prevention of Terrorism*, of 16 May 2005, also addressed this issue and Art. 13—entitled "protection, compensation and assistance to victims of terrorism"—says:

> Each Party shall adopt such measures as may be necessary to protect and support the victims of terrorism that has been committed within its own territory. These measures may include, through the appropriate national schemes and subject to domestic legislation, *inter alia*, financial assistance and compensation for victims of terrorism and their close family members.

Within the framework of the Council of Europe, and outside of the *Guidelines on the Protection of Victims of Terrorist Acts* adopted by the Committee of Ministers of the Council of Europe on 2 March 2005, the right of victims to compensation—as the Guidelines themselves show—had been previously formulated in guideline No. XVII of July 2002 with regard to the compensation of victims of terrorist acts. This guideline reminds Member States that:

> When compensation is not fully available from other sources, in particular through the confiscation of the property of the perpetrators, organisers and sponsors of terrorist acts, the State must contribute to the compensation of the victims of attacks that took place on its territory, as far as their person or their health is concerned.

Compensation of victims is also part of the object of various recommendations of the Committee of Ministers of the Council of Europe. Thus, the *Recommendation (83) 7* of June 23, 1983, *On Participation of the Public in Crime Policy* under the heading entitled "D. criminal policy taking into account the interests of the victim" says that the Member States of the Council of Europe should facilitate the compensation of victims by offenders, "for example by providing, as an alternative to a custodial sentence, the payment of such compensation"[193] and make "state compensation more widely available to victims in the absence of compensation by offenders".[194]

[192] Cf. Article 2.1 a) and b).

[193] On point 30.

[194] On point 31.

The compensation of victims is also covered by the *Recommendation (2006) 8* of the Committee of Ministers of 14 June 2006, *On Assistance to Crime Victims*. Point No. 8 of it aims precisely "State compensation"and under this heading it addresses four issues: the beneficiaries of the compensation, the compensation fund, the damage to compensate and subsidiary compensation by the State.

With regard to the *beneficiaries of the compensation*, point 8.1 of this Recommendation considers both the *direct victims*[195] and the immediate family and dependants of victims who have died as a result of such crime.[196]

With regard to the *Fund of Compensation*, the Recommendation points out that States should adopt a compensation scheme for the victims of crimes committed on their territory, irrespective of the victim's nationality (point No. 8.2.).[197] Second, the compensation awarded to victims should be based on the principle of social solidarity (point No. 8.3). Third, the compensation should be granted without undue delay, "at a fair and appropriate level" (point No. 8.4). Since many persons are victimized in European States other than their own, the States are finally encouraged to co-operate to enable victims to claim compensation from the State in which the crime occurred by applying to a competent agency in their own country (point No. 8.5).

The damage subject to compensation is both the physical and the psychological understanding as also, the treatment and rehabilitation for physical and psychological injuries (point No. 8.6). Likewise, States should consider compensation for loss of income, funeral expenses and loss of maintenance for dependants. States may also consider compensation for pain and suffering (point No. 8.7). Ultimately, the Recommendation says that States may consider means to compensate damage resulting from crimes against property (point No. 8.8).

Last but not least, point No. 8.9 of this Recommendation states that State compensation to victims should be awarded to the extent that the damage is not covered by other sources such as the offender, insurance or state funded health and social provisions. That is, with a *subsidiary character*.

In the framework of the *European Union*, compensation to crime victims is contemplated both by *Directive 2004/80/EC* of 29 April 2004 relating to *compensation to crime victims* and by *Council Framework Decision 2001/220/JHA*, of 15 March 2001,[198] even in the cross-border dimension of the problem. That is,

---

[195] "Victims of an intentional offence with violence, including victims of sexual offences".

[196] "To the immediate family and dependants of victims who died as a result of such crime".

[197] This question is partially covered by the *European Convention on the Compensation of Victims of Violent Crimes*, of 24 November 1983.

[198] Recent studies underline evidence of a lack of effective victim access to compensation and restoration: "Divergent national policies mean that restorative justice services are not equally accessible, and are not available at all to victims of crime in six Member States. (…). Although basic standards and principles have been established by the UN in 2002 (…) and by the Council of Europe in 2006 (…), there is widely expressed concern that such principles are not fully adhered to and that restorative justice processes are prone to losing an appropriate focus on the victim. Commentators are concerned that restorative justice services are becoming too identified with

when the crime has been suffered in the territory of a State other than that in which the victim resides.[199]

In relation to this cross-border dimension of compensation to crime victims, mention shall be made of the judgement of the EUCJ (Second Chamber) of 5 June, 2008 where it clearly states that "Community law precludes legislation of a Member State which excludes nationals of other Member States who live and work in its territory from the grant of compensation intended to make good losses resulting from offences against the person where the crime in question was not committed in the territory of that State, on the sole ground of their nationality."[200]

With regard to the *American regional system* related to victims, the *Inter-American Convention on Forced Disappearance of Persons* of 9 July 1994 has no provision on this matter. It is not surprising given that this Convention contains, above all, obligations for the States and the possible compensation, which a victim could obtain would come through the mechanism of the petitions and communications provided for in the American Convention on human rights, 1969, to which that Convention refers.[201]

Finally, compensation is also the subject of *international treaties of human rights* but with different approaches. As emphasized by Bottigliero, in contrast to the right to effective remedies referred in all of them with the view of obtaining compensation, only some treaties expand this right of appeal to include more

---

one particular party, whether victims, offenders or communities" (European Commission, Commission Staff Working Paper, Impact Assessment Accompanying the document "Communication from the Commission to the European Parliament, the Council, The European economic and social Committee and the Committee of Regions", Proposal for a DIRECTIVE OF THE EUROPEAN PARLIAMENT AND OF THE COUNCIL establishing minimum standards on the rights, support and protection of victims of crime, SEC(2011) 580 final, Brussels, 18.5.2011), 14.

[199] Situation envisaged in Article 12.2 of *Directive 2004/80/EC* of 29 April 2004 relating for compensation for crime victims, which states: "All Member States shall ensure that their national rules provide for the existence of a scheme on compensation to victims of violent intentional crimes committed in their respective territories, which guarantees fair and appropriate compensation to victims." Article 1 of this same Directive provides: "Member States shall ensure that where a violent intentional crime has been committed in a Member State other than the Member State where the applicant for compensation is habitually resident, the applicant shall have the right to submit the application to an authority or any other body in the alter Member State." On the same lines, Article 11 of Council Framework Decision 2001/220/JHA, of 15 March 2001, provides that Member States shall ensure that its competent authorities "can take appropriate measures to minimize the difficulties faced where the victim is a resident of a State other than the one where the offence has occurred, particularly with regard to the organization of the proceedings."

[200] Cf. http//:curia.europa.eu., case C-164/07. This judgement is the result of a preliminary ruling on the interpretation of Article 12 EC. The reference was made in the course of proceedings brought by Mr Wood, a British national, against the "Fonds de garantie des victimes des actes de terrorisme et d'autres infractions" (Guarantee Fund for the Victims of Acts of Terrorism and Other Crimes 'Guarantee Fund') concerning the latter's refusal to grant him compensation, on the ground of his nationality, to make good damage caused by a crime committed outside French territory.

[201] Obviously, it is also opened the way of individual communications in the framework of other international treaties of human rights, but this option depends on the previous acceptation of the competence of the international concerned treaty-body by the State Party in question.

specific provisions on reparation in their various possible forms: restitution, compensation, rehabilitation, satisfaction and guarantees of non-repetition.[202]

In the field of international human rights law, it should therefore distinguish several situations. The *first* is characterized by the fact that the majority of international treaties in the field of human rights are limited to establish the competence of the international body to fix an indemnity for the victim of the violation of the treaty.

With regard to the *international treaties of human rights of the UN general or universal system*, on the basis of Article 2.3 of the *International Covenant on Civil and Political Rights* of 16 December 1966, the Human Rights Committee has considerably clarified the statute and the components of the right of victims to reparation for violations of the Covenant.[203] Thus, although the Committee's mandate does not include the crimes of international law and other violations of human rights than the rights covered by the Covenant its "jurisprudence",[204] issued on the occasion of individual complaints relating to the most serious violations of human rights—such as torture and disappearances—has substantially contributed to the gradual expansion and the best definition of the right of victims to reparation for crimes under international law.[205] This is the case, for example, of their pronouncements on the cases *Rodriguez v. Uruguay,*[206] *Zelaya v. Nicaragua,*[207] y *Laureano v. Perú.*[208] In the first, the Human Rights Committee states that *the States, obligation to effectively investigate the violation* of the Covenant is part of the obligation of the State to ensure an effective remedy; a circumstance that does not occur when allegations of violations are not investigated in a rapid and impartial manner by the competent authorities. In the second, the Committee goes still further in stating that the victim has the right to an "effective remedy", calling on Nicaragua not only to ensure "adequate compensation" to the victim but also to carry out official investigations on alleged violations and to ensure that similar violations do not recur in the future.[209] In the third, in connection with the disappearance of a minor when he was in a military prison in Peru, the Committee urged Peru to open an investigation into the disappearance to grant compensation appropriate to the victim and his family and to bring to justice those responsible for the disappearance whatever the amnesty adopted in this regard in the domestic system.

---

[202] Cf. Bottigliero, *Redress for Victims. . ., op. cit.*, 113.

[203] Cf. Bottigliero, *Redress for Victims. . ., op. cit.*, 115.

[204] I put in quotation marks for the term "jurisprudence" because although the Committee is not a judicial body, it is the interpreter of the Covenant.

[205] Cf. Bottigliero, *Redress for Victims. . ., op. cit.*, 116.

[206] Comm. No. 322/1988, CCPR/C/51/D/322/1988, of 9 August 1994.

[207] Comm. No. 328/1988, CCPR/C/51/D/328/1988, of 14 August 1994.

[208] Comm. No. 540/1993, CCPR/C/56/D/540/1993, of 16 April 1996.

[209] The Human Rights Committee has pronounced on the same line in the following cases: *Irene Bleier Lewenhoff and Rosa Valiño de Bleier v. Uruguay*, Communication No. 30/1978; *Guillermo Ignacio Dermit Barbato and Hugo Haroldo Dermig Barbato v. Uruguay*, Communication No. 84/1981; *John* Khemraadi Baboeram et al. V. Suriname, Comm. No. 146/1983 y 148-154/1983.

At the regional level, this type of regulation—compensation fixed by the international treaty body—is possible only in the American Convention on human rights of 1969, being a result of the exercise of the right of effective remedy.[210] In this sense, Art. 63.1 says:

> 1. If the Court finds that there has been a violation of a right or freedom protected by this Convention, the Court shall rule that the injured party be ensured the enjoyment of his right or freedom that was violated. It shall also rule, if appropriate, that the consequences of the measure or situation that constituted the breach of such right or freedom be remedied and that fair compensation be paid to the injured party.

On the same lines, Article 9 of the *Inter-American Convention to Prevent and Punish Torture*, of 9 December 1985, imposes upon the States Parties the obligation to incorporate into their national laws regulations guaranteeing suitable compensation for victims of torture adding that "none of the provisions of this article shall affect the right to receive compensation that the victim or other persons may have by virtue of existing national legislation."

The *European Convention on Human Rights*, of 4 November 1950, however, does not give to the Court the possibility to rule on compensation, limiting it to indicate in Article 41 that "If the Court finds that there has been a violation of the Convention or the Protocols thereto, and if the internal law of the High Contracting Party concerned allows only partial reparation to be made, the Court shall, if necessary, afford just satisfaction to the injured party."

In this regard, Fernández Sola argues that the mechanism for the protection of the European Convention on human rights has become outdated and that its reparation system does not adhere to the requirements of the principles of the United Nations on reparation to the victims of violations of human rights, having been "at least at this point, far short of the minimum requirements to make material justice for the victims".[211] Therefore, she proposes amendment of the current legal regulation or, if not, a more flexible interpretation of this provision "that, when referring to the domestic law of the parties as a first source of repair, should allow the Court impose obligations on States, as does the IACHR and complete them, if necessary, with a compensation."[212]

---

[210] Ruled, respectively, in Articles 13 and 25.

[211] Fernández Sola, "El derecho a la reparación de las víctimas de desaparición forzada: hacia la justicia a través del Derecho internacional", *op. cit.*, 413. From the perspective of the victims of enforced disappearance that she examines, she considers that Article 41 is insufficient because although sometimes victims need an economic compensation for the losses generated by the disappearance, "major damages are not of an economic nature". Indeed, "the deprivation to minors to know or to grow with one of their parents, distress and psychological problems generated by the uncertainty, marginalization or social stigma on occasions, the threat latent on the rest of the family if they denounce what has happened or insist to inquire about their authors, the right to know those guilty of such an outrage and other collateral damage are not covered by compensation. It is necessary a satisfaction, in the broad sense, to repair, the aforementioned damage" (*ibid.*, 409).

[212] *Ibid.*

Unlike the European Convention of 1950 (which provides for equitable satisfaction) and the American Convention of 1969 (which provides for compensation), the *African Charter on Human and Peoples' Rights* of 27 July 1981 lacks provisions on compensation. Only Article 25 of the *Protocol to the African Charter on Human and Peoples' Rights on the Rights of Women in Africa* of 11 July 2003 provides for it but obviously only for the purposes of the Protocol. In accordance with it, the States assume a dual obligation. On the one hand, they undertake to provide for "appropriate remedies" to any woman whose rights or freedoms, as recognized by the Protocol, have been violated. On the other hand, they are obliged to ensure that such remedies are determined by competent judicial, administrative or legislative authorities, or by any other competent authority provided for by law.

The second situation that exists between the different human rights treaties is determined by those treaties dealing only with certain forms of reparation, the modalities of reparation being linked to the objective and the purpose pursued by the treaty in question. In the *general or universal* level of the United Nations, for example, is the *Convention on the Rights of the Child*, of 20 November 1989, whose Article 39 states that the States Parties have the obligation to take:

> all appropriate measures to promote physical and psychological recovery and social reintegration of a child victim of: any form of neglect, exploitation, or abuse; torture or any other form of cruel, inhuman or degrading treatment or punishment; or armed conflicts. Such recovery and reintegration shall take place in an environment which fosters the health, self-respect and dignity of the child.

Finally, also at the level of the UN, a third group of treaties incorporates, with compensation, references reparation for victims of violations pursued by the treaty in question. This is the case of the *International Convention on the Elimination of All Forms of Racial Discrimination* of 21 December 1965, whose Article 6 obliges the States Parties to assure everyone within their jurisdiction "the right to seek from such tribunals just and adequate reparation or satisfaction for any damage suffered as a result of such discrimination."

More recently, and on the same lines, Article 14 of the UN *Convention Against Torture and Other Cruel, Inhuman or Degrading Treatment or Punishment* of 10 December 1984, says:

> 1. Each State Party shall ensure in its legal system that the victim of an act of torture obtains redress and has an enforceable right to fair and adequate compensation including the means for as full rehabilitation as possible. In the event of the death of the victim as a result of an act of torture, his dependents shall be entitled to compensation.
> 2. Nothing in this article shall affect any right of the victim or other person to compensation which may exist under national law.[213]

---

[213] This Convention is considered by Bottigliero as one of the pillars in the codification of the fundamental principle concerning the right of victims to reparation for violations of human rights (*Redress for Victims*. . ., *op. cit.*, 123).

Right to the Protection of Private and Family Life

International norms relating to victims claim the right to protection of private and family life. However, this fact should not make us forget that, as in other rights previously examined, in this also we face a fundamental human right proclaimed on international human rights treaties. Among them are the International Covenant on Civil and Political Rights of 16 December 1966[214] and the European Convention for the Protection of Human Rights and Fundamental Freedoms, of 4 November 1950.[215] In contrast to these two treaties, both the American Convention on Human Rights, of 22 November 1969 and the African Charter on Human and Peoples' Rights, of 27 June 1981, only allude to the protection of the family without reference to the protection of private and family life.[216]

What the different international norms concerning the different categories of victims do by proclaiming the right to respect for private and family life in a specific way is nothing but giving a particular application to this right with respect to the victims. Thus, *with regard to victims* this right has a content linked with the consequences of the victimizer fact that focuses on the respect for the private and family life of the victims at the time of the research, assistance and information activities subsequent to the victimizer fact as well as within the framework of the procedures initiated by the victims. On a complementary basis, this right is linked with the right to effective remedy that they could use to claim that their right to private and family life has been violated, when they deem that there has been such a circumstance.

In the universal frame of the *UN*, paragraph 6 of UN *Declaration of Basic Principles of Justice for Victims of Crime and Abuse of Power*, of 29 November 1985, formulates this right in the following terms:

> 6. The responsiveness of judicial and administrative processes to the needs of victims should be facilitated by: . . .
> d) Taking measures to minimize inconvenience to victims, protect their privacy, when necessary, and ensure their safety, as well as that of their families and witnesses on their behalf, from intimidation and retaliation;

On the same lines, with regard to *victims of gross violations of international human rights law and serious violations of International Humanitarian Law* is also paragraph 10 of the UN General Assembly Resolution 60/147, adopted on 16 December 2005, through which the *Basic principles and guidelines of the right to a remedy and reparation for victims of gross violations of international human*

---

[214] In Article 17.

[215] In Article 8, which states: "Everyone has the right to respect for his private and family life, his home and his correspondence". In the opinion of Saura Estapa, this Article 8.1 contains only the elements that constitute the right to privacy, relegating the reputation to a secondary place (cf. Saura Estapa 1998, p. 228).

[216] Respectively in Articles 17 and y 18.

rights law and serious violations of International Humanitarian Law adopted by the UN Commission on Human Rights on 19 April 2005, by Resolution 2005/35, are adopted. This paragraph says:

> 10. Victims should be treated with humanity and *respect for their dignity* and human rights, and appropriate measures should be taken to ensure their safety, physical and psychological well-being and *privacy*, as well as those of their families. The State should ensure that its domestic laws, to the extent possible, provide that a victim who has suffered violence or trauma should benefit from special consideration and care to avoid his or her re-traumatization in the course of legal and administrative procedures designed to provide justice and reparation.

On the *European regional frame* of the Council of Europe, several recommendations of the Committee of Ministers, examined in relationship to other rights, also envisage this right related to the protection of the private and family life of victims. It is the same in the case, for example, of *Recommendation 85 (11)*, of 28 June de 1985, *On the Position of the Victim in the Framework of Criminal Law and Procedure*[217]; of *Recommendation (87) 21*, of 17 September 1987, *On Assistance to Victims and the Prevention of Victimization*[218]; and, more recently, of *Recommendation (2006) 8*, of 14 June 2006, *On Assistance to Crime Victims*, which updates and replaces the previous two. Paragraphs 10 and 11 of this latter envisage both the protection of victims' private life and confidentiality.

With regard to the *protection of victims' private life*, paragraph 10 says:

> 10.8. States should take appropriate steps to avoid as far as possible impinging on the private and family life of victims as well as to protect the personal data of victims, in particular during the investigation and prosecution of the crime.
>
> 10.9. States should encourage the media to adopt and respect self regulation measures in order to protect victims' privacy and personal data.

With regard to *confidentiality* the criteria on which is based *Recommendation (2006) 8*, of 14 June 2006, *On Assistance to Crime Victims* is that the victim's interest must always prevail. That is why the disclosure of data relating to the victim should be admitted only if there is explicit consent of the victim or by virtue of a legal requirement or authorization to do so. But even in these three exceptions, the disclosure should be governed by clear rules and respect the principle of proportionality.

On this matter, paragraph 11 of Recommendation (2006) 8 says:

> 11.1. States should require all agencies, whether statutory or non-governmental, in contact with victims, to adopt clear standards by which they may only disclose to a third party information received from or relating to a victim under the condition that:

[217] Paragraph 8 of which states: "At all stages of the procedure, the victim should be questioned in a manner which gives due consideration to his personal situation, his rights and his dignity. Whenever possible and appropriate, children and the mentally ill or handicapped should be questioned in the presence of their parents or guardians or other persons qualified to assist them;".

[218] Paragraph 9 of which says that States "take steps to prevent victim assistance services from disclosing personal information regarding victims, without their consent, to third parties;".

> – the victim has explicitly consented to such disclosure;
> – there is a legal requirement or authorisation to do so.
>
> 11.2. In these two cases of exception, clear rules should govern the disclosure procedures. Complaints procedures should be published for dealing with alleged breaches to the rules.

With regard to *victims of terrorism*, the right to the protection of their private and family life is formulated in the following terms by the *Guidelines on the Protection of Victims of Terrorist Acts* adopted by the Committee of Ministers of the Council of Europe on 2 March 2005:

> 1. States should take appropriate steps to avoid as far as possible undermining respect for the private and family life of victims of terrorist acts, in particular when carrying out investigations or providing assistance after the terrorist act as well as within the framework of proceedings initiated by victims.[219]

As I have just stated, the *Guidelines on the Protection of Victims of Terrorist Acts* adopted by the Committee of Ministers of the Council of Europe on 2 March 2005 complete the formulation of this right with reference to the need that the States, in full compliance with the principle of freedom of expression, encourage the media and journalists to adopt self-regulatory measures in order to ensure the protection of the private and family life of victims of terrorist acts in the framework of their information activities. It also asks the States to ensure that victims of terrorist acts have an effective remedy when they raise an arguable claim that their right to respect for their private and family life has been violated.

In paragraph VIII entitled *Protection of the private and family life of victims of terrorist acts*, the Guidelines state:

> 2. States should, where appropriate, in full compliance with the principle of freedom of expression, encourage the media and journalists to adopt self-regulatory measures in order to ensure the protection of the private and family life of victims of terrorist acts in the framework of their information activities.
>
> 3. States must ensure that victims of terrorist acts have an effective remedy where they raise an arguable claim that their right to respect for their private and family life has been violated.[220]

In the framework of the *European Union*, the victims' right to the protection of privacy is formulated on Council Framework Decision 2001/220/JHA, of 15 March 2001, on the standing of victims in criminal proceedings Article 8 of which states:

> 1. Each Member State shall ensure a suitable level of protection for victims and, where appropriate, their families or persons in a similar position, particularly as regards their

[219] As we shall see later, points 2 and 3 of the Guideline regarding this right include aspects relating to the same such as self-regulation measures to be taken by journalists and the media for communication in relation to the victims of terrorism, as well as the right of these victims to an effective remedy for violation of his right to private and family life.

[220] Completing the appointment, to strengthen it, with the reference to the following recommendations of the Committee of Ministers: *Recommendation No. (97) 19 On the Suppression of violence in the electronic media*, and *Recommendation No. (99) 5. On the protection of privacy on the Internet.*

safety and protection of their privacy, where the competent authorities consider that there is a serious risk of reprisals or firm evidence of serious intent to intrude upon their privacy.[221]

In the *American regional system*, the Inter-American Convention on Forced Disappearance of Persons of 9 July 1994 has no provision on the protection of victims' private and family life probably because its priority is the repression of the practice of forced disappearance.

Whatever the previous considerations it should be, however, insisted that the right to private and family life is a human right guaranteed by international treaties that make up this section of the international law of human rights. Therefore, and contrary to international norms relating to victims, from the particular perspective of the State as the perpetrator of the violation. In the *UN system*, this right is enshrined in Article 17 of the International Covenant on Civil and Political Rights of 16 December 1966.[222] At the *European regional level*, for example, it is formulated in Article 8 of the European Convention for the Protection of Human Rights and Fundamental Freedoms, of 4 November 1950.[223] Given the particularity, moreover, that such treaties contain control techniques that fulfil specific conditions and requirements, both individuals and States may resort to them when the rights referred to therein are breached by a State Party to the treaty.

Prior to these treaties, the right to private and family life already had been proclaimed in Article 12 of the Universal Declaration of Human Rights, of 10 December 1948; unlike those, this Article 12 contains two different but interrelated subjective rights: the right to privacy and the right to honour.[224] As it can be seen,

---

[221] Paragraphs 2, 3 and 4 of this Article 8 provided for the right of the victim to protection in the context of the proceedings taking into account, too, the dimension of the privacy of the victim. Vid. 205 et seq. of the present work.

[222] That states: "1. No one shall be subjected to arbitrary or unlawful interference with his privacy, family, home or correspondence, nor to unlawful attacks on his honour and reputation. 2. Everyone has the right to the protection of the law against such interference or attacks." As pointed out by Saura Estapà, article 17 of the International Covenant on Civil and Political Rights reproduces almost literally article 12 of the Universal Declaration of Human Rights. In his opinion, the only substantive alteration is to add 'illegal' as modulator trait of the interference or attacks not permitted against privacy or honour. It is a change which has "the potentiality to highlight the possibility of attacks 'legal' against honour and reputation of the people;" "attacks that can come under the freedom of information" (J. Saura Estapà, "Artículo 12", *op. cit.*, 228).

[223] That states: "1. Everyone has the right to respect for his private and family life, his home and his correspondence. 2. There shall be no interference by a public authority with the exercise of this right except such as is in accordance with the law and is necessary in a democratic society in the interests of national security, public safety or the economic well-being of the country, for the prevention of disorder or crime, for the protection of health or morals, or for the protection of the rights and freedoms of others."

[224] That states : "No one shall be subjected to arbitrary interference with his privacy, family, home or correspondence, nor to attacks upon his honour and reputation. Everyone has the right to the protection of the law against such interference or attacks." This article 12 is based upon article 5 of the American Declaration of the Rights and Duties of Men that states: "Every person has the right to the protection of the law against abusive attacks upon his honor, reputation, and his private and family life."

its proclamation is accompanied by an obligation on the part of the States to take legislative measures that are necessary to ensure their *effective* protection.

Both the private and family life are protected against arbitrary interference or illegitimate intromission—in both cases of public or private character—of any kind whatever, which can invade them inappropriately.[225] However, as with other human rights, this may also be subject to limitations or restrictions in the form of interference that are neither arbitrary nor unlawful.

In terms of content, *the right to respect for private and family life* includes both the protection of privacy—which "is the most intimate sphere of the personality of human beings"—such as family life, implying that "the family as a unit must be protected, both for parents and for parents and children".[226]

As noted by Martin y Pérez de Nanclares, three different areas within the legal content of this right can be seen in the current case-law of the ECHR. Thus, the *private sphere*, which constitutes the fundamental dimension of this right and implies a requirement of guarantee against the interference of public authorities in the private individual sphere,[227] is to be linked with other rights such as those relating to the protection of the individual and private communications with third parties, postal correspondence, the inviolability of the home, the right to the image itself or the right to preserve the name of children.[228]

With regard to the *concept of "family"*, the ECHR has pointed out in its jurisprudence that the interpretation of the concept of "family" has to be done in the broad sense, "as it not only protects the family life of the marriage or situations of assimilable couples, but it also covers children and even the life in common between grandparents and grandchildren".[229] What the ECHR requires is that there is a real common life, so that protection in itself is not projected to the course in life to separately. As Martin y Pérez de Nanclares pointsout, what is protected is family life whose determination depends more on reality than on law. In the same vein, Saura Estapà says that the family "includes stable couples (regardless of which have been formalized or not in the bond of marriage), parents and children, and even close relatives such as grandparents and grandchildren, always and when maintaining active linkages".[230]

More recently, the right to respect for private and family life has been added in the framework of the European Union by Article 7 of the *Charter of Fundamental*

---

[225] As, for example, recordings, mechanisms for listening or other technical means, etc. Unlike the honour, which is protected from "attacks" (cf. J. Saura Estapà, *op. cit.*, 232).

[226] Newmann and Vasak (1984), 230.

[227] Martin y Pérez de Nanclares (2008), 213.

[228] Within the private sphere is also the physical and psychological integrity of the individual in his private sphere and the right of everyone to freely conduct their lives.

[229] Cf. ECHR, Judgement of 13 June 1979, *Marckx v. Belgium*, para. 56.

[230] Saura Estapà, *op. cit.*, 232.

Rights of the European Union.[231] In the Charter, the objective of this law has a triple nature. First, to protect everyone from interference by public authorities in their intimate sphere.[232]

Second, and in the field of the European Convention on human rights of 4 November 1950, the aim is also to protect the individual from interference by a third individual in their private sphere, which implies that public authorities must intervene to prevent the action of a particular person if it involves a violation of the legal content guaranteed by this right.[233]

Finally, this right also entails the existence of specific guarantees against interference in the private and family life arising from proceedings, although this existence is not disclosed explicitly in the wording of the provision.[234]

So, he concludes that the right to respect for private and family life contains two elements. On the one hand, it imposes a negative duty of respect. On the other hand, it also imposes positive duties of guarantee of this right by public authorities.[235]

As to the interpretation of this right in the field of European Community law, in accordance Article 52.3 of the Charter of Fundamental Rights of the European Union with regard to *all* the rights contained therein, it must be taken as per the case-law of the ECHR, and as provided for in the aforementioned Article 52.3, that the meaning and scope of the rights contained therein shall be the same as those laid down by the European Convention on human rights.[236] As a result, the limitations that can legitimately limit this right are the same as those allowed in the framework of Article 8 of the European Convention on human rights, which proclaims the same right in the framework of that Convention.[237]

---

[231] Which states: "Everyone has the right to respect for his or her private and family life, home and communications." In the opinion of J. Martin y Pérez de Nanclares, this right contains, in fact, four different guarantees: the right to respect for private life, the right to respect for family life, the right to respect for the home and the right to respect for communications (cf. *op. cit*., p. 213).

[232] In this regard, J. Martin y Pérez de Nanclares emphasizes that ECHR jurisprudence on the matter has remained constant since the well-known Belgian affair on languages (judgment of 23 July 1967) until now (judgement of 24 June 2004, *Carolina v.Germany*) (cf. *op. cit*., 211).

[233] Cf., in this respect, ECHR, judgement of 9 September 1979 *Airey v. Ireland*, para. 32; judgement of 26 March 1985 *X and Y v. Netherlands*, Series A 91, para. 23; judgement of, 24 June 2004, *Carolina v.Germany*, just quoted, para. 57. *Ibid*., p. 212.

[234] Cf. ECHR, decisión of 11 July 2000, *Ciliz v. Netherlands, Reports of Judgements and Decisions*, VIII.

[235] Cf. Martin y Pérez de Nanclares, "Artículo 7...", *op. cit*., 215.

[236] Article 52.3 states: "3. In so far as this Charter contains rights which correspond to rights guaranteed by the Convention for the Protection of Human Rights and Fundamental Freedoms, the meaning and scope of those rights shall be the same as those laid down by the said Convention. This provision shall not prevent Union law providing more extensive protection."

[237] Cf. the *Explanations relating to the Charter of Fundamental Rights* (*OJ* C 303, 14 December 2007).

The Right to the Protection of Dignity and Security

The right to the protection of dignity and security of the victims proclaimed by international norms relating to the various categories of victims is linked with the various phases of court proceedings and takes place within the framework of this, specifying the adoption by the States of measures for the protection of the identity of the victim and granting special treatment to vulnerable victims and protecting them when they need to act as witnesses. At the same time, and for the purposes of ensuring their security, the States must adopt measures of protection for the victims where competent authorities consider that there is a serious risk of reprisals or clear signs of the intention to disrupt their private life.

The dignity of victims is worthy of protection and the international norms have addressed this as an additional requirement. The inherent dignity of every person is important and therefore these norms have specified criteria according to which the victims should be treated within the framework of the different phases of the proceedings. In accordance with this standard, the treatment that victims should receive at any time must be respectful of their status as such and take into account all kinds of consequences (physical, psychological, emotional) that yield the victimizer fact. It is, at least, an approach which must be observed and respected by all those professionals (police, judicial, medical, media, etc.) who have to interact—in however small a measure—with the victim.

In the framework of the *United Nations*, the protection of the identity of the victim is the object of the *Declaration of Basic Principles of Justice for Victims of Crime and Abuse of Power* of 29 November 1985, adopted by the General Assembly of the United Nations. To that end, paragraph 6 States that the responsiveness of judicial and administrative processes to the needs of victims should be facilitated, "taking measures to minimize inconvenience to victims, protect their privacy, when necessary, and ensure their safety, as well as that of their families and witnesses on their behalf, from intimidation and retaliation".

The General Assembly Resolution 60/147 adopted on 16 December 2005 through which the *Basic principles and guidelines of the right to a remedy and reparation for victims of gross violations of international human rights law and serious violations of International Humanitarian Law* adopted by the UN Commission on Human Rights on 19 April 2005, by Resolution 2005/35, is adopted also takes into account this right to protection and security of the victims. In paragraph 10 of Principle VI which affirms that victims should be treated with humanity and *respect for their dignity* and human rights, and "appropriate measures should be taken to ensure their safety, physical and psychological well-being and privacy, as well as those of their families". Moreover, the States should ensure "that its domestic laws, to the extent possible, provide that a victim who has suffered violence or trauma should benefit from special consideration and care to avoid his or her re-traumatization in the course of legal and administrative procedures designed to provide justice and reparation."

Other recent and most relevant international norms covering the protection of the victims at the time of the process are the Statute of the International Criminal Court and the Statute of the international criminal tribunals for the former Yugoslavia and for Rwanda, with relevance for the *victims of violations of International criminal law* referred to in their respective statutes and subject to the jurisdiction of these courts.

In accordance with Article 43.6 of the *Statute of the International Criminal Court*, the Registrar of the Court shall set up a Victims and Witnesses Unit within the Registry. This Unit, in consultation with the Office of the Prosecutor, "shall provide protective measures and security arrangements, counselling and other appropriate assistance for witnesses, victims who appear before the Court, and others who are at risk on account of testimony given by such witnesses." As stated by this same article, "the Unit shall include staff with expertise in trauma, including trauma related to crimes of sexual violence."

As a *general principle* Rule 86 states that both the Chamber, in making any direction or order, and other organs of the Court in performing their functions under the Statute or the Rules, shall take into account the needs of all victims and witnesses in accordance with Article 68, in particular, those of children, elderly persons, persons with disabilities and victims of sexual or gender violence.[238]

Article 68 of the Statute and Rules 87 and 88 are charged with *the protection of the victims* and witnesses and their participation in the proceedings.[239] According to Article 68.1, the Court shall take appropriate measures to protect the safety, physical and psychological well-being, dignity and privacy of victims and witnesses but the Prosecutor shall also take such measures particularly during the investigation and prosecution of such crimes.

As an exception to the principle of public hearings provided for in Article 67, Article 68.2 states that the Chambers of the Court may, "to protect victims and witnesses or an accused", conduct any part of the proceedings in camera or allow the presentation of evidence by electronic or other special means. On the same lines, Rule 87.3 allows the Chambers to hold a hearing, which shall be conducted in camera, to determine whether to order measures to prevent the release to the public or press and information agencies, of the identity or the

[238] According to Rule 86: "A Chamber in making any direction or order, and other organs of the Court in performing their functions under the Statute or the Rules, shall take into account the needs of all victims and witnesses in accordance with Article 68, in particular, children, elderly persons, persons with disabilities and victims of sexual or gender violence."

[239] According to Rule 87.1: "1. Upon the motion of the Prosecutor or the defence or upon the request of a witness or a victim or his or her legal representative, if any, or on its own motion, and after having consulted with the Victims and Witnesses Unit, as appropriate, a Chamber may order measures to protect a victim, a witness or another person at risk on account of testimony given by a witness pursuant to Article 68, paragraphs 1 and 2. The Chamber shall seek to obtain, whenever possible, the consent of the person in respect of whom the protective measure is sought prior to ordering the protective measure."

location of a victim, a witness or other person at risk on account of testimony given by a witness.[240] Moreover, in line with what is established by Article 68.2 of the Statute of the Court, Rule 88 establishes that upon the motion of the Prosecutor or the defence, or upon the request of a witness or a victim or his or her legal representative, if any, or on its own motion, and after having consulted with the Victims and Witnesses Unit, as appropriate, a Chamber may, taking into account the views of the victim or witness, order *special measures* "such as, but not limited to, measures to facilitate the testimony of a traumatized victim or witness, a child, an elderly person or a victim of sexual violence". On the same lines, the Chamber shall seek to obtain, whenever possible, the consent of the person in respect of whom the special measure is sought prior to ordering that measure.

Finally, and inside the frame of the special measures envisaged in Rule 88, "taking into consideration that violations of the privacy of a witness or victim may create risk to his or her security, a Chamber shall be vigilant in controlling the manner of questioning a witness or victim so as to avoid any harassment or intimidation, paying particular attention to attacks on victims of crimes of sexual violence."

With regard to the *Statutes of the international criminal tribunals for the former Yugoslavia and for Rwanda*, they provide victims a very small role in that they conceive of them only as witnesses of the Prosecutor. As I have already pointed out elsewhere in this work, the foundation and the description of the status of the victim in these courts is in the Statute of the Prosecutor. The Prosecutor is the person who runs the public action aiming to defend International law and the repression of crime. The result is that the two Statutes have provided a device for the protection of the victim as witness, but have not referred to a special status for the victim. As a result, since it is the Prosecutor who directs the international public action the victim cannot be the civil party.[241]

The *International Convention for the Protection of All Persons from Enforced Disappearance*, of 20 December 2006, follows the way of the most recent

[240] Rule 87.3 states: "3. A Chamber may, on a motion or request under sub-rule 1, hold a hearing, which shall be conducted in camera, to determine whether to order measures to prevent the release to the public or press and information agencies, of the identity or the location of a victim, a witness or other person at risk on account of testimony given by a witness by ordering, inter alia: (a) That the name of the victim, witness or other person at risk on account of testimony given by a witness or any information which could lead to his or her identification, be expunged from the public records of the Chamber; (b) That the Prosecutor, the defence or any other participant in the proceedings be prohibited from disclosing such information to a third party; (c) That testimony be presented by electronic or other special means, including the use of technical means enabling the alteration of pictures or voice, the use of audio-visual technology, in particular videoconferencing and closed-circuit television, and the exclusive use of the sound media; (d) That a pseudonym be used for a victim, a witness or other person at risk on account of testimony given by a witness; or (e) That a Chamber conduct part of its proceedings in camera."

[241] C. Jorda, "L'accès des victimes à la justice pénale internationale", in *Terrorisme, victimes et...*, *op. cit.*, 363. Cf. also C. Tournaye, "L'apport des Tribunaux *ad hoc* pour la repression du terrorisme", *ibid.*, pp 416 et seq.

international norms related to victims. With regard to the protection of this category of victims Article 12.1 obliges the States Parties to take "appropriate steps to ensure that the complainant, witnesses, relatives of the disappeared person and their defence counsel, as well as persons participating in the investigation, are protected against all ill-treatment or intimidation as a consequence of the complaint or any evidence given." On the same lines, Article 12.4 states that the States Parties to the Convention shall ensure in particular that persons suspected of having committed an offence of enforced disappearance "are not in a position to influence the progress of an investigation by means of pressure or acts of intimidation or reprisal aimed at the complainant, witnesses, relatives of the disappeared person or their defence counsel, or at persons participating in the investigation."

But the obligations on the charge of the States Parties do not disappear with the release of the person deprived of liberty because in this case they shall also take necessary measures to assure the physical integrity of such persons and their ability to exercise fully their rights at the time of release, "without prejudice to any obligations to which such persons may be subject under national law".[242]

In the *European regional frame*, and related to *victims of terrorism*, the right to the protection of the dignity and security is ruled in the *Guidelines on the Protection of Victims of Terrorist Acts* adopted by the Committee of Ministers of the Council of Europe on 2 March 2005; Guidelines make reference to it on number "*IX. Protection of the dignity and security of victims of terrorist acts*", in the following terms:

1. At all stages of the proceedings, victims of terrorist acts should be treated in a manner which gives due consideration to their personal situation, their rights and their dignity.
2. States must ensure the protection and security of victims of terrorist acts and should take measures, where appropriate, to protect their identity, in particular where they intervene as witnesses.[243]

In this regard, and in relationship to the *respect of the personal situation of the victims, of their rights and their dignity*, the Guidelines do nothing other than repeat what the Committee of Ministers of the Council of Europe had already stated in recommendations prior to it, for example, in the case of *Recommendation 85 (11)*, of 28 June 1985, *On the Position of the Victim in the Framework of Criminal Law and Procedure*, paragraph 8 of which states that "at all stages of the procedure, the victim should be questioned in a manner which gives due consideration to his personal situation, his rights and his dignity."

In the frame of the *European Union*, the respect to the personal situation of the victims, their rights and their dignity constitute the object of Article 2 of *Council*

---

[242] Article 21 of the Convention.

[243] In line with what has been stated previously by the Committee of Ministers of the Council of Europe, but from another perspective, in *Recommendation (97) 13*, of 10 September 1997, *On the intimidation of witnesses and the rights of the defence*. In particular, in paragraph 25: "25. Vulnerable witnesses should, whenever possible, be examined at the earliest stage of the criminal proceedings, as soon as possible after the facts have been reported. Such examinations should be carried out in a particularly careful, respectful and thorough manner".

Framework Decision (2001/220/JHA) of 15 March 2001 on the Standing of Victims in Criminal Proceeding. Article 2, entitled "Respect and recognition", states:

1. Each Member State shall ensure that victims have a real and appropriate role in its criminal legal system. It shall continue to make every effort to ensure that victims are treated with due respect for the dignity of the individual during proceedings and shall recognise the rights and legitimate interests of victims with particular reference to criminal proceedings.
2. Each Member State shall ensure that victims who are particularly vulnerable can benefit from specific treatment best suited to their circumstances.

The second issue that *the Guidelines on the Protection of Victims of Terrorist Acts* adopted from the recommendations by the Committee of Ministers of the Council of Europe on 2 March 2005 is that related to the *protection of the identity* of victims in order to guarantee their protection and security when they have to act as witnesses, which is also present in other international norms. In the same framework of the Council of Europe, this issue is repeated after the Guidelines in *Recommendation (2006) 8* of the Committee of Ministers of 14 June 2006, *On Assistance to Crime Victims*, paragraph 10.1 of which states:

States should ensure, at all stages of the procedure, the protection of the victim's physical and psychological integrity. Particular protection may be necessary for victims who could be required to provide testimony.

In the framework of the *European Union*, the protection of the identity of victims in order to guarantee their protection and security when they have to act as witnesses is the object of Article 3 of *Council Framework Decision (2001/220/JHA)* of 15 March 2001 *on the Standing of Victims in Criminal Proceedings*. This article, entitled "Hearings, and provision of evidence", states:

Each Member State shall safeguard the possibility for victims to be heard during proceedings and to supply evidence.
Each Member State shall take appropriate measures to ensure that its authorities question victims only insofar as necessary for the purpose of criminal proceedings.

But this Council Framework Decision specifically envisages the protection of the security and dignity of victims in Article 8, entitled "Right to protection". In fact, the need for such a protection is one of the justifications of the Framework Decision as it is clearly declared on paragraph 4 of the Preamble:

(4) Member States should approximate their laws and regulations to the extent necessary to attain the objective of affording victims of crime a high level of protection, irrespective of the Member State in which they are present.

The right of victims to protection implies a plurality of measures drawn up in Article 8:

1. Each Member State shall ensure a suitable level of protection for victims and, where appropriate, their families or persons in a similar position, particularly as regards their safety and protection of their privacy, where the competent authorities consider that there is a serious risk of reprisals or firm evidence of serious intent to intrude upon their privacy.

2. To that end, and without prejudice to paragraph 4, each Member State shall guarantee that it is possible to adopt, if necessary, as part of the court proceedings, appropriate measures to protect the privacy and photographic image of victims and their families or persons in a similar position.
3. Each Member State shall further ensure that contact between victims and offenders within court premises may be avoided, unless criminal proceedings require such contact. Where appropriate for that purpose, each Member State shall progressively provide that court premises have special waiting areas for victims.
4. Each Member State shall ensure that, where there is a need to protect victims—particularly those most vulnerable—from the effects of giving evidence in open court, victims may, by decision taken by the court, be entitled to testify in a manner which will enable this objective to be achieved, by any appropriate means compatible with its basic legal principles.

Nevertheless, and despite the Council Framework Decision quoted above, according to a EU Commission Staff's recent working paper on the matter "victims are not sufficiently recognized and treated with dignity and respect. Victims need to be recognized as victims and to be acknowledged for their suffering. Victims also need to be treated with dignity and respect in all communications with all persons involved in the judicial process. Particular attention should be given to the needs of vulnerable victims, e.g. children, disabled person, victims of sexual violence. Indirect victims (e.g. family members) also need to be recognized as the consequences of the crime affect them too."[244]

In any case, and without prejudice to the preceding legal references, in relationship with the protection of the dignity of victims it should be remembered that the dignity of the victim proclaimed in different international norms[245] necessarily presides over and informs all actions related to victims. This is why the respect of the dignity of the victim is an obligation that permeates everything related to it, in reality, the inherent dignity of the human being—whether a victim or not. In other

[244] European Commission, Commission Staff Working Paper, *Executive summary of the Impact Assessment Accompanying the document Communication from the Commission to the European Parliament, to the Council, to the European economic and social Committee and to the Committee of the Regions—Strengthening victim's rights in the EU* {COM(2011) 274 final}and {SEC(2011) 580 final}, Brussels, 18.5.2011, SEC(2011) 581 final, 2.

[245] Paragraph 4 of the *Declaration of Basic Principles of Justice for Victims of Crime and Abuse of Power* of 29 November 1985, adopted by the General Assembly of the United Nations: "4. Victims should be treated with compassion and respect for their dignity. They are entitled to access to the mechanisms of justice and to prompt redress, as provided for by national legislation, for the harm that they have suffered". Also, paragraph 10 of General Assembly Resolution 60/147 adopted on 16 December 2005 through which *the Basic principles and guidelines of the right to a remedy and reparation for victims of gross violations of international human rights law and serious violations of International Humanitarian Law* adopted by the UN Commission on Human Rights on 19 April 2005, by Resolution 2005/35, are adopted: "10. Victims should be treated with humanity and respect for their dignity and human rights, and appropriate measures should be taken to ensure their safety, physical and psychological well-being and privacy, as well as those of their families. The State should ensure that its domestic laws, to the extent possible, provide that a victim who has suffered violence or trauma should benefit from special consideration and care to avoid his or her re-traumatization in the course of legal and administrative procedures designed to provide justice and reparation."

words, in situations of victimization the dignity of the victim acquires additional significance in that it expressly requires protection by the State, but that "highlighted" dignity of the victim is inseparable from the inherent dignity of every human being. It is the victimizer fact which makes clear the requirement of respect for the dignity of the victim in such circumstances.

Finally, the protection of the dignity and security of the person is also included in treaties that make up the *International law of human rights*, for example, for the protection of especially vulnerable people as in the case of children. In this regard, the *Convention on the Rights of the Child* of 20 November 1989 gives general protection while it proclaims a number of rights that the States Parties have an obligation to ensure. In connection with the object of this work, special attention should be devoted to Article 39 of the Convention, which obliges the States Parties to take "all appropriate measures to promote physical and psychological recovery and social reintegration of a child victim from any form of neglect, exploitation, or abuse; torture or any other form of cruel, inhuman or degrading treatment or punishment; or armed conflicts. Such recovery and reintegration shall take place in an environment which fosters the health, self-respect and dignity of the child."

On the same lines, Article 13 of the *Convention against Torture and Other Cruel, Inhuman or Degrading Treatment or Punishment* of 10 December 1984 and Article 13 of the UN Convention against torture and other cruel, inhuman or degrading treatment or punishment, of 10 December 1984, provide for the protection both of the complainant of the act of torture and of the witnesses and oblige the States Parties to take steps "to ensure that the complainant and witnesses are protected against all ill-treatment or intimidation as a consequence of his complaint or any evidence given."

Right to Information

In the International law of human rights, the right to information is linked with the freedom of expression and has a dual dimension. On the one hand, a positive dimension consisting of communicating information and ideas and on the other hand, a passive dimension consisting of receiving such information or ideas. Thus, it conceived the International Covenant on Civil and Political Rights,[246] the European Convention on human rights,[247] the American Convention on human rights[248] and the African Charter on Human and Peoples' Rights.[249] In the frame of the

[246] In Article 19.

[247] In Article 10.

[248] In Article 11.

[249] In Article 9.

European Union, however, freedom has emerged in the jurisprudence of the Court of Justice almost always linked with the freedom of the single market.[250]

Prior to these treaties, the right to private and family life was picked up in Article 12 of the Universal Declaration of Human Rights of 10 December 1948.[251]

In addition to other human rights, the right to information may be subject to certain restrictions, limitations, conditions or formalities, sanctions; all circumstances that have to be provided for by law and are necessary in a democratic society.

In contrast to the formulation of the right to information in international human rights treaties, the right to information referred to by various international norms *in relation to the various categories of victims has a different dimension* linked with the litigation and parcels in the following field. First, the obligation of the State to inform the victims on any matter linked with the process related to the victimizer fact, namely the status of the investigation, the way in which the victim can obtain free legal assistance, the final decision of the proceedings, the date and place of hearings, the way in which it is possible to know the decisions handed down, the time of the release of the accused person, etc.

Second, the right to information of which victims are titular is reflected in the establishment by the State of contact points to provide information to victims about their rights, on the existence of support agencies, on the possibilities of obtaining assistance, practical and legal advice, as well as on the repair of the damage or compensation.

Third, the State's obligation to inform victims also includes the possibility that they may have to renounce such information.

Finally, in the case of enforced disappearance, the right to information to which such victims are titular is reflected in the right that, in certain circumstances, the family of a missing person have to be informed by the State of the investigations and the whereabouts of the victim in question.[252]

As pointed out by Sanz Hermida, the main objective of this right is ensuring that the victim has access as soon as possible, effectively and by means deemed appropriate, to relevant information for the protection of his interests.[253] Such information should come from the competent authorities according to national law. That is, the judicial authority, police authority or the Prosecutor's Office.

In the general or universal level of the United Nations, the *Declaration of Basic Principles of Justice for Victims of Crime and Abuse of Power* of 29 November

---

[250] In this regard, cf. Martín y Pérez de Nanclares (2008), 277.

[251] In Article 19.

[252] In this regard, cf. Articles 17 y 18 of the *International Convention for the Protection of All Persons from Enforced Disappearance*, of 20 December 2006. For its part, article XI of *the Inter-American Convention on Forced Disappearance of Persons* obliges States Parties to establish and maintain official up-to-date registries of their detainees and, in accordance with their domestic law, shall make them available to relatives, judges, attorneys, any other person having a legitimate interest, and other authorities.

[253] Sanz Hermida, *op. cit.*, 64.

1985, adopted by the General Assembly of the United Nations, this right is located within the framework of the right relating to access to justice and fair treatment. Within it, paragraph 6 of the Declaration sets forth that judicial and administrative procedures adequate to the needs of the victims will be provided. In particular, informing victims "of their role and the scope, timing and progress of the proceedings and of the disposition of their cases, especially where serious crimes are involved and where they have requested such information."

As we have seen, in the case of the *Statute of the International Criminal Court*, and as a result of the participation of the victim and his representative in all proceedings, both the victims and their representatives must be notified of all proceedings of the Court. That is why, in order to allow victims to apply for participation in the proceedings in accordance with rule 89, the Court shall notify victims regarding the decision of the Prosecutor not to initiate an investigation or not to prosecute pursuant to Article 53.[254] In addition, the Court shall notify its decision to hold a hearing to confirm the charges.

For its part, the Registrar of the Court must notify in a timely manner to the victims or their legal representatives participating in the proceedings and in connection with them all the proceedings before the Court (including the dates of hearing and any postponement thereof, and the date of delivery of the decision) as well as requests, submissions, motions and other documents relating to such requests, writings or motions.

On the same lines, Resolution 60/147 of the General Assembly of 16 December 2005 through which the *Basic principles and guidelines of the right to a remedy and reparation for victims of gross violations of international human rights law and serious violations of International Humanitarian Law* adopted by the UN Commission on Human Rights on 19 April 2005, by Resolution 2005/35, is adopted to establish that the States should "develop means of informing the general public and, in particular, victims of gross violations of international human rights law and serious violations of international humanitarian law of the rights and remedies addressed by these Basic Principles and Guidelines and of all available legal, medical, psychological, social, administrative and all other services to which victims may have a right of access."[255] Moreover, it states that victims and their representatives should be entitled to seek and obtain information on the causes leading to their victimization and on the causes and conditions pertaining to the gross violations of international human rights law and serious violations of international humanitarian law and to learn the truth in regard to these violations.[256]

With regard to the case of victims of enforced disappearance, Article 18.1 of the *International Convention for the Protection of All Persons from Enforced Disappearance*, of 20 December 2006, envisages three types of information. One

---

[254] Cf. Rule 92.2.

[255] In Principle X, entitled "Access to relevant information concerning violations and reparation mechanisms".

[256] Cf. *ibid.*

concerns any person with a legitimate interest in this information, such as relatives of the person deprived of liberty, their representatives or their counsel; persons to whom States Parties shall guarantee the access to a minimum of information.[257]

A second type of information is that provided to any judicial or other competent authority or institution authorized for that purpose by the law of the State Party concerned or any relevant international legal instrument to which the State concerned is a party.[258]

Finally, the Convention envisages another type of information that may only be used in criminal proceedings relating to an offence of enforced disappearance or the exercise of the right to obtain reparation but the collection, processing, use and storage of such information (personal information, including medical and genetic data), "shall not infringe or have the effect of infringing the human rights, fundamental freedoms or human dignity of an individual."[259]

---

[257] Whose content is specified by the article 18.1 itself: "1. Subject to articles 19 and 20, each State Party shall guarantee to any person with a legitimate interest in this information, such as relatives of the person deprived of liberty, their representatives or their counsel, access to at least the following information: (a) The authority that ordered the deprivation of liberty; (b) The date, time and place where the person was deprived of liberty and admitted to the place of deprivation of liberty; (c) The authority responsible for supervising the deprivation of liberty; (d) The whereabouts of the person deprived of liberty, including, in the event of a transfer to another place of deprivation of liberty, the destination and the authority responsible for the transfer; (e) The date, time and place of release; (f) Elements relating to the state of health of the person deprived of liberty; (g) In the event of death during the deprivation of liberty, the circumstances and cause of death and the destination of the remains."

Only where a person is under the protection of the law and the deprivation of liberty is subject to judicial control may the right to information referred to in Article 18 be restricted, on an exceptional basis, where strictly necessary "and where provided for by law, and if the transmission of the information would adversely affect the privacy or safety of the person, hinder a criminal investigation, or for other equivalent reasons in accordance with the law, and in conformity with applicable international law and with the objectives" of this Convention (cf. article 20).

[258] It is the mínimum information envisaged in Article 17.3: (a) The identity of the person deprived of liberty; (b) The date, time and place where the person was deprived of liberty and the identity of the authority that deprived the person of liberty; (c) The authority that ordered the deprivation of liberty and the grounds for the deprivation of liberty; (d) The authority responsible for supervising the deprivation of liberty; (e) The place of deprivation of liberty, the date and time of admission to the place of deprivation of liberty and the authority responsible for the place of deprivation of liberty; (f) Elements relating to the state of health of the person deprived of liberty; (g) In the event of death during the deprivation of liberty, the circumstances and cause of death and the destination of the remains; (h) The date and time of release or transfer to another place of detention, the destination and the authority responsible for the transfer.

[259] It is the case of information quoted in Article 19: "1. Personal information, including medical and genetic data, which is collected and/or transmitted within the framework of the search for a disappeared person shall not be used or made available for purposes other than the search for the disappeared person. This is without prejudice to the use of such information in criminal proceedings relating to an offence of enforced disappearance or the exercise of the right to obtain reparation. 2. The collection, processing, use and storage of personal information, including medical and genetic data, shall not infringe or have the effect of infringing the human rights, fundamental freedoms or human dignity of an individual."

In the *European regional frame*, and with regard to *victims of terrorism*, the *Guidelines on the Protection of Victims of Terrorist Acts* adopted by the Committee of Ministers of the Council of Europe on 2 March 2005 deals with the information to be facilitated to victims of terrorism in the following terms:

> States should give information, in an appropriate way, to victims of terrorist acts about the act of which they suffered, except where victims indicate that they do not wish to receive such information. For this purpose, states should:
>
> (i) set up appropriate information contact points for the victims, concerning in particular their rights, the existence of victim support bodies, and the possibility of obtaining assistance, practical and legal advice as well as redress or compensation;
> (ii) ensure the provision to the victims of appropriate information in particular about the investigations, the final decision concerning prosecution, the date and place of the hearings and the conditions under which they may acquaint themselves with the decisions handed down.

The recommendation the Guidelines make to the Member States are to establish contact points to provide information to victims about their rights, about the existence of support bodies, about the possibilities to obtain assistance, practical and legal advice, as well as redress or compensation—subject of point (i) of this guideline—follows the line of precedent recommendations adopted by the Committee of Ministers of the Council of Europe. This is the case in *Recommendation 85 (11)*, of 28 June 1985 *On the position of the Victim in the Framework of Criminal Law and Procedure* and of *Recommendation (87) 21*, of 17 September 1987 *On Assistance to Victims and the Prevention of Victimization.*

The first, on paragraph 2, states that "the police should inform the victim about the possibilities of obtaining assistance, practical and legal advice, compensation from the offender and state compensation". With regard to the second, paragraph 4 recommends that the governments of the Member States "ensure that victims and their families, especially those who are most vulnerable, receive in particular (. . .) information on the victim's rights".

Finally, the obligation on the charge of the States to provide the victims appropriate information about the investigations, the final decision concerning prosecution, the date and place of the hearings and the conditions under which they may acquaint themselves with the decisions handed down is also supported by the Committee of Ministers on precedent recommendations. *Recommendation 85 (11)*, of 28 June 1985, *On the position of the Victim in the Framework of Criminal Law and Procedure*, paragraphs 3, 6 and 9 of which treat these questions. So, paragraph 3 states that "the victim should be able to obtain information on the outcome of the police investigation". Paragraph 6 adds that "the victim should be informed of the final decision concerning prosecution, unless he indicates that he does not want this information". Finally, paragraph 9 says that the victim should be informed of the date and place of a hearing concerning an offence which caused him suffering, of his opportunities for obtaining restitution and compensation within the criminal justice process, legal assistance and advice, as well as of how he can find out the outcome of the case.

Like in the rights examined in the preceding pages, the obligation on the charge of the State to provide the victims appropriate information about the investigations, the final decision concerning prosecution, the date and place of the hearings and the conditions under which they may acquaint themselves with the decisions handed down is repeated in *Recommendation (2006) 8 of the Committee of Ministers of* 14 June 2006, *On Assistance to Crime Victims*, which substitutes the preceding recommendations *85 (11)* and *87 (21)*. In this sense, *Recommendation (2006)* establishes that unless victims indicate that they do not wish to receive such information:

> 6.5. States should ensure in an appropriate way that victims are kept informed and understand:
> – the outcome of their complaint;
> – relevant stages in the progress of criminal proceedings;
> – the verdict of the competent court and, where relevant, the sentence
>
> Victims should be given the opportunity to indicate that they do not to receive such information.[260]

On the other hand, and in the frame of the general heading entitled "6. Information", *Recommendation (2006)* also treats other issues namely, the access of victims to information relevant to their case and necessary for the protection of their interests and the exercise of their rights; the information that should be provided to victims as soon as the victim comes into contact with law enforcement or criminal justice agencies or with social or health care services. Such information should be communicated orally as well as in writing, and as far as possible in a language understood by the victim.[261] *Recommendation (2006)* also envisages the *content of the information* that should be facilitated to victims.[262]

The violation—by the State—of the victims' right to receive information is treated in the *Guidelines on the Protection of Victims of Terrorist Acts* in the frame of the case-law of the ECHR related to a case of disappearance. In it, the Court admitted that in certain circumstances relatives of a missing person may suffer inhuman treatment (in the sense of Article 3 of the European Convention on human rights) if the authorities of the State remain silent despite attempts by family

---

[260] Paragraph 6.5 of *Recommendation (2006)*, placed inside the heading entitled: "Information on legal proceedings".

[261] Questions treated in paragraphs 6.1 y 6.2 of this Recommendation.

[262] Basically, two large blocks of issues. On the one hand, the services or organizations which can provide support and the type and, where relevant, the costs of the support (all this, in paragraph 6.3). On the other hand, when an offence has been reported to law enforcement or criminal justice agencies, the information provided to the victim should also include as a minimum: the procedures which will follow and the victims' role in these procedures; how and in what circumstances the victim can obtain protection; how and in what circumstances the victim can obtain compensation from the offender; the availability and, where relevant, the cost of legal advice, legal aid, or any other sort of advice; how to apply for state compensation, if eligible; and if the victim is resident in another state, any existing arrangements which will help to protect his or her interests (all of it in paragraph 6.4).

members to obtain information about the missing person. This statement concerns the *case Cyprus v. Turkey*, where the ECHR affirms:

> 156. The Court recalls that the question whether a family member of a "disappeared person" is a victim of treatment contrary to Article 3 will depend on the existence of special factors which give the suffering of the person concerned a dimension and character distinct from the emotional distress which may be regarded as inevitably caused to relatives of a victim of a serious human rights violation. Relevant elements will include the proximity of the family tie—in that context, a certain weight will attach to the parent–child bond—, the particular circumstances of the relationship, the extent to which the family member witnessed the events in question, the involvement of the family member in the attempts to obtain information about the disappeared person and the way in which the authorities responded to those enquiries. The Court further recalls that the essence of such a violation does not so much lie in the fact of the "disappearance" of the family member but rather in the authorities' reactions and attitudes to the situation when it is brought to their attention. It is especially in respect of the latter that a relative may claim directly to be a victim of the authorities' conduct (see Çakici v. Turkey [GC], no. 23657/94, § 98, ECHR 1999-IV).
>
> 157. The Court observes that the authorities of the respondent State have failed to undertake any investigation into the circumstances surrounding the disappearance of the missing persons. In the absence of any information about their fate, the relatives of persons who went missing during the events of July and August 1974 were condemned to live in a prolonged state of acute anxiety which cannot be said to have been erased with the passage of time. The Court does not consider, in the circumstances of this case, that the fact that certain relatives may not have actually witnessed the detention of family members or complained about such to the authorities of the respondent State deprives them of victim status under Article 3.

In the frame of the *European Union*, Article 4 of *Council Framework Decision (2001/220/JHA)* of 15 March 2001 on the Standing of Victims in Criminal Proceedings rules the "right to receive information". This right implies that victims in particular have access, as from their first contact with law enforcement agencies, by any means it deems appropriate and as far as possible in languages commonly understood, to information of relevance for the protection of their interests. The content of this information deals with a plurality of issues quoted above—the type of services or organizations to which they can turn for support; the type of support which they can obtain; where and how they can report an offence; procedures following such a report and their role in connection with such procedures; how and under what conditions they can obtain protection; to what extent and on what terms they have access to legal advice or legal aid, or any other sort of advice if, in the two first cases envisaged, they are entitled to receive it; requirements for them to be entitled to compensation; and, if they are resident in another State, any special arrangements available to them in order to protect their interests.[263]

In addition, if victims have expressed a wish to this effect, the States shall ensure that they are kept informed of the outcome of their complaint; of the relevant factors enabling them, in the event of prosecution, to know the conduct of the criminal proceedings regarding the person prosecuted for offences concerning them (except

[263] In Article 4.1.

in exceptional cases where the proper handling of the case may be adversely affected); and, at least, of the court's sentence.[264]

Like in the case of the Council of Europe, *Council Framework Decision (2001/220/JHA)* of 15 March 2001 on the Standing of Victims in Criminal Proceedings rules, in Article 4.3, the obligation that Member States have to take necessary measures to ensure that, at least in cases where there might be danger to the victims, when the person prosecuted or sentenced for an offence is released, a decision may be taken to notify the victim if necessary.

Finally, Article 4.4 envisages the possibility for the victim not to receive the information referred to in paragraphs 2 and 3, unless communication thereof is compulsory under the terms of the relevant criminal proceedings.[265]

The whole text of Article 4 states:

1. Each Member State shall ensure that victims in particular have access, as from their first contact with law enforcement agencies, by any means it deems appropriate and as far as possible in languages commonly understood, to information of relevance for the protection of their interests. Such information shall be at least as follows:

   (a) the type of services or organizations to which they can support;
   (b) the type of support which they can obtain;
   (c) where and how they can report an offence;
   (d) procedures following such a report and their role in connection with such procedures;
   (e) how and under what conditions they can obtain protection;
   (f) to what extent and on what terms they have access to:

      (i) legal advice or
      (ii) legal aid, or
      (iii) any other sort of advice, if, in the cases envisaged in point (i)and (ii), they are entitled to receive it;

   (g) requirements for them to be entitled to compensation;
   (h) if they are resident in another State, any special arrangements available to them in order to protect their interests.

[264] In Article 4.2. Nevertheless, this Framework Decision "has not been effective in meeting, or moving towards the desired outcomes of addressing the needs of victims and achieving minimum standards for victims across the EU. No Member State can claim to have fully implemented the Framework Decision. The ineffectiveness of this legislation is due to ambiguous drafting, a lack of concrete obligations and a lack of infringement possibilities against Member States." (European Commission, Commission Staff Working Paper, *Executive summary of the Impact Assessment Accompanying the document Communication from the Commission to the European Parliament, to the Council, to the European economic and social Committee and to the Committee of the Regions—Strengthening victim's rights in the EU* {COM(2011) 274 final}and {SEC(2011) 580 final}, Brussels, 18.5.2011, SEC(2011) 581 final, 2.

[265] That is, information concerning the course of the complaint, to the elements, in the event of prosecution, to continue the development of the criminal process, the information concerning the judgement of the Court and information relating to the release of the specified indicted or convicted of the offence.

2. Each Member State shall ensure that victims who have expressed a wish to this effect are kept informed of:

   (a) the outcome of their complaint;
   (b) relevant factors enabling them, in the event of prosecution, to know the conduct of the criminal proceedings regarding the person prosecuted for offences concerning them, except in exceptional cases where the proper handling of the case may be adversely affected;
   (c) the court's sentence.

3. Member States shall take the necessary measures to ensure that, at least in cases where there might be danger to the victims, when the person prosecuted or sentenced for an offence is released, a decision may be taken to notify the victim if necessary.
4. In so far as a Member State forwards on its own initiative the information referred to in paragraphs 2 and 3, it must ensure that victims have the right not to receive it, unless communication thereof is compulsory under the terms of the relevant criminal proceedings.

Right to Specific Training for Persons Responsible for Assisting Victims

The need that the persons responsible for assistance to victims receive specific training is envisaged in various international norms relating to victims.

In the general or universal plane of the *UN*, the need for a specific training for persons intervening in the proceedings or having contact with victims is envisaged in the *Declaration of Basic Principles of Justice for Victims of Crime and Abuse of Power* of 29 November 1985, adopted by the General Assembly of the United Nations, paragraph 16 of which states:

> 16. Police, justice, health, social service and other personnel concerned should receive training to sensitize them to the needs of victims, and guidelines to ensure proper and prompt aid.

On this issue, Article 23.1 of the *International Convention for the Protection of All Persons from Enforced Disappearance*, of 20 December 2006, imposes upon the States Parties the obligation "to ensure that the training of law enforcement personnel, civil or military, medical personnel, public officials and other persons who may be involved in the custody or treatment of any person deprived of liberty includes the necessary education and information regarding the relevant provisions of this Convention".[266]

In the *European regional frame*, and in the Council of Europe, the need for a specific training for persons intervening in the proceedings or having contact with victims is envisaged in paragraph 12 of *Recommendation (2006) 8* of the

[266] All this with the aim to: "(a) Prevent the involvement of such officials in enforced disappearances; (b) Emphasize the importance of prevention and investigations in relation to enforced disappearances; (c) Ensure that the urgent need to resolve cases of enforced disappearance is recognized."

Committee of Ministers of 14 June 2006, *On Assistance to Crime Victims*, under the title "Selection and training of personnel". Under it, three types of questions are treated: training, specialized training and the training of personnel in other services.

With regard to *training*, paragraph 12.2 states:

> Training should as a minimum include:
> - awareness of the negative effects of crime on victims;
> - skills and knowledge required to assist victims;
> - awareness of the risk of causing secondary victimization and the skills to prevent this.

In dealing with *specialized training*, paragraph 12.3 states:

> Specialized training should be provided to all personnel working with child victims and victims of special categories of crime, for example, domestic or sexual violence, terrorism, crimes motivated by racial, religious or other prejudice, as well as to families of murder victims.

Finally, and with regard to *training of personnel in other services*, paragraph 12.4 states:

> Member states should ensure that appropriate training is provided for:
> - the police and personnel involved in the administration of justice;
> - the emergency services and others attending the scene of a major incident;
> - relevant staff in health, housing, social security, education and employment services.

According to paragraph 12.5 of *Recommendation (2006) 8*, the personnel belonging to the three precedent categories should be trained "to a level which is appropriate" to their contact with victims. Training should include, as a minimum:

- General awareness of the effects of crime on a victim's attitudes and behaviour, including verbal behaviour;
- The risk of causing secondary victimization and the skills required to minimize this risk;
- The availability of services providing information and support specific to the needs of victims and the means of accessing these services.

Later, and with regard to victims of terrorism, the *Guidelines on the Protection of Victims of Terrorist Acts* adopted by the Committee of Ministers of the Council of Europe on 2 March 2005 affirms that the States "should encourage specific training for persons responsible for assisting victims of terrorist acts, as well as granting the necessary resources to that effect".[267]

In the frame of the *European Union*, the specific training of persons charged with the assistance of victims is envisaged both in the preamble and in Article 14 of *Council Framework Decision (2001/220/JHA)* of 15 March 2001 on the Standing of

[267] It is striking that the norms adopted by the Committee of Ministers of the Council of Europe are the only ones that use this language. Those of the EU, for example, use a clearly mandatory language. The explanation may lie in the different nature (of cooperation, in the first case, of integration, in the second) of these international organizations.

Victims in Criminal Proceedings. In its preamble, paragraphs 10 and 11 echo this necessity and proclaim it:

> (10) The involvement of specialized services and victim support groups before, during and after criminal proceedings is important.
>
> (11) Suitable and adequate training should be given to persons coming into contact with victims, as this is essential both for victims and for achieving the purposes of proceedings.

Article 14 treats this issue "with particular reference to the needs of the most vulnerable groups" and applying in particular to police officers and legal practitioners:

1. Through its public services or by funding victim support organizations, each Member State shall encourage initiatives enabling personnel involved in proceedings or otherwise in contact with victims to receive suitable training with particular reference to the needs of the most vulnerable groups.
2. Paragraph 1 shall apply in particular to police officers and legal practitioners.

Ultimately, with the exception of the norms of the Committee of Ministers of the Council of Europe—using a merely recommendatory language for the States ("should promote")—the rest of the international norms concerning victims clearly express the importance and the necessity that persons who are in contact with the victims receive appropriate and sufficient training. In particular, police officers, legal professionals and workers in health services. The corollary of this concept is the configuration as an obligation on the State of the right of victims to be assisted by individuals with specific training.

In *International Law of human rights*, this concern for the specific training of persons responsible for assisting victims or treating them is present in the UN *Convention against Torture and Other Cruel, Inhuman or Degrading Treatment or Punishment*, of 10 December 1984. So, Article 10 obliges the States Parties to "ensure that education and information regarding the prohibition against torture are fully included in the training of law enforcement personnel, civil or military, medical personnel, public officials and other persons who may be involved in the custody, interrogation or treatment of any individual subjected to any form of arrest, detention or imprisonment."[268] With this aim, the States Parties shall include this prohibition in the rules or instructions issued in regard to the duties and functions of any such person.[269]

On the other side, and according to Article 11, each State Party shall keep "under systematic review interrogation rules, instructions, methods and practices as well as arrangements for the custody and treatment of persons subjected to any form of

[268] On the same lines, Article 7 of the Inter-American Convention on Forced Disappearance of Persons, of 9 December 1985, states: "Criminal prosecution for the forced disappearance of persons and the penalty judicially imposed on its perpetrator shall not be subject to statutes of limitations. However, if there should be a norm of a fundamental character preventing application of the stipulation contained in the previous paragraph, the period of limitation shall be equal to that which applies to the gravest crime in the domestic laws of the corresponding State Party."

[269] Cf. Article10.2.

arrest, detention or imprisonment in any territory under its jurisdiction, with a view to preventing any cases of torture."

The Right to Truth

The first thing to be said for the right to the truth is that it is a right recognized in the field of International law concerning human rights in the event of *serious violations of human rights* as genocide, crimes against humanity, war crimes, forced disappearances, extrajudicial executions or terrorism. Second, that the objective of this right is, through the knowledge of the facts and perpetrators who produced them, none other than the consolidation of peace and reconciliation processes in societies where such crimes were committed.

Therefore, the right to the truth is not raised with regard to all kinds of crimes but only for the most serious. Perhaps, it is this fact which explains that the right to the truth is mentioned in some international norms specifically related to victims. They are in all cases victims of grave violations of human rights.

This is the case both of the General Assembly Resolution 60/147 adopted on 16 December 2005 through which the *Basic principles and guidelines of the right to a remedy and reparation for victims of gross violations of international human rights law and serious violations of International Humanitarian Law* adopted by the UN Commission on Human Rights on 19 April 2005, by Resolution 2005/35, is adopted and of the *International Convention for the Protection of All Persons from Enforced Disappearance*, of 20 December 2006.

The first of these international norms, the basic principles and guidelines deal with the right to truth in the triple context of the victim's right to remedies, right to access to relevant information to know the causes and conditions of the victimization and right to *satisfaction* as a form of reparation for the harm suffered. In relation to this last question, paragraph 22.b) states that satisfaction should include, where applicable, any or all of the following measures:

> Verification of the facts and full and public disclosure of the truth to the extent that such disclosure does not cause further harm or threaten the safety and interests of the victim, the victim's relatives, witnesses, or persons who have intervened to assist the victim or prevent the occurrence of further violations.

With regard to the Convention, this treaty reaffirms and develops the *Declaration on the protection of all persons from Enforced Disappearance*, of 18 December 1992, ruling in article 24.2 the right of victims to know the truth and to claim reparation for the harm suffered. According to it:

> 2. Each victim has the right to know the truth regarding the circumstances of the enforced disappearance, the progress and results of the investigation and the fate of the disappeared person. Each State Party shall take appropriate measures in this regard.

Beyond international norms specifically concerning the victims, the right to the truth has been the subject of exhaustive examination within the framework of the UN resulting in the *Study on the right to the truth*, which is a Report from the Office of the United Nations High Commissioner for Human Rights, of 9 January 2006. The report explains that the *right to truth* implies "knowing the full and complete truth as to the events that transpired, their specific circumstances, and who participated in them, including knowing the circumstances in which the violations took place, as well as the reasons for them".[270] In addition, "in cases of enforced disappearance, missing persons, children abducted or during the captivity of a mother subjected to enforced disappearance, secret executions and secret burial place, the right to the truth also has a special dimension: to know the fate and whereabouts of the victim".[271]

According to this study, the right to truth is an inalienable and autonomous right linked with the State's duty to protect and guarantee human rights and to the State's obligation to conduct effective investigations and to guarantee effective remedies and reparation. It is a right which has individual and collective aspects and that, moreover, does not support suspension nor is it subject to restrictions. In this sense, it is an imprescriptible right "to know the truth about the circumstances in which violations took place and, in the event of death or disappearance, the victims' fate."[272]

As is the case with many of the rights discussed above, the right to the truth is closely linked with other rights. As concluded by the *Study on the right to the truth*, the right to truth is linked to the following: the right to an effective remedy; the right to legal and judicial protection; the right to the family life; the right to an effective investigation; the right to a hearing by a competent, independent, and impartial tribunal; the right to obtain reparation; the right to be free from torture and ill-treatment; and the right to seek and impart information. In short, "truth is fundamental to the inherent dignity of the human person."[273]

The reverse side of the right to the truth *is the State's duty* to protect and guarantee human rights as well as the State's obligation to conduct effective investigations into gross human rights violations and serious violations of humanitarian law and to guarantee effective remedies and reparation. The right to the truth is also closely

[270] UN, Economic and Social Council, Commission on Human Rights, Sixty-second session, Item 17 of the provisional agenda, PROMOTION AND PROTECTION OF HUMAN RIGHTS, *Study on the right to the truth, Report of the Office of the United Nations High Commissioner for Human Rights*, 9 January 2006, (E/CN.4/2006/91, 8 February 2006), para. 59. For the construction of this section, I will abundantly use this study as the most complete one to date in relation to this right. Also, because it has been open to the participation of the States and these have had the possibility to demonstrate their opinions on the matter.

[271] *Ibid.*

[272] Principle 4 of the *Set of principles for the protection and promotion of human rights through action to combat impunity (E/CN.4/2005/102/Add.1)* 7), recommended by Commission resolution 2005/81.

[273] *Ibid.*, para. 57.

linked with the rule of law and the principles of transparency, accountability and good governance in a democratic society."[274]

With regard to its *legal basis*, it is based on the International law in general (customary, conventional and institutional) and International humanitarian law in particular, having also been recognized by the international jurisprudence emanating from international courts of human rights (ECHR and Inter-American Court of Human Rights), international criminal tribunals and international supervisory bodies for human rights.

In the frame of the *UN*, the right to truth is formulated in a plurality of norms coming from different organs (General Assembly, Security Council, Commission on Human Rights, Committee of Human Rights).

As far as the *General Assembly* is concerned, it has addressed issues related to the right to the truth in numerous resolutions since 1974 regarding missing persons or those subjected to enforced disappearances,[275] the most recent being the *Declaration on the protection of all persons from Enforced Disappearance,* of 18 December 1992, adopted through Resolution 47/133 of 18 December 1992.

However, this Declaration is not the first instrument in which the General Assembly dealt with this issue (as emphasized by the preamble to this Declaration),[276] it had earlier been the object both of resolution 43/173 of 9 December 1988 containing the *Body of Principles for the Protection of All Persons under Any Form of Detention or Imprisonment* and of resolution 44/162 of 15 December 1989, which adopted the *Principles on the Effective Prevention and Investigation of Extra-legal, Arbitrary and Summary Executions* that was formulated by the Economic and Social Council of the United Nations in the annex to its resolution 1989/65 of 24 May 1989.

With regard to the *Security Council*, this organ of the United Nations has also reiterated in various resolutions that the determination of the truth about the crimes against humanity, genocide, war crimes and gross violations of human rights is necessary to consolidate the peace process and forms part of the reconciliation process[277]; a line followed by the *Secretary-General*, as proved in his bulletin

[274] *Ibid.*, para. 56.

[275] Cf. UN, Economic and Social Council, Commission on Human Rights, Sixty-second session, Item 17 of the provisional agenda, PROMOTION AND PROTECTION OF HUMAN RIGHTS, *Study on the right to the truth*, *op. cit.*, para. 12.

[276] As I have pointed out, it has been doing it since 1974. The proof of this lies in resolutions 55/118, 57/105 and 57/161. Also, in its resolution 33/173, of 20 December 1978, on which it stated: "*Deeply concerned* by report of various parts of the world relating to enforced or involuntary disappearances of persons as a result of excesses on the part of law enforcement or security authorities or similar organizations, often while such persons are subject to detention or imprisonment, as well as of unlawful actions or widespread violence" (on third para.).

[277] Is the case of the resolutions of the Security Council 1468 (2003) of 20 March 2003, concerning the Democratic Republic of the Congo (S/RES/1468 (2003), 1470 (2003) of 28 March 2003, concerning Sierra Leone (S/RES/1470 (2003), and 1606 (2005) of 20 June 2005, on Burundi (S/RES/1606 (2005).

entitled *Observance of International Humanitarian Law by United Nations forces*, which sets the rule that the United Nations shall respect the right of families to know the whereabouts of their sick, wounded and deceased members. [278] On other occasions, the Secretary-General has also indicated that the peace processes must fully respect the right of victims to truth, to justice and to reparation having also highlighted the importance of truth in the context of transitional justice.[279]

As I have noted above, the assertion of the right to the truth has not been limited to the principal organs of the United Nations. The competent bodies of this international organization in the field of protection of human rights also provide examples, as for instance the *Commission on Human Rights*, which has various resolutions on the subject. It is worth mentioning in this regard that both the *Set of principles for the protection and promotion of human rights through action to combat impunity* recommended through Resolution 2005/81of the Commission on Human Rights[280] and the General Assembly Resolution 60/147 adopted on 16 December 2005 through which the *Basic principles and guidelines of the right to a remedy and reparation for victims of gross violations of international human rights law and serious violations of International Humanitarian Law* was adopted by the UN Commission on Human Rights on 19 April 2005, by Resolution 2005/35, have been adopted as I have already mentioned at the beginning of this section.

A day after the latter, on 20 April 2005, the *Commission on Human Rights* devoted its resolution 2005/66 exclusively to the right to the truth. In it, it recognizes "the importance of respecting and ensuring the right to the truth so as to contribute to ending impunity and to promote and protect human rights".[281] At other times, it has also been noted that "the legal framework governing the disarmament, demobilization and reintegration process of illegal armed groups should guarantee the rights to truth, justice and reparations".[282]

Completing this tour of the scope of the United Nations, can be examples from both the *Human Rights Committee*,[283] and the *United Nations High Commissioner for Human Rights*[284]; both bodies that also recognize and affirm the right of victims to the truth.

---

[278] Cited on paragraph 18 by *Study on the right to the truth, op. cit.*

[279] Vid. *ibid.*

[280] UNO, E/CN.4/2005/102/Add. 1.

[281] Para. 1.

[282] Regarding the human rights situation in Colombia, April 22, 2005. Vid. UN, Economic and Social Council, Commission on Human Rights, *Study on the right to the truth, op. cit.*, para. 16.

[283] Both the Human Rights Committee (cf. CCPR/C/79/Add.63 and CCPR/C/19/D/107/1981) and the Working Group on Enforced or Involuntary Disappearances (cf. E/CN.4/1999–1962) on several occasions have acknowledged the right of victims of gross violations of human rights and their families to know the truth about the events, including the identity of the perpetrators of the events that led to violations.

[284] With regard to The High Commissioner for Human Rights, the best example is his report cited in the preceding pages of this work.

At the *regional level* also, the right of victims to truth is recognized. In Europe, both the Council of Europe[285] and the European Union[286] have done so. In America, at least since 1983 various resolutions of the General Assembly of the Organization of American States have urged the States to inform the family about the fate of the victims of enforced disappearances.[287]

At the same time, as I have mentioned earlier, the right to the truth is also picked up in international treaties pertaining to the field of International law made up of International Humanitarian law and International Law of human rights; treaties that I examine below.

With respect to *International Humanitarian law*, the right to the truth is codified in Article 32 of the Additional Protocol to the Geneva Conventions of 12 August 1949 (Protocol I of 1977) relative to the protection of victims of international armed conflicts. The Geneva Conventions of 12 August 1949 also incorporate several provisions that require the warring parties to solve the problem of missing combatants and establish a central search agency.[288] The Geneva Conventions and Protocol I deal with the question of missing persons In the same vein.

In the framework of the *International Law of human rights* and at the *universal level*, for example, the UN Human Rights Committee has, based on the International Covenant on Civil and Political Rights, urged a State party "to guarantee that the victims of human rights violations know the truth with respect to the acts committed and know who the perpetrators of such acts were".[289]

Although, perhaps as a result of the date on which they were concluded, the oldest human rights international treaties do not expressly claim the right to the truth, in the practice of international human rights bodies its invocation takes place *indirectly* through the other rights enshrined in those treaties. Thus, within the United Nations, the right to know the truth has been invoked in relation to the *International Covenant on Civil and Political Rights* of 16 December 1966 with regard to the following

[285] For example, the following resolutions of the Parliamentary Assembly of the European Council: 1056 (1987), 1414 (2004), paragraph 3, and 1463 (2005), paragraph 10 (2).

[286] For example, the European Parliament resolution related to the missing in Cyprus, January 11, 1983, or the conclusions of the European Council of the European Union, October 3, 2005, on Colombia, paragraph 4.

[287] In this respect, see UN, Economic and Social Council, Commission on Human Rights, *Study on the right to the truth*, *op. cit.*, paras. 20 y 21.

[288] It is the case of the three followings: Geneva Convention (IV), of 12 August 1949, on the Protection of Civilian Persons in Time of War (Articles 16 and 17); Geneva Convention (I), of 12 August 1949, for the Amelioration of the Condition of the Wounded and Sick in Armed Forces in the Field (articles 136 et seq.); Geneva Convention (II), of 12 August 1949, for the Amelioration of the Condition of Wounded, Sick and Shipwrecked Members of Armed Forces at Sea (articles 122 et seq.).In this respect cf. ICC, Pre-Trial Chamber (PTC I), Decision ICC-01-04-01/07, 13 May 2008. In this Decisión, the Chamber states that the right of victims to the truth can be deduced from Articles 32 and 33 of Additional Protocol I to the Geneva Conventions.

[289] *Vid.* UN, Economic and Social Council, Commission on Human Rights, *Study on the right to the truth, op. cit.*, para. 8.

rights: the right to life (art. 6), the right not to be subjected to torture (art.7), the right to liberty and security (art. 9), the right to recognition everywhere as a person before the law (art. 16) and the right to the protection of the family (art. 23).

Also, in relation to the *Convention on the Rights of the Child* of 20 November 1989, on the basis of the right of the child to preserve his or her identity, including nationality, name and family relations (art. 8), the right of the child not to be separated from his or her parents (art. 9) and other provisions of this Convention.[290]

Finally, the right to the truth is invoked also within the framework of the UN *Convention against Torture and Other Cruel, Inhuman or Degrading Treatment or Punishment*, of 10 December 1984, that obliges the States Parties to adopt effective measures to prevent and suppress acts of torture.[291]

At the *European regional level*, and within the framework of the *European Convention on human rights*, of 4 November 1950, the ECHR has not expressly addressed the right to the truth. However, it has inferred it from the following rights: the right to be free from torture or ill-treatment (art. 3), the right to an effective remedy (art. 13) and the right to an effective investigation and to be informed about the results of the same (linked with the right to an effective remedy of art. 13).[292] In addition, as we have seen in relation to the right of victims to an effective investigation, the ECHR has stated that the fact that the State has not made an effective investigation to ascertain the whereabouts and fate of persons in circumstances that were endangering their lives constitutes a violation of its obligation to protect the right to life (under art. 3 of the European Convention). Also, and for the purposes of the concept of "effective remedy", the ECHR has indicated that this involves, in addition to the payment of compensation where appropriate, comprehensive and effective investigation leading to the identification and punishment of those responsible as well as the effective access of the victim's relatives to the inquiry procedure.[293]

In the *African regional frame*, the *African Commission on Human and Peoples' Rights* has followed an approach similar to ECHR. So, in its *Principles and Guidelines on the Right to a Fair Trial and Legal Assistance in Africa*, it infers that the right to the truth forms a constitutive part of the right to an effective remedy.[294]

But where the right to the truth has obtained greater jurisprudential precision has been in the *American regional frame*, through the *Inter-American Commission on Human Rights* and the *Inter-American Court of Human Rights* (later I/ACHR).

[290] It has done so the Special Rapporteur on the question of human rights and states of emergency, in its 1991 report (UN, E/CN:4/Sub.2/1993/6, paragraph 16).

[291] This treaty is invoked in that the suffering of the relatives of the missing victim is equated to torture and to cruel and inhuman treatment.

[292] Cf. ECHR, judgements 14 November, *Tas v. Turkey*, request No. 24396/94, and of 10 May 2001, *Cyprus v. Turkey*, request No. 25781/94.

[293] Cf. ECHR, judgement of 18 December 1996, *Aksoy v. Turkey*, request No. 21987/93.

[294] Cf. UN, Economic and Social Council, Commission on Human Rights, *Study on the right to the truth*, op. cit., para. 28.

This was as a result of the enforced disappearances of persons that happened in some States in this continent, while the jurisprudential analysis has not been limited to this type of behaviour.

In the case of the *Inter-American Commission on Human Rights*, the recognition of the right to the truth was initiated from the decade of the eighties of the last century, both with respect to the victims of human rights violations and their families and with regard to enforced disappearances. However, in cases of gross violations of human rights, such as torture and extrajudicial executions, the Inter-American Commission on human rights has now reached the conclusion that the right to the truth arises essentially from the general duty of the States to respect and guarantee human rights, the right to be heard by a Court of competent jurisdiction that is independent and impartial, the right to an effective remedy and judicial protection and the right to request information.[295]

With regard to the *I/ACHR*, this international judicial body has repeatedly recognized the right to the truth. For example, in its Judgement of 7 September 2004, case *Tibi v. Ecuador*, it ruled that the right to the truth is not limited to cases of enforced disappearances but applies to any violation of human rights. In this regard, and in the same case cited above, the I/ACHR stated that the right to the truth is also based on the obligation which States have to respect and ensure human rights and, in particular, the obligation that they have to carry out an effective investigation of gross violations of human rights; obligations incompatible with amnesty laws and similar measures that impede the investigation and/or prosecution of perpetrators of violations of human rights.[296]

On the same lines, in its Judgement of May 11, 2007 in the *Case of the Rochela Massacre v. Colombia*, the I/ACHR held Colombia responsible for violating Articles 8(1) and 25 of the Convention, in relation to Article 1(1) thereof because the domestic proceedings conducted in the present case:

> have not constituted effective recourse to ensure true access to justice for the surviving victims and the next of kin declared to be victims.[297]

[295] Cf. *ibid.*, para. 29.

[296] In fact, such laws and measures violate the right to the truth, as it has highlighted international jurisprudence in the field of human rights. In the words of the Inter-American Court, the obligation to investigate shall be undertaken "in a serious manner and not as a mere formality preordained to be ineffective. An investigation must have an objective and be assumed by the State as its own legal duty, not as a step taken by private interests that depends upon the initiative of the victim or his family or upon their offer of proof, without an effective search for the truth by the government" (cf. *Case of the "Street Children" (Villagrán-Morales et al.) v. Guatemala. Merits.* Judgement of November 19, 1999. Series C No. 63, para. 226; *Case of Godínez-Cruz v. Honduras. Merits.* Judgement of January 20, 1989. Series C No. 5, para. 188; and *Case of Velásquez-Rodríguez v. Honduras. Merits.* Judgement of July 29, 1988. Series C No. 4, para. 177.

[297] *Case of the Rochela Massacre v. Colombia. Merits, Reparations and Costs.* Judgement of May 11, 2007. Series C No. 163, para 287. This why the State must, "within a reasonable time, effectively conduct the criminal proceedings currently underway and those that have yet to begin, and must adopt all measures necessary that reveal the facts of the present case in order to

According to the jurisprudence of the Inter-American Court, the right to the truth "is subsumed in the right of the victim or his next of kin to obtain clarification of the facts relating to the violations and the corresponding responsibilities from the competent State organs, through the investigation and prosecution established in Articles 8 and 25 of the Convention".[298]

This is why the "historical truth" included in the reports of the above-mentioned Commissions "is no substitute for the duty of the State to reach the truth through judicial proceedings. In this sense, Articles 1(1), 8 and 25 of the Convention protect truth as a whole".[299]

Hence, no law or provision of domestic law may be invoked to exempt from the obligation to investigate and punish criminally those responsible for the violations of human rights.[300]

Regarding the *content* of the right to truth, the *Report of the Office of the United Nations High Commissioner for Human Rights*, of January 9, 2006, entitled *Study on the right to the truth* concludes that the right to the truth "implies knowing the full and complete truth as to the events that transpired, their specific circumstances, and who participated in them, including knowing the circumstances in which the violations took place, as well as the reasons for them. In cases of enforced disappearance, missing persons, children abducted or during the captivity of a mother subjected to enforced disappearance, secret executions and secret burial place, the right to the truth also has a special dimension: to know the fate and whereabouts of the victim."[301]

In short, as noted by the *Report of the Office of the United Nations High Commissioner for Human Rights*, of January 9, 2006, entitled *Study on the right to the truth*,

> Given that historically the right to the truth was initially linked to the missing and disappeared, the content was focused on knowing the fate and whereabouts of disappeared persons. However, as international law on the right to the truth has evolved to apply in all

determine the responsibility of those who participated in the mentioned violations. . . The results of these proceedings shall be released to the public by the State, so that the Colombian people may know the truth of the events of the present case." (para. 9 of the Jugdement).

[298] I/ACHR, *Case of Bámaca-Velásquez v. Guatemala. Merits.* Judgement of November 25, 2000. Series C No. 70, para. 201. Also in *Case of Almonacid-Arellano et al. v. Chile*, Judgement of 26 September 2006, para.148. In this judgement, the I/ACHR repeats its jurisprudence established in the *Case Barrios Altos*, Judgement of 14 March 2001, para. 48 and in the *Case of Bámaca Vélasquez*, Judgement of 25 November 2000, Series C No. 70, para. 201.

[299] I/ACHR, *Case of Almonacid-Arellano et al. v. Chile. Preliminary Objections, Merits, Reparations and Costs.* Judgement of September 26, 2006. Series C No. 154, para. 150.

[300] *Ibid.*, para. 151. Identical conclusion was reached in the UN. The UN Secretary General in his report on the establishment of a Tribunal for Sierra Leone, stated that the amnesty granted in Sierra Leone, "given its illegality in accordance with international law" is not recognized as legal effects. Similarly the peace agreements approved by the United Nations can never promise amnesties for crimes against humanity.

[301] UN, Economic and Social Council, Commission on Human Rights, *Study on the right to the truth*, op. cit., para. 59.

> situations of serious violations of human rights, the material scope of the right to the truth has also expanded to include other elements. These may be summarized as the entitlement to seek and obtain information on: the causes leading to the person's victimization; the causes and conditions pertaining to the gross violations of international human rights law and serious violations of international humanitarian law; the progress and results of the investigation; the circumstances and reasons for the perpetration of crimes under international law and gross human rights violations; the circumstances in which violations took place; in the event of death missing or enforced disappearance, the fate and whereabouts of the victims; and the identity of perpetrators.[302]

As a result, we can conclude that it is an autonomous right at the same time closely *connected with the obligation* of the State to conduct effective investigations into gross violations of human rights and serious breaches of International Humanitarian law, as well as the obligation to ensure effective remedies and reparation. At the same time, the right to the truth also fosters close *relationship with the rule of law and the principles* of transparency, accountability and good governance in a democratic society, as well as with *other rights*,[303] but this relationship does not affect their autonomous existence.

But the right to the truth is a right that also has a societal dimension: "society has the right to know the truth about past events concerning the perpetration of heinous crimes, as well as the circumstances and the reasons for which aberrant crimes came to be committed, so that such events do not reoccur in the future."[304]

Finally, it is a right inconsistent with the amnesty laws and similar measures that impede the investigation and/or prosecution of perpetrators of violations of human rights. Such laws and measures violate the right to truth and are null and void, as it has highlighted international jurisprudence in the field of human rights.[305]

---

[302] *Ibid.*, para. 38.

[303] The following: the right to an effective remedy; the right to legal and judicial protection; the right to the family life; the right to an effective investigation; the right to a hearing by a competent, independent, and impartial tribunal; and the right to obtain reparation (cf. *ibid.*, para. 42). With regard to this last issue, the Human Rights Committee, the ECHR, the IACHR and the African Commission on Human and Peoples' Rights have all considered that the failure to give information about the fate and whereabouts of disappeared persons or of the circumstances of an execution and the exact place of burial of the executed persons can amount to torture or ill-treatment (cf. *ibid.*, para. 42).

[304] *Ibid.*, para. 58.

[305] Cf., between others, *Case of Barrios Altos v. Peru (Meritsf)*, Judgement of March 14, where—for the first time—an international court states that amnesty laws are incompatible with International law and, consequently, lack legal effect (para. 4 of the decision); *case of Barrios Altos (Interpretation)*, Judgement of 3 September 2001, para. 17; *Case of Almonacid-Arellano et al. v. Chile. Preliminary Objections, Merits, Reparations and Costs.* Judgement of September 26, 2006. Series C No. 154; and *Case of La Cantuta v. Perú*, Sentencia de 29 de noviembre de 2006.

In the opinion of Tomushat, however, that nullity is not so clear. He agrees with those authors who are of the view that such amnesties, "if they have been responsibly enacted by people wishing to make a fresh start after having lived through a period of national cataclysm, should also be respected by other States and by the institutions of the international community". And he adds: "To decide on methods suited to reckon with the wrongs inflicted by a dictatorial regime is an act

Right to Memory

In relation to this right, the first thing to note is that, as so with the right to the truth, its invocation takes place in connection with *serious violations of human rights*: genocide, crimes against humanity, war crimes, forced disappearances, extrajudicial executions and terrorism. Like other rights already examined, too, it is linked with other rights of the victims; more so to the right to the truth.

It must be stressed that the right to memory is inseparable from the personal dignity of victims as proclaimed by the international norms and the recognition of the rights and legitimate interests of the victims. They are, as we are seeing in this work, rights and legitimate interests largely developed by international norms adopted within the framework of the United Nations and regional international organizations (Council of Europe and European Union, for example).

In the framework of the UN, the dignity of the person is already present in the Universal Declaration of Human Rights, of 10 December 1948, whose preamble bases justice in the dignity of the person declaring that:

> . . . recognition of the inherent dignity and of the equal and inalienable rights of all members of the human family is the foundation of freedom, justice and peace in the world.

Article 1, taking the Declaration of the rights of man and the citizen of the French constituent Assembly of 1789 as reference, declares that

> All human beings are born free and equal in dignity and rights. They are endowed with reason and conscience and should act towards one another in a spirit of brotherhood.

As Carrillo Salcedo points out, this statement was a milestone in the history of contemporary International Law because the assertion that every human being is the owner of rights, opposable legally by all States, including the State of which he is a national, "constitutes a legal revolution in that, unlike the classical International Law, the person cannot already be regarded as a mere object. It is not, however, assert that the individual is now full subject of International Law, but to recognize the supreme place of human interest in the order of the values".[306]

Subsequently, the preambles to the Universal Declaration of Human Rights and the international treaties on human rights legally based these rights on the dignity of the person. The international supervisory bodies under those treaties also made this the basis of their intrepretation of the rights. Examples of this are the two first general human rights treaties adopted within the framework of the UN. In fact, both the International Covenant on Civil and Political Rights and the International Covenant on Economic, Social and Cultural Rights (both of 16 December 1966), reproduced what was stated by the Universal Declaration of Human Rights in its

of national self-determination", but he excludes from this reflexion the crime of genocide. ("The Duty to Prosecute International Crimes. . .", *op. cit.*, 347).

[306] Carrillo Salcedo (1999), 16.

preamble and alluded to human dignity as a separate principle and as a basis of rights and freedoms set forth therein.

In this regard, it is indicated that "in accordance with the principles proclaimed in the Charter of the United Nations, recognition of the inherent dignity and of the equal and inalienable rights of all members of the human family is the foundation of freedom, justice and peace in the world" and to then recognize that these rights derive from the "inherent dignity of the human person." At the same time it is recognized that "in accordance with the Universal Declaration of Human Rights, the ideal of free human beings enjoying civil and political freedom and freedom from fear and want can only be achieved if conditions are created whereby everyone may enjoy his civil and political rights, as well as his economic, social and cultural rights".

Subsequently, other treaties continued along these lines. This is the case with, among others, the *International Convention on the Elimination of All Forms of Racial Discrimination*, of 21 December 1965[307]; the *Convention on the Elimination of All Forms of Discrimination Against Women* of 18 December 1979[308]; the *International Convention on the Protection of the Rights of All Migrant Workers and Members of Their Families*, of 18 December 1990[309]; the *Declaration on the*

---

[307] In paragraphs second and third of the Preamble.

[308] The Preamble of which states that: "that discrimination against women violates the principles of equality of rights and respect for human dignity, is an obstacle to the participation of women, on equal terms with men, in the political, social, economic and cultural life of their countries, hampers the growth of the prosperity of society and the family and makes more difficult the full development of the potentialities of women in the service of their countries and of humanity". On the same lines, and in relation to Article 6 of the Convention which requires the States to take all appropriate measures, including legislation, to suppress all forms of traffic in women and exploitation of prostitution of women, the Committee on the Elimination of Discrimination Against Women has noted that "poverty and unemployment increase opportunities for trafficking in women. In addition to established forms of trafficking there are new forms of sexual exploitation, such as sex tourism, the recruitment of domestic labour from developing countries to work in developed countries and organized marriages between women from developing countries and foreign nationals. These practices are incompatible with the equal enjoyment of rights by women and with respect for their rights and dignity. They put women at special risk of violence and abuse." (Vid. para. 14 of General Recommendation No. 19 (llth session, 1992). General recommendation can be consulted on: http://www.un.org/womenwatch/daw/cedaw/recommendations/recomm-sp.htm#recom24.

About this Convention vid. V. Mayordomo Rodrigo, "La lucha contra la discriminación de la mujer", in C. Fernández de Casadevante Romani (dir.), *Derecho Internacional de los Derechos Humanos*, *op. cit.*, 370 et seq.

[309] Article 17 of which states that migrant workers and members of their families who are deprived of their liberty shall be treated with humanity and with respect for the inherent dignity of the human person and for their cultural identity. On the other hand, Article 70 affirms that the States Parties shall take measures not less favourable than those applied to nationals to ensure that working and living conditions of migrant workers and members of their families in a regular situation are in keeping with the standards of fitness, safety, health and principles of human dignity. Cf. http://www.unhchr.ch/spanish/html/menu3/b/m_mwctoc_sp.htm.

Protection of all Persons from Enforced Disappearance, of 18 December 1992[310]; and the *Convention on the Rights of Persons with Disabilities*, of 13 December 2006.[311]

At the institutional level of the UN, various resolutions of the General Assembly have been pronounced in the same direction, for example, resolution 40/34, adopted on 29 November 1985, containing the *Declaration of Basic Principles of Justice for Victims of Crime and Abuse of Power* of 29 November 1985, and also of the *Principles on the Effective Prevention and Investigation of Extra-legal, Arbitrary and Summary Executions* recommended by Economic and Social Council resolution 1989/65 of 24 May 1989 and Resolution 47/133, of 18 December 1992, containing the *Declaration on the Protection of all Persons from Enforced Disappearance.*

In the framework of the *Council of Europe*, the affirmation of the dignity of the person and its recognition is found both in conventional and in institutional norms. Among them for example, some of those discussed in this work can be quoted as the *Guidelines on the Protection of Victims of Terrorist Acts* adopted by the Committee of Ministers of the Council of Europe on 2 March 2005, and *Recommendation (2006) 8* of the Committee of Ministers of 14 June 2006, *On Assistance to Victims of Crime*, which substitutes Recommendation No. R (87) 21, of 17 September 1987.

In the conventional plane, for example, the *Social Charter* revised in 1996 refers to dignity at work (art. 26). With regard to dignity, and from the perspective of health care, the international body provided for in this agreement (the Committee of Social Rights) has stated that:

> human dignity is the fundamental value that is located in the heart of positive European law in the field of human rights and health care is a basic previous condition for their preservation by which the Committee has estimated that a law or practice that denies the

[310] Whose Article 1, paragraph 1, affirms that any act of enforced disappearance is an offence to human dignity, while paragraph 2 of the same article states that "2. Any act of enforced disappearance places the persons subjected thereto outside the protection of the law and inflicts severe suffering on them and their families. It constitutes a violation of the rules of international law guaranteeing, inter alia, the right to recognition as a person before the law, the right to liberty and security of the person and the right not to be subjected to torture and other cruel, inhuman or degrading treatment or punishment. It also violates or constitutes a grave threat to the right to life."

[311] The Preamble of which, for example, states that discrimination against any person on the basis of disability is a violation of the inherent dignity and worth of the human person. Article 16.4—related to freedom from exploitation, violence and abuse—obliges the States to take all appropriate measures to promote the physical, cognitive and psychological recovery, rehabilitation and social reintegration of persons with disabilities who become victims of any form of exploitation, violence or abuse, including through the provision of protection services. Such recovery and reintegration shall take place in an environment that fosters the health, welfare, self-respect, dignity and autonomy of the person and takes into account gender- and age-specific needs.

> right to health care to foreign nationals in the territory of a State party, even when they are in an irregular situation, is contrary to the Charter.[312]

In this area of the Council of Europe the dignity of the person is referred to in more recent treaties such as the *Convention for the Protection of Human Rights and Dignity of the Human Being with regard to the Application of Biology and Medicine* (Convention on human rights and Biomedicine), of 4 April 1997; Convention complemented by two protocols: the Protocol of 1998 on *Prohibition of Cloning of Human Beings* and the 2005 *Protocol on Biomedical Research.*[313]

Finally, the European *Convention on Action against Trafficking in Human Beings*, adopted in Warsaw on May 16, 2005 considered trafficking in human beings as a violation of human rights and an attack on the dignity and integrity of persons. On the other hand, the Convention refers to dignity in connection with measures that the States are required to take to discourage the demand that fosters all forms of exploitation of persons (especially women and children) and that leads to trafficking in them (art. 7), both in terms of measures of repatriation and return of victims (art. 20).

With regard to the *European Union*, the dignity of the person and, therefore, the dignity of the victims, is not only present in three of the most important acts adopted in connection with the victims and their rights (I have looked over this work) the *Council Framework Decision 2001/220/JHA*, of 15 March 2001, *on the standing of victims in criminal proceedings*; the *Council Framework Decision (2002/475/JHA)* of 13 June 2002 *on combating terrorism* and *Directive 2004/80/EC* of 29 April 2004 *relating to compensation to crime victims*, but it is also the foundation of the European Union. Thus it proclaims in the preamble, the *Charter of Fundamental Rights of the European Union*, of 7 December 2000, stating that:

> Conscious of its spiritual and moral heritage, the Union is founded on the indivisible, universal values of human dignity, freedom, equality and solidarity; it is based on the principles of democracy and the rule of law. It places the individual at the heart of its activities, by establishing the citizenship of the Union and by creating an area of freedom, security and justice.[314]

Consistent with the preceding paragraph of the preamble, Article 1 of the Charter affirms human dignity categorically:

> Human dignity is inviolable. It must be respected and protected.

In the opinion of Sobrino Heredia, this wording contains two important statements. On one side, the inviolability of human dignity. On the other, the twofold commitment to human dignity that it shall be respected and protected. Ultimately, he argues that it is an absolute and non-derogable or permanent principle which

---

[312] *International Federation of Leagues of Human Rights v. France*, Claim No. 14/2003, Decision of 7 September 2004, para. 31 et seq.

[313] The three declared as one of its objectives the protection of the dignity and identity of all human beings.

[314] Second paragraph of thePreamble.

implies that a human being can never be exploited, that is, treated as a mere object.[315]

In respect to this Article 1, the *Explanations relating to the Charter of Fundamental Rights* specifies: "The dignity of the human person is not only a fundamental right in itself but constitutes the real basis of fundamental rights... It results that none of the rights laid down in this Charter may be used to harm the dignity of another person, and that the dignity of the human person is part of the substance of the rights laid down in this Charter. It must therefore be respected, even where a right is restricted."[316]

This shows that in the *Charter of Fundamental Rights of the European Union* human dignity is not only an inspiring value of the rights and freedoms but that it is also conceived as a fundamental right to which an essential and absolute dimension is given. As highlighted in the commentary on this Charter prepared by the network of independent experts in the field of fundamental rights of the Union, its location in an exclusive article not linked with other fundamental rights (like freedom or integrity) nor sharing their space with other rights (such as the prohibitions of torture or the death penalty) reinforce *its absolute and autonomous nature*[317] that allows—as has already happened—[318] it to be invoked before the courts of the European Union.[319]

At the same time, the Charter itself stands for dignity as a basis for the rights contained in Title I.[320] But it also set it up as an autonomous human right within the same Title I (Article 1 is dedicated to *Human dignity*).[321]

---

[315] "Idea anchored, in the Judeo Christian tradition common to the Member States, according to which man has been created in the image of God" Sobrino Heredia (2008), p. 108. Cf. also MATHIEU, (de Mathieu 2005, 35 et seq).

[316] For Sobrino Heredia, such a clear statement explains the reason that the Charter of Fundamental Rights of the Union, "after the relevant preamble starts, precisely, with the first title dedicated to the dignity" and with his article concerning human dignity (*op. cit.*, 108).

[317] Cf. 25 of the commentary deaft by W. Heyde. See the text in http://ec.europa.eu/justice_home/doc_centre/rights/charter/docs/network_commentary_final%20_180706.pdf.

[318] Thus, for example, in the case C-377/98, in which the ECJ confirmed that the fundamental right to human dignity is part of Union law (cf. judgement of 9 October 2001, case C-377/98, *Netherlands v. European Parliament and Council*, Rec. 2001, I-7079, para. 70–77).

[319] But as far as the Charter of Fundamental Rights of the European Union is concerned, it does not specify what is meant by dignity as an autonomous right. Sobrino Heredia stresses that there are specific applications. In other words, "cases in which the legislative institutions or, ultimately, the Court of Justice claim that a certain conduct violates it" (cf. *op. cit.*, 124). In any case, it is—according to this same author—human dignity and not the dignity "of the human person".

[320] Title that bears the statement "The dignity" and includes the following articles: Article 1 Human dignity; Article 2 Right to life; Article 3 Right to the integrity of the person; Article 4 Prohibition of torture and inhuman or degrading treatment or punishment and Article 5 Prohibition of slavery and forced labour.

[321] Apart from the Charter, in the Law of the EU there are also a number of provisions which could serve as a legal basis for the protection of human dignity: provisions that enable the protection of individual rights; provisions relating to cooperation for development; provisions relating to the

This, in the opinion of Sobrino Heredia, can draw the following conclusions: human dignity has a double content. On the one hand, it is foundation of human rights as a whole. On the other hand, and at the same time, it is an autonomous human right which allows—as has already happened—[322] it to be invoked before the courts of the European Union.[323]

The EU Treaty, following its reform by the Treaty of Lisbon, presents the respect for human dignity with a double dimension: as a value of the European Union and as a principle of its external action.[324] In its *internal aspect*, Article 2 of the EU Treaty states that:

> The Union is founded on the values of respect for human dignity, freedom, democracy, equality, the rule of law and respect for human rights, including the rights of persons belonging to minorities. These values are common to the Member States in a society in which pluralism, non-discrimination, tolerance, justice, solidarity and equality between women and men prevail.

In its *external* aspect human dignity is envisaged in Article 21 with regard to EU external action. According to it:

> 1. The Union's action on the international scene shall be guided by the principles which have inspired its own creation, development and enlargement, and which it seeks to advance in the wider world: democracy, the rule of law, the universality and indivisibility of human rights and fundamental freedoms, respect for human dignity, the principles of equality and solidarity, and respect for the principles of the United Nations Charter and international law.

---

other relations of cooperation with third countries; more general provisions relating to the approximation of laws; provisions relating to the subsidiary powers; as well as certain provisions of the third pillar. In this framework acts affecting human dignity are adopted. Thus, as we have already seen, in the framework of the third pillar was adopted the status of the victim in the criminal proceedings, which emphasizes the need to treat victims with due respect for their personal dignity (cf. art. 2 of the Council Framework Decision 2001/JHA/JHA, with regard to the standing of victims in criminal proceedings (*OJ* L 82, March 22, 2001). Also, in the framework of this same pillar terrorism is presented as a serious violation of human dignity (cf. paragraph 8 of the preamble of the Council Framework Decision of 15 March 2001, concerning the standing of victims in the criminal proceedings). Cf. also the recitals 1 and 2 of Council Framework Decision 2002/475/JHA on combating terrorism (*OJ* L 164, 22 June 2002).

[322] Thus, for example, in case C-377/98, in which the ECJ confirmed that the fundamental right to human dignity is part of Union law (cf. judgment of October 9, 2001, *case* C-377/98, *The Netherlands v. European Parliament and the Council of the European Union*, Rec., 2001, I-7079, paras. 70–77).

[323] As an autonomous right, and on the same lines of what is happening at the national level, at the international level dignity is often presented as a basis for fundamental rights, but not as an independent fundamental right. It is reflected, for example, in the preambles of the Universal Declaration of Human Rights, of the International Covenant on Civil and Political Rights and the International Covenant on Economic, Social and Cultural Rights, and in the case law of the ECHR (cf. Sobrino Heredia "Dignidad...", *op. cit.*, 123). But, unlike the two aforementioned International Covenants and the Universal Declaration of Human Rights, the Charter of Fundamental Rights of the European Union takes a step further to configure the human dignity as an autonomous right.

[324] See the text in http://europa.eu/lisbon_treaty/index_es.htm

The jurisprudence of the ECJ also dealt with this issue and has done so from a double perspective: on the one hand, as a fundamental value; on the other hand as a right (but only in two cases). As a *fundamental value*, in the judgement of the ECJ of 6 March 2001, case C-274/99.[325] As a *right*, the approac varies from one matter to another. Thus, in the first case, the ECJ presents human dignity as a *general principle of Community law*[326] while in the second the Court refers to dignity as a *general principle of the law*.[327] In the first case, the standard of protection used by the Court was the community,[328] while in the second the standard of protection was the national because national authorities considered that homicidal simulations violated human dignity. In addition, in the latter case there is the fact that German law recognizes human dignity as an *autonomous fundamental right* and not only as a basis for fundamental rights.[329]

With regard to the contents of human dignity within the scope of the European Union, it is worth bringing here the words of Attorney General Polares Maduro in the preliminary ruling *Case Coleman* on the application of Directive 2000/78/EC of

---

[325] Cf. *case Connolly/Comisión, C-274/99* related to the Staff Regulations of officials and the dignity of the role of officer of the Commission (*European Court reports 2001*, I-01611; (cf. http://curia.europa.eu).

[326] ECJ, Judgement of 9 October 2001, case C-377/98, *Kingdom of the Netherlands v.European Parliament and Council of the European Union*, para. 70. It was an issue related to biotechnology (cf. *European Court reports 2001*, I-07079).

[327] Cf. *case C-36/02, Omega*, Judgement of 14 October 2004. Omega Spielhallen- und Automatenaufstellungs-GmbH ('Omega') is a German company which operated a facility in Bonn under the name 'Laserdrome'. That facility was normally used to run a leisure occupation known as 'Lasersport', inspired by the film *Star Wars* and using modern laser technology. The equipment provided for the players consisted of sub-machine-gun-type laser targeting devices and fabric jackets to which one sensory tag was affixed in the chest area and one at the back. In order to portray the 'shots' optically, a laser beam was simultaneously projected with an infrared beam. Hits were indicated by an acoustic and optical signal. The aim of the contest was to obtain as many points as possible within a playing time of 15 min. Players were awarded points for each hit on a fixed sensory tag. Players who were hit had points deducted. Players who received five hits had to get their targeting devices recharged at a recharging point.

The ECJ was of the opinion that an individual national public order notice banning a commercial activity found by the national courts to be incompatible with basic principles of constitutional law is compatible with the provisions of the Treaty establishing the European Community relating to freedom to provide services if that order is genuinely justified for public policy purposes relating to the public interest and it is ensured that that purpose cannot be achieved by measures that are less restrictive of the freedom to provide services. (cf. para. 34).

Later, in case C-341/05 *Laval a Partneri Ltd v. Svenska Byggnadsarbetareförbundet and Others*, judgement of December 18, 2007, the Grand Chamber of the ECJ reiterated that as the Court of Justice stated in the Omega ruling the exercise of the fundamental right, which was the subject of that issue, namely, respect for human dignity, is not excluded from the scope of the provisions of the Treaty. The judgement of Chamber 1 of the ECJ in case C-36/02 *Omega* is of 14 October 2004.

[328] To determine if the patentability of products where some element of the human body forms part of it violates human dignity or not (judgment of 9 October 2001, case C-377/98, *Netherlands/Parliament and Council*, paragraphs 69–77)

[329] Cf. Sobrino Heredia, "Dignidad", *op. cit.*, 121.

the Council of 27 November 2000 establishing a general framework for equal treatment in employment and occupation. On the occasion of the same, the Attorney General stated that "at its bare minimum, human dignity entails the recognition of the equal worth of every individual. One's life is valuable by virtue of the mere fact that one is human, and no life is more or less valuable than another. As Ronald Dworkin has recently reminded us, even when we disagree deeply about issues of political morality, the structure of political institutions and the functioning of our democratic states we, nevertheless, continue to share a commitment to this fundamental principle. Therefore, individuals and political institutions must not act in a way that denies the intrinsic importance of every human life."[330] In other words, as noted by Serna, the dignity of the individual does not require reasons of power to be respected as it is contrary to the dignity to reduce man to a mere object of the performance of the State.[331]

Finally, both the *jurisprudence of the ECHR* and of the *Inter-American Court of Human Rights* solidly based the rights of victims in international obligations contained, respectively, in the European Convention on human rights, of 4 November 1950, and the American Convention on human rights, of 22 November 1969.

Accordingly, the personal dignity of victims continues to be a dimension of the inherent dignity of the person that forms the basis of their rights and fundamental freedoms. The different catalogues of human rights proclaimed by international norms, which have led progressively to the formation of this specific sector of International lawas also the catalogues of fundamental rights and freedoms of the person that are present in the constitutions of democratic States have been on this basis.[332]

The fact that terrorism, torture, enforced disappearances, extrajudicial executions, serious violations of human rights and International humanitarian law such as genocide, crimes against humanity and war crimes, abuses of power, etc.—whoever commits them—are acts that attempt to lower the dignity of the person is clear. It is also a fact that the actions or omissions of the State, of individuals and of private groups aimed to prevent, hinder or eliminate the right of victims to the memory, constitute an affront to the dignity of the victims and contradict international norms

---

[330] Opinión of the Advocate General Poiares Maduro delivered on 31 January 2008, *Case C-303/06, S. Coleman v. Attridge Law and Steve Law*, para. 9.

[331] Cf. Serna (2004), 221.

[332] It is the case, for example, in Article 10.1 of the Spanish Constitution of 1978: "1.The dignity of the person, the inviolable rights inherent, the free development of personality, the respect for the law and the rights of others are foundation of political order and social peace."

The dignity of the person is also present in the Constitutions of the States members of the European Union. It is the case, for example, in the following: Germany (art. 1), Ireland (in the preamble), Italy (art. 41), Sweden (art. 2), Greece (art. 2) Poland (art. 30), Finland (art. 1), Lithuania (art. 21), Latvia (95), Hungary (art. 54), Slovenia (arts. 21 and 34), or Spain (in the preamble and in article 10 cited above).

on the subject. In fact, acts of exaltation or lifting of the perpetrators, tributes and acts of welcome as well as the denial of acts of recognition to the victims or the removal of monuments built in their memory, for example, are behaviours diametrically opposed to the moral and legal requirements that victims are to be treated with humanity, compassion and respect for their dignity. They are not only diametrically opposed but that can also be considered as a new victimization of victims (so-called secondary victimization).[333] They are acts whose aim is to forget or deny the fact of victimization to avoid having to face reality or assume any responsibility. It also serves to avoid the disapproval and punishment of the criminals and the assumption by them of their specific responsibility to the society, in general, and with respect to the victims to whom they caused damage, in particular.

At the same time, the right to memory is linked with the right of victims to reparation for harm suffered because the right to memory is one of the means through which repair is intended, albeit partially, for the harm suffered. This is expressed in the *Basic principles and guidelines of the right to a remedy and reparation for victims of gross violations of international human rights law and serious violations of International Humanitarian Law* adopted by the UN Commission on Human Rights on 19 April 2005, by Resolution 2005/35, and later adopted through General Assembly Resolution 60/147 of 16 December 2005, with regard to "satisfaction" as a form of reparation that States should include, as a form of satisfaction, "commemorations and tributes to the victims".[334]

As it has been pointed out by Cuesta with respect to the victims of terrorism—although her statement is equally valid in general for any situation of violation of human rights—it is unworthy to want to throw earth on so many unsolved crimes, complicity, supports, and silences; the silence that is wanted for the victims, not only because they seek moral satisfaction, but also because their testimony is essential to understand what has happened to us and guide our future well. It is muted to victims because they did not want to delegitimize terrorism and the supposed cause that leads to practice it."[335]

The right to memory, as the right to the truth, intends—moreover a certain compensation—to contribute to regain the humanity of the victims; all of them innocent and unfairly victimized. For this reason, fight against oblivion "is progress in the knowledge of a damaged society which has damaged much to others, who has not deserved it suffered and which failed to react in time. Oblivion, as well as impossible, is antipedagogical." We should add that it is also unfair because it is an uncritical and inpunesh acceptance of the victimization act and, accordingly, giving it justification and social legitimacy.[336]

---

[333] Cf., respectively, para. 8 and 5 of the Preamble of Council Framework Decision 2001/JHA/JHA, of 15 March 2001, just quoted. Cf. also point No. 5 of UN *Declaration of Basic Principles of Justice for Victims of Crime and Abuse of Power* of 29 November 1985.

[334] On paragraph 22.g).

[335] Cristina (2000), p. 219 et seq. About victims of terrorism, from the perspective of victims of the Basque nationalist terrorist organization ETA vid. the excellent work of Domínguez et al. (2010).

[336] *Ibid.*, 221.

As a result, and despite the fact that the right of victims to memory is not expressly formulated in any international rule, I dare to clarify its content in the following terms:

1. Victims have the right to memory. This right is inseparable from the individual dignity of the victims, from the recognition of their rights and legitimate interests and from their right to the truth. The right to memory is oriented to denounce the wrongful act of victimization and to preserve the memory of the victims to present and future generations.
2. In the context of the right to memory, the States shall take all measures to preserve the memory of the victims and prevent any act of any nature, that violates the same or constitutes an offence or disrespect to them. Also, the States will promote all kinds of events to honor and preserve the memory of the victims to present and future generations.

Increased Protection

The catalogue of rights listed in various international norms pertaining to the sector of the International Law of human rights as well as the norms concerning the different categories of victims that I have examined throughout this work are often completed with a final clause of closure that is confined to asserting that nothing prevents the States Parties to such treaties from adopting further protection measures. This is what is called "increased protection".

It is a common formula used as a closing clause belonging to the International Law of human rights treaties, but it is also possible to find it in other material areas regulated by treaties. The content of this is nothing more than an assertion that the rights proclaimed in the international norm in question, and the way they are, is not incompatible with the adoption by States Parties (in the case of treaties) or by States addressees of the international norm in question (in the case of institutional norms) of favourable or more stringent protective measures; this already takes place through the domestic law of the State or through the existing international law with respect to that State.

Within the International Law of human rights, this clause is present, for example, in the *Convention on the Elimination of All Forms of Discrimination Against Women* of 18 December 1979, and in the *Convention on the Rights of the Child*, of 20 November 1989; in both cases with the same formula.[337]

---

[337] Respectively in Articles 23 and 41. Article 23 states : "Nothing in the present Convention shall affect any provisions that are more conducive to the achievement of equality between men and women which may be contained: (a) In the legislation of a State Party; or (b) In any other international convention, treaty or agreement in force for that State." Article 41 states : "Nothing in the present Convention shall affect any provisions which are more conducive to the realization of the rights of the child and which may be contained in: (a) The law of a State party; or (b) International law in force for that State."

With regard to the international norms on the different categories of victims, the clause of increased protection is present in Article 37 of the *International Convention for the Protection of All Persons from Enforced Disappearance*, of 20 December 2006. It is written in the same terms as this clause is in the human rights treaties. So, Article 37 states:

> Nothing in this Convention shall affect any provisions which are more conducive to the protection of all persons from enforced disappearance and which may be contained in:
> (a) The law of a State Party;
> (b) International law in force for that State.

In the *European regional frame*, the "*Guidelines on the Protection of Victims of Terrorist Acts*" adopted by the Committee of Ministers of the Council of Europe on 2 March 2005 contains this clause under the heading "*XII. Increased protection*". According to this guideline:

> Nothing in these Guidelines restrains states from adopting more favourable services and measures than described in these Guidelines.

As a result, the rights that the international norms discussed in this work recognize as due to victims—rights having obligations to be carried out by the States—are only of a minimum international standard that can be the object of benefits and more favourable measures by those States that so wish. As in other areas of International law, in this also the greater or lesser degree of commitment depends entirely on the States. They are those who make the norms and it is they who are responsible.

References

Ascensio H (2009) Les droits de victimes devant les juridictions pénales internationales In: Flauss J-F (ed) La protection internationale des droits de l'homme et les droits des victimes, Bruylant, Bruxelles, 77–110

Carrillo Salcedo JA (1999) Dignidad frente a Barbarie. La Declaración Universal de Derechos Humanos Cincuenta Años Después, Tecnos, Madrid

Cristina C (2000) Contra el olvido, ed. Temas de Hoy, Madrid

de Mathieu B (2005) Article II-61 In: Burgorgue-Larsen A, Levade A, Picod F (2005) Traité Établissant une Constitution pour l'Europe. Partie II, La Charte des droits fondamentaux de l'Union, Tome 2. Bruylant, Bruxelles, 35–41

Domínguez F, Alonso R, García Rey M (2010) Vidas rotas, Espasa-Calpe, Madrid

Fernández de Casadevante Romani C, Mayordomo Rodrigo V (2011) Código de normas internacionales relativas a las víctimas, Tecnos, Madrid

Heins Ch, Killander M (2009) The african regional human rights system In: Gómez Isa F, De Feyter K (eds) (2009) International human rights law in a global context. Humanitarian Net, Bilbao

Jeangène Vilmer J-B (2009) Réparer l'irréparable. Les réparations aux victimes devant la Cour Pénale Internationale. PUF, Paris

López Escudero M (2008) Artículo 47. Derecho a la tutela judicial efectiva y a un juez imparcial In: Mangas Martin A (ed) Carta de los Derechos Fundamentales de la Unión Europea. Comentario artículo por artículo, Fundación BBVA, Bilbao, 739–758

Martin y Pérez de Nanclares J (2008) Artículo 7. Respeto de la vida privada y familiar In: Mangas Martin A (ed) Carta de los Derechos Fundamentales de la Unión Europea. Comentario artículo por artículo

Martín y Pérez de Nanclares J (2008) Artículo 11. Libertad de expresión y de información In: Mangas Martin A (ed) Carta de los Derechos Fundamentales de la Unión Europea. Comentario artículo por artículo, Fundación BBVA, Bilbao, 209–222

Mutua M (2009) The transformation of Africa. A critique of the rights discourse In: Gómez Isa F, De Feyter K (eds) (2009) International human rights law in a global context. Humanitarian Net, Fundación BBVA, Bilbao, 899–924

Newmann F, Vasak K (1984) Derechos civiles y políticos. In: Vasak K (ed) Las dimensiones internacionales de los derechos humanos, vol. I. Unesco, Serbal, Barcelona, 227–240

Saura Estapa J (1998) Artículo 12 In: Pons Rafols X (coord.) La Declaración Universal de los Derechos Humanos. Comentario artículo por artículo, Icaria edn, Barcelona, 226–236

Serna P (2004) La dignidad humana en la Constitución Europea. In: Alvarez Conde E, Garrido Mayol V (dir.) Comentarios a la Constitución Europea, Libro II, Tirant lo Blanch, Valencia, 191–239

Sobrino Heredia JM (2008) Dignidad. In: Mangas Martin A (ed) Carta de los Derechos Fundamentales de la Unión Europea. Comentario artículo por artículo, Fundación BBVA, Bilbao, 107–145

Tomuschat C (2002) The duty to prosecute international crimes committed by individuals In: Tradition und Weltoffenheit des Rechts. Festschrift für Helmut Steinberger. Beiträge zum ausländischen öffenlichen Recht und Völkerrecht, Band 152. Springer, Berlin, 315–349

Conclusions

1. The process of humanization of International law after the Second World War in the progressive formation of the sector of this law on the protection of human rights has been enriched and expanded since the middle of the decade of the eighties of the last century by the presence of the victims and the attention given to them by many international norms of different legal nature (conventional, institutional and customary), even though with a different approach. Indeed, while in the field of International law concerning the protection of human rights the centre is the person who has suffered the violation of the right or freedom recognized by the international norm against the State to which such breach is attributed, in the case of the victims the breach of the obligation or the commission of the offence—in other words, the victimizer fact—may be the result of a behaviour attributable to the State or to an individual or to a group of individuals. But, as opposed to the International human rights law that has both organs of control, to which the victims of the violation of human rights can go, and control techniques, depending on the circumstances, these same victims can be sued, for victims' recourse to such bodies and to such techniques is possible only if the rights violated by the victimizer behaviour belong to this sector of International law and they have been committed by the State. Otherwise, the legal framework for possible action by the victim lies exclusively in the internal order of the State and such action depends on whether the victimizer conduct in question has been established previously by the State as a criminal offence in its Criminal Code. Without this definition, there is no offence and the commission of such an act does not generate any kind of rights to the victim. In other words, the victim is powerless and helpless.

With regard to the specific case of victims only the *International Convention for the Protection of All Persons from Enforced Disappearance,* of 20 December 2006, and the *Inter-American Convention on Forced Disappearance of Persons*, of July 9, 1994, in the American regional system, have set up bodies and control techniques in line with international treaties on human rights. Nevertheless, this last convention has not created specific organs but it refers to the bodies of the American Convention on human rights (Inter-American Court of Human Rights and Inter-American Commission on Human Rights). As a result, in this case, the access to the Inter-

C. Fernández de Casadevante Romani, *International Law of Victims*,
DOI 10.1007/978-3-642-28140-2_7, © Springer-Verlag Berlin Heidelberg 2012

American Court of Human Rights will be conditioned by the acceptance or not of its jurisdiction by the State concerned.

2. As a result of the humanization process described above, an important set of international norms relating to the victims has been progressively seeing the light of day. They are rules that are intended for eight categories of victims: victims of crime, victims of abuse of power, victims of gross violations of international human rights norms, victims of serious violations of International Humanitarian law, victims of enforced disappearances, victims of trafficking, victims of terrorism and, finally, victims of violations of International Criminal law.

Most of the international norms relating to the various categories of victims take the criminal legislation in the domestic order of States as the criterion the violation of which determines the acquisition of the status of victim. Criterion and prerequisite because without defining the conduct in question as crime in the domestic order of the State the person concerned does not satisfy the status of victim and, consequently, may not exercise the rights granted to it by the international norm.

Therefore, the definition in the domestic order of the State of behaviours such as terrorism, genocide, war crimes, crimes against humanity, forced disappearances, extrajudicial executions, torture (all of them acts included in the international norms relating to the various categories of victims), as crimes, is absolutely essential to ensure that victims can exercise the rights which are recognized as due to them by international norms. At the same time, that legislative action would also work positively to a broader concept of victim. In effect, the criminal legislation of the State being the gold standard, all criminal conduct referred to in it leads to consideration as victims of crime all those who have suffered damages arising from such criminal behaviour. And this, in the triple dimension adopted by examined international norms: the persons who have suffered damage, family members or dependants who have an immediate relationship with the direct victim, as well as persons who have suffered harm in intervening to assist the victim in danger or to prevent victimization.

3. Consequently, the regulatory revolution and the impact that supposes the presence of the victim in International law can be felt,; a revolution similar to that in the domestic law of the State on the occasion of its recognition. On the one hand, inserting the victim and making him visible in the context of a process traditionally conceived as an adversarial and articulated process between the accused and the accuser (the State or its organs); a process, too, in which previously the victim (the passive subject of the victimizer conduct) was not envisaged by the legal system (either domestic or international).

In other words, the bilateralism that characterized the process (both domestic and international) has been—fortunately—altered by the presence of the victim not only as a subject of rights, but also, as a third party who has much to say in the framework of a process, which will determine both the responsibility and the consequences of a (illicit and criminal) fact that the victim has been unwittingly, the taxable person.

On the other hand, because against the void above, now, international norms recognize as due to victims a catalogue of rights that, on its reverse, constitutes obligations on the charge of the State.

4. Both international jurisprudence and the various existing international norms (customary, conventional and institutional) echo this reality and recognize, a catalogue of rights of victims regardless of what may be the origin of the victim; because he resides in a terrorist act, in a violent crime, in an abuse of power, in a flagrant violation of international norms of human rights, in a violation of International Humanitarian law, in a violation of International Criminal law or an act of enforced disappearance.

It is a catalogue of rights that constitutes the minimum common denominator above which sits the international legal statute of the victims, irrespective of the origin of the victimizer cause. The States have, in consequence, the obligation to make those rights "effective" in the respective national legal systems, which implies an obligation to take all necessary and appropriate measures to ensure that such rights can be "effectively" exercised by the victims. On the lines of what was stated at that time by the ECHR, we have rights that are not "illusory" or "theoretical" but "concrete" and "effective", corresponding to which the States ensure that effectiveness and make them possible.

They are rights, on the contrary, which are linked to each other; many of them are intertwined and interact mutually. Accordingly, in such scenarios, the violation of one of them takes other rights with which one relates.

5. The legal nature of most of the international norms relating to the different categories of victims is of an institutional nature. Except in the case of international norms emanating from the bodies of the European Union—which do not pose any question or doubt about its binding legal effects because it is established in the foundation treaties (the case of the *Council Framework Decision 2001/220/JHA, of 15 March 2001, on the standing of victims in criminal proceedings; the Council Framework Decision (2002/475/JHA) of 13 June 2002 on combating terrorism and the Directive 2004/80/EC of 29 April 2004 relating to compensation to crime victims)*—both those adopted by the UN General Assembly and those adopted by the Council of Europe are debtors of the questions that raise the institutional rules of international cooperation organizations.

With regard to those of the General Assembly of the United Nations it can be said, however, that they all declare existing norms of customary nature that are in force in the international order. Therefore, from this perspective their legal effects are clear. This is the case of both resolution 40/34 of the General Assembly, adopted on 29 November 1985, containing the *Declaration of Basic Principles of Justice for Victims of Crime and Abuse of Power,* of 29 November 1985, and General Assembly Resolution 60/147 adopted on 16 December 2005 through which the *Basic principles and guidelines of the right to a remedy and reparation for victims of gross violations of international human rights law and serious violations of International Humanitarian Law* adopted by the UN Commission on Human Rights on 19 April 2005, by Resolution 2005/35, as well as of the *Declaration on the protection of all persons from Enforced Disappearance*, adopted through Resolution 47/133 of 18 December 1992.

With regard to institutional norms adopted by the Committee of Ministers of the Council of Europe with the form of a "recommendation", the favorable vote of the Member States and the language adopted by them to address the object to which they relate also allow us to conclude that they have legal effects. That the fulfillment by Member States of the obligation that the institutional norm provides is delayed in time does not allow us to conclude its failure.

6. Alongside these institutional norms, there are also some—a few still—conventional norms. This is the case in the frame of the United Nations of the *International Convention for the Protection of All Persons from Enforced Disappearance, of 20 December 2006*, of the *Statute of the International Criminal Court*, adopted at the Rome Conference on 17 July 1998, as well as of the statutes of the *ad hoc International Criminal Tribunals for the former Yugoslavia and for Rwanda*, both adopted in the framework of Chapter VII of the Charter. In the *European* regional frame, the *European Convention on the Compensation of Victims of Violent Crimes*, of 24 November 1983, drawn up by the Council of Europe and the first international treaty on victims. Finally, in the *American* regional frame this is the case of the *Inter-American Convention on Forced Disappearance of Persons*, of July 9, 1994.

All these must be added to the *Geneva Conventions and their protocols* which contain norms applicable to the victims in the field of International Humanitarian law.

7. In the international legal order there does not exist a single general concept of victim but almost as many definitions as categories of victims covered by international norms.

In fact, the absence in the international legal order of a comprehensive and unique concept of victim does not constitute any problem. On the one hand, because there are definitions specific for each of the categories of victims; on the other hand, because the definition of victims contained in resolution 40/34 of the General Assembly, adopted on 29 November 1985, containing the *Declaration of Basic Principles of Justice for Victims of Crime and Abuse of Power*, is the widest, and also the most complete. This fact is significant given the nature of crime of all victimizer behaviours covered by the international norms relating to the victims. In other words, the elements present in that definition cover the silences and gaps that occur in some of the existing definitions.

Otherwise, the strict application of the definition of victim in the particular norm (on the category of victim in question) would lead in certain cases to adverse results for the victims. This is the case of victims of terrorism (definition lacking in international norms) and, also, indirect victims in the case of enforced disappearance (as international norms relating to this category of victims do not cover them).

Such adverse effects can be solved through the combined and complementary implementation of the specific definition of the category of victim in question and the more general crime victim, bearing in mind that all behaviours referred to in the norms that give rise to victimization are criminal behaviours that need to be categorized as such by the States in the respective criminal codes. Without such action by the State, the proposal I am putting forward would not be possible.

8. In general, by '*victims*' is understood natural persons (only the ICC Statute includes legal persons in the definition of victim) who, individually or collectively, suffered harm (including physical or mental injury), emotional suffering, economic loss or substantial impairment of fundamental rights as a result of actions or omissions that violate the criminal law in the State in which the fact happens. International norms relating to the victims attributes to all of them the status of *direct victims*.

With regard to the *indirect victims*, it is understood to refer to family members or dependants who have immediate relationship with the direct victim and persons who have suffered harm in intervening to assist victims in distress or to prevent victimization.

At the same time, the different definitions are informed by three fundamental principles. On the one hand, the principle in accordance with which the status of victim is independent of the fact that the perpetrator of the violation has been identified, arrested, tried or sentenced and the family relationship that can exist between the author and the victim; on the other hand, *the principle of non-discrimination*. Under the same, the rights inherent to the condition of victim shall apply to all persons without distinction of any kind, whether of race, colour, sex, age, language, religion, nationality, political opinion or other, beliefs or cultural practices, economic status, birth or family situation, ethnic or social origin, or physical handicap. At least, the principle according to which the States shall treat victims with respect for their dignity and their private and family life.

9. Despite the fact that terrorism is an international crime which severely violates human rights, there are still no international norms of universal scope relating to the victims of terrorism. I find it inconceivable that the United Nations has still promoted no norm that contemplates them, unless they can serve as an excuse or justification the political difficulties in defining terrorism because, as we have seen, in the field of International law the legal definition not only is not a problem, but there are also at least basic elements that have been defined (either explicitly, or by referral to the international treaties to combat terrorism). Therefore, the decisions carried out within United Nations both by the Security Council and the General Assembly, by the Commission on Human Rights, and by the High Commissioner for Human Rights, which are limited to expressing the solidarity of the United Nations with the victims of terrorism and to seek the views of Member States to possibly establish a United Nations voluntary fund for victims of terrorism are totally inadequate. Faced with this heavenly music what victims of terrorism call for and claim is justice, and at the same time they reject the exercise of impunity.

The inactivity of the United Nations with respect to the victims of terrorism is still more poignant, given that this international organization has legislated or has promoted treaties in relation to other categories of victims. Therefore it is urged that the United Nations, in line with its action with regard to other categories of victims and following the example of the Council of Europe, also adopt an international norm that is intended to be the legal statute of victims of terrorism. A statute, consisting of a catalogue of rights inherent to the condition of being a victim of terrorism, based on the right to justice and the banning of impunity and connected to the jurisdiction of the International Criminal Court. Only in this way the "universal" right of all victims of terrorism to justice could be ensured regardless of the State in whose territory or under whose jurisdiction the victim has suffered the victimizer fact.

10. The status of victim is accompanied in the international legal order by an international legal statute made up of a catalogue of rights recognized by a plurality of international norms and international jurisprudence in the field of human rights. It is a set of rights that are held by the victims that on its reverse constitutes obligations for the States. The main obligation is to make those rights effective and really exercisable in practice.

Most of the rights that make up the international legal statute of the victim are already existing rights in the field of International human rights law. From this perspective, therefore, they are consolidated rights whose legal nature and effects do not pose any problems. Others, such as the right of emergency assistance or the right of continuing assistance, however, are rights closely linked with the status of victim that would only link the States that decide to be bound by the international norms that envisage them.

11. The catalogue of rights constituting the international legal statute of the victims is comprised of the following rights: right of emergency assistance, right of continuing assistance, right of investigation and prosecution, right of effective access to the law and to justice, right to reparation and compensation, right to the protection of the private and family life of victims, right to the protection of the dignity and security, right to information, right to the specific training for persons responsible for assisting victims; right to the truth and right to memory.

This catalogue is closed with the optional clause of "increased protection" that allows States recipients of the international norm to give to victims greater protection than that required in the norm in question.

12. The *right to emergency assistance* is a right closely linked with the status of victim. Given the recent nature of international norms relating to victims, it is not among the rights enshrined in International human rights treaties. The recent nature of attention of International Law to victims confirms the fact that this right is affirmed in international norms relating to them.

By virtue of this right, victims—in particular the most vulnerable—are entitled to receive material, medical, psychological, legal and social assistance as necessary; assistance that will be provided through governmental, voluntary, community-based and indigenous means. To this end, the States should inform the victims of the availability of existing services and facilitate access to them.

The most recent international norms state that such assistance should be free, at least during the period of the immediate consequences of the victimizer fact.

13. Like in the case of the right of emergency assistance, the *right to continuing assistance* is also a right directly linked to the status of victim. Asserted and

recognized by international norms relating to the victims, it is intended to be an obligation on the State to establish mechanisms and services in order to reduce the negative effects arising from the victimizer fact. To this end, the States should ensure that such services (medical, psychological, social, legal, police) provide the victims and their families—in particular to the most vulnerable—continued aid.

14. The *right of investigation and prosecution* that are held by the victims is a right that as its reverse thrusts the obligation on the State to investigate and prosecute violations of human rights. It is an obligation established in the field of International Law concerning human rights that is also formulated by international norms relating to the various categories of victims. It is also an obligation that the State has even if the victim has not officially lodged a complaint.

To comply with the standards determined by the international bodies of control in the field of human rights, investigation has to be serious, rapid, effective, exhaustive and impartial.

When it is decided not to take action to prosecute a suspected perpetrator, only the *Guidelines on the Protection of Victims of Terrorist Acts adopted by the Committee of Ministers of the Council of Europe on 2 March* recognize the right of victims to ask for this decision to be re-examined by a competent authority

Like other rights of the victims, the right to the investigation of the facts which gave rise to their victimization also has links with some of them. In particular, with the right to justice (including the right to a fair trial), the right to effective access to justice (including the right to effective remedy) and the right to redress and compensation. As a result, if there is no investigation or if it does not meet the above standards, the concerned State will not only violate this obligation but also the other.

With respect to a hypothetical *obligation to punish* that would be implicit in the obligation of the State to investigate and prosecute, only the General Assembly Resolution 60/147 adopted on 16 December 2005 through which the *Basic principles and guidelines of the right to a remedy and reparation for victims of gross violations of international human rights law and serious violations of International Humanitarian Law* adopted by the UN Commission on Human Rights on 19 April 2005, by Resolution 2005/35, is adopted, as well as international norms related to the enforced disappearance of persons (the *Declaration on the protection of all persons from Enforced Disappearance*, adopted through Resolution 47/133 of 18 December 1992, and the *International Convention for the Protection of All Persons from Enforced Disappearance*, of 20 December 2006) configures the charge of the State the obligation to punish the perpetrator of such acts.

Therefore, for the time being, it is not possible to assert the existence of a right of victims to insist on the punishment of the author of the victimizer act. In this regard, within the European regional frame the ECHR has pointed out that there is no autonomous right of the victim to prosecute or convict criminally third parties.

15. In general, the *right to the effective access to the law and to justice* is a fundamental human right existing in the field of International Law of human rights that treaties of human rights (both of a universal and regional scope) proclaim with

respect to "any person" and that it has been specified and developed by the interpretation made by different international treaty bodies in relation to the respective treaty (ECHR, I/ACHR, Committee on Human Rights, etc.).

It implies the right to a prompt and effective judicial remedy as well as the participation of the victims in civil and criminal proceedings with the right to obtain a judicial decision within a reasonable time. With regard to remedies, in accordance with the criteria set out by international supervisory bodies in the field of human rights, they must be adequate, effective and rapid. They should also include all the procedures available and appropriate to attack the victimizer fact suffered. If they do not meet these characteristics, the effectiveness of the rights protected by those treaties is non-existent. In other words, given the obligation the States Parties to the treaty have to make effective the rights in question and also, given the obligation to ensure that every person has accessible and effective remedies to justify those rights, the absence of such resources entails the violation of such obligations.

In relation to the victims, one of the most important advances in this area is the visibility of the victim in the criminal process; visibility that formalized various international norms recognizing victims' participation in criminal proceedings (Council Framework Decision 2001/220/JHA On the standing of the victim in criminal proceedings, of 15 March 2001, the ICC Statute, recommendations of the Committee of Ministers of the Council of Europe and the Guidelines On the Protection of Victims of Terrorist Acts (also of the aforementioned Committee of Ministers)).

The inclusion of the victim in the criminal proceedings is a development of great importance in view of the fact that, previously, the criminal proceedings was limited to relations between the accused and the Prosecutor. In the design of that process, the victim did not exist.

This right to the effective access to the law and to justice is linked with the obligation the States have to investigate the violation committed (the victimizer fact), so a non-existent investigation or an investigation without the characteristics of seriousness, rapidness, effectiveness, completeness and impartiality required by International Law also entails a violation of the right to effective remedy.

The right to effective access to justice also means, the right to obtain a judicial resolution "within a reasonable time". In this regard, international norms relating to victims do nothing more than reiterate a right which forms part of the human right to effective judicial protection, recognized as due to everyone by international human rights treaties. They have also been international supervisory bodies in the field of human rights which have specified the criteria in the light of which specific cases must be assessed whether reasonable or not (the circumstances of the case, the complexity of the dispute and the behaviour of litigants) and this for all processes (civil, criminal, administrative or others).

16. In contrast to the international human rights norms, which do not cover it (the only one that specifically mentions compensation is the American Convention on Human Rights), the *right of victims to reparation and compensation*, is proclaimed by all international norms relating to the victims. This is a new event connected

with the recent and novel character of the attention given by the international norms to victims. The object of this right is the repair of material damage and immaterial or moral damages to the victims.

Under the general heading of the right of victims to reparation, the international norms relating to them include various forms of reparation, classifiable into two blocks. On the one hand, *individual measures* (restitution, compensation and rehabilitation). On the other hand, *collective measures* of a symbolic nature—but not less relevant—whose objective is the moral reparation for the victims (request for forgiveness, recognition of responsibility by the State or by the perpetrators, restoration of the dignity of the victims, tributes, etc.).

Restitution being the main objective of reparation and given that this is almost always impossible because it is not possible to fully restore the victim to the state (moral and material) before the victimization (especially in cases of serious violations of human rights), international norms relating to victims proclaim unanimously the right to compensation.

With regard to the characteristics of the compensation, international norms relating to victims indicate they must be fair, appropriate and prompt. These norms also affirm subsidiary payment by the State.

As regards its links with other rights, international human rights supervisory bodies underline that the right to reparation is connected with the obligation on the charge of the State to carry out a prompt and effective investigation and the right of effective remedy. As a consequence of it, without these prerequisites, there is no possible redress.

17. The *right to the protection of private and family life* is a fundamental human right proclaimed by international human rights treaties and to which international norms relating to victims grant particular application—linked with the consequences of the victimizer fact—which focuses on the respect for the private and family life of the victims when carrying out investigations or providing assistance and information after the victimizer fact, as well as within the framework of the proceedings initiated by the victims. In this context, the States should take appropriate measures to ensure the safety, physical and psychological well-being of victims, as well as privacy (protection of personal data, for example), so that the legal and administrative procedures to render justice and grant compensation do not give rise to a new victimization (secondary victimization).

International norms both belonging to the sector of International human rights law and international norms relating to the victims recognize the need to grant special protection to the most vulnerable victims.

On a complementary basis, this right is linked to the right of effective remedy that victims can use to claim when their right to private and family life has been violated, when they deem that there has been such a circumstance.

18. The *right to the protection of the dignity and security of the victims* proclaimed by international norms relating to the various categories of victims is linked to the various phases of court proceedings and takes place within this framework. It is specified in the adoption by the States of measures for the protection of the identity

of the victim, granting special treatment to particularly vulnerable victims and protecting them when they need to act as witnesses. Also, and for the purposes of ensuring their security, the States shall adopt measures of protection for the victims where competent authorities consider that there is a serious risk of reprisals or clear signs of an intention to disrupt their private life. Such measures of protection and safety shall be taken in particular to those victims who are particularly vulnerable.

The dignity of the victims worthy of protection to which international norms refer is an additional requirement for the inherent dignity of every person. It is not in this case the dignity that underpins human rights, but the criterion according to which the victims in the framework of the different phases of the proceedings should be treated. According to him, the treatment that victims receive at any time should be respectful of their status as such and should take into account the consequences of all kinds (physical, psychological, emotional), which brings about the victimizer fact. It is, finally, a criterion which must be observed and respected by all those professionals (police, judicial, medical, media, etc.) which have intervention—however small—in dealing with the victim.

19. In contrast to the content that the *right to information* has in the field of International Law concerning the protection of human rights, with regard to victims the essential objective of this right is to ensure that the victim has access as soon as possible, effectively and by any means deemed appropriate, to relevant information for the protection of their interests. This information must come from the competent authorities in accordance with the domestic law of the State concerned (the judiciary, the police authority or any other to be determined by the domestic law of the State concerned).

It is a right, which the victim may waive because international norms covering it are unanimous in allowing victims to choose not to receive such information.

As for the content of the information, it is linked with the procedural area and concretized in the obligation on the charge of the State to inform victims about any matter related to the proceedings relating to the victimizer fact (the state of the investigation, the way in which the victim can obtain free legal assistance, the final decision concerning the proceedings, the date and place of the hearings, the way in which it is possible to know the decisions handed down, the time of the release of the accused person, etc.).

Second, the right to information to which victims are entitled is also concretized in the establishment by the State of contact points to provide information to victims about their rights, the existence of support agencies, the possibilities to obtain assistance, practical and legal advice as well as reparation or compensation.

Finally, in the case of enforced disappearance, the right to information to which victims are entitled is concretized in the right that, in certain circumstances, the family of a missing person has to be informed of the investigations and the whereabouts of the victim in question by the concerned State.

20. The *right of victims to the specific training for persons responsible for assisting* them echoes the need and the importance that people who are in contact with victims receive suitable and sufficient training (police, justice, health, social

services and other interested personnel services); the necessity and importance of which are recognized by all international norms relating to the victims.

Only the recommendations of the Committee of Ministers of the Council of Europe envisage this right as an obligation on the charge of the State. It would be, thus, one more objective to achieve rather than an obligation to be complied with by Member States.

Unlike the Council of Europe, both the norms of the EU and other international norms specify this right of the victims in imperative terms. It is logical, given the physical and psychological trauma resulting from the victimizer fact. It is, ultimately, an obligation of the State which has as a corollary the right of victims to be treated by trained personnel.

21. The *right to the truth* is an autonomous right recognized in general International Law in sectors relating to International Humanitarian law and International human rights law. It is also a right recognized by international human rights jurisprudence.

Its recognition takes place always in a specific context of grave violations of human rights as genocide, crimes against humanity, war crimes, forced disappearances or terrorism.

In terms of content, it focuses on the right of victims to have full and complete knowledge of the facts that gave rise to their victimization, the specific circumstances that led to them, those who were responsible for, it and the declaration as such.

On its reverse, it entails the obligation on the State for protection of human rights, to carry out effective investigation, to ensure that there are effective remedies and that victims obtain reparation.

Through the knowledge of the facts and the determination of those responsible for, it this right usually aims at achieving the consolidation of peace and reconciliation processes in societies where the crimes listed above were committed.

Therefore, its scope is limited to the most serious crimes (crimes under International Law) which is why it is expressly included in some international norms relating to victims. In all cases it is for victims of serious violations of human rights.

The right to the truth is linked to other rights of the victims. In particular, the right to an effective remedy, the right to legal and judicial protection, the right to family life, the right to an effective investigation, the right to be heard by a competent, independent and impartial tribunal, the right to reparation, the right not to suffer torture or ill treatment and the right to seek and disseminate information.

Finally, the right of victims to the truth is incompatible with the amnesty laws and similar measures of pardon or forgiveness that are intended to prevent the investigation and/or prosecution of perpetrators of serious violations of human rights. Such laws and measures violate the right to the truth and are invalid, according to international jurisprudence in the field of human rights.

22. The *right to memory*, as the right to the truth, does not preach any offence but is relevant only with regard to serious violations of human rights (genocide, crimes against humanity, war crimes, extrajudicial executions, forced disappearances and terrorism). As a result, only the victims of such violations are holders of the same.

As is the case with the other rights of the victims, the right to memory is also linked to other rights of the victims; in particular, with the right to the truth.

The right to the memory of the victims of serious violations of human rights is an autonomous right of such victims which is founded in the dignity of the person. In terms of content, it is oriented to denounce the wrongful act on the victim with a permanence over time effect and to preserve the memory of the victims to present and future generations. On its reverse, the States shall take all measures to preserve the memory of the victims and are obliged to prevent any act of any nature that is injurious to the same or constitutes an offence or a disregard for the victims. Also, States will promote all kinds of events to honour and preserve the memory of the victims.

Although it is not covered explicitly by any international norm, the right to the memory of the victims of serious violations of human rights follows international jurisprudence in the field of human rights, also being as a result of the right to the truth.

23. The facility permitting the States—if they so wish—by international norms to adopt stricter protective measures than those provided for the specific case by the conventional or institutional norm in question is called *increased protection*. It is a common formula used as a closing clause belonging to the International law of human rights treaties, but which is also found in other material areas regulated by treaties.

With respect to such treaties, as well as with those related to victims which include this clause, its content is reflected in the affirmation that the rights proclaimed by the international norm in question, and the way they are, is not incompatible with the adoption by the States Parties (in the case of treaties) or by the States addressees of the international norm in question (in the case of the institutional norms) of measures of protection more stringent or favourable; through the domestic law of the State or through existing International law with respect to that State.

Therefore, it is the responsibility of the States to use or not to use it, consistent with the greater or lesser degree of compromise the States wish to adopt in the specific case.

As a result, the increased protection clause is not a right of victims but a facility the State has and that it uses if it deems it appropriate.

International Norms

United Nations

Institutional Norms

General Assembly

- Universal Declaration on Human Rights, adopted by Resolution 217 A (III) of 10 December 1948
- Declaration of the Rights of the Child adopted by the General Assembly on 20 November 1959.
- Declaration on the Elimination of All Forms of Racial Discrimination adopted by A/RES/1904 (XVIII) of 20 November 1963.
- Declaration on the Protection of All Persons from being subjected to Torture and Other Cruel, Inhuman or Degrading Treatment or Punishment adopted by A/RES/3452 (XXX) of 9 December 1975
- A/RES/ 33/173, of 20 December 1978, on disappeared persons.
- Declaration of Basic Principles of Justice for Victims of Crime and Abuse of Power adopted by General Assembly resolution 40/34 of 29 November 1985
- A/RES/43/173 of 9 December 1988, containing the Body of Principles for the Protection of All Persons under Any Form of Detention or Imprisonment
- Principles on the Effective Prevention and Investigation of Extra-legal, Arbitrary and Summary Executions set forth in the Annex to the Economic and Social Council resolution 1989/65 of 24 May 1989, adopted by the GA on A/RES/44/162 of 15 December 1989.
- Declaration on the Protection of All Persons from Enforced Disappearance adopted by A/RES/47/133 of 18 December 1992.
- A/RES/48/122 of 20 December 1993, adopted under the heading "Human Rights and Terrorism" which makes reference to victims of terrorism.
- A/RES/49/185 of 23 December 1994, adopted under the heading "Human Rights and Terrorism" which makes reference to victims of terrorism.

C. Fernández de Casadevante Romani, *International Law of Victims*,
DOI 10.1007/978-3-642-28140-2, © Springer-Verlag Berlin Heidelberg 2012

– A/RES/50/186 of 22 December 1995, adopted under the heading "Human Rights and Terrorism" which makes reference to victims of terrorism.
– A/RES/52/133 of 12 December 1997, adopted under the heading "Human Rights and Terrorism" which makes reference to victims of terrorism.
– A/RES/54/164 of 24 February 2000, adopted under the heading "Human Rights and Terrorism" which makes reference to victims of terrorism.
– A/RES/56/160 of 19 February 2001, adopted under the heading "Human Rights and Terrorism" which makes reference to victims of terrorism.
– A/RES/58/174 of 22 December 2003, adopted under the heading "Human Rights and Terrorism" which makes reference to victims of terrorism.
– A/RES/ 55/118, of 1 March 2001, on the situation of human rights in Haiti. It contains references to the right to truth.
– A/RES/ 57/105, of 13 February 2003, on Assistance for humanitarian relief, rehabilitation and development for Timor-Leste. It contains references to the right to truth.
– A/RES/ 57/161, of 28 January 2003, on United Nations Verification Mission in Guatemala. It contains references to the right to truth.
– A/RES/ 60/147 adopted on 16 December 2005 through which the Basic principles and guidelines of the right to a remedy and reparation for victims of gross violations of international human rights law and serious violations of International Humanitarian Law adopted by the UN Commission on Human Rights on 19 April 2005, by Resolution 2005/35, are adopted.

Security Council

– *Statutes* of the international criminal courts *ad hoc* for the *former Yugoslavia* and for *Rwanda* adopted by Security Council resolutions in the frame of Chapter VII of the Charter.
– Resolution 1566 (2004), adopted on 8th October 2004 that considers the possibility of establishing an international fund to compensate victims of terrorist acts and their families.
- Resolution 1377 (2001), of 12 November 2001 (S/RES/1377 (2001).

Commission on Human Rights

– Resolution 1994/46, adopted on 4 March 1994, on Human rights and terrorism and qualifying terrorism as a violation of human rights.
– Resolution 1995/43, adopted on 3 March1995, on Human rights and terrorism and qualifying terrorism as a violation of human rights.
– Resolution 1995/44, adopted on 3 March1995, on Human rights and terrorism and qualifying terrorism as a violation of human rights.
– Resolution 1996/47, adopted on 19 April 1996, on Human rights and terrorism and qualifying terrorism as a violation of human rights.

- Resolution 1997/42, adopted on 28 August 1997, on Human rights and terrorism and qualifying terrorism as a violation of human rights.
- Resolution 52/133, adopted on 12 December 1997, on Human rights and terrorism and qualifying terrorism as a violation of human rights.
- Resolution 1998/47, adopted on 21 April 1998, on Human rights and terrorism and qualifying terrorism as a violation of human rights and qualifying terrorism as a violation of human rights.
- Resolution 1999/26, adopted on26 August 1999, on Terrorism and human rights and qualifying terrorism as a violation of human rights.
- Resolution 2000/30, adopted on 20 April 2000, on Human rights and terrorism and qualifying terrorism as a violation of human rights.
- Resolution 2001/37, adopted on 23 April 2001, on Human rights and terrorism and qualifying terrorism as a violation of human rights.
- Resolution 2002/35, adopted on 22 April 2002 and entitled "Human Rights and Terrorism" which envisages compensation to victims of terrorism.
- Resolution 2003/37, adopted on 23 April 2003, related to the establishing of an international fund to compensate victims of terrorist acts.
- Resolution 2003/68 about "Protection of Human Rights and Fundamental Freedoms while Countering Terrorism."
- Resolution 2004/87 about "Protection of Human Rights and Fundamental Freedoms while Countering Terrorism."
- Resolution 2005/35, adopted on 19 April 2005, containing the Basic principles and guidelines of the right to a remedy and reparation for victims of gross violations of international human rights law and serious violations of International Humanitarian Law

Sub-Commission on the Promotion and Protection of Human Rights

- Resolution 1993/23, adopted on 23 August 1993, on the situation of human rights in Peru and condemning the violations of human rights in Peru by the terrorist groups Sendero Luminoso and Movimiento Revolucionario Tupac Amaru.
- Resolution 1994/18, adopted on 25 August 1994, on Human rights and terrorism and qualifying terrorism as a violation of human rights.
- Resolution 1996/20, adopted on 29 August 1996, on Human rights and terrorism and qualifying terrorism as a violation of human rights.
- Resolution 1997/39, adopted on 28 August 1997, on Human rights and terrorism and qualifying terrorism as a violation of human rights.
- Preliminary Report drafted by Special Rapporteur K. Koufa on Terrorism and Human Rights, (Doc. E/CN.4/Sub.2/1999/27 of 7 June 1999).
- Progress Report drafted by Special Rapporteur K. Koufa on Terrorism and Human Rights, (Doc. E/CN.4/Sub.2/2001/31 of 27 June 2001).
- Second Progress Report drafted by Special Rapporteur K. Koufa on Terrorism and Human Rights (Doc. E/CN.4/Sub.2/2002/35 of 17 July 2002).

- Additional progress report with two addenda drafted by Special Rapporteur K. Koufa on Terrorism and Human Rights (Doc. E/CN.4/Sub.2/2003/WP.1 and Add.1 and 2 of 8 August 2003).
- Final Report drafted by Special Rapporteur K. Koufa on Terrorism and Human Rights (Doc. E/CN.4/Sub.2/2004/40 of 25 June 2004).

United Nations High Commissioner for Human Rights

- Report to the General Assembly according to Resolution 48/142 entitled "Human rights: a unity framework report" (Doc. E/CN.4/2002/18 of 27 February 2002).
- Economic and Social Council, Commission on Human Rights, Promotion and Protection of Human Rights. Study on the right to the truth. Report of the Office of the United Nations High Commissioner for Human Rights, 9 January 2006 (E/CN.4/2006/91).

International Treaties

- Convention on the Prevention and Punishment of the Crime of Genocide of 1948.
- Geneva Convention On the Protection of Civilian Persons in Time of War, of 12 August 1949.
- Geneva Convention (I), of 12 August 1949, for the Amelioration of the Condition of the Wounded and Sick in Armed Forces in the Field.
- Geneva Convention (II), of 12 August 1949, for the Amelioration of the Condition of Wounded, Sick and Shipwrecked Members of Armed Forces at Sea.
- Additional Protocol I to the Geneva Conventions of 12 August 1949, On the Protection of Victims of International Armed Conflicts of 8 June 1977.
- Additional Protocol II to the Geneva Conventions of 12 August 1949, On the Protection of Victims of Non International Armed Conflicts of 8 June 1977.
- International Convention on the Elimination of All Forms of Racial Discrimination, of 20 December 1965.
- International Covenant on Civil and Political Rights of 16 December 1966.
- First Optional Protocol to the Covenant on Civil and Political Rights of 16 December 1966.
- International Covenant on Economic, Social and Cultural Rights of 16 December 1966.
- Convention for the Suppression of Unlawful Seizure of Aircraft of 16 December 1970.
- Convention for the Suppression of Unlawful Acts against the Safety of Civil Aviation of 23 September 1971.
- Convention on the Prevention and Punishment of Crimes against Internationally Protected Persons of 14 December 1973.
- International Convention against the Taking of Hostages of 17 December 1979.

- Convention on the Elimination of Discrimination against Women of 18 December 1979.
- Convention on the Physical Protection of Nuclear Material of 3 March 1980.
- Convention against Torture and Other Cruel, Inhuman or Degrading Treatment or Punishment of 10 December 1984.
- Protocol for the Suppression of Unlawful Acts of Violence at Airports Serving International Civil Aviation, supplementary to the Convention for the Suppression of Unlawful Acts against the Safety of Civil Aviation of 24 February 1988.
- Convention on the Rights of the Child of 20 November 1989.
- Convention on the Protection of the Rights of All Migrant Workers and Members of Their Families, of 18 December 1990.
- Convention on the Marking of Plastic Explosives for the Purpose of Detection of 1 March 1991.
- International Convention for the Suppression of Terrorist Bombings of 15 December 1997.
- Statute of the International Criminal Court (ICC) adopted by the Conference of Rome on 17 July 1998.
- International Convention for the Suppression of the Financing of Terrorism of 9 December 1999.
- Protocol for the Suppression of Unlawful Acts against the Safety of Fixed Platforms Located on the Continental Shelf of 10 March 1988 and its Protocol for the Suppression of Unlawful Acts against the Safety of Fixed Platforms Located on the Continental Shelf of 14 October 2005.
- International Convention for the Suppression of Acts of Nuclear Terrorism of 13 April 2005.
- Convention on the Rights of Persons with disability of 13 December 2006.
- International Convention for the Protection of All Persons from Enforced Disappearance adopted on 20 December 2006.

European Union

- Resolution of the European Parliament on the missing in Cyprus, of 11 January 1983.
- Charter of Fundamental Rights of the European Union, of 7 December 2000.
- Explanations relating to the Charter of Fundamental Rights of the European Union, of 7 December 2000.
- Council Framework Decision (2001/220/JHA) of 15 March 2001 on the Standing of Victims in Criminal Proceedings.
- Council Framework Decision (2002/475/JHA) of 13 June 2002, on combating terrorism.
- Conclusions of the European Council of the EU, of 3 October 2003, Colombia.

- Council Directive 2004/80/EC of 29 April 2004 Relating to Compensation to Crime Victims.
- Council Framework Decision (2008/919/JHA) of 28 November 2008 adding other offences linked to terrorist activities.

Council of Europe

Institutional Norms

- Resolution 77 (27) On the Compensation of Victims of Crime adopted by the Committee of Ministers on 28 September 1977.
- Recommendation (81) 7E On Measures Facilitating Access to Justice, adopted by the Committee of Ministers on14 May 1981.
- Recommendation (83) 7, adopted on 23 June 1983 On Participation of the Public in Crime Policy.
- Recommendation (85) 11, adopted on 28 June 1985 On The Position of the Victim in the Framework of Criminal Law and Procedure.
- Recommendation No. R (87) 21 on the Assistance to Victims and the Prevention of Victimisation.
- Recommendation No. R (93)1 On Effective Access to the Law and to Justice for the Very Poor, adopted by the Committee of Ministers on 8 January 1993.
- Recommendation No. R (97) 13, concerning Intimidation oo Witnesses and the Rights of the Defence, adopted by the Committee of Ministers on 10 September 1997.
- Guidelines on the Protection of Victims of Terrorist Acts adopted by the Committee of Ministers of the Council of Europe on 2 March 2005.
- Recommendation (2006) 8 of the Committee of Ministers On Assistance to Crime Victims which substitutes Recommendation No. R (87) 21 on the Assistance to Victims and the Prevention of Victimisation.

International Treaties

- European Convention for the Protection of Human Rights and Fundamental Freedoms of 4 November 1950.
- European Social Charter, of 18 October 1961.
- Additional Protocol to the European Social Charter, of 5 May1988.
- European Social Charter, revisited, of 1996.
- European Convention on the Compensation of Victims of Violent Crimes of 24 November 1983.
- European Convention on the Prevention of Terrorism, of 16 May 2005.
- Convention for the protection of Human Rights and dignity of the human being with regard to the application of biology and medicine: Convention on Human Rights and Biomedicine, of 4 April 1997 (CETS No.: 164).
- Additional Protocol to the Convention for the Protection of Human Rights and Dignity of the Human Being with regard to the Application of Biology and

Medicine, on the Prohibition of Cloning Human Beings, of 12 January 1998 (CETS No.: 168).
- Additional Protocol to the Convention on Human Rights and Biomedicine, concerning Biomedical Research, of 25 January 2005 (CETS No.: 195).

Organization Of American States(OAS)

International Treaties

- American Declaration of the Rights and Duties of Man, of 1948.
- American Convention on Human Rights, of 22 November 1969.
- Inter-American Convention to Prevent and Punish Torture, of 9 December 1985.
- Inter-American Convention on the Forced Disappearance of Persons, of 9 June 1994.
- Inter-American Convention Against Terrorism, of 2002.

African Union

International Treaties

- African Charter on Human and Peoples' Rights of 27 June 1981.
- Protocol to the African Charter on Human and Peoples' Rights On the Rights of Women in Africa, of 11 July 2003.
- African Convention on the Prevention and Combating of Terrorism, of 14 July1999 and its Protocol of 2004.
- Principles and Guidelines on the Right to a Fair Trial and Legal Assistance in Africa, African Commission on Human and Peoples' Rights.

Other Regional Systems

International Treaties

- Arab Convention on Suppression of Terrorism, of 22 April 1998.
- Convention against Terrorism, of 4 May 2004, adopted by the Cooperation Council for Arab States of the Gulf.
- Convention of the Organization of the Islamic Conference on combating international terrorism of the 1st July 1999.
- Regional Convention on Suppression of Terrorism of 4 November 1987 and the Additional Protocol to it of 6 January 2004, both adopted in the frame of the South Asian Association for Regional Cooperation (SAARC).
- ASEAN Convention on Counter Terrorism, of 13 January 2007, adopted in the frame of the Association of South East Asian Nations (ASEAN).

Table of Cases

European Court of Human Rights

- Case *Wemhoff v. Germany*, Judgement of 27 June 1968.
- Case *Neumeister v. Austria*, Judgement of 27 June 1968.
- Case *Ringeisen v. Austria*, Judgement of 16 July 1971.
Case *Klass and others v. Germany*, Judgement of 6 September 1978.
- Case *König v. Germany*, Judgement of 28 June 1978
- Case *Marckx v. Belgium*, Judgement of 13 June 1979.
- Case *Buchholz v. Germany*, Judgement of 6 May 1981.
- Case *Foti and Others v. Italy*, Judgement of 10 December 1982.
- Case *Zimmermann and Steiner v. Switzerland*, Judgement of 13 July 1983.
- Case *Leander v. Sweden*, Judgement of 26 March1987.
- Case *Lechner and Hess v. Austria*, Judgement of 23 April 1987.
- Case *Nölkenbockhoff v. Germany*, Judgement of 25 August 1987.
- Case *Inze v. Austria*, Judgement of 28 October 1987.
- Case *Capuano v. Italy*, Judgement of 25 June 1987.
- Case *Vijayanathan et Pusparajah v. France*, Judgement of 27 August 1992.
- Case *Open Door y Dublin Well Woman v. Ireland*, Judgement of 29 October 1992.
- Case *Hurtado v. Switzerland*, Judgement of 28 January 1994.
- Case *McCann and others v. United Kingdom*, Judgement of 27 September 1995.
- Case *Aksoy v. Turkey*, Judgement of 18 December 1996.
- Case *Kaya v. Turkey*, Judgement of 19 February 1998.
- Case *Kurt v. Turkey*, Judgement of 25 May 1998.
- Case *L.C.B. v. the United Kingdom*, Judgment of 9 June 1998.
- Case *Aerts v. Belgium*, Judgment of 30 July 1998.
- Case *Yaşa v. Turkey*, Judgement of 2 September 1998.
- Case *Çakıcı v. Turkey (GC)*, Judgement of 8 July 1999.
- Case *Kudla v. Poland*, Judgement of 26 October 2000.

C. Fernández de Casadevante Romani, *International Law of Victims*,
DOI 10.1007/978-3-642-28140-2, © Springer-Verlag Berlin Heidelberg 2012

- Case *Brudnicka and others v. Poland*, Judgement of 3 March 2005.
- Case *Senator Lines v. EU States (GC)*,
- Case *Dalban v. Rumania* [GC], Judgement of 28 September 1999.
- Case *Büyükdag v. Turkey,* Judgement of 21 December 2000.
- Case *Berktay v. Turkey*, Judgement of the 1st March 2001.
- Case *McKerr v. United Kingdom*, Judgement of 4 May 2001.
- Case *Cyprus v. Turkey*, Judgement of 10 May 2001.
- Case of *The Christian Federation of Jehovah's Witnesses in France v. France*, Judgement of 6 November 2001.
- Case *Nitecki v. Poland*, Judgement of 21 March 2002.
- Case *Larioshina v. Russia*, decision as to the admissibility of 23 April 2002.
- Case *Ulku Ekinci v. Turkey*, Judgement of 16 July 2002.
- Case *McGlinchey and Others v. The United Kingdom*, Judgement of 29 April 2003.
- Case *Kudła v. Poland* [GC], Judgement of 29 April 2003.
- Case *Tepe v. Turkey*, Judgement of 9 May 2003.
- Case *Finucane v. United Kingdom*, Judgement of the 1st July 2003.
- Case *Karner v. Austria*, Judgement of 24 July 2003.
- Case *Perez v. France (GC)*, Judgement of 12 February 2004.
- Case *Mutimara v. France,* Judgement of 8 June 2004.
- Case *Slimani v. France*, Judgement of 27 July 2004.
- Case *Gorraiz Lizarraga and others v. Spain*, Judgement of 27 April 2004.
- Case *Fairfield and others v. United Kingdom*, Judgement of 8 March 2005.
- *Case Issayeva v. Russia*, Judgement of 24 February 2005.
- Case *Marie-Louise Loyen et Bruneel v. France*, Judgement of 5 July 2005.
- Case *Biçand others v. Turkey*, Judgement of 2 February 2006.
- Case *Thévenon v. France*, Judgement of 28 February 2006.
- Case *Paşa et Erkan Erol v. Turkey,* Judgement of 12 December 2006.
- Case *Amuur v. France*, Judgement of 12 December 2006.
- *Case of Sandru and Others v. Romania*, Judgement of 8 December 2009.
- *Case of Carabulea v. Romania*, Judgement of 13 July 2010.
- *Case Silih v. Slovakia (GC)*, Judgement of 9 April 2011.
- Case *McKerr v. United Kingdom*, Judgement of 4 May 2011.
- *Case Association 21 December 1989 and Others v. Romania (GC)*, Judgement of 24 May 2011.
- *Case Al-Skeini and Others v. United Kingdom (GC)*, Judgement of 7 July 2011.
- Case *Tas v. Turkey*, Judgement of 14 November 2000.

Court of Justice of the European Union

- *Case Johnston*, 222/84, Judgement of 15 May 1986, [1986] ECR 1651.
- *Case Heylens and others*, 222/86, Judgement of 15 October 1987, [1987] ECR 4097.

- *Case Commission/Austria*, C-424/99, Judgement of 27 November 2001, [2001] ECR I-9285.
- *Case Unión de Pequeños Agricultores/Council*, C-50/00, Judgement of 25 July 2002, [2002] ECR I-6677.
- *Case Eribrand*, C-467/01, Judgement of 19 June 2003, [2003] ECR I-6471.
- *Case Unibet (London) Ltd. And Unibet (International) v. Justitiekanslern*, Case C-432/05, Judgement of 13 May 2007.
- *Case, "Les Verts" v. European Parliament*, C -294/83, Judgment of 23 April 1986, [1988] ECR 1339).
- *Case Baustahlgewebe/Commission*, C-185/95, Judgement of 17 December 1998, (1998) ECR I-8417.
- *Case Netherlands and Van der Wal/Commission*, C 174/98 P and C-189/98, Judgement of 11 January 2000, Rec., p. I-1.
- *Case Eurofood IFSC Ltd.*, C-341/04, Judgement of 2 May 2006, (2004) ECRI-3813.
- *Case Salzgitter Mannesmann/Commission*, C-411/04 P, Judgement of 25 January 2007.
- *Case Ordre des barreaux francophines et germanophone*, C-305/05, Judgement of 27 June 2007.

Inter-American Court of Human Rights

- *Case of Velásquez-Rodríguez v. Honduras*. Reparations and Costs, Judgment of July 21, 1989. Series C No. 7.
- Caso *Godínez Cruz v. Honduras*, Judgement of 20 January 1989.
- *Case of the "Street Children" (Villagrán-Morales et al.) v. Guatemala*, Merits. Judgment of November 19, 1999. Series C No. 63
- *Case of Barrios Altos v. Peru,* Merits. Judgment March 14, 2001. Series C No. 75.
- *Caso Barrios Altos (Interpretación)*, Judgement of 3 September 2001.
- *Case of 19 Tradesmen v. Colombia*, Judgment of July 5, 2004. Series C No. 109.
- *Case of the Serrano-Cruz Sisters v. El Salvador*, Judgment of March 1, 2005. Series C No. 120.
- *Case of the "Mapiripan Massacre" v. Colombia,* Judgment of September 15, 2005. Series C No. 134.
- *Caso Almonacid Arellano et al. v. Chile*, Judgement of 26 September 2006.
- *Case of Nogueira de Carvalho et al. v. Brazil,* Preliminary Objections and Merits, Judgment of November 28, 2006, Series C No. 161.
- *Case of La Cantuta v. Peru,* Merits, Reparations and Costs. Judgment of November 29, 2006. Series C No. 162.

Bibliography

Abbott KW, Snidal D (2000) Hard and soft law in International Governance. Int Org 54 (3):421–456

Aguirrezábal Quijera I (November 2005) 'The United Nations' Responsibility towards Victims of Terrorist Acts', working paper, FRIDE 16, 2

Almqvist J (2006) Facing the Victims in the Global Fight against Terrorism. Working paper, FRIDE (November)

APAV (2009) Project victims in Europe. Implementation of the EU Framework Decisión on the standing of victims in the criminal proceedings in the Member States of the European Union. Lisboa

Ararteko/Defensor del Pueblo, Atención institucional a las víctimas del terrorismo en Euskadi, Special Report to the Basque Parliament, Vitoria, June 2009

Ascensio H (2009) Les droits de victimes devant les juridictions pénales internationales. In: The collective work edited by Flauss, J.-F., La protection internationale des droits de l'homme et les droits des victimes. Bruylant, Bruxelles, 77–110

Bandrés JM (1998) Artículo 8, in the collective work of the Association for the United Nations in Spain, coord. Pons Rafols, X., La Declaración Universal de los Derechos Humanos. Comentario artículo por artículo, Icaria ed., Barcelona, 186 192

Barberis J (1994) Formación del derecho internacional, ed. Ábaco de Rodolfo De Palma, Buenos Aires

Bassiouni Ch (2002) Reconnaissance internationale des droits des victimes. In: The collective work of SOS Attentats: Terrorisme, victimes et responsabilité pénale internationale. Calmann-Lévy, Paris, 134–185

Berger V (2007) Le 'préjudice important' selon le Protocole nº 14 à la Convention européenne des droits de l'homme. Questions et réflexions, in the collective work, Promoting Justice, Human Rights And Conflict Resolution Through International Law. Liber Amicorum Lucius Caflish, M. Nijhoff Pub., Leiden, 81–91

Beristain Ipiña A (2000) Victimología. Nueve palabras clave. Tirant lo Blanch, Valencia

Beristain Ipiña A (2004) Protagonismo de las víctimas de hoy y mañana. Tirant lo Blanch, Valencia

Beristain Ipiña A (2008) Transformación del Derecho Penal y la Criminología hacia la Victimología. ARA Editores, Perú

Bollo Arocena MªD (2004) Derecho Internacional Penal. Estudio de los Crímenes internacionales y de las técnicas para su represión. Servicio Editorial de la Universidad de País Vasco, Bilbao

Bonet Pérez J, Alija Fernández A (2009) Impunidad, derechos humanos y justicia transicional, Cuadernos de Deusto de Derechos Humanos, Núm. 53, Bilbao

Bottigliero I (2004) Redress for victims of crimes under International Law. M. Nijhoff, Leiden/ Boston

C. Fernández de Casadevante Romani, *International Law of Victims*,
DOI 10.1007/978-3-642-28140-2,

Bou V, Fernández de Casadevante C (2009) La inclusión del terrorismo entre los crímenes internacionales previstos en el Estatuto de la Corte Penal Internacional. MINIM, Valencia

Burgorgue-Larsen L, Úbeda de Torres A (2009) Las decisiones básicas de la Corte Interamericana de Derechos Humanos. Estudio y jurisprudencia, Civitas & Thomson Reuters, Cizur Menor

Burgorgue-Larsen L, Úbeda de Torres A (2011) The Inter-American Court of Human Rights. Case law and commentary. Oxford University Press, Oxford

Cario R (2002) Terrorisme et droit des victimes. In: The collective work of SOS Attentats: Terrorisme, victimes et responsabilité pénale internationale. Calmann-Lévy, Paris, 342–361

Carnerero R (2007) La inmunidad de jurisdicción penal de los Jefes de Estado extranjeros. Iustel, Madrid

Carrillo Salcedo JA (1991) Curso de Derecho Internacional Público. Tecnos, Madrid

Carrillo Salcedo JA (1993) Algunas reflexiones sobre el valor jurídico de la Declaración Universal de Derechos Humanos, in the collective work Hacia un nuevo orden internacional y europeo. Homenaje al Profesor M. Díez de Velasco, Tecnos, Madrid, 167–178

Carrillo Salcedo JA (1999) Dignidad frente a Barbarie. La Declaración Universal de Derechos Humanos Cincuenta Años Después, Trotta, Madrid

Castañeda J (1970-I) Valeur juridique des résolutions des Nations Unies. R. des C t. 129:205–232

Clapham A (2007) The jus cogens Prohibition of Torture and the Importance of Sovereign State Immunity. In: The collective work Promoting Justice, Human Rights and Conflict Resolution Through International Law. Liber Amicorum Lucius Caflish, M. Nijhoff Pub., Leiden, 151–169

Conseil de l'Europe (2006) Soutien et aide aux victimes. éditions du Conseil de l'Europe, Strasbourg

Cruz Ortiz de Landázuri LM (2010(1)) La reparación a las víctimas en el Convenio Europeo de Derechos Humanos. REDI, LXII:89–117

Cuesta C (2000) Contra el olvido, ed. Temas de Hoy, Madrid

D'argent P (2009) Les réparations pour violations historiques, in the collective work edited by Flauss, J.-F., La protection internationale des droits de l'homme et les droits des victimes, Bruylant, Bruxelles, 195–220

Díaz Pérez IL (2009) El rostro de los invisibles. Víctimas y su derecho a la verdad, justicia, reparación y no repetición, in the collective work coord. by Bondia García, D., and Ramiro Muñoz, M., Víctimas invisibles, conflicto armado y resistencia civil en Colombia, Huygeds ed., Barcelona, 37–72

Doucet G (2005) Terrorisme: définition, juridiction pénale internationale et victimes, Victimes et Terrorisme. Rev Int Droit Penal 3/4 trimestre(76e année nouvelle série):250–273

Dungel J (2009) Defining victims of crimes against humanity: *Martic* and the International Criminal Court. Leiden J Int Law 22:727–752

Dupuy PM (1992) Droit International Public. Dalloz, Paris

Dupuy RJ (1975) Droit déclaratoire et Droit programmatoire: de la coutume sauvage à la soft law. In: The collective work L'élaboration du droit international public. A. Pedone, Paris, 132–148

Espósito C (2007) Inmunidad del Estado y Derechos Humanos. Civitas, Madrid

Estévez Araujo JA (1998) Artículo 1, in the collective work of the Association for the United Nations in Spain, coord. Pons Rafols, X., La Declaración Universal de los Derechos Humanos. Comentario artículo por artículo, Icaria ed., Barcelona, 104–109

Feldman T (2009) Indirect victims, direct injury: recognising relatives as victims under the European Human Rights System. Eur Hum Right Law Rev 6:50–69

Fernández de Casadevante Romani C (dir) (2011) Derecho Internacional de los Derechos Humanos, 4th edn., Dilex, Madrid, 421–450

Fernández de Casadevante Romani C (dir) (2011) El Derecho Internacional de las Víctimas. Porrúa, México

Fernández de Casadevante Romani C (dir) (2006) La nación sin ciudadanos. El dilema del País Vasco. Dilex, Madrid

Fernández de Casadevante Romani C, Jiménez García F (2005) Terrorismo y Derechos Humanos. Una aproximación desde el Derecho Internacional. Dykinson, Madrid

Fernández de Casadevante Romani C, Mayordomo Rodrigo V (2011) Código de normas internacionales relativas a las víctimas. Tecnos, Madrid

Fernández Sola N (2008/2) El derecho a la reparación de las víctimas de desaparición forzada: hacia la justicia a través del Derecho internacional. REDI LX:397–425

Ferreiro Bahamonde X (2005) La víctima en el proceso penal. La Ley, Madrid

Flauss J-F (ed) (2009) La protection internationale des droits de l'homme et les droits des victimes. Bruylant, Bruxelles

Fundación Miguel Angel Blanco (2010) International Action, Terrorism: a crime against humanity. Palais des Nations, Geneva

Fundación Miguel Angel Blanco (2011) International action, terrorism: a crime against humanity. Palais des Nations, Geneva

García San José D (2006/1) El derecho a la justicia de las víctimas de los crímenes más graves de trascendencia para la Comunidad Internacional. R.E.D.I, LVIII:119–145

Gil-Robles A (2001) Report by Mr. Alvaro Gil-Robles, Commissioner for Human Rights, on his visit to Spain and the Basque Country 5–8 February 2001, for the Committee of Ministers and the Parliamentary Assembly. Council of Europe, CommDH(2001)2

Gómez Bermúdez J (2010) No destruirán nuestra libertad. Planeta, Madrid

Gómez Isa F, De Feyter K (eds) (2009) International human rights law in a global context. Humanitarian Net, Bilbao

González Campos JD, Sánchez Rodríguez LI (2008) Andrés Sáenz de Santa Maria, M^{a}. P., Curso de Derecho Internacional Público, 4th ed. Revisited. Thomson & Civitas, Madrid

Gozzi M-H, Laborde J-P (2005) Les Nations Unies et le droit des victimes du terrorisme. Rev Int Droit Pénal 76(3e/4e trimestre):275–298

Groenhuijsen MS, Pemberton A (2009) The EU Framework Decision on Victims. Does hard law make a difference? Eur J Crime Criminal Law Criminal Justice 17:43–59

Hamilton M (2009) Transitional justice in an age of legal pluralism, in the collective work edited by, J.-F., La protection internationale des droits de l'homme et les droits des victimes, Bruylant, Bruxelles, 165–194

Heyns Ch, Killander M (2009) The African Regional Human Rights System. In: Gómez Isa F, De Feyter K (eds) International human rights law in a global context. Humanitarian Net, Bilbao, 858–898

Hinojosa Martínez LM (2008) La financiación del terrorismo y las Naciones Unidas. Tecnos, Madrid

Jacque J-P (1991-II) Acte et norme en Droit International Public. R. des C t. 227:361–417

Jeangène Vilmer J-B (2009) Réparer l'irréparable. Les réparations aux victimes devant la Cour Pénale Internationale. PUF, Paris

Jiménez de Aréchaga E (1978-I) International law in the past third of a century, R. des C., t. 159: 4–343

Jiménez Luque T (2009) El observatorio del conflicto: Una forma de conservar la memoria de las víctimas invisibles, in the collective work ewdited by Bondia García, D., and Ramiro Muñoz, M., Víctimas invisibles, conflicto armado y resistencia civil en Colombia, Huygeds ed., Barcelona, 73–102

Kailliopi K Koufa, Special Rapporteur on Terrorism and Human Rights, UN Subcomissionon on the Promotion and Protection of Human Rights, Report of 2001, Doc. E/CN.4/Sub.2/2001/31

Kirsch Ph (2002) Terrorisme, crimes contre l'humanité et Cour pénale internationale, in the collective work of SOS Attentats. Livre Noir, Paris, 111–124

Landrove Díaz G (2002) La moderna Victimología. Tirant lo Blanch, Valencia

Letschert R, Staiger I, Pemberton A (eds) (2010) Assisting victims of terrorism. Towards a European Standard of Justice. Springer, Dordrecht

López Escudero OPEZ, M., "Artículo 47. Derecho a la tutela judicial efectiva y a un juez imparcial", in the collective work dir. by Mangas Martín, A., Carta de los Derechos Fundamentales de la Unión Europea. Comentario artículo por artículo, Fundación BBVA, Bilbao, 2008, 739–758

de Lucas J (1998) Artículo 2, in the collective work of the Association for the United Nations in Spain, coord. Pons Rafols, X., La Declaración Universal de los Derechos Humanos. Comentario artículo por artículo, Icaria ed., Barcelona, 1998, 110–123

Macgibbon I (1982) Means for the identification of International Law. General assembly resolutions: custom, practice and mistaken identity. In: The collective work of Bin Cheng (ed.) International law: teaching and practice. Stevens, London, 10–26

Mangas Martín A (dir) (2008) Carta de los Derechos Fundamentales de la Unión Europea. Comentario artículo por artículo, Fundación BBVA, Bilbao

Martín y Pérez de Nanclares J (2008) Artículo 7. Respeto de la vida privada y familiar. In: The collective work of Mangas Martín, A. (dir.), Carta de los Derechos Fundamentales de la Unión Europea. Comentario artículo por artículo, Fundación BBVA, Bilbao, 209–222

Martín y Pérez de Nanclares J (2008) Artículo 11. Libertad de expresión y de información. In: The collective work of Mangas Martín, A. (dir.), Carta de los Derechos Fundamentales de la Unión Europea. Comentario artículo por artículo, Fundación BBVA, Bilbao, 271–286

Mate R (2002) La mirada de la víctima, *Estudios de Deusto*, vol. 50/1

Mayordomo Rodrigo V (2003) Aspectos criminológicos, victimológicos y jurídicos de los malos tratos en el ámbito familiar. Servicio de Publicaciones de la Universidad del País Vasco, Bilbao

Mayordomo Rodrigo V (2005) La violencia contra la mujer: un estudio de Derecho comparado. Dilex, Madrid

Mayordomo Rodrigo V (2011) La lucha contra la discriminación de la mujer, in the collective work coord. by de Mathieu B (2005) Article II-61. In: Burgorgue-Larsen A, Levade A, Picod F (eds) Traité Établissant une Constitution pour l'Europe. Partie II, La Charte des droits fondamentaux de l'Union, Tome 2. Bruylant, Bruxelles, 35–41

Momtaz D (2007) De l'incompatibilité des amnisties incoditionnelles avec le droit International, in the collective work Promoting Justice, Human Rights And Conflict Resolution Through International Law. Liber Amicorum Lucius Caflish, M. Nijhoff Pub., Leiden, 2007, 353–368

Mubiala M (2007) L'accès de l'individu à la Cour africaine des droits de l'homme et des peoples, in the collective work Promoting Justice, Human Rights And Conflict Resolution Through International Law. Liber Amicorum Lucius Caflish, M. Nijhoff Pub., Leiden, 369–378

Mutua M (2009) The transformation of Africa. A critique of the rights discourse. In: The collective work of Gómez Isa, F. and Feyter, K. De, (eds.), International Human Rights Law in a global context. Humanitarian Net, Bilbao, 899–924

Pastor Ridruejo JA (2010) Curso de Derecho Internacional Público y Organizaciones Internacionales, 14th edn. Tecnos, Madrid

Pemberton A, Groenhuijsen MS (2012) Developing victim's rights within the European Union: past, present and future. In: Kirchhoff G et al (eds) Proceedings of the 13th world society of victimology symposium. Wolf Legal Publishers, Nijmegen

Pemberton A, Rasquete C (2010) Victims in Europe-Assessment of the implementation on the Framework Decision on the standing of victims in criminal proceedings: preliminary results. In: Hartmann J (ed) Perspektiven professionneller Opferhilfe. VS Verlag, Wiesbaden, 99–112

Pinto M (2009) Dealing with the past – democracies and victims' struggle to deal with gross human Rights violations, in the collective work e. by Flauss, J.-F., La protection internationale des droits de l'homme et les droits des victimes, Bruylant, Bruxelles, 111–128

Pons Rafols, X. (coord.) (1998) La Declaración Universal de los Derechos Humanos. Comentario artículo por artículo, Icaria ed., Barcelona

Quoc Dinh N, Daillier P, Pellet A (1992) Droit international public, 4th edn. LGDJ, Paris, 356–372

Requejo Isidro M (2009) Violaciones graves de derechos humanos y responsabilidad civil (transnational human rights claims). Thomson & Aranzadi, Cizur Menor

Roucunas E (1987-VI) Engagements parallèles et contradictoires. R. des C t. 206:9–288

Requejo Isidro M (2007/1) Las instituciones comunitarias ante las reclamaciones civiles por violaciones graves de derechos humanos frente al Estado, R.E.D.I., LIX:153–174

Salado Osuna A (1998) Artículo 3, in the collective work of the Association for the United Nations in Spain, coord. Pons Rafols, X., La Declaración Universal de los Derechos Humanos. Comentario artículo por artículo, Icaria ed., Barcelona, 124–136

Sanz Hermida AM (2009) Víctimas de delitos: derechos, protección y asistencia. Iustel, Madrid

Saura Estapá J (1998) Artículo 12. In: The collective work of the Association for the United Nations in Spain, coord. Pons Rafols, X., La Declaración Universal de los Derechos Humanos. Comentario artículo por artículo. Icaria ed., Barcelona, 226–236

Seibert-Fohr A (2009) Prosecuting serious human rights violations. Oxford University Press, Oxford

Sepúlveda C (1990) Methods and procedures for the creation of legal norms in the International System of States: an inquiry into the progressive development of International Law in the present Era. German Y.I.L. 33:432–459

Serna P (2004) La dignidad humana en la Constitución Europea. In: en Comentarios a la Constitución Europea, Libro II, E. Álvarez Conde y V. Garrido Mayol (dirs.). Tirant lo Blanch, Valencia, 191–239

Shelton D (1999) Remedies in International Human Rights Law. Oxford University Press, Oxford

Shelton D (2009) The jurisprudente of human Rights tribunal son remedies for human rights violations, in the collective work edited by Flauss,, J.-F., La protection internationale des droits de l'homme et les droits des victimes, Bruylant, Bruxelles, 57–76

Sloan B (1987) General Assembly Resolutions revisited (forty years later), B.Y.I.L., 39–150

Sobrino Heredia JM (2008) Dignidad. In: Mangas Martin A (ed) Carta de los Derechos Fundamentales de la Unión Europea. Comentario artículo por artículo, Fundación BBVA, Bilbao, 107–145

SOS Attentats (2003) Terrorisme, victimes et responsabilité pénale internationale. Calmann-Lévy, Paris

SOS Attentats (2002) Livre Noire, Paris

Subijana Zunzunegui IJ (2006) El principio de protección de las víctimas en el orden jurídico penal. Del olvido al reconocimiento, Ed. Comarés, Granada

Stern B (2007) Vers une limitation de l' 'irresponsabilité souveraine' des Etats et chefs d'Etat en cas de crime de droit International?, in the collective work Promoting Justice, Human Rights And Conflict Resolution Through International Law. Liber Amicorum Lucius Caflish, M. Nijhoff Pub., Leiden, 511–548

Tomuschat C (2002) The duty to prosecute international crimes committed by individuals. In: The collective work Tradition und Weltoffenheit des Rechts. Festschrift für Helmut Steinberger. Beiträge zum ausländischen öffenlichen Recht und Völkerrecht, Band 152. Springer, Berlin, 315–349

Tomuschat C (2007) Reparation in favour of individual victims of gross violations of human rights and international humanitarian law. In: The collective work Promoting Justice, Human Rights and Conflict Resolution Through International Law. Liber Amicorum Lucius Caflish. M. Nijhoff Pub., Leiden, 569–590

Tomuschat C (2009) La protection internationale des droits des victimes. In: The collective work edited by Flauss, J-F La protection internationale des droits de l'homme et les droits des victimes. Bruylant, Bruxelles, 1–29

UNODOC (2011) The criminal justice response to support victims of acts of terrorism. United Nations, New York

Vallat FA (1959-II) The competence of the United Nations General Assembly. R des C t. 97:203–292

Van Boven T (2009) The right to a remedy as contained in international instruments: access to justice and reparation in treaties and the new United Nations principles. In: The collective work edited by Flauss J-F La protection internationale des droits de l'homme et les droits des victimes. Bruylant, Bruxelles, 31–55

Vandermeersch D (2009) Violations graves des droits de l'homme (crimes internationaux) et competence pénale universelle, in the collective work edited by Flauss, J.-F., La protection internationale des droits de l'homme et les droits des victimes, Bruylant, Bruxelles, 129–164

Vasak K (1984) Las Dimensiones Internacionales de los Derechos Humanos. In: Editor General K Vasak, Traducción Hernán Sabat y María José Rodellar, vols I–III. UNESCO Serbal, Barcelona

Virally M (1984) Résolution et accord international. In: The collective work Essays in International Law in honour of judge Manfred Lachs. Nijhoff, The Hague, 299–306

Zappalá S (2009) The rights of victims of terrorism: teachings of international law. In: The collective work edited by Flauss J-F La protection internationale des droits de l'homme et les droits des victimes. Bruylant, Bruxelles, 221–236

MIX
Papier aus verantwortungsvollen Quellen
Paper from responsible sources
FSC® C105338

Printed by Books on Demand, Germany